EVALUATING SOCIAL PROGRAMS

QUANTITATIVE STUDIES IN SOCIAL RELATIONS

Consulting Editor: Peter H. Rossi

UNIVERSITY OF MASSACHUSETTS
AMHERST, MASSACHUSETTS

EVALUATING SOCIAL PROGRAMS

THEORY, PRACTICE, AND POLITICS

Edited by
PETER H. ROSSI

Department of Social Relations
The Johns Hopkins University
Baltimore, Maryland

WALTER WILLIAMS

Graduate School of Public Affairs and
Institute of Governmental Research
University of Washington
Seattle, Washington

SEMINAR PRESS   New York   San Francisco   London   1972

A Subsidiary of Harcourt Brace Jovanovich, Publishers

SEMINAR PRESS, INC.
111 Fifth Avenue, New York, New York 10003

United Kingdom Edition published by
SEMINAR PRESS LIMITED
24/28 Oval Road, London NW1 7DD

LIBRARY OF CONGRESS CATALOG CARD NUMBER: 75-183473

PRINTED IN THE UNITED STATES OF AMERICA

For

    STUART AND DAVID

    PETER, KRIS, AND NINA

CONTENTS

III. EVALUATIVE RESEARCH: PRACTICE

IV. ORGANIZING FOR LARGE-SCALE EVALUATIVE RESEARCH

LIST OF CONTRIBUTORS

Numbers in parentheses indicate the pages on which the authors' contributions begin.

GLEN G. CAIN, Department of Economics and Institute for Research on Poverty, University of Wisconsin, Madison, Wisconsin (73,109)

JAMES S. COLEMAN, Department of Social Relations, The Johns Hopkins University, Baltimore, Maryland (97)

JOHN W. EVANS, Assistant Commissioner, Planning and Evaluation, U.S. Office of Education, Washington, D.C. (247)

THOMAS K. GLENNAN, JR., Director, National Institute of Education, Department of Health, Education and Welfare, Washington, D. C.

ROBINSON G. HOLLISTER, Department of Economics, Swarthmore College, Swarthmore, Pennsylvania (109)

TOM R. HOUSTON, JR., San Francisco, California (51)

DAVID N. KERSHAW, Mathematica, Incorporated, Princeton, New Jersey (221)

EDWARD L. McDILL, Department of Social Relations, The Johns Hopkins University, Baltimore, Maryland (141)

MARY S. McDILL, University of Maryland, School of Medicine, Baltimore, Maryland (141)

PETER H. ROSSI, Department of Social Relations, The Johns Hopkins University, Baltimore, Maryland (11,267)

J. TIMOTHY SPREHE, Office of Population, Agency for International Development, Washington, D.C. (141)

JULIAN C. STANLEY, Department of Psychology, The Johns Hopkins University, Baltimore, Maryland (67)

HAROLD W. WATTS, Department of Economics, University of Wisconsin, Madison, Wisconsin (73)

WALTER WILLIAMS, Graduate School of Public Affairs and Institute of Governmental Research, University of Washington, Seattle, Washington (3, 247, 287)

PREFACE

The government and the academic community have recently focused much attention on evaluative research asking the basic question: How well does a social program or project work? This is hardly a surprise. First, it is difficult to argue with the fundamental proposition that social agencies, or for that matter any large enterprise, ought to seek evidence of the effectiveness of existing programs and proposed program alternatives as a basic guide to decision making. Second, the experience of the 1960's raised serious doubts about the effectiveness of most existing major social action programs and a lessening of the confidence in what seemed to be an implicit premise of the early years of the War on Poverty that programs can be launched *full scale* without testing and yield significant improvements in the lives of the disadvantaged. Third, the evaluative issues raised by the newer social programs are as conceptually and methodologically challenging as any now faced by social scientists.

Yet few sound evaluations and even fewer rigorous field experiments have been undertaken. Moreover, serious questions exist concerning the capacity of the government both to develop and use evaluative results and of the social science research community to carry out the needed studies. The short supply of competent policy-oriented researchers both within and outside of the government, the inadequacy of available methods and concepts for carrying out evaluative studies, and the shortage of organizations with the capacity to undertake large-scale evaluative activities raise the very serious question of whether the current use of evaluative results directly in the policy process may not cause more harm than good.

The editors of this volume starting from the premise that sound evaluative research is badly needed to improve the social policy process have chosen a number of essays addressed to three related questions. First: Why have the quantity and quality of evaluative activity to date been so low? Second: What are the problems and risks associated with developing more evaluation research and using results in the social policy process? Third: What steps should be taken by the government and the social science research community to increase significantly the level of soundly conceived and executed evaluative studies and to reduce the dangers attendant in the use of the results?

In many respects, the first issue dominates the volume. That is, there are many problems and risks in developing and using evaluative results, and positive recommendations are hard to derive because numerous conceptual, methodological, bureaucratic, political, and organizational problems have hindered the undertaking of a significant quantity of sound evaluative research. Let us briefly outline each of these problems.

1. *Conceptual Problems*: The social policy areas are inherently complex and difficult to cope with either in developing programs or research. Social scientists seem to be stuck with the fact that pigeons, genes, and even elementary particles appear to be easier to understand in a rigorous way than people in complex social situations.

2. *Methodological Problems*: No doubt in part because of the sheer complexity of the problems to be faced, social science methods and field procedures often are not adequate for producing evaluative results sufficiently sound to warrant use in the social policy process. In some policy areas methodological deficiencies rule out work that will be directly relevant to decisions. Furthermore, even where direct policy studies are warranted, various technical defects will make them subject to legitimate attack on methodological grounds.[1]

---

[1] The term "methodology" is used here in a very broad sense to include experimental design, statistical measurement, variable specification (the conversion of a variable into meaningful, measurable terms), and field procedures (e.g., sampling including the very difficult problems of maintaining treatment and control groups over time). Certainly in these broad terms severe methodological problems exist. But it is also important to recognize that these problems should not be overplayed in that in some areas such as education and manpower present methods are adequate for reasonably sound evaluative studies and that methodological deficiencies are frequently more a result than a cause of the other four problems listed here. For example, the deficiencies in methods in the education area are brought about more by conceptual problems of not understanding the educational process and by bureaucratic-organizational factors that have blocked extensive evaluative research than by deficiencies in statistical theory per se. In short, we suspect that a real commitment to evaluative research—a political and bureaucratic commitment—would pro-

3. *Bureaucratic Problems*: Program and project managers in general do not like to be graded. It is a bit disconcerting to find out that one's program has a benefit-cost ratio of .3, and hardly the kind of information the aspiring manager wants brought to public attention (unless, perhaps, he inherited his job from someone whose last score was minus .3). Nor are program people likely to stand in awe of an evaluative statistic, but instead may well do battle either to thwart a proposed evaluation or to call into question the validity of a completed study.

4. *Political Problems*: All public programs are political in the sense that elected officials make life and death decisions about them. And social programs are often highly visible—little kids in Head Start, or people on welfare often alleged to be stealing tax dollars—making evaluative studies even more difficult to carry out.

5. *Organizational Problems*: Evaluative studies in the social areas will frequently require a large-scale, multidisciplinary effort demanding high levels of technical, administrative, and organizational skills. But neither government at various levels nor the social science community are organized to develop and carry out such studies. Furthermore, there are severe shortages of competent people to supervise or perform evaluative studies.

Moreover, these factors become intertwined as witnessed by the New Jersey negative income tax experiment and the Westinghouse Head Start evaluation discussed in several of the essays in this volume. The New Jersey experiment came about because of a lack of evidence concerning whether people would decrease work if they received a negative income tax allowance. It was clearly a difficult conceptual-methodological question requiring a longitudinal investigation of particular labor supply responses to various negative income tax schemes that offered the researchers who were to develop the project an unusual opportunity for rigorous academic research. The prime reason, however, for undertaking the study from the perspective of the government officials who funded it was the political need to be able to counter the claim that able-bodied "bums" would stop work and just collect welfare checks and not the scientific need to learn about socioeconomic behavior. In essence science and policy had the same information needs. In order to answer the policy question, the researchers had to design a seminal study getting at questions of fundamental importance in economic theory (note and remember, as it is a key point, evaluative research is not necessarily low-level applied work but often requires very basic research). But the study came again into the political realm as preliminary evidence from it was hurriedly processed to provide evidence to the

---

duce significant methodological improvements. We mention our views at this point because subsequent essays will present the thesis that deficient methods over time block sound evaluations, a view that we reject in some areas and are skeptical of in other substantive areas.

House Ways and Means Committee in support of the Family Assistance Plan. And, as this book was being prepared for publication, David Kershaw, the Chief of Field Operations for the experiment and a contributor to the volume, had just avoided being charged by Mercer County, New Jersey with conspiring with experimental families to misreport welfare payments (more of this later).

The Westinghouse Head Start evaluation was a bureaucratic and political donnybrook from beginning to end with strong opposition to the study arising from the Head Start staff almost immediately. Yet much of the controversy was cast in methodological terms. As one of us has observed elsewhere:

> As the controversy developed, the principal weapons in the battle were the esoteric paraphernalia of modern statistics. One cannot help but find some irony in the spectacle of one academic person accusing another of the mortal sin of an unrepresentative sample, not in the cloistered halls of some professional meeting but on page 1 of the *New York Times*.
>
> But far more important than the barbs in methodological raiment was that the limitations of current methodological capability structured much of the debate . . . . It is a near certainty that a competent methodologist can call into question such things as the test used, the drawing of the sample, the comparability of the control group. In short, no evaluation can be expected to be unassailable in terms of its methodological and field development. And these deficiencies open up the debate so that ideological or political concerns can be pursued in a methodological framework.[2]

This then is the stuff of evaluation research. It blends many factors ranging from esoteric statistical concerns that the reader will appreciate fully only if he has a solid methodological background through bureaucratic-political process issues probably perceived in all their subtleties only if one has been burned a few times in that process. Moreover, if one is to understand the complexity of evaluative research, he must confront both methodology and politics. These requirements present problems in a volume such as this meant for a diverse readership. The problem is particularly difficult for those whose methodological skills are now low. For them, some of the papers in the section entitled *Evaluative Research: Theory* will be both hard and tedious. We have tried to ease the pain by summarizing some of the difficult points in nontechnical terms in Rossi's introductory paper. But we feel the reader should be prepared for the journey.

Policy research can be as methodologically and conceptually challenging as anything presently done in the social sciences. At the same time, if it is to have an impact on policy, it ultimately must come under bureaucratic and political scrutiny and probable attack. If the reader is now serving on a government policy or evaluation staff he cannot avoid these controversies. If instead he is a university researcher or a graduate student in the social sciences, he can choose

[2] Walter Williams, *Social Policy Research and Analysis: The Experience in the Federal Agencies,* American Elsevier, New York, 1971, pp. 103–104.

to stay away. There are many other career choices, but whether or not they will be as interesting as policy research or as potentially valuable remains a moot point.

If we may for a moment intrude explicitly with our tastes and values, we would make a couple of points. First, evaluative research is exciting. Political and bureaucratic infighting can be good fun. Second, evaluative research can be a serious and important activity, a whole lot more important than most of the research now done in the social sciences. To be blunt, a good evaluative study may be worth more to society than the total yearly wisdom set down in a prestigious academic journal. Actually, more and more, good evaluative work makes the right journals. For example, two of our essays are reprinted from the *American Sociological Review*. But such a statement diverts us from the key point that sound evaluative research may allow social science to make a far greater contribution to society than it has in the past.

The development of this book reflects the overlapping government and social science research community concerns. The common starting point for the two editors was the problem of the organizational requirements in the social sciences necessary in order to perform the large-scale evaluative research required for social policy-making. We got together when Williams, who was in the process of preparing the essay entitled "The Capacity of Social Science Organizations to Perform Large-Scale Evaluative Research" and had read Rossi's earlier paper "Observations on the Organization of Social Research" (both in this volume), suggested that they meet to discuss the organizational issue. In the course of our conversations we found that both of us were thinking of an edited volume on evaluative research, and under quite different circumstances had collected a number of essays. It also became clear that neither group of essays alone quite covered the topic, but that a melding of the two would overcome this deficiency. Let us now touch briefly on the origins of these two sets of essays.

The Williams group of papers might be termed the "RPP&E set" because all of the authors were either on the staff or had close contact with OEO's Office of Research, Plans, Programs, and Evaluation, the first central analytical office in a social agency.[3] Of the group of people who were on the RPP&E staff (Cain, Evans, Hollister, Watts, and Williams), all except Evans are now on university faculties. Thus, while the primary focus of the RPP&E set is that of a central analytical office, the papers also reflect a strong social science research organization interest (particularly as manifested by people on university faculties).

The other group of papers may be termed the "AAAS set" since they are drawn from the American Academy of Arts and Sciences sponsored "Evaluation

---

[3] These papers include the ones by Cain and Hollister, Cain and Watts, Glennan, Kershaw, and Williams and Evans. It might be noted that when the Cain and Watts paper was printed in the *American Sociological Review*, that issue contained a comment on the paper by James Coleman, which is also included in this volume.

of Social Action Program Conference," May 2–3, 1969.[4] The papers selected for this volume were chosen primarily on the basis that they complement the RPP&E set and the papers on organization. The AAAS papers are all prepared by university faculty members; however, as will be clear from Rossi's summary paper of the conference, a good part of the discussion at the conference was provided by members of social agency policy staffs.

It is these two groups that are the primary audiences of the essays, or more particularly the graduate students of today who will occupy key social agency staff and social science research positions of tomorrow. And it certainly follows from some of the more pessimistic remarks made earlier in this Introduction that the new group will need to do much better than those of us concerned with evaluative research in the past if social science is to make a truly significant contribution to social policy-making.

[4]These papers include the ones by Huston, Stanley, McDill *et al.*, and Rossi.

I

AN OVERVIEW

1

THE ORGANIZATION OF THE VOLUME
AND SOME KEY DEFINITIONS

Walter Williams

This chapter has these purposes: to rationalize decisions concerning the organization of the book, to introduce very briefly the articles in the volume, including some discussion of the relationship among them, and to try to make sense out of the terminology used in the various papers. The definitional issue is clearly the starting point since there is no standard usage in the area of evaluative research and social policy and we have not tried to impose a set of definitions on the authors.

This chapter will (1) present some definitions from a recent book of mine; (2) show how these definitions differ from other types of activities labeled as evaluation; and (3) make a critical distinction between two activities defined below, policy analysis and evaluation research. Also, the discussion of each paper that follows this section will indicate how its key terms are related to the definitions spelled out below.

The definitions are as follows: (Williams, 1971, pp. 12-13).

Policy analysis (or simply analysis) describes a policy-oriented approach, method, and collection of techniques of synthesizing available information including the results of research: (a) to specify alternative policy and program choices and preferred alternatives in comparable, predicted qualitative and quantitative cost/benefit type terms as a format for decision making; (b) to assess organizational goals in terms of value

3

inputs and to specify the requisite output criteria for organizational goals as a basis of goal determination and measurement of outcome performance; and (c) to determine needed additional information in support of policy analysis as a guide for future decisions concerning analytical and research activities. . . .

The term *research* will be used to delineate all studies using scientific methodologies to describe phenomena and/or to determine relationships among them. Within the broad category of "research" two types will be distinguished, *outcome evaluations* and [*field experiments*], because they are particularly important aspects of social science research vis-à-vis social policy analysis.

Outcome evaluations assess the effects of an organization's *existing* projects or programs on their direct participants, other designated groups, and/or specific institutions (e.g., a relationship between benefits and costs). [*Field experiments*] assess the merits of *new* ideas with programmatic implications in terms of *outcomes* in a setting corresponding at least in part to actual field operating conditions. Both of these types of research can be placed in a larger categóry entitled [*evaluation or evaluative research*] in which the distinguishing characteristic is that the measurement of outcomes takes place either under actual operating conditions or under conditions that reflect in some reasonable degree the problems associated with operating actual programs.

Outcome evaluations need to be distinguished from on-site monitoring. The latter focuses primarily on the quality and use of inputs in considering such factors as administrative management practices, adherence to stated program guidelines and staff capability. The on-site monitoring evaluation stresses inputs in asking how well the project is being administered; the outcome evaluation emphasizes outputs in asking if the project changes the situation in a desirable direction.

In the past, small-scale projects aimed at investigating the feasibility of new programmatic ideas in a field setting have gone under a variety of labels including "E&D" (experimental and demonstration), "R&D" (research and demonstration or development), and "Demonstration." Many such projects have not attempted to evaluate outcomes but rather have determined whether or not the proposed idea can be carried out in the sense of administrative or political feasibility. The focus, as in monitoring, has been on inputs, particularly administrative viability (the capacity to continue in operation). These projects aimed at showing administrative and/or political feasibility are termed "Demonstration" projects to distinguish them from field experiments. In this volume the papers will focus almost exclusively upon outcome evaluations and field experiments rather than monitoring and demonstration projects.

In terms of understanding some of the distinctions made in the volume, it is important to keep clear the distinction between policy analysis and evaluative research and to recognize that the results of research are an input to analysis that may limit severely its successful application. As the author observed (Williams, 1971, pp. 13-14):

A basic conceptual distinction is between policy analysis and research. The former is a means of synthesizing information to draw from it policy alternatives and preferences stated in comparable, predicted quantitative and qualitative terms as a basis or guide for policy decisions; conceptually it does not include the gathering of information. A similar statement might be made concerning regression "analysis" and research in that the regression methodologies are not research but rather are a means of manipulating information.

The analogy to regression analysis and research may be extended. . . . Any application of regression techniques is bounded and limited by the available information including the results of research. No matter how sophisticated the regression techniques become, an input of inferior theory and data will produce a relatively inferior product. The application of regression techniques may increase the understanding of the implications of the limited data. But the superiority of the techniques should not obscure the inferiority of the information—certainly a critical point for policy analysis.

In some cases the use of policy analysis has improved the social agency decision-making process in that central analytical offices have derived from limited programmatic and socioeconomic data, feasible alternatives (and, if not a precise estimate of benefits and costs, at least a reasonable estimate of consequences) and recommended courses of actions. These efforts have been limited by the deficiencies in the available data. However adroit a central analyst may be in synthesizing available information as a guide to decision-making, the fact remains that policy analysis is limited by that information. As time passed it became clear that the critical missing element was research treating specifically issues of program conceptualization, design, operation, and measurement. In short, the central analyst in social agencies could not show to policy makers evaluative research results indicating that a current program worked or that an alternative to that program was likely to work better. (Williams, 1971, pp. 5-9).

THE ESSAYS IN THE VOLUME

This volume of readings is divided into four sections: An Overview; Evaluative Research: Theory; Evaluative Research: Practice; and Organizing for Large-Scale Evaluative Research. The first and the last sections present no problems in sorting out the papers; the first is an introduction and the last topic is a special case that can clearly be distinguished. And, of course, in the abstract so can theory and practice be separated, with the latter covering such issues as field procedures and bureaucratic and political problems. What is difficult in terms of the edited volume, however, is that several articles discuss both theory and practice, and we must make an arbitrary judgment putting them into one or another category.

I shall discuss briefly the scope of the papers that follow in the volume; point out special features, including the orientation and experience of the authors that are important for other papers or for a contrast in perspective in papers covering similar topics; alert the reader to possible definitional problems; and set out the rationale for putting certain articles under either the theory or practices sections:

EVALUATIVE RESEARCH: THEORY

Rossi, "Testing for Success and Failure in Social Action," (1) introduces the topic of evaluative research, providing an historical perspective and a brief discussion of current problems, and (2) summarizes both the papers and the discussion at the American Academy of Arts and Sciences' "Evaluation of Social Action Programs Conference."

The two short papers by Houston, "The Behavioral Sciences Impact Effectiveness Model," and Stanley, "Controlled Field Experiments as a Model for Evaluation," present a succinct summary (and the best one I have seen) of the statistical design requirements for developing sound outcome evaluations and field experiments. Impact effectiveness is equivalent to the term "outcomes" used in my definitions.

Cain and Watts, "Problems in Making Inferences from the Coleman Report," discuss the weaknesses of the methodological and field procedures used in the Office of Education-sponsored study, *Equality of Educational Opportunity* (Coleman *et al.*, 1966), usually referred to as the Coleman Report because of its senior author. Cain and Watts consider why the present deficiencies in research techniques, particularly the inability to build sophisticated models, make it so difficult to assess the unique effect of various treatment (e.g., schools) and nontreatment variables. Since this paper discusses a major attempt to assess elementary and secondary schools, it might well be included in the Practices section. But it is predominantly theory oriented in discussion and thus, in our view, qualifies for this section. In "Reply to Cain and Watts" Coleman responds to many of the criticisms of the previous paper and broadens our understanding of the difficult problems of mounting a major evaluative effort in the field.

Cain and Hollister, "The Methodology of Evaluating Social Action Programs," is a good exposition of methodological problems (relying primarily on manpower program examples) written by two top-flight academic economists who also have sound experience in developing outcome evaluations. However, the approach is distinctly that of the academic methodologist, and for that reason is included in the Theory section. Unfortunately, in terms of the previously discussed definitions, Cain and Hollister used the term "cost-benefit analysis" to include both policy analysis (termed by them *"a priori* analysis") and outcome evaluations (termed *"ex post* analyses"). The reader should simply disregard the use of their term "cost-benefit analysis," and recognize that *a priori* analysis is similar to policy analysis, and that ex post analyses are outcome evaluations.

EVALUATIVE RESEARCH: PRACTICES

McDill, McDill, and Sprehe, "Evaluation in Practice: Compensatory Education," provides a useful overview both of previous outcome evaluations and field experiments in the area of compensatory education. The paper presents a critique of recent evaluation efforts highlighted by an extensive and insightful summary of the methodological controversy surrounding the Westinghouse Learning Corporation evaluation of the Head Start program.

Glennan, "Evaluating Federal Manpower Programs: Notes and Observations," reviews recent efforts to evaluate manpower programs and tries to draw some policy inferences from this experience. Glennan's background is similar to that of Cain and Hollister, but his perspective in this paper is much more in terms of an organization conducting an evaluation or responsible for such an evaluation in a social agency.

Kershaw, "Issues in Income Maintenance Experimentation," is written by the chief of field operations for the New Jersey Negative Income Tax experiment and discusses a number of problems faced by researchers in implementing the project in the field. Included as an addendum is a section (prepared several months later) taken from Kershaw's statement before the Mercer County (New Jersey) Grand Jury on charges that he had conspired with experimental families to misreport welfare payments. In many respects this section is a far distance from Houston and Stanley's scholarly discussions of experimental design requirements, and yet at basic issue is the integrity (in a statistical, not a moral sense) of the experiment.

Williams and Evans, "The Politics of Evaluation: The Case of Head Start," looks at the severe political/bureaucratic problems raised by the recent Westinghouse Learning Corporation evaluation of the Head Start program.

ORGANIZING FOR LARGE-SCALE EVALUATIVE RESEARCH

Rossi, "Observations on the Organization of Social Research," is a discussion of the university's role in social policy research drawing in part on Rossi's experience as Director of the National Opinion Research Center.

Williams, "The Capacity of Social Science Organizations to Perform Large-Scale Evaluative Research," considers the problems of developing such studies from the perspective both of the government as principal demander and the social science research community as the main potential supplier of this badly needed research.

REFERENCES

Coleman, J. S. (1966). *Equality of Educational Opportunity*. U.S. Govt. Printing Office, Washington, D.C.
Williams, W. (1971). *Social Policy Research and Analysis: Experience in the Federal Agencies*. American Elsevier, New York.

II

EVALUATIVE RESEARCH: THEORY

2

TESTING FOR SUCCESS
AND FAILURE IN SOCIAL ACTION*

Peter H. Rossi

INTRODUCTION

In the last two decades behavioral scientists have joined economists in the policy-making arena. Although far from the center stage of the policy makers, social scientists are playing some of the supporting roles and are significant parts of the crews of stage hands and supporting technicians in the drama of public affairs. Being first on the scene, economists are playing the most important role through their participation in the Council of Economic Advisors, the Office of Management and Budget, the Treasury Department, and the Federal Reserve Board. In the last decade, sociologists, psychologists, and anthropologists have found places as advisors to the Executive Branch, the Congress, numerous governmental agencies, and the courts.

The special competences of the social sciences have been put to use in a variety of ways. This paper is concerned with the most important of these, *policy analysis* and the *evaluation* of social policy. We will examine these roles both from descriptive and prescriptive points of view to assess how the social

*This chapter is based upon a conference on evaluation research sponsored by the American Academy of Arts and Sciences and held May 2-5, 1969. The conference was supported by a grant from the Ford Foundation, whose support is gratefully acknowledged.

sciences are used and to examine the strategies that would maximize the contributions social science could make to such programs.

The development of this country in the direction of a liberal welfare-oriented state is connected intimately with the growing importance of social science in public policy. With the exception of the economists, social scientists are connected mainly with the health, education, and welfare wings of the national establishment, although there are significant contingents within some of the other agencies. The heavy participation of social scientists started with the shift toward the welfare state that occurred in the 1930's. Indeed, a good way to measure the growth of social science participation in public policy is to start by examining the roles played by social science in the New Deal period.

In the 1930's, when the New Deal social welfare programs were set up, only economists were involved either in the policy formation process or in running programs. Roosevelt's Brain Trust had several economists as members, but one notes in retrospect that sociologists, psychologists, and anthropologists were conspicuous by their absence. The latter were the recipients of benefits rather than the architects of policy. Much of the best empirical social research that came out of the decade of the 1930's was made possible through Works Progress Administration (WPA) "white collar projects" or National Youth Administration (NYA) funds which paid for research assistants.[1] Some behavioral scientists were unemployed and became part of WPA white collar projects which wrote local histories, conducted surveys of unemployment, and translated large portions of the European (especially German) social science literature.

Policy analysis in the sense that is being used in this volume was not used to any appreciable extent in formulating New Deal programs. The self-conscious laying out of a set of goals and corresponding sets of alternative programs to achieve those goals was not undertaken in any but the most informal way. Similarly, very little evaluation research was undertaken. Moynihan[2] reports that at the time the War on Poverty was designed, a fruitless search was made through the archives for studies that would provide some assessment of the effectiveness of such programs as the Civilian Conservation Corps (CCC),[3] information desired as a guide to the design of the Job Corps program. Little is known also about the other New Deal programs, some of which served as the prototypes for other War on Poverty efforts, except for the grossest measures—numbers of projects funded, persons and families served, and funds expended.

[1] WPA and NYA funds made possible such studies as St. Clair Drake and Horace R. Cayton's *Black Metropolis* (University of Chicago Press, Chicago, 1945) and Robert E. Faris and H. Warren Dunham's *Mental Disease in Urban Areas* (University of Chicago Press, Chicago, 1939).

[2] D. P. Moynihan, *On Understanding Poverty,* Basic Books, New York, 1969.

[3] Another attempt to locate studies of this sort was made under OEO contract by Educational Research Associates (Karen Rosenbaum, "A Second Chance for Youth: A Comparative Study of Federal Youth Programs in the 1930's and the 1960's," Educational

Even very general information on social welfare was not generated routinely in the 1930's. The estimates of unemployment used by policy makers all through these years were informed guesses, better than no information at all, but hardly precise. Systematic, periodic measurement of the labor force did not come about until the establishment of the Current Population Survey in the 1940's, a development which in turn depended on the devising of area probability sampling techniques. Reliable statistics on the educational system did not exist. The United States Census first began collecting detailed information on educational attainment in the 1940 Census and the Office of Education statistical series have only begun to be regarded as of high quality in the past few years.

As a consequence, we know very little about the effectiveness of the New Deal social welfare programs, other than the fact that they existed. In contrast, the social historian of the future will have considerably more primary and secondary materials upon which to base an assessment of the War on Poverty programs. To begin with, there is much better monitoring of social trends. Growing out of the needs that were demonstrated so acutely during the Depression for better information on current social trends, our society tracks monthly the trends of unemployment, has much better morbidity, mortality, and fertility data, statistics on levels of educational attainment and on enrollments in every level of our educational system, statistics on crimes known to the police, and so on. One of the major changes in the postwar period was the widespread acceptance of the concept of gross national product and its measurement, especially as implied by the establishment of the Council of Economic Advisors under the Full Employment Act of 1948.

Some of these series have been established within the last years and others, such as crime statistics, have been improved dramatically both in quality and coverage in that time. The impetus for these developments came from an increased need for information for public policy purposes. The requisite technical inventions were developed to make the statistical series possible.[4]

Research Associates, 1966. A few accounts were found which provided descriptions of the range of activities undertaken in the various youth programs, but firm statistics on, e.g., how many youths were ever enrolled in the CCC, were not found in either the archives or in other sources. In a commentary on an early draft of this paper, Robert Dentler asserted that the National Archives hold considerable documentary materials on the New Deal Programs, especially WPA, and provided a reference to his M.A. thesis, ("The Federal Writers Project" American University, Washington, D.C., 1954), where more precise references to some of the archived materials may be found.

[4]For example, many data handling devices, from the punched card through the electronic computer, have developed in connection with the data processing needs of the U.S. Census. It should be recalled that Hollerith, who invented the punch card sorting machine, was a Census Bureau employee and UNIVAC I (an early model of the vacuum tube generation of electronic computers) was first used extensively in processing the 1950 Census.

The second source of materials for the historian of the future will be the researches explicitly directed at the evaluation of social action programs. The behavioral sciences were invited into the War on Poverty in the enabling legislation, which called for mandatory evaluations and set aside earmarked funds for such research. Similar provisions were incorporated into the Elementary and Secondary Education Act, into the legislation setting up the National Institute of Law Enforcement and Criminal Justice and into many other pieces of legislation.

A third source of materials for future historians arises out of the development and application of the cost-benefit model. Applied with considerable success by Robert S. MacNamara to Department of Defense planning operations, it was introduced into other departments of the Federal government in the modified form of the Program, Planning and Budgeting System (PPBS) by President Johnson. The effect of the introduction of PPBS was to make agency officials conscious of the information they needed on the operations of the programs for which they were responsible.

As a consequence there has been a considerable flowering of applied social research. Social scientists were not merely to be the recipients of benefits in the 1960's round of social legislation but also to be participants in the policy-making process through the exercise of their special professional competences. Social scientists in the universities have been drawn into applied work. New social research firms have been started and ongoing businesses have founded subsidiaries or opened departments which were dedicated to evaluation of social action programs. Federal, state, and local agencies sought to add to their staffs professional social scientists who could aid in policy analysis and help design and carry through evaluation researches.

The development of the evaluation research "industry" has not been without its problems, however. "Applied" research does not have the same appeal to social scientists that "pure" research has. Elegant research designs are easy to devise on paper, but difficult to carry out in the field. Cost benefit studies have only been possible to carry out at the cost of considerable simplification of the basic ideas involved. The politics of evaluation research have turned out to be more of a problem than anticipated. Finally, participation in evaluation research has not brought the social scientist as close into the policy-making process as had been hoped: Some social scientists were on stage, notably in DHEW and OEO, but the preponderance were employed as stage hands.

Out of the successes and disappointments of the 1960's is emerging a more sophisticated view of the role of social science in social action programs. Policy analysis and evaluation research are evolving new techniques and methodologies for grappling with actual field experiences. A better understanding of the politics of evaluation is also developing.

SOME THEORY AND PRACTICE OF EVALUATING SOCIAL POLICY:
A REPORT ON A CONFERENCE

The present chapter grew out of a conference sponsored by the American Academy of Arts and Sciences held in 1969.[5] The purpose of the conference was to bring together persons who had been either in positions of responsibility for policy analysis or evaluation research or who had contributed through their own scholarly work either to the theoretical literature on these topics or actually undertaken work in these areas.[6] The conference was organized around a set of six papers, some of which are reproduced in this volume.[7] The papers provided themes around which grew an important exchange of experiences and opinions among participants. This paper is an attempt to capture both the major themes of the papers and the discussion which they sparked. Brief summaries of the papers presented are given in this paper along with a summary of the discussion among conference participants prepared from a tape recording of the proceedings. The transcript of the conference ran to several hundred manuscript pages. Hence this paper can only pretend to present the highlights, hopefully well selected and fairly presented. The author has also taken this opportunity to present some of his own views, particularly on evaluation research, most of which were presented at the conference.

[5] This conference in turn arose out of a 2-year long seminar conducted under the chairmanship of Daniel Patrick Moynihan on the problem of poverty; the major papers presented at this seminar are reported in D. P. Moynihan *On Understanding Poverty* (Basic Books, New York, 1969) and J. L. Sundquist, *On Fighting Poverty* (Basic Books, New York, 1969). Although participants in the poverty seminar were not at all agreed on the nature of poverty, its causes, and the appropriateness of current social policies, all were in agreement on the importance of policy analysis and evaluation research.

[6] Participants in the conference were as follows: John Banks (The Home Office, United Kingdom), Richard Berk (Johns Hopkins University), Zahava D. Blum (Johns Hopkins University), Norman Bradburn (National Opinion Research Center, The University of Chicago), David Cohen (Graduate School of Education, Harvard University), Robert Dentler (Center for Urban Education), Bettye K. Eidson (Johns Hopkins University), John Evans (Office of Economic Opportunity), John Greve (University of Southampton), W. Eugene Groves (Johns Hopkins University), Marcia Guttentag (Queens College, CUNY), Thomas Houston (Johns Hopkins University), Robert A. Levine (The Urban Institute), Guy Orcutt (The Urban Institute), Edward L. McDill (Johns Hopkins University), Daniel P. Moynihan (The White House), Martin Rein (Bryn Mawr College), Gerald Rosenthal (Brandeis University), William Ross (Dept. of Housing and Urban Development), Jerome Rothenberg (Massacusetts Institute of Technology), Harold Sheppard (Joint Center for Urban Studies), Timothy Sprehe (Florida State University), Edward A. Suchman (University of Pittsburgh), June Tapp (American Bar Foundation), Carol Weiss (Columbia University), Robert Weiss (Harvard Medical School), Joseph Wholey (The Urban Institute), and Robert Wood (Joint Center for Urban Studies). Academy staff participating were Corinne Schelling (who also helped to organize the conference) and John Voss.

[7] See papers by Houston and McDill *et al.*

In planning and organizing the conference it became apparent that there were two distinct problems which had been merged under the general rubric of evaluating social policy. On the one hand, there is the broad class of problems to which economists mainly have addressed themselves, under the heading of policy analysis, concerned with working out ways of making informed and intelligent decisions among alternative social policies. It is this broad problem area with which the methodology of the cost-benefit model and its derivatives is concerned. On the other hand, there is the problem of evaluation, determining the effectiveness of particular social policies, i.e., the extent to which the policies accomplish intended effects. Evaluation has been mainly the concern of the behavioral social scientists, particularly sociologists and psychologists, and the main methodological model used is the controlled experiment and its derivatives.

Although policy analysis and evaluation are addressed to distinctly different problems, it is obvious that they are complementary. The best circumstances under which to conduct policy analyses would be when the effectiveness of alternative social policies are known through evaluation research. Correspondingly, the effectiveness of a program is only one item of information to go into the judgment of whether a particular program is worthwhile. It was surprising to many of the participants to learn that their specialization in a particular area had cut them off from understanding the issues that arose in other areas. Indeed, one of the sources of a major confusion in the first few hours of the conference itself was the fact that both groups used the same set of terms to designate quite different and distinctive approaches.

Another major theme which emerged very early in the conference was the gap between theory and practice in both policy analysis and evaluation. Both the controlled experiment and cost benefit approach are ideal models which can only be more or less faithfully approximated in practice. Hence much of the discussion in the papers and in the conference itself centered around problems of approximation and compromise. Considerable concern was expressed over whether levels of compromise and approximation in the evaluations of the past decade were acceptable. Conference participants were particularly eager to discuss strategies for minimizing compromise and achieving closer approximations to ideal models in the future.

THE MAIN PROBLEMS OF EVALUATION: VAGUE GOALS, STRONG PROMISES, AND WEAK EFFECTS

Although the debate over the New Deal programs could have been phrased in terms of policy analysis or, in some cases, in terms of evaluation, very little was done along these lines, in part because the goals and their achievement were supposedly self-evident and in part because the social science of the time had yet to evolve the appropriate methodologies.

As to goals, the Civilian Conservation Corps, for example, had the dual function of accomplishing conservation and of providing employment to unemployed youths. These ends were seen as obvious and easy to assess by observation alone. Indeed, the U.S. Army, which administered the program, resisted strongly proposals that the Corps offer adult educational programs or even literacy training. The Works Progress Administration provided employment and also undertook a wide variety of public works tasks ranging from the construction of buildings and airports to the writing of local guide books. The philosophy underlying many of the New-Deal programs was that there was nothing "wrong" with the populations that were to be served: The problem lay in the economy. All that such programs as the CCC and WPA were supposed to achieve was the provision of employment and the accomplishment of certain public services, things which the economic system of the time was unable to achieve.

Given these goals, the problems of evaluation were quite simple. The programs either provided income or they did not, and the public works which they accomplished could be counted and arrayed. Of course, the major conflict over the New Deal programs was largely over this social philosophy. Opponents claimed that many of the programs had important negative side effects, for example, the encouragement of sloth and indolence among the unemployed. Furthermore, critics claimed, the diversion of national income into unnecessary public works was hindering the recovery of the private sector.

The social welfare programs of the 1960's, in contrast, were based on philosophical principles which called for evaluation. The economic system was considered to be functioning more or less well. The problem was within the disadvantaged groups. The social action programs were designed to bring about changes in individuals and in institutions which would lead eventually to the disappearance of the problem of disadvantage. Individual rehabilitation and institutional change were often the twin goals of many of the social action programs. Thus the legislative package presented by President Johnson in 1964 as the Economic Opportunity Act contained provisions for vocational retraining, for coordination of social services on the local level, and correcting other presumed deficits either in the characteristics of the poor or in the institutions which were serving them badly. Only the aged and the disabled were seen as having primarily an income deficit problem: It was the other poor and disadvantaged—young and middle-aged who were not suffering from any physical disability—who had problems which went beyond the lack of income and involved serious deficiencies.

Under these conditions, the goals set for the programs were difficult to state with either specificity or clarity. Thus the preambles to enabling legislation tended to refer to very broad objectives—for example, improving the quality of life in urban neighborhoods, or providing better health care for disadvantaged neighborhoods, or improving the quality of education given to poor children, etc. These are objectives for which we do not yet have indicators on which there would be broad consensus. If there is still some controversy over the best way to measure unemployment, consider how much more controversy can be engendered over how to measure improvement in the quality of urban life.

The problem presented by the lack of clearly specified goals compounds the problem presented by defining the task in terms of changing individuals and institutions. It is hard enough to change individuals, but it is even harder to change individuals to an unspecified state. It is almost as if those who devised the social welfare programs were mainly convinced that the present state of affairs was bad, at the same time being unable to indicate what would be a more desirable state of affairs to be achieved. Thus change in and of itself becomes important, perhaps in the hope that some of the changes that take place will prove to be beneficial.[8]

A social welfare program (or for that matter any program) which does not have clearly specified goals cannot be evaluated without specifying some measurable goals. This statement is obvious enough to be a truism. Joseph Wholey's paper[9] illustrates this point very well: The first task that faced the HEW group charged with making recommendations about child welfare programs was to decide what were national goals in the child welfare field. Obviously, the setting of such goals is a matter of policy, but when the policy makers do not specify goals clearly and still require evaluation, the evaluators are put into the uncomfortable position of deciding what were the goals policy makers had (or perhaps should have had) in mind.

Not all social welfare programs suffered to the same degree from ambiguity in the setting of goals. At the one extreme, manpower retraining programs were among the most clearly defined: A manpower retraining program is effective to the extent that it manages to impart marketable occupational skills. There may be some degree of disagreement over what are occupational skills and which ones are marketable, but unless trainees manage to function better on the labor market (if jobs are available), the program has not succeeded. At the opposite extreme, the desired end results of the Model Cities Program cannot be specified very clearly without radical simplification, a process which not only poses almost insurmountable obstacles to evaluators but leaves open the ques-

---

[8] Edward A. Banfield suggests that the present social welfare policy can be summed up in two slogans, "Do Something!" and "Do Something Good!" (*The Unheavenly City*. Little, Brown, Massachusetts, 1970). However unfair this caricature may appear, there is more than a little truth in the fact that policy makers seem to have suffered a failure of nerve in starting up programs with the aim of doing good mainly in response to need but without clear aims.

[9] Not reproduced in this volume. Joseph S. Wholey "The Absence of Program Evaluation as an Obstacle to Effective Public Expenditure Policy: A Case Study of Child Health Care Programs." Copies of this paper may be obtained from the author at The Urban Institute, Washington, D.C. The paper was based upon the work of the author as staff director of the HEW Program Analysis Group on Child Health Care from 1966 to 1968.

tion whether any evaluation that is undertaken is an appropriate one. Thus an evaluation may be made of the extent to which Model Cities Programs reduce unemployment in the target areas, but program administrators can easily counter negative findings by asserting that the programs were effective in some other respect and that these other goals were more important. Indeed, this is a large part of the reason why there is so much controversy over the Westinghouse-Ohio State University evaluation of the Head Start Program.[10] The Head Start Program's announced goals were to compensate for the alleged educational disadvantages suffered by poor children which hindered their functioning when they entered the regular school program. The Westinghouse evaluation showed that Head Start children were not appreciably helped in cognitive skills. But, said the critics, such an evaluation is partly beside the point since there are other important ways in which the program might have been more effective, e.g., in improving the physical condition of the children, etc. In short, the more vaguely phrased the objectives of a program, the more difficult it is to obtain commitment to accept the findings of any evaluation effort.

The 1960's were a difficult period in which to develop a heavy conscience concerning the poor. This was a period of seeming prosperity. The gross national product was increasing at an impressive annual rate, and, although American unemployment rates were not as low as those in some other Western countries, e.g., West Germany, Sweden, or England, they were certainly low enough to be considered not a serious problem. The American educational system had functioned very well for the bulk of the population. For example, the proportions of young people of college age in college had doubled in the first part of the decade.

As more and more families and individuals were brought into relative affluence, those who still remained in poverty, who were uneducated, who found it difficult to get jobs, and who were not being served well by the existing medical system—in short, the "problems"— were more likely to be families and individuals which it would be hard to reach and to help with any program. These were the "hard core" problems of the society, those who were bypassed by the existing system's mode of distributing the valued things of the society, either because of their own inability to "fit in" the system or because the system had no way of reaching them in their present positions. Treatments devised for the problems presented by these groups can hardly be expected to provide remedies

[10] V. G. Cicirelli *et al.*, *The Impact of Head Start. An Evaluation of the Effects of Head Start on Children's Cognitive and Affective Development,* Report to the Office of Economic Opportunity by Westinghouse Learning Corporation and Ohio State University, 1969. An excellent summary of the criticisms made of the Granger *et al.* Report is presented in an expanded version of the conference paper by McDill (E. L. McDill *et al., Strategies for Success in Compensatory Education.* Johns Hopkins University Press, Baltimore, Maryland, 1969).

as easily as treatments designed to affect the less disadvantaged segments of the population.[11]

It appears that we are in much the same situation with respect to social ills as with respect to physical illnesses. The introduction of modern medicine and especially modern public health measures into a country which has had neither can be expected to produce dramatic results in the form of reduced morbidity and mortality. However, in the United States, which has had relatively good public health practices and a very advanced medical care system (at least in the technical sense), each new gain in the reduction of morbidity and mortality can be expected to be achieved only at the expense of considerably increased effort and more complex technical developments. Providing potable water in a community which has used polluted water supplies will achieve dramatic reductions in mortality. Expensive research on lung cancer and attempts to reduce the amount of smoking, even if very successful, will not reduce mortality by very much.

Similarly with respect to our social ills. Dramatic reductions in rates of illiteracy can be achieved by providing schools and teachers to all children and illiterate adults, as the recent experiences in Cuba indicate, and can be achieved within a short period of time.[12] Getting virtually every person to persist long enough in the educational system to achieve at least high school graduation is much more difficult to accomplish. Hence, the higher the average levels of educational attainment, the more difficult it becomes to achieve further advances in the level of educational attainment, without alterations in the educational system itself. Similarly, the smaller the rates of unemployment, the more difficult it is to reduce the rates further, as the unemployed consist more and more of for one reason or another individuals who are difficult to place. The

[11] This statement is intended to mean that it is easier both to reach and to train the less disadvantaged. Hence, the same program administered to persons of different degrees of disadvantage would show less of an effect the more disadvantaged the clientele. Put in another way, to achieve the same effect, it would require more effort both to reach and train the most disadvantaged groups. However, cost-benefit ratios may appear to be more favorable for the most disadvantaged because benefits may increase more than costs the more disadvantaged the personnel. Thus a very disadvantaged person may be more difficult to train, but the increase in his income once trained may more than offset the increased effort involved. Hence there are two senses in which the term effectiveness is used: In the policy analysis context the term means some balance between costs and benefits. In the evaluation context, it means the ability of a program to achieve any effects at all, regardless of the costs or the benefits involved.

[12] See R. R. Fagen, *The Transformation of Political Culture in Cuba* (Stanford University Press, Stanford, 1969) for a description of how it is possible to make dramatic improvements in literacy in a country which has a very high rate of illiteracy. In the space of a few years the Cubans were able to make extremely dramatic inroads in this problem by mounting an all-out campaign that had almost the character of a crusade.

more social services already supplied, the more difficult it is to add to benefits by supplying additional services.

An additional source of skepticism about the efficacy of social action programs is that they are directed at transforming individuals who are relatively autonomous. Such programs are harder to pursue successfully, in contrast to ones designed to change institutions which are under close control. Thus the Armed Forces were able to make greater strides in reducing racial discrimination within the services than it has been possible for the government to effect in the hiring practices of private corporations. One would expect to make much more dramatic changes in the levels of cigarette smoking through controls over the manufacture and sale of cigarettes than through campaigns designed to convince individuals to give up smoking. When individuals are the targets of programs it can be anticipated that success will be harder to achieve.

Dramatic effects can also be produced by the introduction of new "hard-ware." Thus the provision of a modern sanitary sewer can be expected to reduce mortality considerably faster and more efficiently than a campaign to get individuals to install septic tanks. Indeed, the success of hardware measures have led some writers to search for the "technological fixes" which would be easy to install and which would have dramatic effects.[13] For example, noting that civil disorders occur primarily during hot weather when ghetto residents congregate in the streets, Weinberg suggested that supplying inner city residents with home air conditioning would significantly lower the incidence of civil disorders.[14] Obviously, one of the difficulties with the contemporary definitions of our social problems is that they do not lend themselves easily to solutions by technological fixes.[15] Thus the problem of affecting social problems as they are defined in this historical period is that such programs can be expected to yield

[13] A. S. Weinberg, "Social Problems and National Socio-Technical Institutes," in *Applied Science and Technological Progress,* Report to the Committee on Science and Astronautics. U.S. House of Representatives by the National Academy of Sciences, Washington, D.C., 1967.

[14] Recently the Baltimore Chief of Police strongly recommended that new public housing be air-conditioned for much the same reasons advanced by Alvin Weinberg. It should also be noted that one of the most popular technological fixes for urban social problems has been the provision of better housing for the poor. Housing has been viewed in the past as the cause of most of our social ills and low-cost housing has been proposed as the solution to high mortality, crime, juvenile delinquency, marital disorders, and almost any other social ill one might list. Although the public housing movement has dropped most of these presumed benefits as the rationale for support for subsidized low-cost housing, there is still some tendency for public housing supporters to make claims of a close relationship between housing and other social conditions.

[15] Commenting upon an earlier draft of this paper, Julian Stanley pointed out that tranquilizing drugs were a "technological fix" which acted directly on individuals and have served to change drastically the treatment of the mentally ill.

only disproportionately small improvements over existing programs. Hence cost-to-benefit ratios can be expected to be relatively high and also to rise as target problems represent increasingly "hard core" phenomena.

There are two extremely important consequences which flow from the low expected return from new social action programs: First of all, because effects are anticipated to be slight, the questions of the effectiveness of such programs and associated cost-to-benefit ratios become more important. With a few years of experience it is now clear that such programs as the Job Corps, Community Action, Model Cities, and the like may not be working at all or may not be appreciably better than alternative programs. This expectation of low returns is one important source of concern with evaluation.

Second, because most of the effects (if any) can be anticipated to be small, more high-powered evaluation methods are needed to demonstrate effectiveness. In other words, the smaller the effects, the more difficult it is to prove that they exist. At the same time, it is all the more important to look at programs from a cost-benefit viewpoint. This problem is another source for the current surge of interest in evaluation research. Clearly, if the costs of evaluation rise as more potent research designs are needed to attain a given level of confidence in results, then considerable interest will be generated in examining evaluation research from the point of view of reducing costs. Everyone hopes (and some expect) that new and less expensive research techniques will be devised which will make it possible to show at minimum cost that programs work.

By and large, the interest is in finding *positive* effects and *not negative* effects or *no effects* at all. Those who have proposed programs do so with the conviction that the programs are effective; those who administer the programs have an interest in showing that under their leadership the programs have accomplished something; and evaluators who are connected more or less intimately with the programs are not likely to want to offend by showing that programs do not work.[16]

These problems are further compounded by the hyperbole with which programs are presented to funding agencies and often to target populations. The claims made in public for most social welfare programs are ordinarily set at levels much higher than anyone could reasonably expect to be able to attain. Thus the War on Poverty has come to resemble the Viet Nam War. In both cases, unrealistically high expectations for quick and rapid success were stated at the outset; few programs were supported financially to the extent that stated

[16] One of the conference papers (not included in this volume, Robert A. Weiss and Martin Rein) illustrates how evaluators can become involved in the success of a program to the extent that they no longer believe that the program can be evaluated. Similar events occurred in the Mobilization for Youth Project in New York City. A plan to make a longitudinal study of the effects of the program on young people on the Lower East Side was abandoned after an expensive first round of interviewing because the researchers no longer believed that the project could be well served by evaluation.

expectations demanded; and both wars are presently bogged down in ambiguous battles in the field with victories nowhere in sight.

With such high expectations stated in public for the outcome of social welfare programs, evaluations are particularly threatening, especially when they are so likely to show either no effects or very small effects. The controversies that arose over the Head Start evaluation are an excellent case in point. There are too many commitments on the part of large numbers of agencies and individuals for a negative evaluation to be easily accepted.

The main import of the past few pages has been to stress that the evaluation of social action programs is not an easy task. It is fraught with both technical and political difficulties, some arising out of the nature of the social problems to which they are directed and some arising out of the broadly defined political context in which the programs have been devised and are being administered.

A MODEL FOR RATIONAL DECISION MAKING:
COST-BENEFIT ANALYSIS

Given the characteristics of the social problems of the present historical period, alternative social welfare programs (and alternatives to social welfare programs) are not easy to decide among. Target populations are going to be difficult to define and affect, proposed programs are going to be difficult to assess, and alternative programs cannot be easily ordered in terms of their superiority or inferiority. Furthermore, social welfare programs are bound to be relatively expensive. Under these circumstances, decision making, always problematical, becomes especially difficult. How to choose among alternative programs in such a fashion that the chances of achieving desired goals are enhanced is the topic of Jerome Rothenberg's paper.[17] Rothenberg lays out the main features of cost-benefit analysis and proposes that this model can serve as a framework for decision making. The cost-benefit analysis approach is a way of making decision making more explicitly rational. It is designed to answer the question of how to choose among alternative approaches to achieving a particular set of social goals. The model set forth in his paper is a conceptual one, providing a framework for approaching a problem in decision making rather than a set of formulas or other specific rules about how to make decisions in any particular case. Rothenberg's cost-benefit analysis is a similar but more restrictive concept than policy analysis.[18]

[17] Not included in this volume. To be published in a forthcoming handbook of evaluation edited by Marcia Guttentag.

[18] For example, the notion of cost-benefit analysis derived from economic theory places more emphasis upon quantification in money terms than does policy analysis. See Walter Williams *Social Policy Research and Analysis* (American Elsevier, New York, 1971, pp. 5-9) for a more extensive discussion of policy analysis.

The essential elements of cost-benefit analysis are as follows: Rational decisions among alternative policies may be accomplished by ordering all alternatives in terms of the balances or ratios between anticipated costs and the anticipated benefits of the policies in question. The benefits of a particular policy alternative are the anticipated want fulfillment patterns made possible by the proposed change. The costs are the want fulfillments which are possible with alternative usages of the resources involved and which would have to be given up if the proposed policy is to be achieved.

It should be immediately obvious that the key problems in the application of cost-benefit analysis center around the following questions: First, there is the problem of what are the goals of a policy. As we noted earlier, the goals of social welfare programs are not often stated very precisely. In some cases the goals are stated in such wide-spectrum terms (for example, the Model Cities Program) that any cost-benefit analysis would necessarily turn out to be extremely complicated. A proposed policy change whose aims cannot be stated in terms of desired outcome cannot be subjected to cost-benefit analysis, Rothenberg states.

Second, how does one reduce want-fulfillness patterns to a common metric so that the costs and benefits can be calculated? Rothenberg suggests that it should be possible to rely heavily on monetary values. For example, the benefits accruing from subsidized higher education may be converted into increased lifetime income returns to individuals, properly discounted, and into terms of the increased productivity of the labor force resulting from a higher level of educational attainment. Rothenberg also proposes that both costs and benefits may be considered as sets of vectors, each vector representing a particular dimension of outcome. For example, the benefits accruing from subsidizing higher education might be represented in terms of increased income to individuals, increased levels of work satisfaction, increases in the levels of marital happiness, and so on.

The third major problem arising from the model is how to delimit the costs and benefits which are to be considered. It is a truism that any modern industrial society is a complicated interrelated system. A change in policy, however apparently limited in scope, may be traced in its effects quite far from the narrow area apparently directly affected. In part, this question is related to the problem of externalities, the costs (and benefits) imposed upon systems other than the target system. In part, the problem lies in where one draws the line between important and unimportant effects. Thus a proposed program to reduce fertility may have indirect effects on the demand for education, which in turn may affect the publishing industry through changes in the levels of demand for textbooks, and so on.

The fourth major question concerns how to delimit the set of alternative programs. At the one extreme, cost-benefit analysis could be restricted only to those programs which are being placed before authoritative decision makers to decide among. At the other extreme, cost-benefit analysis could be extended to cover not only policies being considered but also all conceivable alternative policies.

The fifth major question concerns how to aggregate costs and benefits to come up with measures relevant to the collectivity in question. Specifically, this question boils down to whether one should be concerned with problems of aggregate levels of well-being or with the distribution of well-being in a social system. Thus the effect of a manpower retraining program may be to increase the aggregate level of income within a society but only at the expense of lowering the incomes of certain portions at the expense of augmented incomes for other portions. Rothenberg's paper suggests no particular solution for this problem other than that a suggested course of action ought to be evaluated both as to its aggregated and its distributional effects.

Rothenberg dwells at considerable length in his paper on these thorny questions, suggesting in the end that practical considerations would tend to restrict considerably the range of specific items to be considered as potential costs, benefits, alternative policies, and so on. Indeed, the specific examples given in the last section of his paper indicate that in practice cost-benefit analysis is applied relatively narrowly.

A rather lively discussion was provoked among participants at the conference by Rothenberg's paper. By and large, there was consensus among participants that cost-benefit analysis provided a useful framework for rational decision making. But there was also considerable agreement that empirical methods lagged far behind theory.

Drawing upon his experience in the Office of Economic Opportunity, Robert Levine[19] argued that there were very severe limitations on the practical use of cost-benefit analysis. One of the more serious problems was the deficiencies of the available empirical information on the impact of programs, which allowed widely different cost-benefit analyses. Levine illustrated this point with examples of cost-benefit analyses conducted by OEO on the Job Corps programs. An analysis by an economist outside the agency estimated the cost-benefit ratio to be about 1.5:1: Job Corps analysts came up with 4:1: The General Accounting Office found that their calculations yielded 0.3:1. Subsequent analysis of the three estimates indicated that the differences stemmed largely from using different sources to establish the effectiveness of the program. In short, the benefits in increased income estimated for Job Corps trainees varied widely depending upon which group of young people were used as "control groups" for estimating effectiveness.

Based on his experience, Levine felt that cost-benefit analysis was a useful framework in terms of which to conceptualize the problem of decision making

---

[19] A list of participants is given in footnote 6 to this chapter.

but that in practice so little firm empirical data were available that the cost-benefit analyses actually undertaken tend to be somewhat fictional in character. Four major problems stand in the way of using cost-benefit analysis in practice. First, the lack of any firm data on the effectiveness of programs; second, the great difficulty in finding control groups with which persons participating in a program can be compared and hence a corresponding inability to estimate the impact effectiveness of programs; third, problems in estimating at a given point in time the benefits that are to accrue in an uncertain future; and fourth, uncertainty about the kind of discount rate that ought to be applied to future earnings. These problems were so great that the proper empirical application of cost-benefit analysis was almost impossible to achieve.

Some fear was expressed by a few participants that the conceptual attractiveness of the cost-benefit framework, coupled with difficulties in empirical application, would give rise to a "pseudo-science" in which so-called cost-benefit analysis would produce results tailor-made to their clients' wishes.

Several participants noted that Rothenberg in his paper explicitly excluded from cost-benefit analysis decisions in which the main goals attempted were concerned with modes of decision making. Both Greve and Ross noted that some of the major controversies over social welfare policy were centered around the roles to be played in decision making by "indigenous" groups, as, e.g., in the Community Action Program and in Model Cities. If cost-benefit analysis was not applicable in such cases, how then does one evaluate such programs?

From the discussion several points of consensus arose. First, it was acknowledged that the mode of thinking in cost-benefit analysis terms had affected deeply policy making within federal agencies. Second, no participant was satisfied that cost-benefit analysis had been applied to empirical cases with any great success. Third, the implementation of cost-benefit analysis at the present time was badly hampered by the lack of data which could provide firm estimates of the impacts of social programs. Finally, the restriction of cost-benefit analysis to situations in which the modes of decision making were not in question meant that this technique was not applicable to some of the more important controversies presently raging about social welfare programs and their control.

Most of the difficulties involved in applying the basic ideas of cost-benefit analysis to a specific decision-making problem are amply illustrated in Joseph Wholey's paper[20] which was based on his experiences as staff director of a group within HEW charged with the task of evaluating proposed maternal and child health programs in 1966, preparatory to introducing new legislation into Congress in 1967.

Wholey states that the first task of his group was to specify the limits within which they were to examine alternatives and to lay out a set of clearly

---

[20] Not included in this volume.

defined national goals in the areas of maternal and child health. The limitations were set in part by the Secretary of HEW who apparently indicated what were the outside fiscal boundaries to whatever might be suggested as new policy. The group also did not consider the full range of costs and benefits that might result from policy changes; the impact of policy changes on the distribution of physicians, changes in income levels, and so on, were excluded.

The goals of the maternal and child health programs were set out by Wholey and his group to be quite specific and highly delimited: (1) reduction of chronic handicapping conditions among children; (2) the reduction of infant mortality rates in health-depressed areas; and (3) reduction of unmet dental needs in depressed areas. It should be noted that it is not clear from Wholey's paper how these particular goals were arrived at. The goals were phrased in distributional terms, i.e., in terms of increasing the amounts of services available to persons living in poverty areas.

The next steps in the analysis involved deriving several estimates. To begin, it was necessary to estimate the level of unmet needs for maternal and child health care services. Such estimates were constructed on the basis of "fragmentary data," the best of which were infant mortality rates for poverty areas.

It was then necessary to survey existing maternal and child health programs and to derive estimates of the per capita cost of delivering services under each of the existing programs. These estimates, as Wholey indicates, were also based on fragmentary data, the programs varying widely in the extent to which they were able to provide data on the sizes of their client populations. Given the types of services rendered and the coverages of the several programs along with the estimates of unmet needs, it became clear to Wholey and his group that a very large proportion of the target population was not receiving adequate care.

The third major step was to estimate the effectiveness of existing child health programs. Here almost no estimates were available, let alone firm data. In short, it was not known whether or not existing health programs in this area were at all effective in improving maternal and child health of target client groups.

Finally, Wholey and his group had to assess the relative cost effectiveness of the alternative programs to be incorporated into the new maternal and child health legislation. Considerable work went into estimating the costs and feasibility of proposed new programs. Some could be rejected on the grounds that they would cost more than the budgetary limitations imposed. Others could be rejected because they called for more manpower in the way of pediatric care than conceivably could be delivered by the existing medical care system. The final results, as incorporated into the Secretary's (HEW) recommendations, included demonstration projects to test the feasibility of using paraprofessional personnel; a program of early case finding and detection in order to locate potentially handicapped children; family planning programs, fluoridation, treatment of Selective Service rejectees, and finally program evaluation.

The legislation enacted contained many of the group's proposals, although (up to the time of the writing of Wholey's paper) adequate funding had not yet been provided to run the programs. The fiscal problems of the federal government were such that an economy-minded administration and Congress did not provide any funds.

Wholey came to the conclusion that while his group worked as well as they could with existing information and data, because so little information was available on the effectiveness of existing programs, their analysis could not be very persuasive. In the absence of firm estimates of program effectiveness, it was all too easy for program administrators to subvert, in effect, the proposed new programs. Over time, given the fiscal situation, maternal and child health programs remained essentially unchanged.

Much of the discussion which followed Wholey's paper was centered around the following topics:

First, participants were impressed by the limitations within which the analysts had to function. The budgetary limit of $100,000,000 by the HEW Secretary on additional appropriations meant that comprehensive medical care programs could not be considered except on a demonstration basis. The existing medical care establishment served as another limit: (e.g., no more doctors could be deployed than already existed in the labor pool) a limitation which also argued in favor of experimentation with medical care delivery systems which were not so dependent on medical doctors.

Second, the analysis presented by Wholey and his group was judged to have had an impact on policy through being incorporated largely in the HEW Secretary's recommendations to the President and Congress. The failure to implement the program as enacted was seen more as a consequence of the fiscal problems of the federal government than of an inability on the part of the report to persuade.

Third, there was considerable agreement that the placement of the analysis group within the higher levels of the HEW Department was a considerable advantage. Because of their status within HEW, Wholey and his group were able to argue directly for their recommendations with the Secretary, the Bureau of the Budget, and the President's Office. All too often, it was remarked, program analyses are carried out at levels too low to provide the analysts with direct access to relevant decision makers.

Finally, all agreed that the lack of good information on program effectiveness severely handicapped the ability of Wholey and his colleagues in preparing a close approximation to the cost-benefit model. The analysis group could not be expected to conduct its own effectiveness researches: It had neither the time nor the resources. It could only rely on existing data, but since the existing programs had never been evaluated (indeed, only a few had relatively good data on program coverage) the estimates of effectiveness had to be based on very incomplete information.

In sum, the application of the cost-benefit analysis model, as illustrated in the work of Wholey and his group, highlighted the difficulties involved in empirical application. Before cost-benefit analysis could be applied in any way remotely approximating Rothenberg's exposition of the model, considerable prior work had to be undertaken to provide reasonable, empirically based estimates of program effectiveness.

THE EXPERIMENTAL MODEL FOR EVALUATION

It is almost always an open question whether a contemporary social action program or project achieves its objectives. Effects can be expected to be small and hence not obvious to casual observation. Furthermore, so much change is occurring spontaneously or in response to larger movements in the society as a whole that it is difficult to separate out the changes which are the result of a particular program from those which have occurred in response to other events. To assess the effects of a program—the degree to which a program or project is achieving its objectives—is therefore a critical part of the evaluation of social welfare programs. Certainly, as we saw earlier in the discussion of Joseph Wholey's paper, policy analysis of any program depends very heavily on evaluations of alternative programs.

For a variety of reasons it is not easy to conduct evaluation studies. As in the case of cost-benefit analyses, there is a wide gap between ideal models of such studies and the kinds which have actually been undertaken studying social welfare programs. On the one hand, there exist elegant models for carrying out evaluation studies, derived mainly from the controlled experiment tradition; on the other hand, there are almost no examples of evaluation studies of current programs which have followed these models with any appreciable degree of fidelity. The main issues in the discussion of this topic centered around this gap between the ideal and the real. Two main positions can be discerned. There are those who center their attention on what are the obstacles to the use of controlled experiments in impact effectiveness studies; and, in contrast, others who propose to abandon the controlled experiment model as either impractical or irrelevant, and who are trying to build alternative models.

Hardly any more persuasive proponent of the controlled experiment model can be found than Houston[21] whose paper argues very strongly for the appropriateness and singular power of controlled experiments as the model for evaluation studies. In broad outline, the essential feature of a controlled experiment is the active intervention of an experimenter who administers a treatment (program or project) to randomly selected subjects arranged in groups that are equivalent in the way in which they were chosen, there being at least one group to whom the treatment is administered and at least one group from whom the

[21] Included in this volume.

treatment in question is withheld or to whom an alternative treatment is given. The method of assuring equality between groups is through requiring that persons would have an equal (or at least known) chance of being placed in either the experimental group (treated) or the control (untreated) group.[22] Measurements made on experimental and control groups allow comparisons to be made from which estimates can be made of the impact effectiveness of the treatment used.

The simplest controlled experimental design consists of one experimental (treated) group and one control (untreated) group, the individuals within each group being selected by equivalent random processes from the same universe before the treatment is given. Measures of a presumed effect of the treatment are taken in each group after the treatment is administered to the experimental group. More elaborate experimental designs (called factorial designs) exist which have the ability to detect differential effects according to the characteristics of individuals treated (e.g., old versus young or male versus female) and according to the single elements (or combinations) of which the treatment is composed (e.g., community control versus manpower training in a Community Action Program). Factorial designs may also be used to compare alternative programs or projects according to their effectiveness.

Houston points out the special relevance of factorial designs to problems of program and project evaluation. Unlike nonexperimental designs (e.g., static or correlational studies), the direction of causality is specified in controlled experiments. It is also possible to use the information resulting from a factorial experiment to build a better program or project by concentrating on those features which either singly or in combination produce the greatest level of desired effects. Furthermore, although such designs are subject to error, the size of the experiment can be adjusted to the desired level of accuracy, and thereby errors of inference from the experiment can be minimized.

Finally, Houston points out that the major obstacle to the employment of experimental designs lies more in the reluctance of public officials to authorize their use than in the difficulties of implementation in the field. Public officials hesitate to allow randomization to be used as the means of allocating individuals to treatments. Even in projects or programs where there are not enough resources to treat everyone in need of treatment, the application of the "first come, first served" rule appears to be more "humane" than assignment by "random" selection.

Most of the discussion about the Houston paper centered around whether it was possible in the "real" world to conduct controlled experiments to evaluate social action programs or projects.

[22] Hence, any differences between the two groups before treatment would be generated by chance alone and the size of posttreatment differences can be compared with the range of differences that might arise through chance alone.

In addition to the reluctance of administrators, another major obstacle lies in the practical difficulty of applying random selection procedures in assigning people (or other units) to experimental and control groups. For example, it would seem at first glance to be quite easy to divide preschool children into experimental and control groups, admitting the former into Head Start programs and withholding admission from the latter. However, Head Start was instituted in such haste that, at least during the first year, institutions had all they could do to fill the Head Start classes that were authorized. In short, initially there was no surplus of potential clients which could have been diverted into control groups. Similar experiences occurred in connection with many of the manpower training programs.

Another situational difficulty lies in the extraordinary empirical diversity of programs produced by local variations in administration. This is especially true of broad spectrum programs (e.g., Title I projects can be called *a* program only by a very charitable stretch of the imagination) since it is generally believed that the variation from project to project is enormous. Because of this variability, dividing clients among control and experimental groups would be fatuous since the treatment to be administered to the experimental groups would not be uniform.[23]

The major obstacle to randomization lies in the political and administrative resistance to the idea of experimentation and to the controls over programs and projects which experimental designs make necessary. The term "experimentation" to some conjures up images of eccentric scientists probing unfeelingly into vulnerable subjects and hence leads to an understandable desire to protect target populations from needless damage inflicted mainly by idle curiosity. To others, the establishment of experimental and control groups means that some persons are arbitrarily and unjustly prevented from receiving aid which they need badly. Indeed, so strong is the sentiment against experimentation that provisions of the Elementary and Secondary Education Assistance Act of 1965 contained specific injunctions against the use of randomization as a means of determining who shall receive services in connection with one of the programs authorized.

To the proponents of experimental designs, this type of argument is seen as based upon misunderstandings. The requirements of experimental designs do not necessarily mean that services be withheld from anyone. The main requirement is that the program or project to be evaluated be different from the services made available to the control groups. Thus, in the evaluation of the impact effectiveness of a manpower retraining project, a control group might be

[23] Part of this objection can be countered by employing more complicated factorial designs, although the proper use of factorial designs requires that systematic variations in project characteristics be planned in the design of the specific projects.

given traditionally available services, e.g., job counseling, registration with employment agencies, etc.

On the administrative level, resistance to experimental designs stems from
a variety of sources. First of all, as several discussants pointed out, it is not clear
that any administrators of projects and programs desire to have their activities
evaluated. Both Bradburn and Guttentag suggested that according to Bayesian
statistical theories it is not worthwhile evaluating programs whose administrators
are completely convinced that the programs are effective. If the subjective
probabilities held by administrators for the effectiveness of their programs
approaches 1.0, then it is not worthwhile evaluating their programs since any
findings are not likely to lead to a change in administrator practices or in
programs.[24] Stated in other terms, where the will-to-believe in the effectiveness
of a program or project is very strong, it is highly likely that an evaluation of
that program will be disregarded.[25] Drawing upon his experiences as Director of
the Center for Urban Education, Dentler stated that to conduct an experimental
evaluation is to ask to be permanently barred from returning to the institution
that has been evaluated: "No good evaluation goes unpunished!"

A second source of resistance lies in the reluctance of program or project
administrators to accept the kinds of controls over their activities that experimental designs make necessary. Wholey illustrated this point by pointing out the
failure of the attempt to evaluate the Follow Through Program by the Office of
Education. A number of different versions of the Follow Through Program were
to be evaluated comparatively, each version allocated to different school systems. School administrators resisted the Office of Education's attempts to
specify which form of the program they were to put into effect within their
system. In the end, local autonomy won out and, although programs varied from
school system to school system, they did so in an unsystematic way.

[24] Of course, this argument rests on the assumption that only evaluations which can
affect policy are worth undertaking. However, even disregarded evaluations, properly
conducted, can be considered contributions to general knowledge and perhaps a guide to
policy making in the future. Indeed, we are only just beginning to see benefits to policy
flowing from the 1967 Coleman Report on public education (J. S. Coleman et al., Equality
of Educational Opportunity. U.S. Govt. Printing Office, Washington, D.C., 1966).

[25] This appears to be the main source of resistance to evaluation reports when they are
issued. Every evaluation study has some methodological vulnerabilities and the advocates of
a program have been exceedingly diligent in finding methodological experts who can mount
an attack on an evaluation. Thus the Coleman Report (J. S. Coleman et al., Equality of
Educational Opportunity. U.S. Govt. Printing Office, Washington, D.C., 1966) has been
subject to extraordinary amounts of methodological criticism (see paper by Cain and Watts
in this volume), as have the studies showing a strong correlation between smoking and the
incidence of lung cancer, as well as the recent Westinghouse–Ohio State evaluation of Head
Start (loc. cit.), and the recent report of the Presidential Commission on Campus Disorders,
and so on.

A third source of difficulty lies in administrators' proclivities to change details of programs in midstream. Thus, what may have started out as a project using one method of instruction in reading may end up using a totally different method, the change having been made by the administrator of the project who, before the experiment was completed, judged that the first method had not been producing enough in the way of positive results.

The discussion of the experimental model was left somewhat inconclusive. Proponents continued to the end of the discussion to insist that with the proper will and effort, experimental designs in practice as well as theory could be used in evaluations. At the least, comparison of a preexperimental or quasiexperimental design with the ideal designs provided estimates of sources of error and bias. At best, it would be possible to use such designs fully.

The inappropriateness of experimental designs in practice was the theme of the paper presented by Weiss and Rein.[26] Although granting the validity of the experimental model as appropriate to some types of evaluation researches, Weiss and Rein claim in their paper that particularly for broadly aimed social welfare programs (e.g., Model Cities, Community Action, and the like) experimental designs are not only inappropriate but were likely to be somewhat harmful.

The centerpiece of their paper is a particular case, the evaluation of "The Neighborhood Benefit Program" (a pseudonym), whose purpose it was to coordinate youth services of existing social welfare agencies. A research staff was assembled as part of the program staff to design and carry through an evaluation of the program. The research staff designed a sample survey of 1500 youths in the target area and a sample survey of 500 youths from a neighboring city which was not served by the program (or any program). It was planned to re-interview both samples 2 years later to measure changes among both groups. The research, however, was never completed. The researchers became increasingly alienated from the programs. Data from the first wave of interviews became increasingly irrelevant to the action side of the program. Program administrators began to lose interest in the evaluation as they became more and more convinced that there was a very real possibility that their program was having at maximum a negligible effect on area youths. The end came when members of the research staff drifted away before the evaluation was completed.

According to Weiss and Rein there were two main reasons for the failure of the attempt to evaluate the "Neighborhood Benefit Program": First, although the program was designed to affect institutions and agencies in the target area, the research design was aimed at studying effects on individual youths. The

[26] Not included in this volume. See Robert S. Weiss and Martin Rein, "The Evaluation of Broad-Aim Programs: A Cautionary Case and a Moral," *Annals of the American Academy of Political and Social Science,* Vol. 385 (1969).

measurement of organizational changes requires a special approach, so far from the traditional survey technique as to make sample surveys irrelevant. Second, because the research design was focused on measuring the differences between youths at the beginning and at the end of the program, the research was not relevant to the study of the processes involved in the program and hence the research staff had little to give the program administrators until the program was over.

Weiss and Rein note that the research design was an attempt to approximate the controlled experiment.[27] The difficulties that stood in the way of following through on that design were typical and stem, according to the authors, from the essential nature of experimental and quasiexperimental designs.

As a more relevant alternative, Weiss and Rein propose that broadly aimed social welfare programs be evaluated using a method to which they give the title "process oriented qualitative research." This approach consists essentially of employing sensitive observers to monitor the unfolding of a program as it is going on, noting particularly those events which are critical, collecting documents, and sensitively observing the effects of the program on institutions and individuals.

The advantages of the "process oriented qualitative research," say the authors, are several: First, such an approach is able to note institutional as well as individual change. Second, it is more appropriate to studying the process of implementing a program since programs tend to shift and change in response to the trial-and-error groping of program administrators. A broad-aim program is hardly ever designed in any great detail at the outset; rather, it develops as program administrators try one and then another approach. Third, it has the advantage of regarding the target population (usually community or neighborhood) as a system, composed of interacting parts, which reacts organically to programs addressed to it. Finally, such an approach has the advantage of providing information to program administrators in time for the administrators to modify their actions in order to maximize the impact of their program on relevant targets.

Weiss and Rein do not describe their preferred approach in great detail. Indeed, because the essence of the approach is flexibility and adaptability to particular field circumstances, "process oriented qualitative research" cannot be described in outline form in the same way that one can lay out the requirements of experimental designs.[28]

[27] The research design could only have yielded information on presumed institutional effects as manifested in individuals. However, since a major concern of the program was in changing neighborhoods and institutions in the neighborhood, the design was defective since no direct measurements on the institutional level were provided for.

[28] They did refer, however, to the work of Marshall Kaplan in evaluating Model Cities Programs, as an example of their approach. Kaplan has been using teams of researchers who

In the discussion which followed the Weiss and Rein paper, two major positions developed: Some of the discussants interpreted their abandonment of the experimental model as meaning that there were programs which simply could not be evaluated. Accordingly, it is also an abandonment of *any* attempt to evaluate broadly aimed social programs on the grounds that their aims are not specified clearly enough and the activities pursued cannot be described in any systematic way. Bradburn went so far as to say that, for such programs, evaluation is both impossible and irrelevant and that the decision whether or not the program is to be continued rests on other than empirical grounds in the minds of decision makers.

The second major position was to accept the proposal of Weiss and Rein, but in a modified form. One of the major questions that arises is whether or not a program in fact exists after it has been enacted and funds allocated to specific agencies to carry out particular projects. "Process oriented qualitative research," as exemplified in the work of Marshall Kaplan, can provide the decision maker with information about the variety of forms the program is taking in individual projects, information which may be useful in setting up tighter evaluations at a later stage or in modifying policy to bring local practices in line with overall agency aims.

John Evans[29] illustrated the place of such research in an agency's evaluation program by describing the evaluation activities of the Office of Economic Opportunity. Evans distinguished between three types of evaluation researches being carried out by OEO: Type 1 consists of researches designed to measure the overall impact of programs, of which the Westinghouse-Ohio State evaluation of Head Start is a good example. The purpose of Type 1 research is to answer the question whether the program as a whole (or some major element such as summer or full year Head Start) is having any impact. Type 2 researches are designed to evaluate the differential effectiveness of program strategies or techniques (e.g., a Montessori versus a Bereiter approach in Head Start) or the effects of a single program on identifiably different target populations (e.g., a manpower retraining program addressed to young people or to middle-aged persons). Type 3—project monitoring—is designed to be more qualitative and to provide descriptions of what is going on within specific projects, in effect, project monitoring.

Responsibility for conducting the three types of research is located at different levels, Type 1 being the responsibility of the OEO central staff at-

---

visit Model Cities Programs periodically, collecting documents and interviewing participants to obtain running accounts of the Model Cities planning processes. The work in question is proceeding under a contract with the Department of Housing and Urban Development held by Kaplan, Gans, and Kahn, Inc. of San Francisco.

[29]A more detailed exposition of these approaches to evaluation may be found in the paper by Williams and Evans included in this volume.

tached to the Director's Office, Type 2 and 3 being the responsibility of program staff people within OEO. Types 2 and 3 may be carried out by different segments of the program; Type 2 by national program research staff, and Type 3 by the national office or regional office monitoring staffs. Adequate evaluation requires all three types but note that in terms of earlier definitions only Types 1 and 2 are outcome evaluations.

Evans expressed the view that ideal evaluation researches following faithfully the experimental models are probably too difficult both to design and to carry through. It is most likely that the best information one could get would be results from *ex post facto* designs, such as the Westinghouse-Ohio State Head Start study. Despite the patent dangers of *ex post facto* designs, they still provide some information and in the setting of social policy it is better to have some information of some probity than to make decisions based on estimates made up entirely of whole cloth.[30]

It is difficult to summarize the two papers and the discussion which they provoked. On the one hand, there was considerable agreement on what the experimental model provided in principle, the ideal toward which evaluation research ought to be oriented. On the other hand, there was expressed considerable despair that in practice it was possible to design and carry out meaningful experiments. Beyond these two main points, disagreement arose. One position was to look for alternative designs which would be free of the binding restrictions of the experimental model. The opposing position was to continue to strive to get acceptance of the experimental model with the end goal of compromising such designs as little as possible.

THE STATE OF THE ART: A CLINICAL VIEW

Evaluation research has become so prevalent that the social role of evaluator has begun to emerge. Drawing upon his experiences and those of his colleagues at the Center for Urban Education, Dentler[31] explored the characteristics of that role in his paper.

---

[30] A more detailed description of OEO's evaluation activities can be found in John Evans, "Evaluating Social Action Programs," *Social Science Quarterly,* Vol. 50, No. 3 (1969). A recent overview of federal evaluation activities gave very high praise to OEO's evaluation program: Joseph S. Wholey *et al., Federal Evaluation Policy* (The Urban Institute, Washington, D.C., 1970).

[31] Robert A. Dentler "The Phenomenology of the Evaluation Researcher" (not included in this volume).

Dentler's paper drew an analogy between the evaluator and a mendicant friar. Like the friar, he is produced by an institution, in this case a university graduate social science department, which is not oriented toward the "real world." The evaluator is also at the mercy of his clients, just as the friar is dependent on the strength and distribution of Christian charity. But most important, the evaluator judges his own activities in terms of the standards set by his academic mentors and peers in the same way as the mendicant friar retains the other-worldliness of the monastery in which he served his novitiate.

In serving his novitiate within the university, the evaluator is taught a high regard for basic research coupled with a low regard for applied research. According to this view, the applied researcher is in a servile position, in which he serves purposes over which he has little control and has his activities essentially determined by constraints imposed by others. As a consequence, few of the best social scientists go into applied evaluation research and those who do may often quickly withdraw after one or two excursions.

The terms in which the social science community judges professional activities are those which have been set by academic departments. To the extent that one departs from the "pure models" extolled in the graduate departments one is engaged in relatively low prestige work. Thus the evaluators are reluctant to compromise their "principles" for fear that their standing will slip even lower in the minds of their mentors and peers within the university. According to Dentler, the conference itself exemplified deference given to academic standards with almost every paper making proper obeisance to the "pure" models of experimental designs and cost-benefit analysis.

Because the academic social scientists and their satellites are reluctant to enter upon the scene of evaluation research, Dentler points to the development of a special research industry designed to furnish—at a profit—the evaluation researches presently being required of social welfare programs ·and projects. Dentler expressed concern that the evaluation researches provided by private industry may not be of very high quality and may be more in the way of public relations "image management" than adequate evaluations.

Dentler ended his paper with the hope that academic social science departments would undertake to train at least some students directly for the role of evaluation researcher. By providing a place within the academic context for such a role, it might be possible to raise the status of the activity, provide a more realistic orientation on the part of those who will go into evaluation and thereby improve the practice of the art.

The discussion of Dentler's paper produced several important points. First, the British participants indicated that they were puzzled about the distinction between pure and applied research, there being no such clear dichotomy drawn in their British experiences. Because British social scientists have always participated in English politics as social critics and in high quality journalism, working with policy makers does not seem to the British social scientists as especially out of line with the regular activities of academics. According to Greve, it is the separation between policy makers and social scientists in the United States that has produced a lower status for applied work in this country. Paradoxically, the American university is more like a monastery than the British.

A second major topic of discussion centered around the growth of the new health, education, and welfare sectors of private industry. In response to the fear expressed that private firms may be of low quality, several commentators, notably Evans and Orcutt, said that the problem of quality was more a matter of demand than supply. Private industry will supply services of high quality if that is demanded and the high price for quality services is met. If there is a problem of quality (and Evans thought that on the whole OEO received more competent bids from private industry than from the universities), it arises because the policy makers and their advisors have not been properly educated to exercise good judgment in their procurement of social science expertise[32] and because research procurement officials are not competent to make proper judgments on quality grounds.

Finally, most of the participants agreed that serious shortages of competent researchers presently existed. The sources of supply for personnel lie within the staffs of university social science departments and in their graduates. Although the social science graduate departments have been increasing the number of graduates with appropriate training and degrees, applied research has not been accorded a high level of prestige and the best graudates prefer to go into university teaching and research rather than into private or nonprofit research institutes. Nor can we expect that universities will increase their own commitment to applied research. Whether the present leveling off of support for basic research will change appreciably both job preferences of graduates and the research activities of university departments remains to be seen.[33]

---

[32] Indeed, Moynihan criticizes the social scientist for offering poor advice in connection with the poverty program and its predecessors (D. P. Moynihan, *Maximum Feasible Misunderstanding.* Free Press, New York, 1969). In an extended review of Moynihan's book, the present author has turned the criticism around and diagnosed the problem as one of developing the proper procurement policies for social science advice [P.H. Rossi, "No Good Idea Goes Unpunished: Moynihan's Misunderstandings and the Proper Role of Social Science in Social Policy," *Social Science Quarterly,* Vol. 50, No. 3 (1969)].

[33] It should be recalled that this discussion took place just before the present decline in the fortunes of new Ph.D.'s. With fewer jobs opening up in the higher levels of academia, it may well be that the future supply of the best Ph.D.'s may be more available to staff evaluation research units.

THE STATE OF THE ART: A SURVEY OF
COMPENSATORY EDUCATION EVALUATION

The concept of compensatory education flows quite naturally from the social philosophy that is the underpinning of our contemporary social welfare programs. Educational researchers almost invariably find that, on the average, children from poverty families and from disadvantaged minority groups perform relatively poorly in schools. Furthermore, it has also been found that there are few changes in the average intellectual performance of such groups as children progress through the American school system. Confronted with these firm findings, it is only logical to infer that students from poverty and minority backgrounds come to school with an initial deficit in background preparation for education, and that the problem of raising the levels of educational attainment of poor children is one of somehow making up for these deficits.

Based upon this inference, a large portion of our new educational programs have been aimed at compensating for this alleged deficit. Since 1965, annually half a million children have been served by Head Start programs. Another half million children have been aided more indirectly through Title I funds authorized by the Elementary and Secondary Education Act with more than a billion dollars annually being appropriated under Title I. Smaller programs have been designed to encourage older students to stay in school until at least high school graduation and to go on to college.

In their paper, McDill and his colleagues[34] examine the evaluations that have been made of the major compensatory education programs. Starting out by examining the theoretical underpinnings of compensatory programs, they find that there is little direct evidence for the idea of educational deficits. Indeed, there is not very much in the way of firm theory about the effects of family background upon learning ability. We do know that children from underprivileged backgrounds do not achieve as much on the average, but how much of this phenomenon is due to heredity or environment is not well known. Furthermore, it is difficult to unscramble the influences of so many potentially important factors. Maturation is taking place at the same time young children are entering schools; the family and the schools are only part of the socializing influences upon young children; peer groups and the mass media may conceivably play important roles. And so on.

In addition, research on changes in learning levels or abilities are plagued by the lack of sophisticated measuring devices of proven reliability. Although

---

[34] Included in this volume.

relatively good measures of cognitive skills exist,[35] instruments measuring affective domains (e.g., motivation to achieve, self-image, etc.) are less well developed. To the extent that compensatory programs are designed to affect noncognitive areas, this is a serious drawback to the design of sensitive and sophisticated evaluation research.

McDill and his colleagues surveyed evaluations of a variety of compensatory educational programs. Only a few researches stand out as anywhere close to fulfilling the canons of adequate evaluation research.

The authors note a few encouraging signs in the research. First of all, they discern a trend toward increasingly sophisticated research. Better instruments are being developed. Evaluation research was beginning to be accomplished by the federal agencies involved instead of being left to local project personnel to accomplish.

Second, it was abundantly clear that encouraging results had yet to be found. For all practical purposes, neither Head Start or Title I programs could be shown to have noticeable effects on student achievement measures. For Title I projects, which were designed to channel extra resources into schools, there arose the problem of "nonprojects," situations in which the funds allocated were absorbed by a school system but with no visible results in the form of changes in educational practices. Indeed, in some cases, teachers and principals in schools which were supposed to be affected by Title I funds were found not to have been even aware that their schools were participating in Title I programs.

McDill and his colleagues recommend a strategy of evaluation designed to fit the particular circumstances of compensatory education. Because so little is known about the basic underlying processes, they recommend that "trial-and-error experimentation" with different compensatory education techniques be undertaken, with the hope that some of the new techniques developed, if effective, might be usefully adopted on a wide scale. At the same time rigorous experimental studies should be undertaken using the most promising techniques available. This "mixed strategy" they believe will maximize creativity and lead to results which can stand up under methodological scrutiny.

The discussion of McDill's paper centered mainly around issues which had been taken up at considerable length in the discussions of other papers. It was abundantly clear to almost all participants that after 4 years of "experimentation" with compensatory educational programs, the nation was only just beginning to get reasonable (although far from ideal) readings on whether the

---

[35] A very provacative recent paper suggests that existing measurement instruments of cognitive skills may be less useful in measuring changes precisely because they were developed not to measure change but to maximize differentiation among individuals at a given point in time. See Ronald P. Carver, "Special Problems in Measuring Change with Psychometric Devices," in *Evaluative Research: Strategies and Methods,* Amer. Inst. of Research, Pittsburgh, Pennsylvania, 1970).

programs were producing any results. It was also apparent that programs and projects could not be relied upon to evaluate themselves. The locus of evaluation research had to be closer to the seat of fiscal power.

McDill's suggestion for a mixed strategy in approaching evaluation met with a great deal of approval. Few participants were satisfied that the pure models of cost benefit analysis or of experimental designs could be reproduced empirically with great fidelity and hence some degree of compromise was in any event dictated by circumstances. A mixed strategy made it possible to achieve some rigorous data without producing widespread reaction on the part of practitioners.

A STRATEGY FOR THE EVALUATION OF
SOCIAL ACTION PROGRAMS

A particularly important theme which ran through almost all the papers and certainly most of the discussion was one which was centered about what might be called the "politics of evaluation." This theme has two major sub-themes: First, there is the question of what should be the proper relationship between evaluation, policy analysis, and decision makers. Second, how does the evaluator handle his relationships with the programs and projects he may be evaluating?

Cost-benefit analysis places itself squarely in the center of policy making. Indeed, in an ideal sense, as presented in Rothenberg's paper, cost-benefit analysis is synonymous with good decision making, since a properly conducted cost-benefit analysis should yield a rank ordering of policy alternatives in terms of their yield for the public good. Policy analysis and evaluation research activities need to be located as closely as possible to the decision making authority. The success of the analysis of the maternal and child health programs carried by Wholey and his group rested on its being carried out close enough to the DHEW Secretary. Similarly, the very promising evaluation program of the Office of Economic Opportunity is being carried out by an analytical staff reporting directly to the Director's Office and kept out of the control of program and project personnel.

At the other extreme, there is not a single example of adequate cost-benefit analyses or evaluation studies which have been carried out by a group which is responsible for running programs. This is part of the message of the Weiss and Rein paper and lies behind McDill's finding of so little worthwhile evaluation research conducted on Head Start or Title 1 programs, with the notable exception of the Westinghouse—Ohio State evaluation of Head Start.

Thus one of the conclusions of the evaluation conference was that analysis and evaluation should be conducted by groups located close to (and possibly forming the staff of) decision-making authorities. Of course, for national programs, there remains the question of to which decision-making authority should evaluation be connected. Departments and agencies propose legislation through the President's office, the Congress authorizes programs and provides funds; and the Office of Management and Budget advises the President on fiscal matters. Should evaluation be a function attached to the Congress in a form similar to the General Accounting Office? Should evaluation research be conducted by the Secretary of HEW, or by the Director of the Office of Economic Opportunity? At the present time, there are signs that evaluation activities are beginning to be undertaken at almost all these points. The General Accounting Office has undertaken to develop cost-benefit ratios for the Jobs Corps and has been looking into the income maintenance experiment being conducted by the Office of Economic Opportunity. The Office of Education has been developing a very extensive set of researches designed to provide data on the impact effectiveness of a large number of educational programs.

The second aspect of the politics of evaluation concerns relationships between policy analyst, evaluation researchers, and the organizations or persons being evaluated. Instance after instance can be cited of strained relationships between evaluators and the evaluated. Conference papers and the discussion did not provide much in the way of guidelines for handling these relationships. Weiss and Rein come closest with their suggestion that the researcher attached to a program abandon the effort to evaluate and become virtually a project historian feeding information to project administrators in an effort to help them to maximize the efforts of their programs. Of course, changing the location of evaluation tends to avoid some of the problems of relations between evaluators and the evaluated; at least, it tends to insulate the evaluator from the political and fiscal powers of the evaluated. But, until policy analysis and evaluation is taken for granted as one of the "facts of life" for social action program administrators, they will generate considerable tensions.

Although admitting that broad-aimed social action programs were difficult to evaluate, conference participants as a group were somewhat reluctant to give up evaluating such programs. However, some participants took the radical stance that programs such as Community Action, Model Cities, and the like ought not to be evaluated at all, mainly on the grounds that only programs with rather specific aims could be brought properly under scrutiny. A large part of the problem presented by broad aim programs lies in the absence of reasonable social science theories which could serve as a guide to the design of social action programs. There are very few social scientists of any repute who have strongly held ideas of what sorts of social action programs ought to be undertaken to handle most social problems. For example, no social scientist has a clear idea of why the rates of serious crimes have been increasing steeply in the last decade. If social scientists have no clear ideas, then how much more at a loss are members of the Congress or presidential advisors? Perhaps the best thing to do under these circumstances is to provide funds to a diverse set of institutions and hope that trial-and-error experimentation may hit upon some effective program. Indeed, Title I, Model Cities, the Community Action Program, and the like may all be regarded as devices to stimulate trial-and-error experimentation.

The difficulties inherent in attempting to evaluate trial-and-error experimentation have been thoroughly aired through the conference. Bold program innovators who are willing to take risks are also likely to be persons whose strength of conviction about the worth of their programs is likely to be overriding. Trial-and-error experimentation leads to a bewildering diversity of projects, further compounding the problems of evaluation. Finally, this approach tends to center attention more on means than on ends. Maximum feasible participation becomes an end in itself and hence does not need to be evaluated except as to the extent to which it has been achieved in specific projects and programs.[36]

However, if we are to benefit from trial-and-error experimentation, then it is necessary to be able to distinguish programs and projects which show promise from those which are essentially failures. Even those broad aim programs which center on process rather than output need to be evaluated whether the process changes in fact have occurred.[37] The problem of evaluation then becomes one of establishing a monitoring system sufficiently sensitive to detect programs and projects which are having an impact upon their targets.

Monitoring systems for broad aimed programs have begun to be set up within HUD, OEO and OE. The strategy being followed has been away from the sort of case study advocated by Weiss and Rein and more in the direction of comparative studies using rather large numbers of cases. For example, a recent OEO sponsored evaluation of CAP programs compared 50 programs classifying programs into those which emphasized citizen organization (organizing and mobilizing the poor) and those which emphasized the coordination of existing agencies and services. Vanecko[38] found that the former produced more in the way of increased services than the latter. Although this research effort has to be

[36] Rothenberg specifically excludes from the realm of social policies which are amenable to evaluation through cost-benefit analyses all programs which are aimed at altering decision-making procedures as their primary goal. He would also exclude circumstances in which the main aim of the decision maker is to negotiate a satisfactory settlement among contending interest groups. In other words, bargaining as an end in itself does not lead to rational decision making.

[37] For example, if the emphasis in Community Action Programs is on maximum feasible participation on the part of the poor, then it becomes necessary to determine the distribution of participation in decision making if only to be able to distinguish between those CAP programs which have been successful in this sense and those which have failed.

[38] J. J. Vanecko, "Community Mobilization and Institutional Change," *Social Science Quarterly*, Vol. 50, No. 3 (1969).

regarded as a first crude approximation (based on ratings given to the CAP programs by knowledgeable informants within each of the 50 cities) it does provide some data upon which to begin to design more definitive research. Similar programs presently being designed within the Office of Education for its broad-aim programs and within the Department of Housing and Urban Development for Model Cities projects will provide within the next few years comparable information on those programs. These monitoring systems all have the same general design—relatively large numbers of projects will be studied, with efforts being made to measure both the characteristics of specific projects and outputs. Thus, an Office of Education monitoring system now being planned will concentrate on a large sample of school systems (around 500), collecting information from school administrators, teachers, and students.

Monitoring broad-aim programs and projects can be seen as the first step in a graded series of nested researches. Once promising projects have been identified, then it becomes appropriate to employ tighter research designs, using better measures of both programs and outputs. At this point, it seems utopian to expect that we will ever have experimental designs measuring the output of Title I programs or Model Cities. The best that we can aspire to is quasiexperiments, employing reasonable approximations to control groups.

The prospect for evaluating specific aim social action programs has always been more sanguine. The more specific the goal of the program, the more consensus there will be among decision makers, researchers, and program administrators on the measures that can be taken as signs of the failure or success of the program. Thus, the better evaluations conducted have measured the effects of manpower retraining in terms of increments in wages using outcome evaluation models. Similarly, the projected evaluation of OEO family planning programs is among the best-planned evaluations primarily because there is an agreed upon desirable outcome of such programs, namely, the reduction of births in target populations.

There are a number of lessons to be drawn from the papers and the discussions of this conference. It seems clear that given the present state of the art we cannot expect either the best of all possible policy analyses or the best of all possible evaluations. The problem of evaluating social policy then boils down to what constitute reasonable approximations to these ideal models. We need to know how best to set up the conditions for doing the best possible job, producing data which contains powerful enough information to make sensible judgments about the worth of social action programs. We must do this without at the same time making such gross political errors that our data are ignored, and do it within a time phasing that is useful to the process of decision making. In other words, policy analysis or evaluation can be fatuous activities if they produce results which are no better than informed guesses, if they are ignored by policy makers, and they produce results only long after the results can be used.

There is much work to be done in bolstering the context in which policy analysis and evaluation research is conducted. In part, this means that we have to educate decision makers, program and project administrators, and relevant portions of the public about the issues involved. The negative aura surrounding controlled experiments has to be lifted. Decision makers have to learn how to tell the difference between the good and the bad in policy analysis and evaluation research; otherwise the fears expressed by some conference participants about the rise of an industry geared to the production of low grade researches may be realized. But, it is even more important to obtain a higher degree of commitment to pay some attention to the outcomes of these activities. It is part of our responsibility as social scientists and as researchers to make everyone aware that in this period even the best of social action programs are not likely to produce spectacular results. The age of miracles is long over. New programs can be expected when they are successful to be only somewhat better than existing programs. Any new program is not likely to produce spectacular changes, and a good proportion are likely to fail to produce any detectable changes.[39]

By commitment to evaluation is meant that it should be worked out in advance what are the policy changes that will flow from each of the set of possible findings. For example, before evaluating manpower training programs it should be worked out what are the policy implications for the programs if positive, negative, or ambiguous findings result from the evaluation.[40] Commitment does not necessarily mean that evaluation research should take the place of the traditional decision-making process, but it does mean that at least the parties involved will have thought through in advance how they might respond under various likely contingencies. This sort of commitment would do much to lessen the frustrations of the evaluator that was manifested in the conference papers and discussion.

A second lesson that can be drawn is that we have a very long way to go in devising acceptable ways of applying controlled experiments to evaluation even under those circumstances when such experiments would be easy in principle to conduct. Political obstacles to the use of randomization make it difficult to get

[39] This is not to say that programs with small effects cannot cumulatively make significant amounts of change. For example, since the start of the War on Poverty there have been significant improvements in the economic position of blacks and there has been a "spectacular" change in the proportion of blacks who finish high school, i.e., from 40% to 65%.

[40] One of the by-products of such an *a priori* setting forth of decision consequences of evaluation will be to favor the development of programs in which a diversity of specific actions are proposed. For example, one would be more likely to develop several modes of manpower training to be evaluated rather than resting the success of manpower training on whether or not one mode of accomplishing this end is effective or not. (See Glennan's article in this volume.)

acceptance of such designs. The difficulty of maintaining controls in a nonsterile world makes full-fledged use of such designs relatively rare. And so on.

Part of the problem lies in raising the level of sophistication among interested parties about the nature of controlled experiments. But at least part of the problem also lies in developing new ways of devising control groups. For example, one of the major reasons for randomization of assignment to experimental and control groups stems from the fact that such a procedure would eliminate the biases of self-selection. However, one may raise the question of whether this is an important bias to eliminate in the evaluation of a social action program. After all, a program once put into action ordinarily is not free of self-selection biases.[41] Perhaps the proper evaluation of some types of social action programs is to evaluate the combined effects of self-selection and the program. If so, then the problem of devising a control group becomes easier.[42] For example, a control group for a job training program may be a sample of unemployed or underemployed persons living in the same target area from which trainees are attracted.

The proposal for generalized control groups leads to another important theme running through the conference. Quasi-experimental designs are the modes most likely to be used for assessing the outcome of social action programs. The important question which faces evaluation researchers is how defective are such designs? How much credence can be placed in their results and what are the circumstances under which they can be employed with relatively strong confidence in the resulting data?

Implicit in many of the papers and in the discussion of them by participants is a rough hierarchy of evaluation research designs. At the top of the hierarchy are controlled experiments: At the bottom of the hierarchy are unsystematic narrative reports of project administrators. Five distinct levels could be discerned in the hierarchy, as follows:

Most Desired Design: Classical Fisherian experiments, preferable using factorial designs

Quasi-experiments with impure control groups, e.g., training program trainees compared with their unemployed friends

[41] This is especially the case if the program is not designed to cover the totality of a target population.

[42] Generalized control groups can be developed for most of the target populations of contemporary social action programs. Samples of youths living in poverty areas can serve as controls for the Job Corps, Neighborhood Youth Services, Follow Through and other youth-oriented programs. OEO has begun to develop several such generalized control groups. For a description of one such attempt, see Ralph Underhill, *Youth in Poor Neighborhoods* (National Opinion Research Center, Chicago, Illinois, 1967).

> Correlational designs in which statistical controls are used
>
> Program and project audits: Qualitative judgments made by outside observers, e.g., Vanecko's evaluation of CAP programs
>
> Least Desired Design: Project and program administrators' narrative reports

Several principles emerged as guides to how high in the hierarchy of designs one should reach in a particular evaluation study. First of all, when it is the case that massive effects are both desired and expected, softer techniques are just as good as subtle and precise ones. To illustrate: If what is desired as the outcome of treatment is the remission of symptoms in each and every individual subjected to the treatment in question, then it is hardly necessary to have a control group. Thus is a proposed birth control technique is to be judged effective if and only if the technique eliminates any chance of conception, then all that is necessary is to make the technique available to a set of subjects and observe whether or not *any* births occur, for the appearance of a single birth, under these rules, invalidates the effectiveness of the method.

Of course, in the evaluation of social action programs one is rarely confronted with the problem of evaluating a technique which is supposed to accomplish complete remission of symptoms in each and every person subjected to the treatment. But there are approximations to this condition. A program designed to teach reading to young children should produce graduates who can read. Or a project designed to produce computer programmers should produce graduate students who have computer programming competences. Or, an income maintenance program which does not change income levels in a target population is obviously ineffective.[43]

Second, the obverse of the above principle also holds. If a treatment shows no effect when evaluated by a soft method of evaluation, then it is not likely to show any effects when evaluated by a harder method. Thus if a Head Start project produces no effects in a before-and-after type of study, it is highly unlikely that a controlled experiment would show any effects either. Hence, if we grant some validity to this principle, then we can use soft evaluation methods to eliminate programs and projects which are ineffective.[44]

---

[43] An empirical example was provided by Robert Levine; an OEO program designed to provide business loans to poor people was in fact providing loans to persons who could have obtained loans through regular banking channels. See Robert Levine, "Evaluating the War on Poverty," in *On Fighting Poverty* (J. L. Sundquist, ed.). Basic Books, New York. 1969.

[44] It is always possible that some higher order interaction effects may mask the positive benefits of a treatment. However, such interaction effects are encountered empirically very infrequently. For all practical purposes it is reasonably safe to generalize that

Third, the major problem of interpretation of results occurs when a soft method produces positive findings. Thus the finding that smoking and lung cancer were associated statistically had to be followed up by a wide variety of substantiating evidence before the association was accepted as evidence of a causal relationship. Soft methods apparently require either followup using a controlled experiment or sufficient number of replications that all shadows of doubts are eliminated. These considerations lead to a strategy of evaluation in which soft methods are used to eliminate ineffective projects and to detect potentially effective ones. Those found to be potentially effective then need further and more precise evaluation through controlled experiments or close approximations to such designs.[45]

Fourth, there are certain circumstances in which only correlational designs will yield information of use to decision makers. If the desired effects are ones which are postulated to be the result of long-acting treatments, then controlled experiments may take too long to carry out. The best example is discerning the effects of smoking upon the incidence of lung cancer. Smoking is presumed to have its effects over some period of time and the most economical (in terms of time) method of discerning whether smoking has such effects is to compare the cause-specific death rates of smokers and nonsmokers. Or, if there is some interest in the effects of high school graduation on subsequent earnings, a first approximation may be made by comparing adults of different levels of educational attainment with experience in the labor force.

A similar set of considerations can be set down as to cost-benefit (policy) analysis. It seems highly unlikely that an analyst will have available to him all the data necessary to evaluate all the costs and benefits of all the alternatives which may be considered at a decision point. As Wholey's paper indicates, it is still

---

negative effects in a quasi-experiment will be matched by negative effects in a controlled experiment, given the same level of generalizability (i.e., same size samples drawn from the same universe, etc.).

[45] The statements made in this paragraph are not entirely correct in theory. For example, soft research methods may result in biases which cancel out the positive desirable effects of social action programs. Donald T. Campbell has argued that the Westinghouse-Ohio State University Evaluation of Head Start (Donald T. Campbell and Albert Erlebacher, "How Regression Artifacts in Quasi-Experimental Evaluations Can Mistakenly Make Compensatory Education Look Harmful," in *Compensatory Education: A National Debate* (J. Hellmuth, ed.), Vol. 3. *Disadvantaged Child.* Brunner/Mazel, New York, 1970) was biased to underplay whatever positive effects the program had. Although one must recognize that in theory such biases can exist, in practice it is unlikely that the complicated mechanisms that would produce such biases in fact do exist. Hence, I am convinced that for most practical purposes a finding of no positive effects of a program by a soft method would not be reversed using a harder method.

possible to provide better bases for decision by utilizing the best information available at a point in time. Furthermore, the exercise of assembling such information provides a better assessment of what is missing.[46]

In sum, the major message of the conference may be put as follows: The state of the art as practiced lags far behind the ideal. Yet there are significant contributions to policy making that evaluation, even poorly practiced, can make. Even more important, the state of the practiced art is improving in response to the heightened level of demands for evaluation research.

[46]For a detailed discussion of this and related points, see Walter Williams, *Social Policy Research and Analysis* (American Elsevier, New York, 1971).

3

THE BEHAVIORAL SCIENCES
IMPACT-EFFECTIVENESS MODEL*

Tom R. Houston, Jr.

To evaluate a social action program is to collect evidence regarding its effectiveness. The Roman jurists called evidence *argumenta,* and the evaluator's role is inevitably forensic: his evidence should persuade others to continue, or modify, or cancel the program. Any number of strategies are open to the evaluator in this endeavor. He might, for example, collect statements from individuals connected with the program, or obtain the opinion of an experienced authority on such matters, or report his own impressions, as many have done. If his evaluation will serve as the basis of an important decision, however, his arguments should be as convincing as possible. And to the skeptical ears of behavioral scientists, mere human testimony is less persuasive than the mathematical rhetoric of the impact effectiveness model which we will outline here.

In this model, effectiveness is defined as *impact,* the capacity of a program to cause changes in those who are exposed to it. *Effect* is the statistician's equivalent for this term. Validity, a tendency not to be contradicted by subsequent evidence, is the persuasive virtue of this model, in which respect it is rivaled by no other method of evaluation. This validity is available only if the evaluation is conducted under conditions which conform to the model, and we

*Paper presented at The American Academy of Arts and Sciences 1969 seminar on Evaluation Research.

will devote some attention to recent critics who have questioned the usefulness to evaluators of procedures requiring such rigorous control.

In the context of program evaluation, "statistical induction," "controlled, comparative experimentation," the "experimental model," and "analysis of variance and covariance" are virtually synonymous terms for the "impact effectiveness model." The model requires that the evaluator gather observations according to some predetermined plan called an "experimental design," and that he numerically analyze his data using a statistical test appropriate to his experimental design. The statistical analysis attaches a probability to the truth of the hypothesis that "The program had no effect." If this probability is small, then the evaluator has indirect but cogent evidence that the program was effective.

This strategy is now standard procedure in many fields of behavioral, biological, and industrial research, but its historical development was a slow process which Boring (1954) has described. The Rev. Thomas Bayes (1763) first discussed the problem of drawing causal inference from empirical observations in terms of mathematical probabilities. Sophisticated experimental designs, including Latin squares, were used by Danish agricultural researchers as early as 1872 (Fisher, 1935), and a fundamental statistical discovery, the distribution of the mean for small samples, was made in Dublin by the research chemist W. S. Gosset ("Student," 1908). It was, however, the British statistician Sir Ronald Fisher (Fisher, 1935), directing agricultural field trials at the Rothamsted Experimental Station, who between 1919 and 1930 established the methodological canon of controlled, comparative experimentation.

In Fisher's sense an *experiment* is a study in which (1) an investigator *interferes* with a process, so the (2) *random* subsets of the units processed are differently treated, and (3) measurements are collected in such a way that the *variability* among units which were treated the same way can be estimated.

The first point, the necessity of intervention, distinguishes experiments from correlational or status studies, and is a necessary condition for drawing causal inference. Since we are here considering the evaluation of programs which, by definition, have attempted to introduce changes into social processes, the point need not concern us further. Fisher's third requirement, that the data provide all estimates of variability, represented a radical improvement over the statistical methods which preceded Gosset's 1908 paper, but in practice this merely requires the evaluator to replicate observations within his experimental design.

The second point above, however, that the experimental units must be assigned to treatment conditions in such a way that each unit has the same probability as any other of receiving a given treatment, was Fisher's greatest discovery. The purpose of an experiment is to permit valid inference regarding the effect of the antecedent variables upon the consequent variables; an experiment is *controlled* to the extent to which it provides such inference. Randomization permits a valid estimate of variability due to error, which is needed to specify the stability of inference, alias statistical significance. Randomization enables the investigator to extend his inference beyond the data at hand to a conceptual universe of similar units, so that a relatively small sample of observations can be used to evaluate a large program. Randomization makes an experiment unbiased, since it can have no *a priori* tendency to favor one group of experimental units over another. In large experiments randomization tends to equate groups of experimental units with respect to *all possible* antecedent variables; here randomization provides better control than nonrandom matching schemes which attempt to equate groups on the basis of prior measures (see Stanley, 1967).

It should be noted, incidentally, that the randomization requirement defines the experimental unit as that which was randomized. If a group of individuals (such as a classroom or a community) is assigned *en bloc* to one treatment condition, then the number of experimental units is the number of groups, rather than the total number of individuals within the groups. A statistical test of significance which assumes the latter will be more likely to yield positive results, but will be unconvincing to those who recognize the fallacy. This brings us to another principle of Fisher, that the statistical analysis must be determined by the experimental design. While this may seem to be a truism, the literature of the behavioral sciences is rich in counterexamples; the availability of computer routines, which typically can analyze some designs but not others, presents new temptations to the evaluator. It is his responsibility to select beforehand a design which will be sensitive to the anticipated impact of a program, and to perform an analysis which will use, insofar as is possible, all of the information in the data.

The experimental design which he selects must permit the comparison of units exposed to the program with a control group which was not. The evaluator wishes to interpret measured differences between these groups as program impact; but a necessary condition for such inference is the absence of prior differences between the two groups. The burden of proof that no other differences existed lies heavy upon the evaluator. If, for example, his program were conducted in Boston, and his control group were found in San Diego, observed differences between the groups might also be attributable to the differential characteristics (sociological, meteorological, astrological, *ad infinitum*) of the two cities. Similarly, random individuals are not a good control for participants in a voluntary program, if the qualities which prompt one to volunteer could directly affect scores on the outcome measures. A group functions as an experimental control only if it eliminates the plausible alternatives to program impact in assigning a cause to observed outcome differences.

As we indicated above, randomization is an elegant means of equating groups. In general, the impact effectiveness model is implemented by identifying units that can potentially be exposed to the program, and assigning them randomly to the treatment or to the control groups. Especially if the number of available units is small, groups composed by unrestricted randomization may be badly "equated." The evaluator may be well advised to rank the units on some relevant antecedent variable, and then to assign units to the treatment or control groups randomly within blocks of adjacent ranks, a design refinement called *randomized blocks*. Alternatively, he may employ the statistical technique of *covariance analysis*. This compensates for initial differences between groups, as measured on an antecedent variable known to be correlated with the outcome measure, by numerically adjusting scores on the observed outcome measure. In any event, randomization is necessary if the evaluator wishes to conduct a controlled experiment.

Randomization is a recent concept, which has not yet attained the status in our culture that it merits. A major obstacle to its use in evaluation is the popular belief that chance will do a worse job than human judgment in determining who will receive the presumed benefits of a program. Certainly if the capacity of a program is greater than the number of qualified candidates, as may be the case in current college efforts to recruit blacks, the random rejection of applicants is unreasonable, and the evaluator must find another strategy. But in the more typical case, program resources are not sufficient to process all potential units, and some decision rule such as "first come, first served" is used in practice to choose from among those eligible for a program. Here random assignment is unlikely to impair program effectiveness. A less controversial procedure (e.g., Wilner *et al.*, 1962) is to form the control group from among units who applied for the program, but who were rejected. This procedure provides experimental control only under the assumption that administrative decisions to accept or reject will approximate a random process.

Another modern feature of the experimental model is the notion of *"factorial designs."* A "factor" can be any measurable characteristic of the experimental units whose relation to the dependent variables is of interest to the investigator. Fisher showed that it was possible within one experimental design to investigate simultaneously an arbitrary number of factors. The efficiency of this procedure, compared with conducting individual experiments to examine each factor, is very great. Whether the variable selected as a factor is measured on a discrete scale (e.g., sex), or on a continuous scale (e.g., age), measures on each factor are reduced to a small number of categories called "levels." For example, scores on an achievement test might be divided at the median into two levels, "high" and "low." If a design includes both men and women with "high" and "low" scores, then the factors of "sex" and "achievement" are said to be crossed, since every combination of levels of those factors occurs in the design. If individuals are the experimental units, and if several individuals are included at each combination of sex and ability, then "individuals" is a nested factor, since each "level" of "individual" occurs with only one combination of sex and achievement. When all of the factors are mutually crossed or nested, effects can be estimated by well-known statistical procedures.

The factors of greatest interest to the evaluator are those which describe the program. While it can be represented as a single factor having two levels corresponding to exposure and nonexposure, such a design measures only the global impact of a program, and provides no information regarding how a program might be improved. Social action programs typically consist of a "package" of treatments, such as the various social, educational, medical, and dental services offered by the Head Start program. The factorial design should specify the components of the program, and arrange them so that the effectiveness of each part can be individually estimated. In this way effective components can be identified, and ineffective components modified or eliminated. Particularly in the exploratory phases of a program's development, the explicit description required by the factorial design can assist those elsewhere who wish to replicate a successful program.

Most (but not all) of the features of the experimental model which we have discussed above are concerned with internal validity—the lack of bias, logical consistency, absence of ambiguity, and statistical justification of the inferences made by the experimentor. Internal validity is a rare and wonderful commodity, without which an experiment is uninterpretable, but it is not a sufficient condition for a good experiment. It is no doubt possible, given the appropriate assumptions, to construct a model of evaluation which employed the authority of experts, or anecdotal evidence, or the entrails of sacrificial animals in place of experimental data. Such rational exercises must be viewed skeptically unless they also exhibit external validity; this requires the specification of those conditions under which the results hold, and is also known as generalizability. Unless inference can be generalized beyond the data at hand, a study is of little value to others.

The generalizability of an experimental study is specified by the factorial design. If inferences are to be drawn which will apply to more than one sex, race, or socioeconomic level, or which will provide information regarding the differential effects of these variables, they should be explicitly represented as factors in the design. While the number of potential classificatory factors is indefinitely large, in practice the evaluator selects his factors from among three (often overlapping) categories: (1) factors which are of special relevance to the goals of the program; (2) factors of traditional interest; and (3) factors directly affecting the variability of the outcome measures. The latter two types require some comment. Conventional factors are useful in that they make evaluations of different programs more comparable. Factors of the third type improve the precision of the statistical analysis of the data; these include factors likely to influence the process of measurement (such as characterisitcs of the persons who secured the data, or the occasions on which a series of measurements were taken).

Another component of generalizability is the battery of instruments which provide the outcome measures. These can include tests, ratings, reports, or laboratory equipment, but they should be selected to measure with adequate precision all of the important outcomes which the evaluator has reason to anticipate. For purposes of comparability, the use of appropriate traditional instruments should be encouraged.

In addition to the advantages which we have cited, factorial designs permit the evaluator to examine the effects of combinations of factors. If a program had two components and the effect of these in combination differed from the sum of the two separate effects, then a "treatment by treatment interaction" would be said to exist. Interaction effects may be positive or negative, depending on whether the combined effect is greater than or less than the sum. A common type of interaction is a "classificatory variable by treatment interaction." This could occur, for example, if a treatment component were effective with boys but not with girls, or with middle-class communities but not with lower-class communities. Classificatory variables may interact with one another, as would be the case between the factors "age" and "race" if, given the same treatment, 5-year-old blacks outperformed 5-year-old whites, but 10-year-olds of both races performed equally well. Individuals or groups can appear in a design as factors, and interactions may exist between these and the treatment; for example, a program component may be successful in Los Angeles, but ineffective in Philadelphia, while other components do badly in the first city but well in the second. Individuals may interact with individuals; thus the rank order among a group of job trainees might depend upon which instructor they were assigned.

The above are all examples of "first-order" (i.e., two-factor) interaction effects, but it is possible to have significant "nth-order" interactions, in which a combination of $n+1$ factors has an effect which is quite different from the sum of all the lower-order interaction effects involved. Such interactions are rare for n greater than two. (This is fortunate for the evaluator, who must attach some meaning to his results; higher-order interactions are notoriously difficult to interpret.)

Interactions offer the evaluator a very detailed description of the effectiveness of the program. They enable him to detect redundancies within the program components, to recommend which treatments should be used with which units, to identify subsets of the target population who are not benefitting from a program, to recognize certain artifacts of his measurement procedure, and to reduce the unexplained variability of the data in his statistical analysis.

The experimental model outlined above is not the only strategy by which scientists obtain empirical evidence to support assertions regarding the effects of treatments. Followers of the behaviorist B. F. Skinner subject an organism to an operant conditioning program designed to establish a particular chain of responses. If the solitary subject subsequently behaves in the manner specified, no interpretation of the data is plausible, other than that the training procedure was effective. There is no need for control groups or for statistics to demonstrate the effects of unmistakably powerful treatments.

For various reasons, unfortunately, the effects of social action programs are rarely this conspicuous. Program goals, such as improving literacy or reducing delinquency, are often sought by other agencies, so that the baseline against which program impact is measured is the effectiveness of traditional procedures. Large increments are difficult to achieve, and detection of them is obscured by variation among units and by the unreliability of outcome measures.

Under these circumstances, the experimental model provides an analytic procedure for determining whether a factor or interaction had any effect. In general, the data are reduced to a test statistic whose magnitude reflects the likelihood that an effect was present. If the test statistic exceeds a critical value, the investigator concludes that an effect was observed; otherwise he concludes that he has no evidence of an effect.

Since observations are subject to sampling and measurement errors, two types of false inference are possible when statistical tests are used. The first kind occurs if the evaluator decides that an effect exists when in fact it does not. The probability of *not* making an error of this sort is called the *size* of a statistical test. The size depends entirely upon the critical value which the evaluator selects to compare with the test statistic. An evaluator who is eager to report favorably on a program may be tempted to tolerate a fairly high risk of such error. Among behavioral scientists, however, there is a widely held convention that this risk should not exceed 5%. Whatever the wisdom of this custom, the evaluator who uses statistical tests of a size smaller than 95% may find that his results are viewed with skepticism or worse.

Less well appreciated are errors of the second kind: deciding that no effect exists, when in fact one exists. The probability of *not* making an error of this kind is called the power of a statistical test. Four things determine the power of a test: (1) the true magnitude of the effect; (2) the number of experimental units and factor levels; (3) the size of the statistical test; and (4) the unexplained variability of the data. Power is directly related to the first two, and inversely related to the latter pair. Despite his cloak of scientific detachment, the evaluator often has a personal desire to demonstrate that a program of social action is indeed effective, an ambition which will be doomed to frustration by a test which lacks adequate power. While magnitude and size are somewhat out of the evaluator's hands, the unexplained variability can be reduced by careful planning and execution of the evaluation design, and the number of experimental units can in theory be increased until the power is arbitrarily high (provided that the evaluator does not lose control of his experiment).

If a size of 95% is a suitable precaution against errors of the first kind, what is an appropriate value for the power of a test? Decision theory, which was devised after Fisher's contributions to the experimental model, deals with problems of this sort. One must first decide whether an error of the first kind is more or less deplorable than an error of the second kind. To the staff of the program, an error of the second sort is worse, but to those funding the program and to those who are subjected to its possible benefits, the choice is less clear. Unless special circumstances make one type of error clearly more serious than the other, as might be the case if a program were potentially dangerous, a convenient solution is to let the power also be 95%, so that the statistical test will be unbiased with respect to errors of either kind.

This does not settle the issue, since statistical tests have more power for detecting large effects than small ones. To design an evaluation which will have tests of a given power, the evaluator must specify the magnitude of the effect which he considers it worth his while to detect. A reading program, for example, may have at its disposal $6000 to spend on improving the reading of each individual in the program. The evaluator must be able to specify the improvement in reading age (1 month? 1 year?) whose utility would justify this expense.

Several considerations must be taken into account in assigning values to outcomes. Effects may be of immediate value, such as a job which they enable a previously underqualified person to hold. A program may have longer term effects, such as reduction in dental expenses which a hygiene program might cause. The value of effects will often depend on complementary effects outside the program; for example, improved literacy is more valuable to an individual who uses it to finish high school. Effects may accumulate, so that the value of an improvement in cognitive skills is enhanced by an improvement in social skills. Although quantifying in dollars the estimated utility of specific outcomes may seem to be a crass and uncertain undertaking, to do so is the task ·of the evaluator, if he is to make rational decisions regarding statistical power. With too little power, he risks reporting unfavorably on socially useful programs; with too much power, he may report favorably on programs of dubious value, and he wastes effort gathering more information than is necessary.

While we have emphasized the inferential aspects of the experimental model in evaluation, the economic aspects deserve further attention. The evaluator should provide information for the improvement of a program, and the cost of a program is frequently susceptible to improvement. After describing program components as factors within his design, the evaluator can identify those which are effective and those which are not. By subsequent investigation, the critical elements of effective components may be isolated, and simplified procedures, designed to produce the same effects, can be developed and tested. These refined and simplified procedures can be mass produced by concentrating resources in the most effective elements of a program.

PREEXPERIMENTAL DESIGNS

The model of controlled, comparative, variable-manipulating experimentation (Stanley, 1957, 1967, 1971, 1971) has rarely been applied to large-scale social action programs. Evaluations based on preexperimental designs have been used with some frequency, so this nominally related model deserves some comment. A preexperimental design is a procedure for gathering observations which does *not* permit valid inference regarding program effects. While it may seem surprising that such procedures are used at all, they possess the advantage of requiring little effort, and are of some persuasive value among persons unfamiliar with scientific research. They often avoid the problem of statistical power entirely, by making no provision for concluding that a program had no effect. We shall discuss below three preexperimental designs, paying special attention to their internal validity.

The simplest preexperimental design is the "post test only" design. A group is exposed to a program, and measures are subsequently obtained to characterize the group. No explicit comparison is made with any other group, this "case study" being presented as evidence of the program's effectiveness. While the evaluator may argue that the group is different from how it would have been without the treatment, our ignorance of how it was before the treatment gives us no basis for agreement or disagreement with his assertions. The evaluator may assert that the group is different from individuals who were not reached by the program; but such differences, if indeed they exist, might occur because peculiar individuals were selected, or because individuals who lasked certain characteristics dropped out of the program before the measurements were taken. Such studies are woefully lacking in control, meaning, or scientific value.

A somewhat less primitive design is the one-group pretest-posttest design, wherein a group is selected, measured, subjected to a program, and measured again. Since the before and after scores can be compared, it is possible to determine whether any changes occurred between the occasions of measurement. It is generally impossible, however, to show that such changes were the effect of the program, and it may be difficult to show that the units themselves, as distinct from the measurements, changed. Campbell and Stanley (1966) have described eight classes of alternative explanations which jeopardize the internal validity of preexperimental designs, and the present design is often vulnerable to six of these, as the following hypothetical examples will illustrate.

History is any set of events other than the program, occurring between the two occasions of measurement. The effectiveness of a program to encourage community involvement with schools would be obscured if local teachers went on strike during the program. The longer the time interval, the greater the danger of historical events' rivaling the program as a plausible cause of change.

Maturation denotes natural changes which occur with the passage of time. The one-group pretest-posttest design would be inappropriate for evaluating a health program; as people grow older their health tends to decline, so that effects of the program would be underestimated.

Testing is the effect of taking the pretest upon the posttest scores. An ineffective program to improve cognitive skills could report improvement if the same instrument were used as the pretest and posttest since items might be remembered or discussed. Even if different test forms were used, persons who are unfamiliar with tests will perform more efficiently the second time. Testing also includes the general problem of *reactivity;* in the social sciences, as in physics, the act of measurement may change the thing measured. We might question whether a program would have had the same effect if the pretest had not sensitized individuals to the program goals.

Instrumentation refers to changes in the system by which measurements are secured; a synonym is "instrument decay." If a program to improve social adjustment were evaluated by comparing pre- and postprogram ratings by psychologists, any changes in their standards of judgment which occurred between testing occasions would bias the results. Since interviewers tend to become more skillful over time, instrumentation is a persistent threat to validity in social science research.

Statistical regression will bias preexperimental evaluation designs when individuals are selected into a program on the basis of extreme scores on the pretest. Regression effects guarantee that individuals who scored below average on a pretest will appear to have improved upon retesting. Thus the effects of a remedial reading program will be overestimated if the evaluator uses the one-group design on readers whose retardation was determined by a pretest whose reliability is not perfect (i.e., any existing test). Conversely, statistical regression will artificially reduce the observed effectiveness of a program whose participants are selected because of their high scores on the pretest. See Thorndike (1963) for an elementary account of the mechanism by which these effects operate.

Selection-maturation interaction is the selection of individuals whose characteristics will change between the pretest and posttest regardless of whether they participate in a program. A one-group evaluation of a voluntary program to assist narcotics users, for example, would be discounted by critics who believed that such an interaction operated: if some volunteers would have spontaneously discontinued drug use, effects would be reported by the evaluator even if the program itself caused no changes. This is a threat to the internal validity of inference whenever preexperimental designs are used with long-term programs involving non-random selection of participants.

All but the last of these six deficiencies are sometimes avoided by a third type of preexperimental design, the *ad hoc* comparison. Here units who were exposed to a program are compared to units who were not, and differences are interpreted as program effects. This procedure may be refined by selecting the comparison group (it is misleading to call this a *control* group) in such a way that it resembles the program group in various respects. The inadequacy of this strategy stems from lack of random assignment of the units to the groups. Two plausible alternatives to interpreting observed differences as effects of the program follow:

Selection, the procedure by which units were assigned to the program and comparison groups, may have created a bias, so that subsequent differences reflect initial differences, rather than program effectiveness. Regardless of the number of variables upon which the two groups are matched, the evaluator cannot establish that nonrandomly assigned groups were equivalent with respect to *all* variables which critics may regard as relevant.

Mortality, the absence of data on some units, may create observed differences between the experimental and the comparison groups. If, for example, less able individuals withdraw from a program or refuse to submit to measurement, the average score of the remaining units will be raised, even if the only effect of the program is to encourage these dropouts. If no similar process occurs in the comparison group, specious program "effects" will be observed.

While experimental designs provide control against all of these threats to internal validity, the external validity (i.e., generalizability) of experimental designs may be subject to undesirable restrictions, many of which can be avoided by careful planning. Some typical threats to generalizability are listed below.

Units sampled may fail to characterize the program clientele. If a program to combat rural poverty is evaluated on the basis of an experiment in Appalachia, the evaluator has weak evidence regarding the nationwide effects of the program. The population from which the experimental units are sampled should not differ, in characteristics which may interact with the program's effect, from the population about which the evaluator wishes to make his inference.

Factors sampled may inadequately represent the conditions relevant to program impact. Failure to include as a factor the time of year in which a highway safety program was conducted might result in the loss of critically important information.

Outcome measures sampled may fail to tap important program effects. Evaluation studies are notorious for appending to negative results the assertion that useful program effects were unquestionably produced, but that no provision was made for their measurement. By using pilot studies and the technique of fractional designs (Cox, 1958; McLean, 1966, 1967) a researcher can economically examine large numbers of factors and outcome measures, reducing the need for such confessions of incompetency. While it is obviously impossible to foresee all contingencies, a considerable amount of thought should precede any research.

Reactive effects may affect generalizability when all groups are pretested. If pretests affect the outcome measures, as might occur if individuals were thereby sensitized to attitudes which the program attempted to modify, then the program effects might be different if no pretesting occurred. When this is a possibility, the Solomon (1949) four-group design and the Solomon and Lessac (1968) extension of it provide appropriate control. If pretesting is found to enhance the impact of a program, it might be incorporated into the program procedure.

Naturally correlated variables may create special problems if the evaluator attempts to include them in his experimental design as crossed classificatory factors. This is a persistent problem in laboratory research, where effort may be devoted to combination of characteristics which in nature are found only as pathological exceptions (see Willems, 1967). If a proposed design involved "race" and "religion" as crossed factors, the evaluator might be able to secure enough black Buddhists for his analysis, but the other characteristics of these unusual individuals would be likely to distort his inferences regarding whites in general or Buddhists in general. Nested variables or incomplete designs are usually preferable to attempting to "untie" naturally correlated variables.

While the examples which we have used have been fairly blatant, the perils in internal validity and generalizability which they illustrate may lurk in subtler forms. These may elude the evaluator, but antagonists of his fingings and critics of his methodology will be quick to announce them. Bracht and Glass (1968) provide an extensive discussion of twelve common sources of restricted generalizability, which the evaluator would do well to consult while planning his study.

Thus controlled, comparative experimentation is seen to be a powerful model for evaluation. Four basic advantages of the experimental model are as follows:

1. The model provides a specific inference regarding the existence of effects which can be causally attributed to program components and their interactions; estimates of the magnitude of these effects are also provided.

2. The stability of these inferences is known, being specified by the size and power of the statistical tests afforded by the model.

3. The generalizability of these inferences is known being specified by the experimental design.

4. The internal validity of these inferences rests upon assumptions generally accepted by behavioral scientists. (This last point is not an appeal to authority, but indicates the cogency of evidence obtained using the model. There is no similar guarantee, for example, that anyone will give credit to pre-experimental results.)

Why is so excellent a procedure so little used by evaluators? Without attempting to answer this directly, we note that its appropriateness in field evaluations has been questioned. Stufflebeam (1968) has vigorously attacked the utility of the experimental model, offering the three major objections listed below:*

1. The model fails to provide for continual program improvement. It inhibits improvement, since internal validity requires that the treatment not be modified during evaluation.

2. The model provides useful informaiton only after a program has run full cycle, but it is almost useless in planning and implementing a program.

3. As Guba (1965) has pointed out, experimental control is generally unavailable, since randomization is rarely feasible outside the laboratory.

We shall now consider the merits of these accusations. The first, that the model precludes change and improvement of the program, makes the dubious assumption that modifications tend to improve a program, and appears to confuse internal with external validity.

Guba's second contention is that experimental data cannot provide information when it is needed. While there may be problems of power in detecting changes after brief exposures to a program, the experimental model by no means requires that measurement and analysis await the end of the program cycle. Subsets of the sampling units may be examined whenever the evaluator can measure them so that short-term feedback, as well as long-term effects (perhaps years after the program ends) can be inspected.

The third point, that randomization usually cannot be arranged, is of great importance, and appears to be the chief obstacle to the use of the experimental model in evaluation. In the view of the present author, however, the fault lies not in the model, but in those who out of ignorance prevent the random assignment of units to program or control groups. Campbell (1967, 1969) has discussed the political and psychological factors which have tended to preserve the preexperimental status quo in evaluation research, despite the nearly 50 years which have elapsed since the advent of scientifically respectable alternatives. A central problem is that program managers take for granted that their program is effective; from this sanguine assumption the conclusion is reached that to assign an individual to a control group randomly is to deny him social benefits. Yet the model does not require that the members of the control group receive no treatment; it requires that they not receive a treatment whose outcomes are likely to resemble those of the program to be evaluated.

Most of the objections to the experimental model reduce, upon closer examination, to incomplete understanding or unskillful application of the model. A more radical criticism, however, may underlie the last source of dissatis-

*His fourth criticism we omit, since it corresponds to various problems in generalizability discussed earlier.

faction which we shall note. Stufflebeam (1968) expresses this well, though he omits it from his list of charges:

> ... why do the typical 'no significant difference' findings in so many of these [experimental] evaluations contravene the experiences of those who are intimately involved in the program?

Lack of statistical power is doubtless a frequent answer to this complaint, but the *a priori* conclusion that a program benefits its clientele consigns the evaluator to a thankless or superfluous role, in which scientific attitudes may be a handicap. If he reports negative results, he affronts the program staff, reveals the inadequacy of his methodology, and presents other public relations specialists with the chore of discounting his results. If he "succeeds" in obtaining positive results, he has merely confirmed, perhaps at considerable expense, what was "known" beforehand. Working in the context of programs which make no provisions for unfavorable results, the evaluator remembers that evil tidings are a dangerous thing to bear, and seeks some innocuous alternative to the experimental model. That his preexperimental methods yield evidence which carries little weight among scientists need not concern him, if scientific criteria are not used in reaching decisions.

Further perspective on the evaluation controversy can be obtained from Scriven's (1967) long article and Baker's (1967) chapter.

Would utilizing the experimental model improve the evaluation and the quality of social action programs? We have indicated why this might be the case. In the absence, however, of programs employing this technique, the matter remains in the realm of speculation.

REFERENCES

Baker, F. B. (1967). Experimental design considerations associated with large-scale projects. In *Improving Experimental Design and Statistical Analysis* (J. C. Stanley, ed.), pp. 206-256. Rand McNally, Chicago, Illinois.

Bayes, T. (1763). An essay towards solving the problem in the doctrine of chances. *Philosophical Transactions of the Royal Society of London* 53, 370.

Boring, E. G. (1954). The nature and history of experimental control. *American Journal of Psychology* 67, 573-589.

Bracht, G. H., and Glass, G. V. (1968). The external validity of experiments. *American Educational Research Journal* 5, 437-474.

Campbell, D. T. (1967). Administrative experimentation, institutional records, and nonreactive measures. In *Improving Experimental Design and Statistical Analysis* (J. C. Stanley, ed.), pp. 257-291. Rand McNally, Chicago, Illinois.

Campbell, D. T. (1969). Reforms as experiments. *American Psychologist* 24, 409-429.

Campbell, D. T., and Stanley, J. C. (1966). *Experimental and Quasi-experimental Designs for Research.* Rand McNally, Chicago, Illinois. Originally published in *Handbook on Research on Teaching* (N. L. Gage, ed.), pp. 171-246. Rand McNally, Chicago, Illinois, 1963.

Cox, D. R. (1958). *Planning of Experiments.* Wiley, New York.

Fisher, R. A. (1935 et seq.). *The Design of Experiments.* Oliver & Boyd, Edinburgh.

Guba, E. (1965). Methodological strategies for educational change. Paper presented to the Conference for Strategies on Educational Change, Washington, D.C.

McLean, L. D. (1966). Phantom classrooms. *School Review* 74, 139-149.

McLean, L. D. (1967). Some important principles for the use of incomplete designs in behavioral research. In *Improving Experimental Design and Statistical Analysis* (J. C. Stanley, ed.), pp. 157-205. Rand McNally, Chicago, Illinois.

Scriven, M., (1967). The methodology of evaluation. In *Perspectives of Curriculum Evaluation* (R. E. Stake, ed.), pp. 39-83. Rand McNally, Chicago, Illinois, (American Educational Research Association Monograph No. 1 on Curriculum Evaluation.)

Solomon, R. L. (1949). An extension of group control design. *Psychological Bulletin* 46, 137-150.

Solomon, R. L., and Lessac, M. S. (1968). A group control design for experimental studies of developmental processes. *Psychological Bulletin* 70, 145-150.

Stanley, J. C. (1957). Controlled experimentation in the classroom. *Journal of Experimental Education* 25, 195-201.

Stanley, J. C. (1967). Elementary experimental design–an expository treatment. *Psychology in the Schools* 4, 195-203.

Stanley, J. C. (1971). The design of controlled educational experiments. In *Encyclopedia of Education* (L. C. Deighton, ed.), Vol. 3, pp. 474-483. McMillan Co. and Free Press, New York.

Stanley, J. C. (1972). Designing psychological experiments. In *Handbook of Psychology* (B. B. Wolman, ed.). Prentice-Hall, Englewood Cliffs, New Jersey (in press).

"Student" (William S. Gosset). (1908). The probable error of a mean. *Biometrika* 6, 1-25.

Stufflebeam, D. L. (1968). Evaluation as enlightenment for decision making. Address delivered at Working Conference on Assessment Theory, Sarasota, Florida.

Thorndike, R. L. (1963). *The Concepts of Over- and Underachievement.* Bureau of Publications, Teachers College, Columbia University, New York.

Willems, E. P. (1967). Toward an explicit rationale for naturalistic research methods. *Human Development* 10, 138-154.

Wilner, D.M. *et al.* (1962). *The Housing Environment and Family Life.* Johns Hopkins Press, Baltimore, Maryland.

4

CONTROLLED FIELD EXPERIMENTS
AS A MODEL FOR EVALUATION*

Julian C. Stanley

There is a definite though by no means unlimited place in evaluation for controlled, variable-manipulating, comparative experimentation. Modern experimental design and analysis are about 50 years old. By 1923 Ronald Fisher (Stanley, 1966) had devised the randomized-block design, probably the first setup in which one classification of the independent variables was fully crossed with the other in a systematically randomized layout. The general factorial design, which incorporated two or more fully crossed "factors," came soon thereafter. By 1935 most of the basic developments still used today had been completed. Five years later in a pioneering book Lindquist (1940) made them more readily available to educationists and psychologists. Experimental psychologists began quickly after World War II to use the new methods. Controlled experimentation has not, however, been employed in many school-based comparisons of teaching methods or curricula. Why not?

In its simplest form, experimentation of the kind mentioned requires the assignment of sampling units to several different treatments randomly and independently of each other. The unit may, for example, be an individual pupil

*Based on papers presented at the 1969 Invitational Conference on Testing Problems of Educational Testing Service, Hotel Roosevelt, New York City, November 1, 1969 (see Stanley, 1970), and the Second Annual Conference on Educational Research of the Virginia State Department of Education, Natural Bridge, Virginia, May 21, 1970.

or a single classroom. Treatments might be several ways to teach physics or biology or mathematics, several different preschool curricula, two or more levels of reinforcement, praise versus blame, etc. Randomized assignment of units to treatments is crucial, because it prevents *systematic* biases in the initial status of the groups. The expected mean of each group is identical with that of any other, though of course if the number of units is small the actual group means may differ considerably at the start of the experiment. (For further explanation, see Campbell and Stanley [1966] and Stanley [1957, 1967, 1971, 1972].)

Controlled experimentation in schools seems to have foundered on the requirements of randomization and independence. Most school administrators seem to resist randomization as being an abdication of their obligation to be authoritative. Nearly all school classes are formed without random assignment of pupils to them, even when several teachers teach the same subject at the same period. Certain teachers are assigned the "better" pupils because those teachers are more senior or more powerful or presumed to be better teachers of such pupils. Some pupils or their parents prefer one teacher to another and insist on assignment to his class. Also, pupils must be in those classes they can schedule, and this depends on what other courses they are taking. For example, if physics comes only at the sixth period, those students who enroll for it cannot take American history that same period.

These and other restraints on the randomized assignment of pupils are features of the school environment that cannot be ignored by the educational experimenter. Usually, the sampling unit for a school experiment must be the intact classroom, rather than the individual pupil. Yet few experiments in educational settings are well enough planned, administered, and financed to involve enough classrooms to give much promise of detecting among treatments differences of the magnitude likely to be produced with the curricular resources and efforts used. Many educational experiments lack statistical power and therefore lean toward producing findings of "no difference."

Despite the problems of securing randomness and independence, however, much experimentation could be done in school settings but seldom is. For instance, how much rigorous published literature is there on the benefits of cursive versus manuscript ways of teaching handwriting, despite the fact that each year several million children in a given age group must be taught to write? Any school system could research this area well with its own resources, but practically none does. Instead, each new language-arts supervisor tends to plan the reading curriculum as she wishes on the basis of arm-chair speculation—not worthless, of course, but leading often to conclusions that fail to convince others.

In an article entitled "Reforms as Experiments," Campbell (1969) has pointed out how threatening to administrators scientific method, particularly controlled experimentation, can be. Powerful methods can yield results from which the administrator may have no place to hide. Weak methods yield results that can be interpreted to his advantage. To many administrators, weak methods seem better for survival, at least over the short term, than strong ones do.

A somewhat related political consideration is that frequently the prospect of experimentation in schools conjures up thoughts of Frankenstein's monster, inhuman physicians in concentration camps, and the Antivivisection League. A new curricular treatment is judged *a priori* to be either dangerous (e.g., new-fangled modern mathematics that has no obvious relationship to balancing a checkbook) or so likely to be beneficial that to withhold it from any pupils would be educationally foolish (e.g., team teaching, classroom TV, or computer-assisted instruction). This widespread carryover from pre-Baconian days glorifies pure thought far beyond the limits found for it in science. Yet it reflects the attitudes of many administrators, teachers, and parents. The researcher may nullify this particular objection by promising to remediate members of the control group if they are found at the end of the experiment to perform appreciably poorer than do members of the experimental group.

Prejudging experimental results may be due considerably to the treatment-versus-control dichotomy that implies a comparison of something with nothing, whereas in actual practice various alternative ways are compared. An illustration may help: Does taking 2 years of Latin improve one's knowledge of English vocabulary more than taking 2 years of direct vocabulary training? Couched in this fashion, the contrast is not between taking Latin versus not taking Latin, but taking Latin versus a potentially effective competitive method. One might find a considerable number of Latin-eligible students at the beginning of the ninth grade and assign at random half of them to study Latin while the other half get vocabulary training. If at the end of the tenth grade one group is superior to the other, members of the lower-scoring group may get special attention until they have caught up. Also, those who studied vocabulary may take Latin in the eleventh and twelfth grades, if they wish. In principle, this kind of experiment is feasible, but so far as I know it has never been done, despite arguments for many years about the vocabulary-building value of Latin.

Of course, most teachers are not equipped technically to plan an experiment and analyze the results therefrom, and surprisingly few school systems have research personnel who can help them adequately. Most of the typical educational psychologist's graduate training has been in testing, rather than in designing experiments and analyzing ensuing data. Measurement competence is necessary to do good experimentation on most educational problems, but it is far from sufficient. Fortunately, a number of doctoral programs are now producing persons with both sets of competencies.

For a long time I have argued that controlled experimentation has not failed to be of use in evaluation, but instead that for various reasons such as those just mentioned it has seldom been tried. Long-term research in school systems is infrequent. When anything is done, it tends to be too little and not pursued long enough to allow both the novelty of new procedures and the disruption they cause to dissipate. Some nice examples of classroom experimentation such as the doctoral-dissertation studies by Page (1958) and Goodwin (1966) do appear in the literature, but too often they are one-shot affairs that lack crucial followthrough.

Apparently, there is more lack of intent, money, and technical resources than of available, applicable methodology. Those critics of experimentation for evaluation who say that controlled, variable-manipulating experimentation may be splendid for stands of alfalfa and weights of pigs but inapplicable to education do not adequately appreciate the generality of Fisherian and neo-Fisherian methods. If, for example, 10% of the Physical Science Study Committee's budget from the start had been for rigorous evaluation, undoubtedly a great deal of experimentation could have been done along with other procedures. Wittich (Pella, Stanley, Wedemeyer, & Wittich, 1962) at the University of Wisconsin a decade ago did much with far less money in 6 months.

In conclusion, I agree with Scriven (1967) and Suchman (1970) that the requisite methodological tools for educational evaluation are already at hand. One of these, controlled comparative experimentation, can be of value at any stage of a program, though most likely in the basic-research early phases and the field-experimentation phases. The powerful principle of factorial design can be used to structure the components of a program systematically in order to see which are effective in what combinations. Despite straw men to the contrary, educational experimentation can be as on-going, flexible, and sequential as the cleverness of the evaluators allows it to be. Inflexibility is more in the minds of planners, researchers, and critics than in the methodology itself. Of course, there is no royal road to new knowledge; it is not easy to experiment with human beings, whether they be medical patients or school pupils. In my opinion, however, controlled experimentation and some quasi-experimental designs are important methodological tools of the educational evaluator. Recent attempts to rule experimentation inapplicable because other methods are useful, too, seem misguided.

REFERENCES

Campbell, D. T. (1969). Reforms as experiments. *American Psychologist* **24,** 409-429.
Campbell, D. T., and Stanley, J. C. (1966). *Experimental and Quasi-experimental Designs for Research.* Rand McNally, Chicago, Illinois.
Goodwin, W. L. (1966). Effect of selected methodological conditions on dependent measures taken after classroom experimentation. *Journal of Educational Psychology* **57,** 350-358.
Lindquist, E. F. (1940). *Statistical Analysis in Educational Research.* Houghton Mifflin, Boston, Massachusetts.

Page, E. B. (1958). Teacher comments and student performance: A seventy-four classroom experiment in school motivation. *Journal of Educational Psychology* **49**, 173-181.

Pella, M.; Stanley, J. C.; Wedemeyer, C. A.; and Wittich, W. A. (1962). The uses of the White films in the teaching of physics. *Science Education* **46**, 6-21.

Scriven, M. (1967). The methodology of evaluation. In *Perspectives of Curriculum Evaluation* (R. E. Stake, ed.), pp. 38-83. Rand McNally, Chicago, Illinois. (American Educational Research Association Monograph No. 1 on Curriculum Evaluation.)

Stanley, J. C. (1957). Controlled experimentation in the classroom. *Journal of Experimental Education* **25**, 195-201.

Stanley, J. C. (1966). The influence of Fisher's *The design of experiments* on educational research thirty years later. *American Educational Research Journal* **3**, 223-229.

Stanley, J. C. (1967). Elementary experimental design—an expository treatment. *Psychology in the Schools* **4**, 195-203.

Stanley, J. C. (1970). Controlled experimentation: Why seldom used in evaluation? *Proceedings of the 1969 Invitational Conference on Testing Problems,* pp. 104-108.

Stanley, J. C. (1971a). The design of controlled educational experiments. In *Encyclopedia of Educational Research* (L. C. Deighton, ed.), pp. 000-000. Crowell-Collier, New York.

Stanley, J. C. (1971b). Designing psychological experiments. In *Handbook of Psychology* ings of the 1969 Invitational Conference on Testing Problems, pp. 104-108.

Stanley, J. C. (1971). The design of controlled educational experiments. In *Encyclopedia of Educational Research* (L. C. Deighton, ed.), Vol. 3, pp. 474-483. McMillan Co. and Free Press, New York.

Stanley, J. C. (1972). Designing psychological experiments. In *Handbook of Psychology* (B. B. Wolman, ed.). Prentice-Hall, Englewood Cliffs, New Jersey (in press).

Suchman, E. A. (1970). The role of evaluative research. *Proceedings of the 1969 Invitational Conference on Testing Problems,* pp. 93-103.

5

PROBLEMS IN MAKING POLICY INFERENCES FROM THE COLEMAN REPORT*

Glen G. Cain and Harold W. Watts

INTRODUCTION

The aim of the Coleman Report (Coleman *et al.*, 1966) is twofold—(1) to describe certain aspects of our educational system, and (2) to analyze the way it is related to education achievement—with the objective of prescribing policies to change the system. In its purely descriptive aspects, it presents a very dismal picture of the effectiveness of our educational system in securing equal opportunities for all our citizens. Looking at educational outcomes for children from different backgrounds, one finds wide discrepancies which the American dream has assumed capable of elimination through the public school system. These discrepancies, authoritatively established in the Report, and the indictment and challenge they present are a crucial contribution. Although we take a critical view of this Report, nothing in our subsequent commentary can detract from

*This research has been supported by funds granted to the Institute for Research on Poverty pursuant to the provisions of the Economic Opportunity Act of 1964. The authors would like to acknowledge the helpful comments from Dennis Aigner, Arthur Goldberger, W. Lee Hansen, Robinson Hollister, M. J. Lefcowitz, Burton Weisbrod and Walter Williams. We are most grateful to Mrs. Felicity Skidmore for editorial help.

Reprinted from *American Sociological Review,* Vol. 35, No. 2, April 1970, pp. 228-242.
The principal theme of this paper is that the analytical part of the Coleman Report

the importance of the findings regarding the inequalities in the education of children of different races, ethnic groups, and socioeconomic classes.

Our criticism of the Report is directed toward its analysis, mainly found in Chapter 3, in which an implicit theory of the determinants of educational achievement is posited, tested, and used to point up prescriptive policy implications. The principal theme of our discussion is that the analytical part of the Coleman Report has such serious methodological shortcomings that it offers little guidance for policy decisions. Other critics have pointed to the shortcomings that resulted from nonresponse to the survey and from errors in measuring certain variables (Bowles and Levin, 1968a; Kain and Hanushek, 1968); and the familiar uneasiness about interpreting nonexperimental data has been expressed (Sewell, 1967, p. 478; Nichols, 1966; Mosteller, 1967a). Our criticism is more fundamental in the following sense. Even if the survey data were uncontaminated by any biases from nonresponse, errors in measurements, and an "uncontrolled experiment," there remain the following two basic defects in the Coleman analysis.

First, the specification of the theoretical model is inadequate to support the regression analysis used in testing the model. Little or no theoretical justification is offered for the selection of explanatory variables, for their functional form, or for the inclusion or exclusion of variables under different specifications of the model. Without a theoretical framework to provide order and a rationale for the large number of variables, we have no way of interpreting the statistical results. We have no way of knowing, for example, whether a variable directly represents a policy instrument or is only indirectly related to policy control through some other unmeasured (or partially measured) relationships; or whether a variable is, indeed, supposed to be subject to policy control or is included in the model to perform a different function. (Examples of this problem are discussed below.)

Second, in those instances where a theoretical justification for the use of a variable in the regression model *is* clear, the criterion used in the Coleman Report to assess or evaluate the statistical performance of the variable is inappropriate. Instead of providing information about the quantitative effect of a variable in altering educational achievement—information which would enable

---

(Coleman, *et al.*, 1966) has such serious methodological shortcomings that it offers little policy guidance: (1) the specification of the theoretical model is inadequate and thus there is no way to interpret Coleman's statistical results; (2) when the Coleman Report does make clear the justification for the use of a variable in the regression model, the criterion used to assess the statistical performance of the variable (namely, its effect on R^2) is inappropriate.

This paper further shows (1) how the role of a variable in affecting objectives *can* be interpretable in the context of a carefully specified, theoretically justified model; and (2) that when such a model is in the form of a regression equation, an appropriately scaled regression coefficient is the most useful single statistic to measure the importance of the variable for policy action.

the reader to assess the feasibility and costliness of operating on the variable—the Report provides information about a statistical measure of the variable's performance (namely, its effect on the coefficient of determination, or R^2, of the regression), which gives no clear guidance for translating the statistical findings into policy action.

The remainder of the paper is organized around the development of these points. In the next section we comment briefly on the policy objectives which determine the choice of a dependent variable—namely, a measure of educational achievement. In the core of the paper we discuss the nature of a statistical-theoretical model necessary to handle any analysis of the determinants of educational achievement. A hypothetical and simplified example is used to indicate a relevant set of questions in terms of the objectives of social policy, and to suggest how the results from testing the statistical model should be translated into terms suitable for policy decisions. We should emphasize, however, that the example *is* hypothetical. The most serious gap concerning educational policy, particularly compensatory education, remains that of an inadequate theory, and we cannot fill that gap. In the last section of the paper we do, however, discuss a few of the many specific variables which are found in the Coleman Report to at least illustrate the points made in our hypothetical example and methodological discussion.

POLICY OBJECTIVES UNDERLYING
THE COLEMAN REPORT

A statement of a desirable, or at least acceptable, objective for social policy is provided by Coleman himself.

> Schools are successful only insofar as they reduce the dependence of a child's opportunities upon his social origins. We can think of a set of conditional probabilities: the probability of being prepared for a given occupation or for a given college at the end of high school, conditional upon the child's social origins. The effectiveness of the schools consists, in part, of making the conditional probabilities less conditional—that is, less dependent upon social origins. Thus, equality of educational opportunity implies, not merely "equal" schools, but equally effective schools, whose influences will overcome the differences in starting point of children from different social groups (Coleman, 1966, p. 72).

The task of translating the objective of equality of educational opportunity into operational terms, however, is a difficult one. The problem is twofold. First, the objective rests on a proposition—that the median levels of ability are roughly similar across racial and class groups[1] —which can be assumed

---

[1] The median is relatively insensitive to the location of the tails of the distribution—a fact that increases the acceptability of this proposition as a working assumption. We set aside the question of how the dispersion of the distribution of innate abilities compares across groups.

but is not proven. Second, the assessment of progress toward that objective requires measuring instruments that have yet to be perfected.[2]

One way to cope with the measurement problem is to rely heavily on the assumption of relative similarity in average abilities. On this basis, changes in factors (other than ability) which bring about educational achievement may be implemented, and the success of this effort may be tested by achievement scores that are correspondingly averaged over relatively large groups.

Such a focus on instruments of public policy to narrow the gaps between average levels of educational attainment across racial and economic groups has several implications:

1. The first priority is to develop a model in which the selection of variables is governed by a distinction between those variables amenable to policy manipulation and those that are not. The use of nonpolicy variables may be desirable for (a) stratifying the population if we think the policy variables have different effects on different groups, and (b) controlling for intervening effects which otherwise may bias the statistical measures of the effects of policy variables. Adding nonpolicy variables also serves to reduce residual variation (i.e., to increase the R^2). But with the current availability of large sample sizes this may not have a high priority, particularly since problems of interpreting the statistical results arise as more and more variables are added, some of which inevitably overlap into the role of a policy variable.

2. A possible conflict arises between the objective of narrowing the gap between groups and the objective of raising the overall average level of each group. Certainly there would be little support for a policy which would lower average levels of performance. If, however, our *prima facie* evidence leads us to the assumption that the lower economic groups and disadvantaged ethnic minority groups are performing well below their potential, then a policy which seeks to raise their performance levels may be both egalitarian *and* an efficient way to raise the overall average level of performance of all the groups combined. (We take up the issue of cost-effectiveness below.)

3. A similar conflict between (a) reducing dispersion and (b) raising the mean level also exists *within* a group. (We should note at the outset that we must expect large variances within groups relative to that between groups. Every ethnic and economic group, after all, includes imbeciles and geniuses, stable personality types and psychotics, hard-working students and lazy students, and so on.) A strategy of compensatory education aimed at a disadvantaged group might call for raising the mean level at the expense of widening the distribution. The acceptability of this outcome would have to be examined in the particular case, but it is difficult to believe that our society is likely to undertake any

---

[2] A serious obstacle to this approach is that our current measuring instruments are clearly not able to discriminate between ability factors and achievement factors (cf. Mosteller, 1967b, pp. 7-8; Kain and Hanushek, 1968, pp. 20-21).

policies to cope with between-group differences that will widen (or indeed severely compress) existing within-group variance.

4. It may appear trivial to suggest that the variables which serve to represent educational achievement ought to be carefully chosen and justified. The Coleman Report gathered data on several measures, but fixed on one—test scores on verbal ability—to carry almost the entire burden of the published analysis. If the several tests of achievement are measuring different "outputs," then theoretical considerations ought to dominate the choice of the most suitable "output" variable. If they are all measuring the same thing (each one imperfectly), then some, indeed almost any, linear combination of the several tests would be better than any one of the tests taken separately.

However, the authors seem to have postulated that one of the tests contained "it" or anyhow more of "it," and then performed the most remarkable feats of statistical augury to discover which one.[3] Perhaps other measures would have performed in the same way as the verbal ability test—we won't know until someone has tried them. But there is no indication that the choice was made on any relevant basis, and any unique properties of the measure that *were* used only add to the concern about the interpretation of the findings.

A SUGGESTED APPROACH TO MEASURING THE DETERMINANTS OF EDUCATIONAL ACHIEVEMENT

The following points about the analysis of specific variables as determinants of educational achievement are developed in this section. The role of a variable in affecting objectives can only take on meaning and be interpretable in the context of a carefully specified and theoretically justified model. When we have such a model in the form of a regression equation, the regression coefficient is our most useful statistic measuring the importance of the variable for the purposes of policy action.

---

[3] One justification for selecting verbal ability was that this variable possessed the largest relative inter-school variances. Another was that among the inter-student variances of test scores, school input variables accounted for more of the variance of verbal ability than of other test scores. It appears that what underlies these puzzling justifications is a preoccupation with "getting large R^2 s," about which we will have a good deal to criticize in the next section. Suffice it to say here, the R^2 criterion is not relevant. What *is* relevant (but nowhere forthcoming in the Report) is a defense of such a verbal ability test as being a valid measure of educational achievement that is related, on the basis of a hypothesis concerning the determinants of educational achievement, to a specified set of school input variables. Instead, the fact that the verbal ability test is *less* likely to be affected by the variation of school curricula and instruction than are some of the other tests is offered as further justification for settling upon the verbal ability test! (cf. Coleman *et al.,* 1966, p. 293 ff).

The Issue of the Significance and Importance
of a Variable

In the analysis of the relation of school factors to achievement, the principal statistic offered in evidence by the Coleman Report is the percent of variance explained. As indicated in their methodological appendix, this is because the authors are interested in assessing the "strength" of various relationships, and they believe that the percent of variance explained provides the best general purpose indicator of "strength." It will be argued below that this measure of strength is totally inappropriate for the purposes of informing policy choices, and cannot provide relevant information for the policy maker.[4]

Consider a general function expressing a relation between y and several x's, $y=f(x_1, x_2, \ldots x_k)$. What conceptual framework can be used to discuss the strength of the relation of y to, say x_2? If we are limited to the information provided by the function $f(x_1, x_2, \ldots x_k)$, the partial derivative $\partial y/\partial x_2 = f'_2 (x_1, x_2, \ldots x_k)$ is both simple and complete. In the case of linear functions, the partial derivative is a constant and expresses the change in y induced by a unit change in x_2.

It should be clear that a change in the unit of measurement will change the magnitude of such derivatives, and that any comparison among them must establish some basis for comparability among the units of measurement. In the context of an analysis of the relation of school factors to pupil achievement, it would seem evident that our interest lies in purposive manipulation of the x's in order to effect an improved performance in terms of y. We can, and should, ask for the expected change in y induced by spending some specific amount of money (or political capital, man hours, etc.) on working a change in x_2, say, as compared with the alternative of spending the same sum on x_3. Budgetary cost is not necessarily the only basis of comparability. But unless *some* such basis is defined and its relevance to policy explained, the question of "strength" has no meaning.

What basis of comparison among the x's is implied by the percent of variance explained—which is the indicator of the "strength" of a variable used in the Coleman Report? To answer this question, we will consider the common case of a linear function, the only type of function investigated in the Report.

The ordinary partial regression coefficients, b_i, for $i=1, 2, \ldots k$, represent the partial derivatives of y with respect to the several x's—where each x is measured in some conventional (perhaps arbitrary) unit. As indicated earlier, some adjustment of these derivatives is generally required in order to establish comparability. By using the percent of variance uniquely explained by x_i, call it

---

[4]That the main purpose of the Coleman Report is to serve as a guide to policy action is made explicit and emphasized repeatedly in a subsequent paper by Coleman (1968b).

ϕ_i, as the measure of strength, the authors have implicitly assumed that x's will be rendered comparable by measuring them in units corresponding to the orthogonal (or uncorrelated) part of their respective sample variances. It is easily shown that:

$$\phi_i = b^2_i \frac{S^2_{x_i}}{S^2_y}(1-R^2_{ai}),$$

where the s symbol refers to the sample standard deviations and R^2_{ai} is the coefficient of multiple determination for the "auxiliary" regression of x_i on the other $(k-1)$ of the x's.[5]

Thus, ϕ_i represents the square of the regression coefficient which would have been obtained if
   (1) each of the x's had been divided by its standard deviation discounted for its relation to other variables,
   (2) y had been divided by its standard deviation, and
   (3) the adjusted y had been regressed on the adjusted $x_1, \ldots, x_k$.

I.e.,

$$\phi_i = \left(\frac{\partial y^*}{\partial x_i^*}\right)^2,$$

$$\text{where } y^* = \frac{y}{S_y} \text{ and } x_i^* = \frac{x_i}{S_{x_1}\sqrt{1-R^2_{ai}}}$$

It seems very difficult to find a reason why x's measured in terms of "dependency-discounted-deviations," or 3-D's, are comparable for any policy purpose. Is a 3-D increment of x_1 equally costly, equally feasible, or equally appealing to the Congress as an increment of x_2? Is there, indeed, *any* basis for

[5] What we refer to as the ϕ_i statistic is labeled the "usefulness" measure of the ith variable (denoted by $p^2 y \cdot x_i(p)$) in Darlington (1968), whose discussion of this statistic parallels much of ours and suggests several references for the interested reader. He uses:

$$\phi_1 = \rho^2_{y.x_i(p)} = b^2_i \frac{S^2_{x_i \cdot (p)}}{S^2_y},$$

where $s^2_{x_i \cdot (p)}$ is the residual variance of x_i—i.e., the variance of x_i after controlling for all other x's in the multiple regression. His $s^2_{x_i \cdot (p)}$ is precisely equal to our $s^2_{x_i}(1-R^2_{ai})$, and was shown in this form for the special case of a multiple regression with two predictor variables. (See equation (6) in Darlington, 1968, p. 163).

The expression, R^2_{ai}, is the same statistic as the C^2 referred to by Coleman (1968a) in his reply to the comment by Bowles and Levin (1968a). Note, however, that Coleman's definition of the "unique contribution" of a variable, which involves C^2, is in error unless the variable whose contribution is being assessed has a unit variance (Coleman, 1968a, p. 241-242).

arguing that these 3-D units form a relevant set of policy alternatives such that one would have some interest, however slight, in how the several variables rank according to ϕ_i?

It should be clear that measuring "strength" by the usual regression coefficients, or by the beta coefficients,[6] is in general no better than using ϕ.

Whether the variables are scaled conventionally or by some equally arbitrary sample-generated unit, they will usually have to be readjusted to secure comparability in the context of a specific choice problem. (This task is usually simpler if the conventional scale hasn't been fiddled with, and it is more likely to be recognized as a necessary step in the analysis.)[7] Although the discussion above was in terms of single variables in a given function, analogous arguments hold for groups of variables or for the same variable in functions describing relations for different groups, regions, years, etc.

How did the choice of such an odd measure of "strength" come about? A plausible explanation is that the investigator is focusing on the "statistical significance" of the relationship. In fact the F-ratio test statistic, which is commonly used to test the hypothesis that one or several coefficients in a linear function are equal to zero, is very simply related to ϕ. When a single coefficient is tested, the F-ratio is strictly proportional to ϕ:

$$F_{1,\ t\text{-}k\text{-}1} = \frac{\phi_i(t\text{-}k\text{-}1)}{1-R^2},$$

where t = sample size, and k = number of independent variables in the regression.

Where F is greater than some critical value, one commonly reports that the variable in question is significantly greater than zero at, say, the 0.05 level. All this means is that in order to maintain a belief that the variable in question has

---

[6] Note that $\phi_i = \beta^2_i(1-R^2_{ai})$. If there is only one x, i.e., $k=1$, or if x_i is orthogonal to all other x's, the term involving R^2_{ai} drops out, and we have:

$$r^2 = \phi_1 = \beta^2_1 = \left[b_1 \frac{s_{x_i}}{s_y}\right]^2 = \text{the squared beta coefficient.}$$

[7] Indeed, an important advantage of the ordinary regression coefficient, b_i, is that, since the units in which x_i are measured are customarily given, the effect of a unit change in x_i on y is, as a matter of course, translated by the user of the statistics into terms relevant for his decision context.

It has been suggested that publication of the regression coefficients produced by Coleman's research would lead to reckless and irresponsible interpretations (Coleman, 1968a, p. 240). This must be because either the statistics themselves, or the users of them, are untrustworthy. If the problem lies with the statistics, it is hardly more responsible to publish statistics which are better behaved simply because they are definitionally limited to the positive numbers between 0 and 1, without revealing the more suspicious-looking joint products of the analysis. If the problem lies with the analysts, why give them any statistics at all?

absolutely no effect, one must believe that the sample analyzed has surmounted odds of 20 to one by showing such a large apparent effect. Clearly, the greater ϕ_i or F is, the greater the *statistical* significance, and the harder it becomes for a betting man to stick to the belief that the partial derivative is zero. This is surely a very restricted and specialized meaning of "significance," since it may bear no relation to the significance (i.e., importance) a variable has for policy purposes.[8]

When the regression model has included all the independent variables, the F-test (or related t-test) of the "net" of "partial" coefficients is not, of course, affected by the order of introduction of the variables into a stepwise calculation of the regression. But, the effect of a variable or set or variables (however "effect" is measured) will show up as different in the case where another set of variables is "held constant," from the case where there is no control over that other set. The only exception is when the variables to be controlled are uncorrelated with the set being examined, but this situation is present so rarely in nonexperimental data that it can be dismissed.[9]

When there is a legitimate interest in testing the zero-effect hypothesis, one of the variants of the F-test is available and nothing else will quite do. There is an entirely unwarranted tendency, however, to use the F-statistic (or its cousin ϕ) to indicate the more relevant kind of policy significance. To take a homely example, one might suppose that an individual's height and sugar consumption are both related to his weight (among other things of course). In most contexts height would explain more variance than sugar consumption. But to a person embarking on a weight-control program this is not the important fact. Anyone who would seriously entertain the hypothesis that weight does not depend on height has more blind objectivity than most of us—but such a person is the only one who should care about the relative size of that test statistic. It is easy to imagine an interest in a test on the "sugar effect," but why say that it is less important or significant or strong, just because it explains less variance?

A second possible defense for the practice of evaluating variables by ϕ_i lies in its similarity to the beta coefficient. The use of such "standardized" regression weights is usually predicated on an assumption (rarely made explicit) that

[8] When ϕ is properly interpreted as a test statistic, one must keep two things in mind: (1) Its relevance is limited to the zero-effect null hypothesis and (2) that, as in all hypothesis tests, the power of the test is as important as the level of significance. A body of data may be unable to reject the hypothesis that some coefficient is zero and be equally consistent with a hypothesis embodying a miraculously high effect. Alternatively, a very powerful test might reject the zero-effect hypothesis, and also reject a hypothesis that the effect is large enough to warrant any further interest in a variable.

[9] An extensive controversy concerning the order of variables has appeared in the literature (Bowles and Levin, 1968a,b; Coleman, 1968a,b; Smith, 1968; Kain and Hanushek, 1968). But neither critic nor defender has presented an adequate theoretical framework within which the objects of their dispute become worth arguing about.

the sample standard deviations used for adjusting the regression coefficients indicate a relatively fixed range of variation for the several variables. There is, in other words, some notion of "normal" limits of variation which are related somehow to the variation actually found in a population. If some x shows little variation in a representative sample drawn from an interesting population—the argument goes—then we must reduce its coefficient in order to achieve comparability with the coefficient of another x that has a larger variance.

The use of ϕ_i for comparing the effects of variables can be interpreted as the result of following this same logic farther into the labyrinth of least-squares regression algebra. Specifically (as seen by the formulas on p. 79), the standardization involved in ϕ_i is in general sensitive to the sample variances *and intercorrelations for all the x's in the regression.* Such a standardization is of interest only if one feels that the entire joint distribution of regressors is both fixed in the population and well represented by the sample.

There are many contexts, particularly in the natural processes studied in the physical sciences, when the persistence of specific sizes of the variances and correlations among some of the variables may be a warranted assumption. But it is patently absurd to postulate such invariance for variables that *can* be affected, directly or indirectly, by the policy alternatives that have motivated the analysis.

The use of beta coefficients (standardized only for variance) is subject to the same sort of criticism—they retain their meaning only so long as there is no intervention by man or nature to change the variances used for standardization. But where β_i is only crippled as a guide to policy, ϕ_i is totally disabled. The latter maintains its relevance as a description of a relationship *only* if we stand aside and wring our hands.

A Hypothetical Numerical Example

A number of the points discussed above can be grasped most readily by a review of a simple numerical example. Suppose that the relation between a suitable measure of school outcomes (y), and indexes of school quality (x_1) and nonschool background and environment (x_2) is as follows:

$$y = 1 + x_1 + 2.0x_2 + u$$

The constant term reflects an arbitrary choice of origin for the outcome measure, and we assume that x_1 and x_2 are standardized scales with zero means and unit variances.[10] The final term, u, is an unobserved disturbance term which must, in part, reflect measurement errors in y and other relevant factors such as "native ability" (whether genetic or irreversibly determined at some earlier time). This disturbance is defined to have a zero mean and to be uncorrelated

---

[10] These scalings merely simplify the numerical calculations and interpretations of the example. It should be noted that since y is not similarly standardized, there is nothing at all unconventional about a coefficient of 2 for the second independent variable.

with x_1 and x_2. (Assuming that x_1 and x_2 are uncorrelated with u, either singly or in a linear combination, permits us to accept the regression coefficients as unbiased measures of the effects of x_1 and x_2.) The variance of u is arbitrarily set at unity.

Now consider several alternative situations which reflect different policies with regard to the allocation of the composite bundle of factors which determine school quality, x_1. For greater simplicity we will not consider allocations that change the variation of x_1 over schools. Only the degree, and sign, of the correlation between x_1 and x_2 (ρ_{12}) will be changed. To make the policy more concrete (and more obviously hypothetical), suppose that all schools have wheels so that a fixed population of schools of various qualities can be moved around to serve an equal number of communities. A zero correlation between x_1 and x_2 ($\rho_{12}=0$) would result from a random assignment of schools to communities. It would be changed to a positive value by moving some of the better schools from "bad" communities (as measured by x_2) to "good" ones, and vice versa. Similarly, ρ_{12} would become negative if the bad communities swapped

TABLE I

Consequences of Varying Correlation Between Regressor
Variables in a Simplified Regression Model

Model: $y = 1.0 + 1.0x_1 + 2.0_2 + u$

$\sigma^2_{x_1} = \sigma^2_{x_2} = \sigma^2_u = 1.0$

$\rho_{ux_1} = \rho_{ux_2} = 0.0$

Number	Parameters	I	II	III	IV	V	VI	VII
1	ρ_{12}	1.00	0.90	0.50	0.0	$-.50$	$-.90$	-1.00
2	ρ^2_{12}	1.00	0.81	0.25	0.0	.25	.81	1.00
3	σ^2_y	10.0	9.6	8.0	6.0	4.0	2.4	2.0
4	$\rho^2_{yx_1}$	0.900	0.712	0.500	0.167	0.0	0.267^a	0.500^a
5	$\rho^2_{yx_2}$	0.900	0.876	0.782	0.666	0.563	0.505	0.500
6	$R^2_{y.x_1x_2}$	0.900	0.896	0.875	0.833	0.750	0.583	0.500
7	ϕ_1	0.0	0.020	0.093	0.167	0.187	0.078	0.0
8	ϕ_2	0.0	0.184	0.375	0.666	0.750	0.316	0.0
9	$R^2_{yx_1.x_2}$	0.0	0.160	0.429	0.500	0.429	0.160	0.0
10	$R^2_{yx_2.x_1}$	0.0	0.432	0.750	0.800	0.750	0.432	0.0
11	β_1	0.312	0.327	0.354	0.408	0.500	0.645	0.707
12	β_2	0.624	0.654	0.708	0.816	1.000	1.29	1.114
13	b_1	1.00	1.00	1.00	1.00	1.00	1.00	1.00
14	b_2	2.00	2.00	2.00	2.00	2.00	2.00	2.00

[a]The squared simple correlation coefficiencies shown here are squares of negative values for ρ_{xy_1}. All other values for ρ_{xy_1} and ρ_{xy_2} in the table are positive.

their bad schools for good ones from the good communities; p_{12} would approach 1.0 if the "best" school served the "best" community, the second best school the second best community, and so on.

Any alteration in the way input variables are combined will change the distribution of the outcomes; for instance, a change in the variance of y is a *necessary* result of a change in the correlation between x_1 and x_2, given our specification of constant variances of x_1 and x_2 and constant effects (b's) of x_1 and x_2. Table 1 shows the consequences for several parameters when the correlation between x_1 and x_2 takes on several different values, ranging from 1.00 to −1.00.

In Column IV one finds the simple case when x_1 and x_2 are uncorrelated—schools have been assigned to communities at random. The variance of y (σ_y^2) is equal to 6.0, and this partitions nicely into a component due to school differences with variance 1.0, another component due to community differences with variance 4.0, and a third due to the combination of factors accounted for implicitly by the disturbance term with variance 1.0. The two variables, x_1 and x_2, together account for 5/6 of the variance—1/6 for x_1 and 2/3 for x_2—as shown in the entries for the simple squared correlations ($\rho^2_{yx_1}, \rho^2_{yx_2}$) and the squared multiple correlation, $R^2_{y.x_1x_2}$.

Because x_1 and x_2 are uncorrelated (orthogonal), the incremental fraction of explained variation that is obtained when x_1, say, is added to the regression ($\phi_1 = R^2_{y.x_1x_2} - \rho^2_{yx_2}$) is equal to the fraction explained when x_1 is used alone ($\rho^2_{yx_1}$). The same is true for the increment due to x_2.

The squared partial correlations are obtained by dividing the increment due to, say, x_1 by the fraction of variance left unexplained by x_2:

$$\rho^2_{yx1 \cdot x2} = \frac{\phi_1}{1 - \rho^2_{yx2}}$$

$$= \frac{R^2_{y.x_1x_2} - \rho^2_{yx2}}{1 - \rho^2_{yx2}}.$$

The beta coefficients, β_i, are simply the partial regression coefficients divided by the standard deviation of y, σ_y, and multiplied by the unitary standard deviation of x_i. The partial regression coefficients shown in the last two rows are constant, of course, because the populations have been generated by maintaining that assumption. (Columns I and VII, where x_1 and x_2 are perfectly correlated, are limiting cases—the multiple regressions would be impossible to carry out with data generated from these cases.)

The values of the various parameters listed in the columns of this table must be regarded as "population" values. A limited sample drawn at random from one of these populations could produce estimates of these parameters which would differ from the "true" values by sampling errors of the usual sort.

If the allocation of x_1 is changed from a random one by matching "good" schools with "good" communities, the correlation between x_1 and x_2 becomes positive. Moving toward the left from Column IV in the table, one finds first that the variance of y gets larger. This is intuitively explained by thinking of the schools as reinforcing and intensifying the inequality found in the environments. The simple correlations shown in the fourth and fifth rows both increase as the two variables become increasingly good substitutes for each other, and the multiple correlation goes up because the constant amount of unexplained variance (from u) becomes a smaller part of the whole variance of y.

The incremental explanatory power or "unique contribution" (measured by ϕ_i) declines as ρ_{12} increases from zero, and ϕ reaches zero in the limit where $\rho_{12}=1$. The squared partial correlations display basically the same pattern. Both are transparent consequences of the increasing interchangeability of x_1 and x_2—as their correlation increases, having both adds very little new information. Finally, the beta coefficients decline as a consequence of increases in the variance of y. Any deeper meaning of this change must be supplied by those who have a penchant for this scaling convention.

Consider now the consequences of allocating relatively more "good" schools to the "bad" locations and vice versa. As ρ_{12} falls from zero to negative values, one finds the variance of y falling also. (See Columns IV to VII.) Here the schools compensate for, or suppress the inequality produced by, unequal backgrounds.

The squared simple correlations, $\rho^2{}_{yx_i}$, both fall initially; $\rho^2{}_{yx_1}$ going to zero at $\rho_{12}=-0.5$.[11] The variance explained by x_2 falls steadily until at the limit it explains only half of the (smaller) variance of y. Beyond $\rho_{12}=-0.5$ (in Columns VI and VII), the simple correlation of x_1 with y becomes negative, and in the limit it is simply a mirror-image of x_2 and thus has the same squared correlation.

The squared multiple correlation falls as the "unexplained" component of the variance becomes relatively more important. The net or unique contributions, ϕ_i, are seen to reach a peak at $\rho_{12}=-0.5$ and then to fall once more to zero as x_1 and x_2 become more identical. The squared partial correlations are seen to fall quite symmetrically on both sides of Column IV where $\rho_{12}=0$.

Finally, the smaller variance in y brings about an increase in the beta coefficients. By this measure the effects of both x_1 and x_2 become more and

---

[11] Intuitively, when $\rho_{12}=-0.5$, we can think of the positive contribution of x_1 to explaining variation in y being exactly negated because of the negative correlation between x_1 and x_2. As the negative correlation between x_1 and x_2 gets larger in absolute value than -0.5, the true positive effect of x_1 is more than offset in the simple relation between x_1 and y (when x_2 is not held constant).

more powerful; by contrast, the regression coefficients measuring their effects remain unchanged at their assigned values.

Now consider a not-entirely-hypothetical society which has shown some tendency to place its "best" schools in the "best" places and to direct its "best" efforts toward its "best" pupils. This produces a ρ_{12} somewhere between 0.5 and 0.9—like Columns II or III. An educational survey might very well find that background and environment are 4–10 times as strong as school quality if it looks at the relative size of the ϕ_i. Less extreme, but no more relevant, statements could be made by comparing the b's or β's. But what is the purpose of such *comparisons?* If the survey is large enough to get decent estimates of the b's, its authors could observe b_1 and infer that school quality *does* make a difference. It follows that moving some schools could change ρ_{12}, and shift the society's educational process toward one described by Columns V or VI. Such a reallocation would substantially reduce the inequality of outcomes and attenuate the correlation of outcomes with social origins; and it would seem to be a proper sort of alternative to consider when interpreting the results of an educational survey.

It must be heavily underscored that, in terms of the model reviewed above, comparisons of the relative explanatory strengths of the two variables x_1 and x_2, whether one uses simple, partial or multiple correlation coefficients, unique contributions or regression weights, adjusted or not, are pointless. If one is concerned with assessing the possible effects of *educational* policy, comparisons of any kind with the effect of "control" (i.e., nonpolicy) variables are pointless. Moreover, all the statistics involved in the comparisons, except for the unadjusted regression coefficients, are dependent upon the particular policies pursued when the data were collected. Their use runs the risk of declaring a policy feeble simply because historically it was not vigorously applied.

In the example shown in Table 1 the "best" allocation to achieve equality calls for a perfect negative correlation between x_1 and x_2. By this allocation the variance of y is reduced to a minimum (=2). It should be noted that educational policy might also change the mean and/or the variance of x_1. With these added degrees of freedom it would be possible, in principle, to eradicate all gross association of y with x_2, and—as an added option—reduce the variance of y to the absolute minimum introduced by the unobservable variable u.

The Need for a Theoretically Justified
Model Relevant to the Policy Context

In general terms one may view the Equality of Educational Opportunity Survey as providing information on the joint distribution of a large number of variables. The analytical effort should be directed toward answering questions about how new or altered policies (more particularly educational policies) would change various characteristics of that joint distribution either directly or indirectly. To do this, one must have a consistent and complete set of specifications concerning: (1) which characteristics of the joint distribution are constant, (2) which can be changed directly by specific activities (policies), and (3) which ones must therefore be determined by the assumed structure and prescribed policy.

This set of specifications is commonly termed a theory or model. In the Coleman Report there is no explicit discussion of a consistent theory of this sort. Some theory, of course, *must* underlie any sort of policy prescription. It is not that one can choose to draw conclusions from the objective facts alone without the aid of any theory, but that if one leaves the theory implicit, ambiguous and obscure, possible nonsensical or even self-contradicting premises go unnoticed.

The theoretical structure of the simple model discussed above asserts that the functional relation between y and x_1, x_2, and u can be approximated satisfactorily by a linear and additive function, with coefficients that would remain fixed under policies designed to change the distribution of x_1 and/or x_2. Similarly, it is assumed that the mean and the variance of the disturbance variable, u, will be unaffected by policies aimed at affecting y via x_1 or x_2. The objective of policy is taken to be some optimal combination of high average level of outcomes (mean of y), minimal inequality (variance of y)—at least as the variance or inequality is affected by intergroup differences—and easy class mobility (minimal correlation of y and x_2).

The tools of educational policy are taken to be measures that would shift the mean of x_1, compress or expand its variability, and/or revise the correlation between x_1 and x_2. If one wished to consider social policy more broadly, similar alternatives for changing the distribution of x_2 would be available. Within the structure so far specified, it is possible to deduce the effects on the marginal and conditional distribution of y for any particular change in the x_1 or x_2 distributions. If no further restriction or relevant information is added, any particular goal in terms of the basic objective can clearly be achieved by a wide range of different manipulations of the x_1 and x_2 distributions. The question of relative strength, in the sense of ability to manipulate y, can now be seen to be meaningless—remembering that the scaling of x_1 and x_2 was arbitrary to begin with. Each of them can be used to achieve the objective so long as unlimited freedom is available for changing the mean, variance, and correlation. If x_2 is not manipulable by educational policy, on the other hand, who cares how effective it might be if it were?

Consider, however, a very simplified situation in which the objective is to close a substantial gap between the mean value of y for blacks and the mean for whites. Assume that the function above holds for blacks, and that one's policy choices are limited to changing—at most—the mean value of x_1 and x_2 for blacks. Which policy or combination of them one chooses will depend on further information about the costs of each alternative. The policy variables which combine to produce the largest gain per unit of cost should be used until the gains from their use diminish (or the costs of using them rise) to the point where the resulting benefit-cost ratio becomes less than that of another combination of policy variables. Costs may be in terms of dollars, time, political consensus or all three—but must be made explicit and must be made a co-determinant of the policy choices.

This necessary inclusion of the cost factor can be achieved within the framework of the regression model we have proposed in this section, by scaling the variables available for manipulation so that a unit change in x_1 is an equally costly alternative to a change in x_2. If an "Iso-chunk" of x_1 is defined to be a $1 billion worth, each one must be a fifth as large as an original unit costing $5 billion—hence its coefficient must be 0.2 (i.e., the old $b_1=1$ coefficient multiplied by its new unit of measure, 0.2). Similarly, an Iso-chunk of x_2 is only 4% of an original unit prices at $25 billion, and hence its coefficient must be 0.08.

A brief example may illustrate the method and will serve to complete our specification of a model which is appropriate for the policy analysis. Take as given the relation between "output," y, and "inputs," x_1 and x_2:

$$y=a+b_1x_1+b_2x_2+u \tag{1}$$

Suppose that the "costs" of alternative mixes of x_1 and x_2, in terms of any scarce item one finds important, are given by:

$$C=c_1x_1+c_2x_2 \tag{2}$$

One may now rewrite equation (1) in terms of "Iso-chunks" which correspond to the amount of x_i obtained by using one unit of whatever "cost" consists of—dollars, man-hours, class-hours:

and
$$x'_1=c_1x_1,$$
$$x'_2=c_2x_2$$

Thus, "Iso-chunks" (read dollars or hours) of C spent in changing x_i can be substituted in (1) for the x_i:

$$y=a+B_1x'_1+B_2x'_2+u,$$
$$\text{where } B_i=\frac{b_i}{c_i}$$

We may call these B_i "bet-coefficients"—derived from Israeli pronunciation of the Hebrew name for the corresponding alphabetic character.[12]

The bet coefficients, which are the equivalents of benefit-cost ratios, give quite direct answers as to which use of the scarce item C yields the largest increment in y. To the extent that relations (1) and (2) adequately reflect the

[12] Professor Arthur S. Goldberger coined this terminology.

way the world works, one could confidently proceed to add to the existing educational process by directing all available C into the x_i for which B_i is the largest.

Unfortunately, one does not usually have that much confidence in a couple of simple linear relations. Commonly, relation (1) will be estimated on the basis of a limited sample, and one's confidence in extrapolations beyond the range of observed combinations of x_1 and x_2 deteriorates rapidly.[13] Moreover, one would rarely encounter a "cost function" as simple as the one in (2)—usually there will be diminishing returns causing marginal costs to rise beyond some point. "Bet coefficients" derived as above ought, therefore, to be interpreted as reflecting, at best, the relative effectiveness of variables in that vicinity of the data over which a linear approximation is deemed to be "sufficiently accurate," taking into account reservations about both relation (1) and relation (2).

INTERPRETING SPECIFIC VARIABLES IN THE COLEMAN REPORT

The absence of any explicit theory of educational achievement is the chief source of the difficulty in interpreting the statistical results of the Coleman Report. We can illustrate the problem by discussing some of the variables used in the Report.

Attitudinal Characteristics of the Student

One remarkable finding of the report's analysis is the high partial correlation of fate control/personal efficacy variables with the verbal ability score used as a measure of educational outcomes.[14] The relation was particularly strong (by

[13] This information on the reliability of the estimate is given by the confidence interval computed for the "bet" or regression coefficient. Our emphasis on the expected value of the B_1 (or b_i) does not imply that we believe a decision maker would have *no* interest in the confidence interval. Indeed, one can imagine cases when a decision maker has some asymmetric subjective utility weighting scheme such that zero or negative values would be deemed so critical—more than offsetting the equally probable high positive values—that a B_1 which was (slightly?) lower than a B_2 would still be selected if the confidence interval of B_1 were sufficiently tighter. Such cases ought to be explicitly argued, however. This proper usage of the confidence interval does not warrant using the ϕ_i statistic, instead of the bet coefficient and classical inferences about that coefficient, as the primary criterion of policy choices.

[14] A number of questions in the survey attempted to measure the student's sense of control over his environment and his sense of fatalism.

the Report's criterion) among minority group children. Without a theory, however, we cannot answer the following types of questions:

1. Is this variable itself merely a *reflection of* (perhaps "caused by") educational achievement? One can easily imagine situations in which educational accomplishment would instill confidence in a youngster and produce a high score on the measure of this variable.[15]

2. Is this variable important only because it is related to various objective factors about the student's family, community, and school environments, which are not fully measured in the model, and which "really" explain *both* school performance *and* the fatalism score? This set of relations would again be quite plausible on *a priori* grounds.[16]

Under situations (1) and (2) above, we can say no more than the following. *Either* changes in the variable, "control over one's fate," are unattainable unless performance on the other objective variables is changed; *or,* if some change in the score could be induced (by, say, counseling), there is no reason to believe educational performance would change.

3. What if—contrary to (1) and (2)—the fatalism variable is a personality trait that does have a separate influence on educational achievement? We still need to know how policy can change the trait to make use of our finding. Clearly these attitudes may be quite congruent with an objective assessment of the situation children find themselves in. If so, the school may be severely limited in its ability to reorient such attitudes (one may have to reintroduce prayer). A verdict of helplessness may have to be passed on the schools. But the evidence in the report supports it *neither* by adding to our knowledge of the causal relation *nor* by indicating a low payoff from interventions within that relation.

Characteristics of the Student's Peer Group

In a review of the Report's findings, Harry C. Bredemeier notes: "More important than all school characteristics and teacher quality for Negro students is the degree to which the *other* students in their schools have the following characteristics: Their families own encyclopedias, they do not transfer much, their attendance is regular, they plan to go to college, and they spend rather much time on homework" (Bredemeier, 1968, p. 21). He notes in a footnote, "I

[15] It is precisely this specification of the causal relationship that is put forward by Wilson (1967, pp. 192 and 206).

[16] The report explicitly notes that the simple correlations of verbal ability and the fate control variable are similar to the intercorrelation among the achievement variables (Coleman *et al.,* 1966, p. 319)—a finding which seems consistent with the interpretation that these attitudinal variables are just another means of measuring the joint output of school and nonschool processes impinging on a child's development.

assume no one will infer from this that the 'solution' is to put encyclopedias in everyone's home."

But, is such an inference less satisfactory than making no inference? Is it any more naive than the presentation of the vague theoretical framework that permits us almost no grounds for saying *how* we should interpret the "significant positive coefficient" of the encyclopedia variable? Consider the following interpretation:

> Encyclopedia ownership is a variable that indicates an intellectual atmosphere in the home conducive to schooling, and/or a measure of affluence that is not fully captured in other measures (of affluence) in the model, and/or a measure of parental attention or affection that contributes to the student's emotional stability and, thereby, to school performance–any or all of which factors creates the positive peer group influence.

Presumably, this interpretation is "more sophisticated" than the inference Bredemeier noted. But is it more helpful? Indeed, what our hypothetical theory has told us up to now is that: (1) if it is intellectual atmosphere that underlies the relation, the variable has probably no policy significance since we do not know much about changing intellectual atmosphere. If we thought we did know something about how to make the change, we would need to know the specification of the relation between encyclopedias and intellectual atmosphere. (2) If it is affluence that underlies the relation, then we need to ask our theory to translate a unit of encyclopedias to a unit of wealth (or income flow) so that we know how much of a change in income will be necessary to yield the changes in educational performance.

We could continue these "if" questions almost indefinitely, but let us summarize the function of our hypothetical theory by saying that it has forced us to consider the possible tortured interpretations we have to make or preposterous policy actions we might have to follow as a consequence of such cavalier inclusion of *ad hoc* variables in our model.

Environmental Characteristics

The Coleman Report stressed that the influence of the regional and urban location of the school and the socioeconomic status of the student body in the school were highly important in explaining a student's educational achievement. A theoretical proposition underlying the authors' interpretation of this finding was that the environment is exogenous and "causally prior" to such factors as school resources; so that an appropriate procedure was to enter the former variables, note the contribution to R^2, and then add the school resource variables and observe their additional contribution to R^2. Other demurrers to this procedure, quite apart from the issue of the R^2 criterion, may be mentioned.

If families select their residence on the basis of the quality of school, residence is neither exogenous to the process nor causally prior to the school resources variable. Particularly with regard to the racial composition of the school, the phenomenon of selective migration may be confounding the results. For example, if a large percentage of whites in a school or a large percentage of high socioeconomic groups appear to have a positive effect on the educational performances of blacks or low SES groups, we should consider the hypothesis that the latter families have strong "tastes" for a high quality education for their children and have moved to a district where the school has a favorable reputation. The observed positive effect of the environment on the educational achievement of disadvantaged groups may therefore be overstated, since some of the effect stems from the unmeasured personal traits of the families; it is further possible that some effect is attributable to the beneficial resources of the school.[17]

What theory of educational achievement justified "urbanness," "Southernness," etc., as causal factors—except insofar as these traits are related to such specific variables as the family characteristics and quality of school found in these areas? There is a real danger that such location variables serve only to attenuate the influence of other variables of interest when such other variables are unmeasured, or measured with a large error component.

Teacher Quality

One type of variable that belongs in the category of school resources over which we have some degree of policy control is "teacher quality"—itself a composite concept made up of several variables. The conclusion in the Report about teacher quality appears to strike a rare optimistic note regarding the beneficial influence school resources can have in compensatory educational efforts. The Report states on page 317 that "a given investment in upgrading teacher quality will have the most effect on achievement in underprivileged areas." Surely, the theoretical justification for this variable should be quite firm. Moreover, the wording of the Report's conclusion exactly fits the criterion we have requested for assessing each variable.

Unfortunately, the statistical evidence in support of the finding the authors present concerns "variance explained": "Given the fact that no school factors (excluding student body composition) account for much variation in achievement, teachers' characteristics account for more than any other." And, "by the 12th grade, teacher variables account for more than nine percent of the variance among Negro students, two percent among white students" (Coleman *et al.*, 1966, p. 325). It is perhaps superfluous to mention again that this ranking

---

[17]The possible misallocation of the effect is more likely if the student family characteristics or the school resources variables are measured with considerable error. That a good deal of error is present in the measure of these variables has been strongly argued by Bowles and Levin (1968a) and by Kain and Hanushek (1968).

of importance of a variable in terms of variance explained does not tell us what the "bet coefficients" are, nor permit us to derive them; therefore, the conclusion about a "given investment in ungrading teacher quality" for underprivileged areas is not supported. If, for example, the variance of verbal ability was large among teachers of black students and the educational achievement scores had a relatively small variance, the large partial correlation coefficient (and ϕ) of this variable would be consistent with a small value for the "bet coefficient"—even setting aside cost considerations. (See the formulas on pp. 79 and 88 of this paper.)

School Resources

Perhaps the single category of variables most susceptible to policy manipulation is that of school resources. Unfortunately, the variables used to measure school resources are very much like the "encyclopedias in the home" we discussed above. It is difficult to know whether, for example, library books or laboratories are supposed to represent their own effects, per se, or whether they are supposed to represent a more extensive collection of items under the rubric of school facilities (or some other concept of school characteristics).

One can argue for either interpretation. On the reasonable assumption that libraries and laboratories are and would be closely linked to an underlying specification of the usage of these facilities, we could treat libraries and labs as proxies for the "usage" concepts, which in turn can be plausibly linked to educational performance. Given this, the reader might further surmise that the two variables must be standing solely for their own effects, for otherwise the authors would have included the other items.

If, on the other hand, it is naive to assume that facilities present are facilities used, and if it would have been overly burdensome to include all relevant items in the survey, then we can more readily accept the argument that the included variables are meant to be representative of some different and/or larger collection. If so, we need to ask: (a) what are these other variables; and (b) what is the specification (i.e., regression equation) by which they are linked to the other variables. This really breaks up into two other questions: how accurate is the representation (i.e., how strongly are they correlated), and what is the quantitative magnitude of the relation (i.e., what are the regression coefficients linking the full set of variables to the proxy variable)?[18]

---

[18] The complexity of this specification need not be exaggerated. There are many decision contexts in which proxy variables may represent a bundle of heterogeneous components, and it may not be worthwhile or expedient for the decision maker to distinguish among the components to determine their separate measures of effectiveness. What is necessary, however, is some translation of a unit of the proxy variable into a unit of the larger bundle (along with, eventually, some measure of the costs of the larger bundle).

The sort of questions we have been posing serves to illustrate the analytical weaknesses noted above. If the questions we have raised are overly demanding of the state of theoretical knowledge about the educational processes, we can only ask that this shaky base be made explicit. Perhaps researchers will be led to work with a more simplified model that can be well specified and interpreted—better this than a complex model that defies interpretation.

Conclusion

We are aware that a demand for theoretical rigor may be likened to a request for virtue. But we hope that the discussion in the last two sections has been sufficiently specific so that both the interpretation of the Coleman Report and the design of further studies will be improved.

Our criticism of the Coleman Report has been aimed at its methods and not at its substantive findings. The questions we have raised about the statistical and methodological techniques in the Report should be viewed as *re-inforcing* the challenge to the "educational establishment"[19] to provide evidence on the effectiveness of their programs, especially compensatory educational programs. Nor should any research into the determinants of educational achievement overlook the potential contribution that may stem, however indirectly, from the simple improvement in economic status of the student or his family or the families of his fellow students.

REFERENCES

Bowles, S. S., and Levin, H. M. (1968a). The determinants of scholastic achievement—an appraisal of some recent evidence. *Journal of Human Resources* 3 (Winter); 3-29.
Bowles, S. S., and Levin, H. M. (1968b). More on multicollinearity and the effectiveness of schools. *Journal of Human Resources* 3 (Summer); 393-400.
Bredemeier, H. C. (1968). Schools and student growth. *Urban Review* April; pp. 21-27.
Coleman, J. S. (1966). Equal schools or equal students? *Public Interest* 1 (Summer); 70-75.
Coleman, J. S. (1968a). Equality of educational opportunity: Reply to Bowles and Levin. *Journal of Human Resources* 3 (Spring); 237-246.
Coleman, J. S. (1968b). *The Evaluation of Equality of Educational Opportunity,* Rep. No. 25. Center for the Study of the Social Organization of Schools, Johns Hopkins University, Baltimore, Maryland.
Coleman, J. S., Campbell, E. Q., Hobson, C. F., McPartland, J., Mood, A. M., *et al.* (1966). *Equality of Educational Opportunity.* US Gov't. Printing Office, Washington, D.C.

[19]The term was used by Daniel P. Moynihan (1968) in the context of his criticism that "educationists"—administrators, teachers, research personnel—have shirked their responsibilities to evaluate their performance and have attempted to use "technical" criticism of the Coleman Report as an excuse for continued inaction.

Darlington, R. B. (1968). Multiple regression in psychological research and practice. *Psychological Bulletin* **69**; 161-182.

Kain, J. F., and Hanushek, E. A. (1968). *On the Value of Equality of Educational Opportunity as a Guide to Policy,* Discuss. Pap. No. 36. Program on Regional and Urban Economics, Harvard University, Cambridge, Massachusetts.

Mosteller, F. (1967a). Preliminary report for Group D (March 29, 1967). In *Report of the Harvard Faculty Seminar on the Equal Educational Opportunity Report, 1967.*

Mosteller, F. (1967b). Report of the Harvard SEEOR Group A (May 11, 1967). In *Report of the Harvard Faculty Seminar on the Equal Educational Opportunity Report, 1967.*

Moynihan, D. P. (1968). Sources of resistance to the Coleman Report. *Harvard Education Review* **38** (Winter); 23-26.

Nichols, R. C. (1966). Schools and the disadvantaged. *Science* **154**, 1312-1314.

Sewell, W. H. (1967). Review. *American Sociological Review* **32**, 475-479.

Smith, M. S. (1968). Comments on Bowles and Levin. *Journal of Human Resources* **3** (Summer); 384-389.

Wilson, A. (1967). Educational consequences of segregation in a California community. In *Racial Isolation in Public Schools,* Vol. 2, pp. 165-206. U.S. Commission on Civil Rights, Washington, D.C.

6

REPLY TO CAIN AND WATTS*

James S. Coleman

Cain and Watts raise a number of criticisms to the report entitled *Equality of Educational Opportunity*—which they call "the Coleman Report"—and I would like to discuss some of these criticisms mostly from a different perspective than theirs.

First, however, let me mention a more personal point: the report is not a "Coleman Report": Ernest Campbell and I were co-directors of the project that culminated in the Report, and Alexander Mood had overall supervision of the study. All three of us, together with other persons in the Office of Education (some of whom are co-authors), spent much time and effort in the analysis and preparation of the report, and the report was a joint product.

Cain and Watts object to one part of the report, an analysis (in Chapter 3) which related an achievement output of school to various input factors. The source of policy interest in this is obvious: if these relationships can give information about the effect of various resource inputs on achievement, then the results are of some aid to policy. This is why we initiated that analysis, and why a number of economists with an interest in "production functions" in education have paid special attention to it.

The first objection of Cain and Watts is to an inadequate specification of the theoretical model on which to base the regression analysis that formed the

*I am indebted to James Fennessey for comments on a draft of this paper. Reprinted from *American Sociological Review,* **35,** No. 2. April, 1970, pp. 228-242.

core of Section 2 of this chapter. The role of a theoretical model in such research is, however, an ambiguous one. If, indeed, it were possible to know which variables have some importance in affecting achievement, and to know the precise functional relationships between these variables—that is, to specify the theoretical model—then a large portion of the policy questions would be re-solved. But neither we, nor Cain and Watts, nor anyone else, is able to specify such a model with any degree of assurance. As with any problem, one must start where he is, not where he would like to be. In such a situation, the specification of a set of relatively simple and straightforward alternative models probably provides more increment to knowledge than a single, more elaborate model with more rigid and more esoteric assumptions. Two models are relatively good candidates. The first, which we chose, is linear regression analysis, in which the output variable (verbal achievement in this case) is taken as the dependent variable, and various inputs, including characteristics of the student, as well as characteristics of his school environment, are potential candidates as factors affecting the dependent variable. The second relatively simple model, often favored by economists because it has the form of a common (Cobb-Douglas) production function, is a multiplicative model, $y=a x_1^{b1} x_2^{b2} \ldots x_n^{bn}$. This becomes an equation that is linear in logarithms, thus allowing estimation of the exponents by linear regression analysis of $\log y$ on $\log x_i$. Although one may be better than the other in a given situation, both are obviously false when carried to the extreme. (The first implies that any input resource is substitutable for any other; the second implies no substitutability: no input resource is substitutable for any other, and if one is missing, all is lost.)

The virtue of multiple regression analysis is, of course, that it allows controlling simultaneously on a number of variables when examining the relation of any one to the dependent variable. If one were certain that variable x_2 has its effect on y through x_{1f} then obviously it would be incorrect to control on x_1 when examining the relation of x_2 to y. But seldom do we have such assurance, particularly in an area as complex as education. It is, in such circumstances, inappropriate to specify a single theoretical model, but rather to examine the relation of x_2 to y both when x_1 is controlled and when x_1 is not. When the number of potential causal variables is quite large, both the alternative models and statistical results may be used not only to estimate parameters—as implied by Cain and Watts—but also to sense the relative importance of these variables under alternative causal structures. This is what we did, and this is what I believe important in an area where the theoretical structure of causation is as poorly known as in education.

Indeed, if I were doing such a study now, I would seriously consider the use of multivariate cross-tabulations, with an even more open perspective toward theoretical models, in place of much of the multiple regression analysis we used.

For in the early stages of the search for knowledge about processes in a given area, it is important to use relatively open models, in which the peculiar quirks of the data that may be highly informative are not lost.

Some part of the difference between this orientation and that of Cain and Watts' may be laid to academic discipline: econometricians ordinarily deal with areas in which there are quite specific theoretical models. Consequently, the task in an empirical analysis becomes one of estimating values of parameters in this causal structure, and the policy results of the study lie in these parameter values. Sociologists ordinarily work in areas without such theoretical models, and the task of their empirical analysis is to gain more information about possibly relevant variables and about plausible causal structures. The policy results of their research lie in such things as uncovering important processes that had previously been unknown or ignored in policy. In this case, for example, the strength of two sets of relationships had that function: the relation between a child's achievement and the educational resources in his schoolmate's families, when his own family characteristics (and various school resources) were controlled; and the relation between his achievement and his sense of control of the environment, again when these factors in the environment are controlled. This kind of policy relevance is unfamiliar to economists: it does not lead directly to budgetary allocations. But it is, I suggest, more valuable than estimation of parameters in a theoretical model that excluded these variables, as one fixed at the outset almost certainly would have. (These variables were in fact not present in early theoretical models that we laid out in preparing the analysis. They came to be present only because we did not let those models blind us to other possibilities.)

One way, however, *not* to specify a theoretical model is that proposed by Cain and Watts: "to develop a model in which the selection of variables is governed by a distinction between those variables amenable to policy manipulation and those that are not." A causal model is independent of the circumstance that some variables happen to be policy variables. Excluding from the analysis variables that are part of the causal structure because they are not policy manipulable can easily lead to biased estimates of the effects of the policy variables. The best example of this in the present case is family background variables. They were included among all sets of regression variables when examining school facilities and curriculum resources, teacher characteristics, and student-body characteristics. They were included because of the biases in estimating the relative effects of different school resource variables that would have been introduced by leaving them out. To use a simple example, if the child's own background characteristics had been left out of the regression equation which examined simultaneously the relation of teacher's characteristics and student body's characteristics to a child's achievement, the estimates of student-body effects would have been much higher than they were—a spurious relation, I infer, due to their correlation with the child's own background characteristics and the correlation of the latter with his achievement.

In this same section of their paper, Cain and Watts also object to the way the dependent variable—a verbal achievement test—was chosen. I can say little here beyond the analysis published in the Report. There we reported conclusions from detailed examination carried out with other tests as dependent variables and, by these criteria, chose the one used. I suspect a linear combination of the various tests would, as they suggest, have been better—but if the conclusions of the analysis would have been much different, this would have been evident in the analysis which led to our choice. No authors, including Cain and Watts, have performed this relatively simple activity with the correlation matrices published in the appendix to the report. Their arguments about possible ill effects of our selection would carry more weight if they had done so.

The major portion of Cain and Watts' paper concerns the measures used in the Report to express the strength of various relationships. These were not the raw multiple regression coefficients that are frequently used as such measures, nor the standardized regression coefficients (path coefficients) that are also used with some frequency. Instead, we used a less common measure, the percent of variance accounted for by a variable beyond that accounted for by other variables in the set included in that equation. Cain and Watts point out some of the defects of this measure. Clearly, as they point out, it is not a measure of the strength of the relationship with a straightforward interpretation like that of the raw regression coefficient ("an increase of 1 unit in the independent variable x_i will increase the independent variable by b_i units").

Ideally regression analysis would lead to such simple, straightforward statements. This would be directly policy-relevant, and it would make clear-cut predictions about effects of policy changes.

What one can say is that if all samples were very large (the greater the multicollinearity, the larger the necessary sample), if all errors were due to sampling and none to measurement, and if the causal structure (what Cain and Watts refer to as the theoretical model) were fully specified in form, then we would be in such a happy state, and all the arguments offered by Cain and Watts would hold. In this portion of their paper, as throughout, Cain and Watts proceed as if we were in this state, and therefore that the principal task is to obtain the best estimates of parameters in a known model, so that policy makers can open the correct valves. The analysis of the Report, however, assumed a prior state of knowledge, a state from which one could not hope to give precise policy specifications but, instead, only narrow down the uncertainty about what kinds of educational resources would make the greatest difference in achievement. I believe we did so with reasonable success, even though the task was more nearly one of cleaning the Augean stables than of providing explicit guidelines for policy. Stated most succinctly and generally, I believe the strongest inference that can be drawn from the results is that the resources most important for a child's achievement in school are the cognitive skills in his social environment in school, including his fellow-students as well as his teachers, and that these effects are strongest for the children with least educational resources outside school. Stated thus, the result appears trite, but it could well have been otherwise. Other resources, on which school systems spend much money, appear unimportant; and lower-class students do better in absolute terms rather than worse (as one might have predicted) in schools where their *relative* achievement is low due to the presence of higher-performing middle-class students.

Cain and Watts argue for using raw regression coefficients (or regression coefficients converted to a common denominator such as dollars) in place of standardized regression (path) coefficients or percent of additional variance accounted for. They show, in their Table 1, how the coefficients of a linear equation may be recovered exactly from perfect data. But there are several difficulties to this approach, some of them arising from the fact that data are never perfect, others from different sources, which I will point out below.

First of all, unless the raw regression coefficients are converted to some common denominator, they are noncomparable. The usual conversion is to standardized regression coefficients, but they reject this for a standardization in terms of dollar costs. I will mention shortly some of the numerous problems that would arise with this cost-standardization. But even with standardized regression coefficients, there arise some problems which led to our use of percent of variance accounted for. One of these was particularly troublesome. It became evident early in the analysis that no single school resource measure would have more than a very small regression coefficient unless we eliminated from the equation other resource measures that were highly correlated with it. Gordon (1968) shows how regression coefficients are depressed by using several measures which are highly correlated, and may in part be proxy measures for other unobserved variables. This is not evident in Cain and Watts' analysis, because they begin by assuming a causal structure in which the variables in the equation are in fact the causal variables, and not partial proxies for other unobserved variables. Thus when the correlation between two variables increases, this increases the zero-order correlation of both (Rows 4 and 5 of their table), because each has an independent effect on the dependent variable. What happens when one makes the other assumption—that the zero-order correlation of each with the dependent variable does *not* increase as their correlation increases—is that the regression coefficient of each declines. (See, for example, Gordon, 1968, Table 3.) This meant that we had to reduce our aspirations, and make our principal inferences only about clusters of variables that were both highly correlated and had some sensible content similarity. The clusters that we used were school facilities and curriculum, teacher characteristics, and student body characteristics (all examined in equations in which the child's own family background characteristics were controlled). We could do this in any of three ways: first, by selecting one of the variables as a proxy for the cluster; second, by forming a single index for each which was a linear combination of the variables in the cluster; or third, to keep the variables distinct in the regression equation. We chose the last of these methods, because of the additional flexibility it permitted. But it dictated that we use, as a measure of the effect of several variables together, the percent of additional variance they jointly accounted for rather than regression coefficients, the reason being that regression coefficients cannot be added to give a combined measure for the effect of several correlated variables. While the regression coefficient of each is depressed by the presence of the others, the sum of the regression coefficients is an inflated measure of their combined effect. If we had used either of the other approaches, it would have been possible to use regression coefficients for measures of effect (though we would have used standardized, rather than raw coefficients, as the only reasonable way of obtaining comparability). However, this would likely have overstated the effects of the variables in question, and we preferred to err on the conservative side, given that various other aspects of the analysis, such as correlated variables omitted from the equation, were likely to lead in the direction of overattribution of causality to observed variables—as is nearly always the case with analyses from cross-sectional data.

But in empirical fact, it really didn't make that much difference, as Cain and Watts would have seen if they had carried out the analysis they propose with the correlation matrices we provided in the Appendix to the Report. Their academic arguments would have carried more weight if they had shown that they made a difference. I have done so, and the results are shown in Table I, for Grade 12, Negroes and whites, North and South. Standardized regression coefficients for each set of variables considered as a unit are presented, as are unique contributions to the variance.[1] The latter have been proportionately scaled up to equal the total explained variance, R^2.

The inferences drawn from the two sets of measures are very similar if one takes into account that the unique variances and the regression coefficients can only be directly compared if the latter are squared or the square roots of the former are taken. Where they do differ, it appears likely that the unique variance

---

[1] The regression coefficients have been obtained by first carrying out a regression analysis using all 29 original variables in the equation. Then for each of the sets of variables, a new single variable was constructed as a linear combination of the individual variables making up that set (e.g., the 11 variables measuring facilities and curriculum). The linear combination uses as coefficients the regression coefficients in the large equation. This creates then four composite variables which in a regression equation together are equivalent to the original set of 29, but which now give one regression coefficient for each of the four sets of variables.

TABLE 1

Standardized Multiple Regression Coefficients (or Path Coefficients) as Measures of the Importance of Each of Four Clusters of Variables on Verbal Achievement, at Grade 12. Family Background (Six Variables), School Facilities and Curriculum (11 Variables), Teacher Characteristics (7 Variables), and Student Body Characteristics (5 Variables), Negroes and Whites in North and South.

	Grade 12			
	Negro North	Negro South	White North	White South
Family	0.23	0.22	0.34	0.34
Facilities and curriculum	0.13	0.07	0.10	0.07
Teacher	0.13	0.12	0.09	0.04
Student body	0.23	0.23	0.09	0.11

Unique contributions to variance in verbal achievement (scaled up to sum to R^2 in each regression) as measures of the importance of each of four clusters of variables.[a]

Family	0.067	0.119	0.133	0.144
Facilities and curriculum	0.018	0.009	0.014	0.007
Teacher	0.016	0.026	0.009	0.002
Student body	0.046	0.078	0.008	0.013
R^2	0.146	0.232	0.165	0.166

[a]The total explained variance consists of the sum of that uniquely explained by each variable, that explained uniquely by each pair, by each triplet, and that which is explainable only by all four. In this table, only the first of these components are presented, but to facilitate comparison, they are scaled up proportionately to sum to R^2.

contributions give a more accurate picture of the strength of different factors. The principal point of difference is for Negroes in the South, comparing the measures of effect of the child's own family background and the measures of effect of the student body backgrounds. (It is in this group that those two variables are most highly correlated.) The regression coefficients show a stronger effect of the student body characteristics than of his own family characteristics. The unique variance explained, in contrast, shows a considerably higher effect of family background—a result which certainly is in accord with *a priori* considerations.

In short, in a situation where there is differential error in measurement, quite beyond sampling error, where there are causal variables not in the equation correlated with those that are, and where there is multicollinearity among the variables in the equation, the apparent advantages of the straightforward approach suggested by Cain and Watts, where only the last of these conditions is true, evaporate.

I think it is important to emphasize that the difference in the statistical measures used by us and proposed by Cain and Watts is fundamentally related to the difference in our conceptions of the kinds of policy inferences that can be made from a study of this sort. The point can best be made by introducing another property of the measure we used and indicating how it has been used in drawing inferences from this survey. One property of the measure of "additional variance accounted for" which we used is that the total explained variance, R^2, can be partitioned into a sum of portions of the variance attributable to different independent variables and sets of independent variables in the equation. For example, if there is one family background variable, labeled 1, and one school variable, labeled 2, the explained variance can be partitioned as follows, using the symbol "ϕ_i" as Cain and Watts have used it in their paper:

$$R^2 = \phi_1 + \phi_2 + \phi_{12}, ,$$

where ϕ_{12} is the portion of explained variance that is explainable either by the background variable or the school variable. Alexander Mood has developed this linear partitioning for a set of n variables in a mode of analysis termed "commonality analysis."[2] For example, for three variables, this equation would become:

$$R^2 = \phi_1 + \phi_2 + \phi_3 + \phi_{12} + \phi_{13} + \phi_{23} + \phi_{123}$$

It should be emphasized that these coefficients for pairs and triplets are not the same as interaction terms in a regression analysis; they arise not from nonlinearity, but from correlations among the independent variables, which confound the uniqueness of causal attributions.

The importance of this mode of analysis is that it shows directly the degree of overlap in explanation that exists in each subset of the independent variables. For example, with these data, ϕ_{12} is much larger than either ϕ_1 or ϕ_2; that is, the variance in achievement that may either be accounted for by variations in family background or by variations in school, but is not uniquely attributable to either, is much larger than that uniquely attributable to either (though that uniquely attributable to background is much larger than that uniquely attributable to school).

Although this method of analysis was not developed at the time our study was carried out, the survey data have been extensively reanalyzed by Mayeske and others (1969) using this method. Its value then becomes quite apparent. For example, in examining four sets of variables, family background, teacher characteristics, pupil programs and policies, and plant and physical facilities, by far the largest portion of R^2 (56% of the total R^2) was accounted for in common by student background and teacher characteristics. Since the commonalities involving other variables were quite low, this partitioning isolated the major source of variance in achievement due to family background and teachers, with the

---

[2] For a discussion of this same technique, developed independently, see Newton and Spurrell (1967) and Rozeboom (1968).

other variables eliminated. The value of such analysis, which does not accrue from the set of regression coefficients in the equation, lies in the fact that it narrows down the task and sets the stage for a more intensive examination of the effects of family background and teachers' characteristics on achievement.

This illustrates well the different conception of "policy inferences" that we have from that of Cain and Watts, for even though we used only the unique portions of this partitioning, its broader use in the way I have described is consistent with our use. We used the regression analysis along with other methods to gain more understanding of the factors leading to achievement, and to eliminate from consideration various factors that showed little or no relation to achievement. This leaves to a later stage of research the estimation of cost-benefit parameters. I am not suggesting that one should use regression coefficients only for cost-benefit uses; we might well have used them in our analysis. Quite generally, it is much better to use as measures of a substantive phenomenon parameters in explicit models rather than measures that derive from tests used in statistical inference. But if we had used regression coefficients in this case, the kind of policy inferences we would have drawn would have made less strong assumptions about the causal properties of the coefficients than Cain and Watts are willing to make, in part because of the multicollinearity among the potential causes of achievement.

To move to related matters, Cain and Watts suggest a rescaling of the raw regression coefficients in dollar terms, to provide a common denominator for comparison of predicted efficacy of expenditures. They call the resulting re-scaled coefficient a "bet-coefficient." This can be, I believe, a useful approach—assuming we were in the happy state where the regression coefficients could truly be interpreted as parameters in a causal model. However, even in this state, there are enormous complications in such an approach. As the authors indicate, perhaps dollars are not the only costs. Perhaps "political capital" must be expended, or suppose time-consumption is a cost. Unless these costs can all be converted to the same base, the bet-coefficient approach runs into difficulties.

I believe the heart of the difficulty lies in the failure to recognize a division of labor between the researcher and the persons or bodies that make policy. It may be very useful to persons charged with the responsibility of making educational policy for the educational researcher to carry their results one step farther than raw regression coefficients and attach dollar costs to them.[3] But it

---

[3] The fundamental defects of linear regression analysis as an instrument forming the basis for budget allocations becomes, however, ludicrously evident here. For the direct implications are to spend all funds on that resource which has the highest bet coefficient, since in linear regression analysis there are no declining marginal returns. Again, it is clear that the value of such work as we carried out is for the kinds of policy questions prior to that of estimating parameters for budget allocations: the classes of variables that must be taken into consideration, rough estimates of the relative sizes of their effects, and some information about the nature of the process.

is the various interested parties, and parties in a position of political authority, who must amalgamate the various kinds of costs associated with each potential policy and form their own bet-coefficients. There, dollar costs are not comparable: for example, in the political arena, to obtain a dollar for school buildings may cost less political capital than a dollar for teachers' salaries, or a dollar for bussing children to integrate schools.

Thus at some point, the researcher must hand over his results to the policy makers, or more generally, to the public. The more easily interpretable and intellectually digestible he can make them, the better. The political digestion itself, however, is not a task of the researcher, but of the whole political process. The research informs that process, but does no more. It cannot, even if its information is perfect, take the place of that process, as Cain and Watts seem to feel it can.

Somewhat more generally, most of the differences between our approach and that of Cain and Watts' can, I believe, be attributed to a different conception of the state of knowledge about the development of achievement in school. This leads to two minor differences in approach: the general way in which statistical tools are used to draw inferences from the data, and the kind of policy advice that may be drawn from the data. They treat the statistical tool—a linear regression equation—as a rather direct model of the causal process, with all causally relevant variables directly measured without error. We treated the same statistical tool as an aid in the prior process of search for causally relevant variables in a state of knowledge where the structure of the process relating them is not fully known. With this latter approach, that statistical tool is only one such aid in the search: inferences from the differences at different grade levels are valuable; examination of within- and between-school components of variance is also valuable, and even examination of marginal distributions and zero-order correlations is important.

The policy advice they would give from their analysis is about expected benefits of various possible expenditures, deriving directly from their regression coefficients. Our policy-relevant results concern the prior information about what classes of variables must be taken into consideration, what is the order of magnitude of their differential effects (as they are currently differentially distributed over the population of children), and something about the structure of the process through which achievement is generated—with the results of the regression analysis playing only one part in those inferences.

REFERENCES

Cain, G. & Watts, H. W. (1970). Problems in making policy inference from the Coleman Report. *American Sociological Review* 35, 228-242.

Coleman, J. S., Campbell, E. Q., Hobson, C. F., McPartland, J. Mood, A. M., *et al.* (1966). *Equality of Educational Opportunity.* US Govt. Printing Office, Washington, D.C.

Gordon, R. A. (1968). Issues in multiple regression. *American Journal of Sociology* **75,** 593-616.

Mayeske, G. W., Wisler, C. E., Beaton, A. E. Jr., *et al.* (1969). *A Study of Our Nation's Schools.* US Govt. Printing Office, Washington, D.C.

Newton, R. G., and Spurrell, D. J. (1967). A development of multiple regression for the analysis of routine data. *Applied Statistics* **16,** No. 1, 51-64.

Rozeboom, W. W. (1968). The theory of abstract partials: An introduction. *Psychometrika* **33,** No. 2, 133-167.

THE METHODOLOGY OF EVALUATING
SOCIAL ACTION PROGRAMS*

Glen G. Cain and Robinson G. Hollister

Manpower programs used to consist almost entirely of vocational training and various but limited types of assistance for the worker in searching for jobs within local labor markets. But with the recent emphasis on problems of poverty and the disadvantaged worker, manpower programs have come to involve remedial and general education, to intermesh with community action programs providing a variety of welfare services, and, on a trial basis, to assist in migration between labor markets. They are part of a broader class of programs which, for lack of a better term, we might call social action programs. Our paper will include many references to this broader class, and in particular to anti-poverty programs. In so doing, we hope to provide a more general and more relevant perspective of the topic of evaluation methodology.

We hold the opinion, apparently widely shared, that existing evaluations of social action programs (and we are including our own) have fallen short of

*We are grateful to the following persons, who have increased our understanding of the ideas in this paper or have commented directly on an earlier draft (or have done both); David Bradford, Frank Cassels, John Evans, Woodrow Ginsberg, Thomas Glennan, Robert Levine, Guy Orcutt, Gerald Somers, Ernst Stromsdorfer, Harold Watts, Arnold Weber, Burton Weisbrod, and Walter Williams.

Reprinted from *Discussion Papers,* Institute for Research on Poverty, University of Wisconsin, Madison, Wisconsin, 1969.

meeting the standards possible within the disciplines of the social sciences. The reasons for these shortcomings are easy to identify. The programs typically involve investments in human beings, a relatively new area of empirical research in economics. They are aimed at such social and political goals as equality and election victories, as well as economic objectives concerning, say, income and employment. They often attempt to deliver services on a large enough scale to make a noticeable impact upon the community. And at the same time, they are expected to provide a quasi-experimental basis for determining what programs ought to be implemented and how they ought to be run.

It is not surprising then, that evaluations of social action programs have often not been attempted and, when attempted, have not been successful. Despite this background, we believe that existing data and methods permit evaluations which, while not satisfying the methodological purists, can at least provide the rules of evidence for judging the degree to which programs have succeeded or failed. Specifically, the theme we will develop is that evaluations should be set up to provide the ingredients of an experimental situation: a model suitable for statistical testing, wide range in the values of the variables representing the program inputs, and the judicious use of control groups.

This paper reflects several backgrounds in which we have had some experience—the tradition of benefit-cost analyses from economics, the approach of quasi-experimental research from other social sciences; and the perspective of one intiating and using evaluation studies from a governmental agency. Each of these points of view has its own literature which we have by no means covered, but to which we are indebted.[1]

TYPES OF EVALUATION

There are two broad types of evaluation. The first, which we call "process evaluation," is mainly administrative monitoring. Any program must be monitored (or evaluated) regarding the integrity of its financial transactions and

[1] As examples of the benefit-cost literature, see R. Dorfman, ed., *Measuring Benefits of Government Investments* (Brookings Institution, Washington, D.C., 1965), and A. R. Prest and R. Turvey, "Cost-Benefit Analysis: A Survey," *Economic Journal* 75, 683-735 (1965). As examples of the evaluation research literature, see E. A. Suchman, *Evaluation Research* (Russell Sage Foundation, New York; 1967), D. T. Campbell and J. C. Stanley, *Experimental and Quasi-experimental Designs for Research* (Rand-McNally, Chicago, Illinois, 1966), G. H. Orcutt and A. G. Orcutt, Incentive and disincentive experimentation for income maintenance policy purposes. *American Economic Review* 58, 754-772, (1968), and H. Watts, *Graduated Work Incentives: Progress toward an Experiment in Negative Taxation,* Discuss. Pap. Ser. Institute for Research on Poverty, University of Wisconsin, Madison; 1968). For examples of the point of view of officials of governmental agencies, see W. Gorham, "Notes of a Practitioner," and E. Drew, HEW grapples' with PPBS, in *Public Interest* 8, Summer (1967).

accounting system. There is also an obvious need to check on other managerial functions, including whether or not accurate records are being kept. A component of process evaluations is progress reports aimed at determining the need for possible administrative changes in the operation of the program. In sum, "process evaluation" addresses the question: Given the existence of a program, is it being run honestly and administered efficiently?

A second type of evaluation, and the one with which we are concerned, may be called "outcome evaluation," more familiarly known as "cost-benefit analysis." Although both the inputs and outcomes of the program require measurements, the toughest problem is deciding on and measuring the outcomes. With this type of evaluation the whole concept of the program is brought into question, and it is certainly possible that a project might be judged to be a success or a failure irrespective of how well it was being administered.

A useful categorization of cost-benefit evaluations draws a distinction between *a priori* analyses and *ex post* analyses. An example of *a priori* analysis is the cost-effectiveness studies of weapons systems conducted by the Defense Department, which have analyzed war situations where there were no "real outcomes" and, thus, no *ex post* results with which to test the evaluation models. Similarly, most evaluations of water resource projects are confined to alternative proposals where the benefits and costs are estimated prior to the actual undertaking of the projects.[2] Only in the area of "social action" programs such as poverty, labor training, and to some extent housing, have substantial attempts been made to evaluate programs, not just in terms of before-the-fact estimates of probable outcomes or in terms of simulated hypothetical outcomes, but also on the basis of data actually gathered during or after the operation of the program.

A priori cost-benefit analyses of social action programs can, of course, be useful in program planning and feasibility studies, but the real demand and challenge lies in *ex post* evaluations. This more stringent demand made of social action programs may say something about the degree of skepticism and lack of sympathy Congress (or "society") has concerning these programs, but this posture appears to be one of the facts of political life.

Two additional differences between human investment programs and physical investment programs deserve mention—although whether these differences are real or merely apparent is a debatable point. One is the complexity of behavioral relations which the social action programs try to change. Is it correct

---

[2] There does seem to be a developing literature in which the *a priori* benefit-cost estimates are compared with the *ex post* results for water projects. See Maynard Hufschmidt, "'Systematic Errors' in Cost Estimation in Public Investment," to appear in the Universities-National Bureau of Economic Research Conference volume, *The Economics of Public Output*. It may be that similar follow-up studies are being undertaken for defense projects—one can at least say that Congressional committees are determined to carry out their own follow-up evaluations on projects such as the TFX.

to say that these relations are more difficult to analyze and predict than the technological relations which appear in defense and water resource analysis? Perhaps, but if the analysis of the latter really requires data on propensities of aggressive behavior or on values of recreational activities, respectively, then we may question whether these are easier to analyze than, say, employment behavior. A second difference is the shorter history and subsequent dearth of analytic studies of social action programs, a fact clearly related to the weaknesses of our theory and empirical knowledge of the behavioral relationships affected by the policies.

An awareness of these rather basic differences between the evaluations (or benefit-cost analyses) which have been carried out allegedly with some speed and success in other areas and the evaluations which have been looked for and generally not been forthcoming in the social action area is important in understanding the relatively "poor performance" of evaluators in the latter area. We can then be better prepared to recognize that the methodology for evaluation of social action programs will have to be developed in new ways to cope with their special difficulties.

PROBLEMS OF THE DESIGN OF THE EVALUATION

Specification of the Objectives

In the methodology of program evaluation which has been constructed, one of the principal tenets is that the first step in the analysis must be to specify the objectives of the program. Unfortunately, agreement on this principle has not facilitated its implementation, the problem being that few programs have a clearly defined single objective or even one dominant objective.

It becomes necessary to assign weights to the different objectives and to guard against both double-counting and under-counting. Arguments arise concerning "ultimate" objectives and "intermediate" objectives, and there will usually be a struggle to agree upon some measurable intermediate objectives which can serve as proxies for (practically speaking) unmeasurable ultimate objectives. Economists, who deal theoretically with the concepts of "welfare" and "utility," while their empirical work involves incomes and prices, should not find it difficult to appreciate the legitimacy of nonmeasurable entities.

We suggest, however, that in general the measures of program outputs, which may be proxies for ultimate objectives, should be measures of behavior and of tangible changes, such as income change, employment gain, and educational attainment. Lower priority should be given to the less tangible measures of self-images, community images, and opinion polls of peoples' attitudes toward the programs. The defense of this position rests mainly on the practical grounds of choosing outcomes which may be more accurately measured, both immediately and in terms of measures of outcomes, and choosing those which are more stable as predictors of a longer run or permanent assessment. We would argue that the relatively hard measures of cognitive educational gain are a more reliable and valid measure of the benefits of a Head Start program than are surveys of parents' or teachers' attitudes about the program. The latter should not be ignored, only given less weight. We suggest that, over the long run, *but not necessarily in the short run,* attitudes will closely correlate with the more tangible performance indicators. So, why not aim right from the beginning at measuring the program's substance rather than its public relations effects?

Although some measurable objectives are necessary for all but the crudest, journalistic type of evaluation, not all such objectives provide an obvious or easy translation into dollars to permit the desired benefit-cost calculation. In our judgment and experience, however, the problem of assigning dollar values is a step we seldom reach because we are unable to measure in the first instance the more direct or specific program outcome. Our failures in this respect are numerous—witness Head Start, health programs, and many of the manpower programs in which we simply do not know what difference the program has made. It is absolutely necessary that we first concentrate on assessing the change in educational attainment, in health, in employment and earnings or in whatever the program objective is. If this is done, we as economists may then offer some guides regarding the dollar worth of these changes, but even if the policy maker decides on his own system of pricing, we will have constrained the possibilities for mistaken judgments.

Indeed, the problems of specifying objectives will not disappear even if there is agreement on a translation of program outcomes to dollar values. Consider a program which provides for a simple transfer of money to the participant, who let us assume, is poor. Obviously, the objective of improving the economic status of the participant is unambiguously attained, but are we satisfied with this objective? It is instructive to begin any discussion of the objectives of social action programs aimed at the poor or disadvantaged person with a simple income-transfer program, because all the arguments about self-help, noneconomic goals, and community-wide goals can be explicitly aired. Economists in particular are forced to face these issues and will be better prepared for them when they arise, sometimes in disguised forms, in analyzing more complicated programs of assistance. At the same time, when noneconomists are directly confronted with the example of a simple income-transfer program, they will be better able to understand and accept the extent to which such a transfer program is the implicit criterion of a benefit-cost ratio of one, as used in benefit-cost analysis.

Specifying program objectives is an important step, but there is a risk that the attempt to reach unanimous agreement on the whole hierarchy of intermediate and ultimate objectives will become a roadblock to the undertaking of program evaluations. There have been numerous cases in which months, and even years, have been taken up in arguments over what the program objectives "really are" or how multiple objectives are to be "weighted" to add up to some overall goal measure. In the meantime, programs have stumbled on with no evaluation or new programs have been forestalled because no *a priori* evaluation was undertaken to assess the feasibility of the program. Wily bureaucrats have been able to prevent evaluation of their programs for many months by refusing to "sign off" on a defined set of objectives. (The legislative history of a program, like the Scriptures, provides a boundless source of Pharisaical counter-interpretations as to intended objectives.)

In the same vein, it must be recognized that there are some important social action programs for which it is necessary to observe what a program is doing and, in the process of observation, identify what the objectives are. Some programs leave considerable operational discretion to the local level, so that the program as actually implemented may differ considerably from area to area. In others, the legislative or administrative mandate may reflect a compromised mixture of several loosely related program proposals. An obvious example is the Community Action Program of OEO. What is necessary here is something which might be called a "search-evaluation." The first stages of the evaluation must be to find out the actual nature of the program in various areas. Of course, some sort of theory is required defining which objectives are relevant, but the search process may modify our theory. An iterative procedure is called for in which the process of evaluation goes on simultaneously with a "search" for the objectives of various elements of the program. The attempt to follow the usual dogma of evaluation, starting with the definition of a single objective—or a hierarchy of objectives—for the program, are bound to fail.

It may be helpful, in sum, to suggest that the structure of the dogma of evaluation developed in defense and water resources was largely a deductive structure, whereas the structure suggested for "search evaluation" situations is essentially, in its initial phases, inductive in nature. Analysts familiar with the first type are reluctant to accept the latter. In certain situations, however, the choice is between a "search evaluation" or no evaluation.

The Use of Control Groups

Given the objective of the program, the question, "What difference did the program make?", should be taken literally; we want to know the difference between the behavior with the program and the behavior if there had been no program. To answer it, some form of control group is essential. If we want to know what difference the program makes, we must ask: differences relative to what? And the basis for comparison must be some base group that performs the methodological function of a control group. Let us consider some alternatives.

The Before-and-After Study

In the before-and-after study, the assumption is that each subject is his own control (or the aggregate is its own control) and that the behavior of the group before the program is a measure of performance that would have occurred if there had been no program. However, it is well known that there are many situations in which this assumption is not tenable. We might briefly cite some examples found in manpower programs.

Sometimes the "before situation" is at a point in time when the participants are at a particularly low state—lower, that is, than is normal for the group. The very fact of being eligible for participation in a poverty program may, for example, reflect transitory conditions. Under such conditions we should expect a "natural" regression toward their mean level of performance if we measure their status in an "after situation," even if there were no program in the intervening period. Using zero earnings as the permanent measure of earnings of an unemployed person is an example of attributing normality to a transitory status. Another similar situation is when young people are involved, and the "natural" tendency over the passage of time would be expected to be improvement in their wages and employment situation.

There may be some structural change in the personal situations of the participants before and after the program, which has nothing to do with the program but would vitiate any simple before-and-after comparison. We should not, for example, look upon the relatively high earnings record of coal miners or packinghouse workers as characteristic of their "before situation" if, in fact, they have been permanently displaced from their jobs.

As a final example of a situation in which the before-and-after comparison is invalid, there is the frequent occurrence of significant environmental changes, particularly in labor market environments, which are characterized by seasonal and cyclical fluctuations. Is it the program or the changed environment which has brought about the change in behavior?

All of the above examples of invalidated evaluations could have been at least partially corrected if the control groups had been other similar persons who were in similar situations in the pretraining period.

Control Groups Which are not Program Participants:
Small Group Studies Versus Large Group Studies

The particular strength of the small-scale study is that it greatly facilitates the desideratum of random assignments to "treatment groups" and "control groups" or, at least, a closely supervised matching of treatment and control groups. Its particular shortcoming is that it is likely to lack representativeness—both in terms of the characteristics of the program participants and in terms of the character of the program. There is first the problem of a "hot house environment" of the small group study. (See discussion of "replicability" below.) Second, a wide range of values of the program inputs (i.e., in terms of levels of a given treatment or in terms of qualitatively different types of treatments) is less likely to be available in a small group study. (See the discussion on "statistical considerations" below.) The small group study may not be able to detect differential effects on different types of participants (e.g., by age, sex, color, residence, etc.), either because the variety of participant types are not available or because their numbers are too small. Finally, it is both a strength and a weakness of the small scale study that it is usually confined to a single geographic location. Thus, although "extraneous" noise from different environments is eliminated, we may learn little or nothing about how the program would operate in different environments.

The large scale study, which involves gathering data over a wide range of environments, customarily achieves "control" over the characteristics of participants and nonparticipants and over programs and environmental characteristics by statistical methods, rather than by randomization or careful matching, individual by individual. These studies have the capability of correcting each of the shortcomings attributed to the small scale studies in the preceding paragraph. But because they are almost impossible to operate with randomization, the large scale studies run afoul of the familiar problem in which the selectivity of the participants may be associated with some unmeasured variable(s) which makes it impossible to determine the net effect of the treatment. Since this shortcoming is so serious in the minds of many analysts, particularly statisticians, and because the small scale studies have a longer history of usage and acceptability in sociology and psychology, it may be worthwhile to defend at greater length the large scale studies, which are common to economists.

Randomization is seldom attempted for reasons having to do with the attitudes of the administrators of a program, local pressures from the client population, or various logistic problems. Indeed, all these reasons may serve to botch an *attempted* randomization procedure. Furthermore, we can say with greater certitude that the ideal "double-blind experiment with placebos" is almost impossible to achieve. If we are to do something other than abandon evaluation efforts in the face of these obstacles to randomization, we will have to turn to the large scale study and the statistical design issues that go along with it.

The fact that the programs vary across cities or among administrators may be turned to our advantage by viewing these as "natural experiments"[3] which may permit an extrapolation of the results of the treatment to the "zero" or "no-treatment" level. This latter device may be particularly useful if the analyst can work with the administrator in advance to design the program variability in

---

[3] We are indebted to Thomas K. Glennan, RAND Corporation, for his ideas on this point.

ways which minimize the confounding of results with environmental influences. Furthermore, the ethical problems raised by deliberately excluding some persons from the presumed beneficial treatments are to some extent avoided by assignments to differing treatments (although, here again, randomization is the ideal way to make these assignments).

It is difficult, at this stage, to provide more than superficial observations regarding the choice between small and large scale studies. It would seem that for those evaluations that have a design concept which is radically different from existing designs or where there is a quite narrow hypothesis which requires detailed examination, a small group study would be preferable. Conversely, when the concept underlying a program is quite broad and where large amounts of resources are to be allocated, the large group approach is probably more relevant—a point argued in greater detail in our discussion of the "replicability criterion."

The Replicability Criterions

A source of friction between administrators of programs and those doing evaluation research (usually academicians) is the failure to agree upon the level of decision-making for which the results of the evaluation are to be used. This failure, which is all the more serious because the issue is often not explicitly addressed, leads to disputes regarding two related issues—the scope of the evaluation study and the selection of variables to be studied. To deal with these disputes, we suggest applying the "replicability criterion." We apply this name to the criterion because of the large number of cases in which evaluations of concepts have been made on the basis of projects which are not likely to be replicable on a large scale or which focus on characteristics of the project which are not within the ability of decision-makers to control. To take an extreme example, it has sometimes been stated that the success of a compensatory education program depended upon the "warmth and enthusiasm" of the teachers.

In a context of a nationwide program, no administrator has control over the level of "warmth and enthusiasm" of teachers.

It is sometimes argued by administrators that evaluations which are based upon samples drawn from any centers of a program are not legitimate tests of the program concept since they do not adequately take into account the differences in the details of individual projects or of differentiated populations. These attitudes frequently lead the administrators or other champions of the program to select, either *ex ante* or *ex post,* particular "pet" projects for evaluations that "really count." In the extreme, this approach consists of looking at the successful programs (based on observations of ongoing or even completed programs) and then claiming that these are really the ones that should be the basis for the evaluation of the program as a whole. *If* these successful programs have worked with representative participants in representative surroundings and *if* the techniques used—including the quality of the administrative and operational personnel—can be replicated on a nationwide basis, *then* it makes sense to say that the evaluation of the particular program can stand for an evaluation of the overall program. But we can seldom assume these conditional statements. After all, each of the individual programs, a few political plums notwithstanding, was set up because someone thought it was worthwhile. Of course, some will flop because of poor teachers or because one or more operations were fouled up—but it is in the nature of the beast that some incompetent administrative and operational foul-ups will occur. It is a strength of summary, overall measures of performance that they will include the "accidental" foul-ups with the "accidental" successes, the few bad administrators and teachers as well as the few charismatic leaders. As a case in point, consider the success (according to prevailing opinion) of Reverend Sullivan's Operation Industrial Council in Philadelphia with the (as yet) absence of any evidence that the OIC type of manpower program has been successfully transferred elsewhere.[4]

Small scale studies of preselected particular programs are most useful either for assessing radically different program ideas or for providing the administrator with information relevant to decisions of program content *within* the confines of his overall program. These are important uses, but the decisions at a broader level which concern the allocation of resources *among* programs of widely differing concept call for a different type of evaluation with a focus on different variables.

It may be helpful to cite an example of the way in which the replicability criterion should have been applied. A few years ago, a broad scale evaluation of the Work Experience Program[5] was carried out. (The evaluation was of necessity based upon very fragmentary data, but we are here concerned with the issues it raised rather than with its own merits.) The evaluation indicated that on the average the unemployment rates among the completers of the program were just as high as those with similar characteristics who had not been in the program. On the basis of this evaluation, it was argued that the concept of the program was faulty, and that some rather major shifts in the design and in the allocation of

---

[4] Briefly, the OIC concept combines elements of training, job development (often aided by pressure tactics against employers), and a psychological up-lifting of the participants which is conducted with an ideology of militancy and participatory democracy.

[5] The Work Experience program consisted of public employment of welfare recipients and other adult poor under Title V of the Economic Opportunity Act. Only minimal training was offered, but it was hoped that work-for-pay would, by itself, provide a springboard to self-sustaining employment in the private market.

resources to the program were advocated.[6] Other analysts objected to this rather drastic conclusion and argued that the "proper" evaluative procedure was to examine individual projects within the program, pick out those projects which had higher "success rates," and then attempt to determine which characteristics of these projects were related to those "success rates."[7]

The argument as to which approach is proper depends on the particular decision framework to which the results of the evaluation were to be applied. To the administrators of the program, it is really the project by project type of analysis which is relevant to the decision variables which they control. The broader type of evaluation would be of interest but their primary concern is to adjust the mix of program elements to obtain the best results within the given broad concept of the program. Even for program administrators, however, there will be elements and personnel peculiar to a given area or project that will not be replicable in other areas and other projects.

For decision-makers at levels higher than the program administrator the broader type of evaluation will provide the sort of information relevant to their decision frame. Their task is to allocate resources among programs based upon different broad concepts. Negative findings from the broader evaluation argue against increasing allocation to the program, although a conservative response is to hold the line on the program while awaiting the more detailed project-by-project evaluation to determine whether there is something salvageable in the concept embodied in the program. There will always be alternative programs serving the same population however, and the decision-maker is justified in shifting resources toward those programs which hold out the promise of better results.

The basic point is that project-by-project evaluations are bound to turn up some "successful" project somewhere, but unless there is good evidence that that "success" can be broadly replicated and that the administrative controls are adequate to insure such replication, then the individual project success is irrelevant. Resources must be allocated in light of evidence that concepts are not only "successful" on *a priori* grounds or in particular small scale contexts but that they are in fact "successful" in large scale implementation.

The Theoretical Framework—Some Statistical Considerations

The main function of a theoretical framework in cost-benefit evaluations is to provide a statistical model suitable for testing. A discussion of the economic

---

[6] U.S. Congress, House Committee on Ways and Means, *Community Work and Training Program,* 90th Congress, 1st Sess., House Doc. No. 96. US Government Printing Office, Washington D.C., 1967.

[7] W. Bateman, Assessing program effectiveness. *Welfare in Review* 6 (1968).

content of the statistical model is taken up in the next section; here we focus on more general questions of the statistical design of the evaluation. Generally, it makes little or no difference whether the statistical method is analysis of variance, regression analysis, or simply working with cell values in tables, but we will adopt the terminology of the regression model for the purposes of this discussion. The object of the social action program is the dependent variable in this model, and the various variables that describe or represent the program (or program inputs) are the particular set of independent variables which are of most interest to us, and which will sometimes be referred to as "treatment variables."

Usually our theory (which includes the body of substantive findings from previous studies) can tell us *something* about what variability can be expected in the behavior described by the dependent variable, and this information is necessary for determining the appropriate sample size. On the same issue, the theory can tell us what independent variables may be included as statistical controls for the purpose of reducing the unexplained or residual variation in the dependent variable. Clearly, the smaller the residual variation, the smaller is the sample size needed to attain a given level of precision (or statistical significance) in our results. (Another way of making this point is to say that the smaller the residual variation the greater is the statistical significance we achieve for a given sample size.)

As an example of these consideration, assume that the objective of the program is to imporve the wage earnings of a group of low-wage workers. Our dependent variable is some measure of earnings over a period of at least one year after those who were in the training program had left it. We can say at the outset that on the basis of the existing studies of income variability, we should be prepared for large variation in the earnings of our subjects—standard deviations in the hundreds of dollars would be typical. Moreover, these same studies combined with other *a priori* information can indicate what independent variables (like the worker's age, education, etc.) will account for some of this variation and thereby produce a smaller residual variation. We might add that the existing studies of determinants of earnings indicate that we should expect a relatively large residual variation to remain. Thus, we might still have to contend with unexplained variability (or standard errors of estimates) in the hundreds of dollars per subject.

How serious is a large residual variation in terms of preventing the detection of an effect on some training program? This depends on how large an effect we expect the training program to bring about, or, in more technical terms, the size of the partial regression coefficients representing the programs. Here again, our existing theory can narrow the range of our ignorance. Thus, we might be able to combine our information on the amount of variability in the dependent variable, earnings, with educated guesses about the earnings effect of a training program to permit us to decide how large a sample will be required to achieve some selected confidence interval on our estimates.[8] Suppose that we have, for example, relevant studies of the effects of investments in education or training suggesting that rates of return of 5 to 25 percent might be expected. Thus, on an investment of $1,000, the annual earnings of a worker might be raised by $50 to $250.[9] Obviously, for the given level of significance, a larger sample will be required and/or more statistical controls will be necessary to detect changes of this order of magnitude than if the program were expected to increase earnings of the participant by $1,000.

Indeed, it is precisely programs which have large and dramatic effects which can be evaluated with a loose design and an almost journalistic level of evaluation, but we would contend that almost all social action programs, and particularly those in the field of manpower training and education, are unlikely to bring about spectacular changes.[10] Regarding the *results* of a program, the analogy between a Salk vaccine for polio and a social action treatment for poverty does not hold. The irony is that regarding the *means* of evaluation, in many ways the test of the Salk vaccine provides an excellent model for the social scientist to study.

Up to now we have discussed the role of theory in providing information on expected variability in the dependent variable representing the goals of the program and on the expected effect of various independent variables—effects of treatment variables representing the program and of control variables which help reduce the residual variation in the dependent variable. Note that the failure to attain statistical significance of the effect of the treatment variable because of

---

[8] One range for a confidence interval of special interest is almost always that which includes zero for its lower limit (thinking now of a social action program that has some positive effect), so that the investigator is able to test the null hypothesis that the program makes "no difference." This is conventional, and so is the practice of measuring the quantitative magnitude of the effect when the null hypothesis is rejected. We should not overlook, however, the information about the range of quantitative effects of variables even when their confidence intervals include zero and when, therefore, the null hypothesis of "no effect" is accepted. Clearly, we would want to know that the interval was, say, -$5 to $455 rather than -$455 and $5. Furthermore, there are any number of situations when we should be interested in weighing the seriousness of negative effects with the benefits from, possibly, very large positive effects. Put in other terms zero is bracketed by -$5 to +$5 as well as by -$500 to +$500, and there may be situations in which it is important to distinguish between the two cases.

[9] In the absence of an *ex post* evaluation, such *a priori* analysis would be useful in assessing the general feasibility of the project.

[10] We may well have in mind attempting a number of different programs that are radically innovative and for which our *a priori* notions predict either spectacular success or complete failure. A program to cure narcotics addiction might be such a program. Given the costliness of properly designed evaluation schemes, we might justify pushing ahead with the programs without waiting on formal evaluation procedures in the hope that even "casual observation" will render a valid verdict of the program.

either a large unexplained variation in the dependent variable or small effects of treatment variables, can be overcome with sufficiently large sample sizes. But in our opinion, the most serious defect in evaluation studies are biases in the measures of effect of the treatment variables and this error is unlikely to be removed by enlarging the sample size.

One source of bias is inaccurate measures of the treatment variable, but a more pervasive and more serious problem is the presence of variables, not included in the statistical model, which are correlated with both the dependent variable and the treatment variable. Had the assignment to a program been made on a random basis, the laws of probability would have assured a low correlation (zero in the limit of a large enough sample size) between participation in the program and these omitted variables. In the absence of randomization, we must fall back on statistical controls. At this point our theory and *a priori* information are crucially important. The requirements are obvious: to identify the variables whose omission leads to biases in the measured effects of the treatment variables and to include them in the model. These variables may be objectively measurable, such as age or education or previous work experience. Or they may be such difficult-to-measure characteristics as ambition, motivation, or an "appealing personality."[11]

As we know too well, however, our theories are woefully weak in providing us with the correct list of variables for explaining such dependent variables as income change, employment experience, health status, or educational attainment, and we often do not have measures of those we do know about. The latter problem frequently arises because of the unfortunate practice of inviting the evaluator in *after* the program has been run and data have been collected.

Even in the best of situations regarding the availability of objective measures of important variables, if we do not have random assignments we must still admit the possibility that *self-selectivity* or the *selectivity procedures* of the program administrators has introduced a systematic difference between the participants and the nonparticipants. We do not claim, as the purists would, that

[11] An important point to be remembered is that, for any given amount of resources available for an evaluation study, there is a trade-off between an allocation of these resources for increased sample size and allocation for improved quality of measurement, which might take the form of an expanded set of variables, improved measures of variables, or reduced attrition from the sample. Too often we have witnessed a single-minded attachment to larger sample sizes, probably stemming from the analyst's fear that he will end up with "too few observations in the cells" of some only vaguely imagined cross-tabulation. This fear should be balanced by an awareness both of the rapidity with which marginal gains in precision of estimates decline with increases in "medium size" samples and of the extent to which a theoretically justified multiple regression model can overcome some of the limitations which cross-tabulation analysis imposes on a given-sized sample.

nonrandom procedures invalidate all evaluations, although there are cases when they undoubtedly have, but there are immense advantages in randomization and we can do a great deal more to achieve this procedure if we can only convince each other of its importance. It is clear that those responsible for the tests of the Salk vaccine were convinced.

Another important advantage of randomization should be mentioned. We have noted that variables which are correlated with both the treatment variable and the dependent variable must be included in the model to measure treatment effects without bias. However, since our information about the effect of the treatment variable necessarily depends on variability in treatments, and since the only variation we can observe within the framework of the statistical model is the residual variation in treatments—that is, variation which remains after the entire set of independent variables is included, greater efficiency is obtained when the treatment variable is uncorrelated with the other independent variables. In the opposite extreme, if the treatment variables were perfectly correlated with some other variable or combination of variables, we would be unable to distinguish between which of the two sets of factors causes a change. It follows that even in the absence of randomization, designing the programs to be studied with as wide a range in levels and types of "treatments" as possible will serve to maximize the information we can extract from an *ex post* analysis.

There are reasons in addition to those of statistical efficiency for planning for a wide range of values in the treatment of programmatic variables. One is that social action programs have a tendency to change, rather frequently and radically, during the course of their operation. Evaluations designed to test a single type of program are rendered meaningless because the program-type perishes. But if the design covers a wider variety of programs, then a built-in hedge against the effects of change is attained. Indeed, there is an even more fundamental reason why a wide range of inputs and program types should be planned for, and it is simply this: we seldom know enough about what will work in a social action program to justify putting our eggs in the single basket of one type of program. This evaluation model for a single type of project, sometimes described as the analogue of the "pilot plant," is not the appropriate model for social action programs given our current state of knowledge.[12]

The Theoretical Framework—Some Economic Considerations

For operational purposes we will assume that the evaluation of each social action program, can at least in principle, be cast in the statistical model discussed in the previous section, complete with variables representing an objective of the

[12] See the vigorous defense of the experimental method in social action programs in G. H. Orcutt and A. G. Orcutt, *op. cit.*

program, treatment variables representing the program inputs, control variables, and control groups.[13] However, the substantive theoretical content of these models—the particular selection of variables and their functional form—must come from one or more of the traditional disciplines such as educational psychology (e.g., for Head Start), demography (e.g., for a family planning program), medical science (e.g., for a neighborhood health center), economics (e.g., for a manpower training program), and so on.

Sooner or later economics must enter all evaluations, since "costing out" the programs and the setting of implicit or explicit dollar measures of the worth of a program are essential steps in a complete evaluation. And this is true even though the most difficult part of the evaluation may lie in determining what the specific program effects are in terms of educational achievement, health, or some other nonmonetary benefit.

In making the required cost-benefit analysis, the part of economic theory that applies is the investment theory of public finance economics, with its infusion of welfare economics. The function of investment theory is to make commensurable inputs and outcomes of a social action program which are spaced over time. Welfare economics analyzes the distinctions between financial costs and real resource costs, between direct effects of a program and externalities, and between efficiency criteria and equity (or distributional) criteria.

We will say very little about the distributional or equity question of *who pays* and *who receives,* even though we strongly feel that accurate data on the distribution of benefits and costs is essential to an evaluation of social action programs. However, the task of conducting a "conventional" benefit-cost analysis (wherein the criterion is allocative efficiency) is sufficiently complex that we believe it preferable to separate the distributional questions.

Program Inputs

In the investment theory model costs are attached to all inputs of a program and a single number emerges which measures the present value of the resources used. Although the purpose of this procedure is to reduce the potentially infinite variety of program mixes to a common dollar denominator, we (economists especially) should not lose sight of the particular quantitative and qualitative mix of inputs, which, after all, defines a program and which provides the information necessary to determine the ingredients of a program success or

---

[13] This assumption will strike some readers as too positivistic, too restrictive to "things measurable," and too oblivious to the unmeasurable and subjective variables. Let us say in defense of this assumption only that it is a "working assumption" that permits us to discuss an important region of evaluation which covers the measurable portion, that it is desirable to expand this region and, therefore to narrow the area left for subjective judgments, and that, in any case, the objective portion is necessary to an improved overall judgment that spans both measurable and unmeasurable inputs and outputs of a program.

failure. On the other hand, program administrators should recognize that the notion that "every program or particular project is different" can be pushed to the point of stifling all evaluations. Evaluations must be relative and comparative.

Most of the technical problems faced by the analysts on the input side are those of traditional cost accounting. We will confine our remarks to the two familiar and somewhat controversial problems of opportunity costs and transfer payments, which arise in nearly every manpower program. Both of these problems are most effectively dealt with if one starts by asking: What is the decision context for which these input measures are defined?

The most general decision context—and the one to which economists most naturally refer—is that of the productivity of alternative resource utilizations in society or the nation *as a whole*. In this case, one wishes to measure the cost of inputs in terms of the net reduction in value of alternative socially productive activities which is caused by the use of the inputs in this particular activity. Now, the value of most inputs in terms of their alternative use will be more or less clearly indicated by their market price, but there are some inputs for which this will not be true. The most troublesome cases often concern the time of people. A well-known example is the value of the time spent by students in school: since those over 14 or so could be in the job market, the social product (or national income) is less; therefore, an estimate is needed of what their earnings would be had they not been in school. (Such an estimate should reflect whatever amount of unemployment would be considered "normal.")

Sometimes the prices of inputs (market prices or prices fixed by the government) do not adequately reflect their marginal social productivity, and "corrected" or "shadow prices" are necessary. For example, the ostensible prices of leisure or of the housework of a wife are zero and obviously below their real price. By contrast a governmental fixed price of some surplus commodity is too high.

For manpower programs the best evaluation design would provide a control group to measure the opportunity costs of the time spent by the trainees in the program. Or, in measuring the value of the time of teenagers participating in a summer Upward Bound program, at least the question of market earnings foregone would be answered with a minimum of conjecture if control groups were available.

The definition and treatment of transfer payments also depend on the decision context of analysis. From the national perspective, money outlays from the budget of one program that are offset by reduced outlays elsewhere in society do not decrease the value of the social product. When these outlays are in the form of cash payments or consumption goods, they are called transfer payments. An example is the provision of room and board for Job Corps trainees. Since it must be assumed that someone (their parents, themselves or some welfare agency) would be meeting the costs of their room and board if they were not in the program, the provision of these services by the program reflects no *net* reduction in the value of alternative socially productive activities. Whoever was paying these costs before will be relieved of that burden and will spend the money thus saved on other goods and services. If there has been an actual *increase* in the value of food consumed by the trainee or in the quality of this housing, the net increase can be counted as a program input—a cost, but in general, it would be equal to the net increase in the value of food and housing consumed—a benefit.[14] To summarize, if these input costs are simply being *transferred* from one individual or agency to another individual or agency they either represent no real cost of resources of this program or they are a cost which is immediately offset by the benefit it yields to the recipient—remembering that the decision context is the general one which includes members of society, with no one member receiving any different weight in the calculation of benefits.

In a narrower decision context, the accounting basis may shift; some input costs counted in the broader context are not counted in the narrower one and vice versa. One example of a narrow decision context—a favorite of people in government, but repugnant to most economists—is the vaguely defined "public budget." Alternatively, the decision context might be considered that of the "taxpayers' viewpoint" if the program participants and their families are excluded from the group considered as taxpayers. In this context the only costs that are to be counted are those that come from the public budget. Some of the examples we discussed above are now reversed. Presumably, most of the opportunity costs of a student's time spent in school is of no interest to the taxpayer since it is a "cost" which is not directly imposed upon the public budget. (A qualification is that the taxpayer should be interested in the taxes that the student would pay if he were working.) By contrast, the payments for the cost of room and board to a Job Corpsman, which was considered a transfer payment above, would now be considered an input cost from the "taxpayers' viewpoint." The fact that the trainee or his family is relieved of this burden would be of no interest since it would not be reflected in the public budget. However, if the costs of room and board had been met previously by a public welfare agency, then from the "taxpayers' viewpoint," the costs would not be charged to the Job Corps program.

It is not uncommon to see several decision contexts used in one analysis, and used inconsistently. For example, the post-training earnings improvement

---

[14] When the program produces an increase in consumption of goods and services, the treatment of these transfer payments can become more complicated if we do not assume that the goods and service have a value to the recipients equal to their cost. See A. A. Alchian and W. R. Allen, *University Economics,* 2nd ed., pp. 135-140 (Wadsworth, Belmont, California, 1967), for an extended discussion.

from participation in a Job Corps program are considered benefits. We all recognize, of course, that the earnings will be used mostly for consumption by the Job Corps graduate. But in the same study, his consumption during training (room, meals, and spending allowance), is not viewed as conferring benefits to the Corpsman.[15] Or is it that the benefits should not count because, while in training, he is not considered a member of "our society"? We leave this puzzle to those who prefer these restricted decision contexts. There are other such examples and still other and more narrow decision contexts, such as that of a local government or of one project by itself. But it is probably clear that our preference is for the national or total societal perspective.

Program Outcomes

The problems of measurement on the outcome side of the evaluation problem are tougher to handle, and *ex post* evaluations of social action programs face particular problems because these outcomes are likely to involve behavioral relationships which are not well understood. It is particularly difficult to predict long run or permanent behavioral changes from the short run indicators revealed by the ongoing or just completed program.

The outcomes we wish to measure from many social action programs occur months or years after the participants have completed the program. We can use proxy measures, which can themselves be measured during and soon after the program, but follow-up studies are clearly preferred and may in many cases be essential. A good deal depends on the confidence we have in the power of our theories to link the proxies or short-run effects (e.g., test scores, health treatments, employment experience in the shortrun, etc.) with the longer run goals (longer run educational attainment, longevity, incomes, or all of these and perhaps other "softer" measures of "well-being"). It is a role for "basic research" in the social sciences to provide this type of theoretical-empirical information to evaluations, but we can also hope that the more thorough evaluation studies will contribute to our stock of "basic research" findings.

The problems of measuring longer run effects of a program and of conducting follow-up studies make up a long list, and most are familiar to administrators and analysts of social action programs. Some of these arose in our discussion of control groups where we noted the critical importance of identifying characteristics of respondents which would be related to the effects of the program and which may distinguish them from the nonparticipants acting as a comparison group.

---

[15] For just one of many examples of this type of treatment of transfer payments see *The Feasibility of Benefit-Cost Analysis in the War on Poverty: A Test Application to Manpower Programs,* prepared for the General Accounting Office Resource Management Corporation, UR-054, December 13, 1968.

The problems of inadequate measures of variables and those of errors in the data are pervasive, particularly since the participants in the programs are often disadvantaged groups. Employment histories are checkered, making it difficult to determine the respondent's normal income, normal occupation and other variables. Years of schooling completed may be a poor measure of education attainment, police records may be an important source of employment difficulties, and so on. All of the above are examples of the problems encountered in determining relevant data.

Measures of the status of a participant before entering the program usually come from the data gathered as part of the program intake procedure. A problem arises when potential enrollees are aware of criteria for program admittance, for they may report inaccurate data in order to meet these criteria. Merely by sampling the data, the amount of inaccuracies can be approximately determined and appropriate correction factors can be devised.

The major obstacle to follow-up measures is the difficulty in locating people, particularly those from disadvantaged populations who may be less responsive and who may have irregular patterns of living. The biases due to nonresponsiveness may be severe, since those participants who are easiest to locate are likely to be the most "successful," both because of their apparent stability and because those who have "failed" may well be less responsive to requests to reveal their current status. One way around the costly problem of tracking down respondents for earnings data is to use Social Security records for participants and control groups. The rights of confidentiality may be preserved by aggregating the data.

Another problem in measuring outcomes, which also tends to be more talked about despairingly than coped with positively, is the category of external or third-party effects of the program. As a typical illustration consider a youth training program which not only increases the earnings of youths but also reduces the incidence of crime among these groups, which benefits the community through less damage and lower costs of prevention and rehabilitation programs. Another source of third-party effects is those accruing to the participant's family members, including those yet to be born. It is an open question, however, whether the problem for concern is the lack of measurement of these external effects, or the tendency by administrators and others (particularly friends of the programs) to exaggerate their likely importance and to count those effects as external or secondary benefits which, while benefiting some people do so at the expense of others.[16]

---

[16] For a notable exception to the absence of attempted measurement of the type of third-party effects discussed above, see Thomas I. Ribich, *Education and Poverty* (Brookings Institution, Washington, D. C., 1968). Ribich's study also gives us some evidence of the likelihood of relatively small quantitative magnitudes of these effects. A rather free-wheeling listing of third-party effects runs the risk of double counting benefits. For example,

Concerning training and education programs, in particular, two types of effects that have received scant investigation are "negative effects" and those which affect the structure of communities. A discussion, though little measurement, of such effects has appeared in studies and accounts of public housing, urban renewal, and road building programs.[17] The following list of three potential negative effects of manpower programs can serve as examples.

(a) Programs placing the hard-core poor into jobs have had, according to some reports, disruptive effects in the plant—both because of the behavior of the trainee-participants (e.g., disciplinary problems and high rates of absenteeism) and because of the special treatment which the participants received.

(b) Programs which augment the supply of workers in a particular occupation will have the effect of exerting downward pressure on the wages of existing workers in that occupation. It is worth noting that the workers earning high wages are likely to belong to unions which will block these programs in their field (e.g., the building trades), but that low wage workers (like hospital workers) have little or no power to protect their economic interests.

(c) Programs which engender high hopes among some applicants or entrants may lead to a further alienation and hostility for some of those who are rejected or otherwise refused admission or for those who enter and fail. Admission policies are, in fact, just one example of administrative discretionary behavior that can have considerable separate influence on the positive and negative effects of programs—a point brought out in debates about the relative merits of self-help programs, transfer payment programs, and welfare and relief programs.[18]

Community effects of social action programs can be viewed as a special type of external effect, since the changes in the community structure or in various community institutions are assumed to be important because of the

---

although other family members benefit from the better education and earnings of the head of the household, we should not forget that had the investment expenditure been made elsewhere, even if in the form of an across-the-board tax cut, *other* family heads would have had larger incomes, at least, with resulting benefits to *their* families. In his examination of cost-benefit analysis of water resource developments Roland N. McKean gives an extended discussion of the pitfalls of double-counting. See his *Efficiency in Government Through Systems Analysis* (especially Chapter 9) (Wiley, New York, 1958).

[17] An exceptionally good discussion of negative external effects, including disruption to the community structure, is contained in Anthony Downs, "Uncompensated Non-Construction Costs Which Urban Highways and Urban Renewal Impose on Residential Households" which will appear in a Universities-National Bureau of Economic Research Conference volume entitled, *Economics of Public Output*. The literature on urban renewal and public housing is extensive and too well known to require listing here.

[18] For an excellent discussion of many of these issues, see J. F. Handler, Controlling official behavior in Welfare Administration. In *The Law of the Poor* (J. tenBroek, ed.,) Chandler, Chicago, Illinois, 1966. [Also published in *California Law Review* 54, 479 (1966).]

benefits or costs they ultimately provide for third-party individuals in the community. Thus, we are not proposing that the "community" be viewed as an "entity" separate from the individuals who comprise it. However, a separate focus on measures of community institutional changes appears necessary since the present state of our theories of community organization permit us little scope for anything except qualitative linkages between institutional changes and their effects on individuals in the community. We can, for example, consider better communication between the neighborhood populace and the police, school officials, or the employment service as "good things," either in their own right (as expressions of the democratic ethic), or because we believe that such changes will have tangible effects in safety, school achievement, or better jobs.

Evaluations of social action programs may well have to deal with the problems of measuring variables that represent community effects even when such effects are not significant outcomes of a program. This need will arise when we have reason to believe that community institutions or aspects of the community structure are important independent or "control" variables that affect the program's objective. We have relatively well developed measures of some variables of the community structure, such as the components of a transportation system, but we are far less able to measure, for example, the degree of trust and rapport between the local branch of the State Employment Service and the poverty population in the community.

One major barrier to an adequate accounting of "community effects" is the scarcity of data pertaining to the community structure, although here we might argue, at the risk of revealing our prejudices or ignorance, that there is an overriding primary need for better theories of community structure and behavior. Without theory it is hard to know what facts or data we should be collecting.

The discussion of program outcomes again raises the problem of how to weigh and combine multiple objectives. Assuming that the separate objectives have been validly measured, the analyst might present the decision-makers with an array of multiple "effectiveness" measures and let them apply their own weights, explicitly or implicitly, to arrive at an overall assessment, or he can use his own expertise and judgment to reduce the disparate outcomes to reasonably commensurable terms. The latter approach may be rationalized on the grounds that *some* such weighting scheme is inevitable and that an explicit method is better than a subjective one. For a least one aspect of commensurability—that of comparing goods and services that are identical except regarding *time*—the investment theory of economics provides a highly systematized method. Since this concerns the discount rate applicable to governmental investment programs and it is treated elsewhere in this conference, we are happy to by-pass this issue.

Organizational Problems

Timing and the Ability to Hold to Design

The effectiveness of evaluations of social action programs is highly dependent on the manner in which a number of organizational and administrative problems are handled. Although a thorough review of these problems is properly consigned to the literature of public administration, we feel it is important to discuss a few obstacles that can block even the best intentioned evaluator armed with the most sophisticated statistical and economic design.

In the beginning stages of planning and evaluation there are some important questions about the timing of the evaluation. As social action programs are often innovative, it is not surprising that there is often a great clamor for an evaluation almost immediately after the program is begun. This is unrealistic since it takes some time for any program to settle down into "normal" operations, and program administrators are well aware of their tendency to progress along some kind of learning curve toward their maximum performance. In response to these points, it is sometimes argued that a "fair" evaluation of a program concept can only be undertaken a couple of years after a program has begun.

However, when the program to be evaluated is large scale and widespread, the organizational problems of setting up the evaluation can almost equal those of setting up a major project in the program. This means that the evaluative mechanism will need to be developed concurrently with the program organization. A failure to generate adequate information for analysis has been largely responsible for the paucity of meaningful evaluations of social action programs.

A related problem is that of insuring that programs hold to the initial design concept long enough to allow an evaluation to be completed. It is not uncommon to hear administrators complain that the evaluation they receive is well done but irrelevant, since the data used were taken from a period before certain fundamental changes were made in the program. The problem for the evaluator, then, is to complete his evaluation somewhere in the period between the "settling down" of the initial organization and the beginning of fundamental shifts in the program process. (To some analysts this optimum period has begun to appear to be of about a week's duration.) If program evaluation is to become an effective element in decision-making it is important that there be an increased awareness both of the time it takes to set up and carry out an adequate evaluation and of the necessity of holding a program to a given design concept a sufficient length of time to allow such an evaluation process to be completed. Assuming that the design of the evaluation provided for a wide range of variability in treatment variables, it is not likely to be irrelevant.

Internal Data Systems

The modernization of the management of public programs has led to an increasing interest in the internal data systems (sometimes called information systems) of programs. These systems are designed to facilitate the management of programs, including those functions we have characterized as "process evaluations" in section two, but they can also be a great help for benefit-cost evaluations. There are several reasons, however, why an evaluator should not rely totally on an internal data system.

Administrators, especially at local levels, tend to place a low priority on data collection and analysis, and the result is that systems operators are seldom able to deliver on schedule the range of data which they originally promise. We have to recognize, also, that project operations sometimes have incentives to provide biased or simply manufactured data. Finally, internal data systems are notoriously inflexible, since the systems are usually designed with a limited set of users in mind. The result is that the analyst finds it impossible to obtain disaggregations of these data or reaggregations by different sets of classifications. The importance of conserving micro-data has still not been generally appreciated.

For all of these reasons, the analyst is well advised to supplement the internal data system with other information sources, perhaps by sampling from the system and perhaps through an outside source, such as the Social Security system. This procedure has the further advantage of liberating the internal data system from the burden of collecting for every participant all sorts of information vaguely believed to be necessary for "eventual" benefit-cost analyses but where the decisions about the selection of variables are made by others than those who are planning the evaluation. For the purposes of the analyst, an internal data system which permits stratification and sampling may be all that is required.[19]

INTENTIONAL EXPERIMENTS: A SUGGESTED STUDY

Underlying the growing interest in evaluations of social action programs is the enlightened idea that the scientific method can be applied to program experience to establish and measure particular cause and effect relationships

---

[19] It has often proved surprisingly difficult to convince program managers that for the purposes of evaluation small samples of data are perfectly adequate and that, in some cases, data gathered on the entire "universe" of the program are cumbersome or costly to manipulate, are notoriously error-laden, and generally add little additional useful information.

which are amenable to change through the agents of public policy. However, traditional methods in science, whether the laboratory experimentation of the physical scientists, the testing of pilot models by engineers, or field testing of drugs by medical scientists, are seldom models that can be directly copied, helpful though they are as standards of rigor.

In particular, evaluation designs patterned after the testing of pilot models, corresponding to "demonstration projects" in the field of social action programs, have been inadequate for both theoretical and operational reasons. The present state of our theories of social behavior does not justify settling on a unique plan of action, and we cannot, almost by definition, learn much about alternative courses of action from a single pilot project. It is somewhat paradoxical that on the operational level the pilot model has failed to give us much information because the design has frequently been impossible to control and has spun off in different directions.

The combination of, first, loose administration of and rapid changes in the operation of individual projects, and second, a large scale program with many heterogeneous projects (different administrations, different environments, different clientele, etc.), has led to the interesting view that this heterogeneity creates what are, in effect, "natural experiments" for an evaluation design. For economists, who are used to thinking of the measurement of consumers' responses to changes in the price of wheat or investors' responses to changes in the interest rate, the idea of "natural experiments" has a certain appeal. Certainly much of this paper has dealt with the problems and methods of coping with evaluations which attempt to take advantage of "natural experiments" with a program. But what should be clear from this discussion—and others before us have reached the same conclusion—is that a greatly improved evaluation could be obtained if social action programs were initiated in *intentional* experiments.

When one talks of "experiments" in the social sciences what inevitably comes to mind is a small scale, carefully controlled study, such as those traditionally employed in psychology. Thus, when one suggests that social action programs be initiated in intentional experiments, people imagine a process which would involve a series of small test projects, a period of delay while those projects are completed and evaluated, and perhaps more retesting before any major program is mounted. This very definitely is *not* what we mean when we suggest social action programs as intentional experimentation. We would stress the word *action* to highlight the difference between what we suggest and the traditional small scale experimentation.

Social action programs are undertaken because there is a clearly perceived social problem that requires some form of amelioration. In general (with the exception perhaps of the area of medicinal drugs where a counter tradition has been carefully or painfully built up), we are not willing to postpone large scale attempts at amelioration of such problems until all the steps of a careful testing of hypotheses, development of pilot projects, etc. have been carried out. The practice, particularly in recent years, has been to proceed to action on a large scale with whichever seems—on reasonable, but essentially superificial, grounds- —the best design at hand. We would suggest that large scale ameliorative social action and intentional experimentation are not incompatible; that experimental designs can be built into a large scale social action program.

If a commitment is made to a more frankly experimental social action program by decision-makers and administrators, then many of the objectives we have advocated can be addressed directly at the planning stage. If we begin a large national program with a frank awareness that we do not know which program concept is more likely to be most efficacious, then several program models could be selected for implementation in several areas, with enough variability in the key elements which make up the concepts to allow good measures of the differential responses to those elements. If social action programs are approached with an "intentionally experimental" point of view, then the analytical powers of our statistical models of evaluation can be greatly enhanced by attempts to insure that "confounding" effects are minimized—i.e., that program treatment variables are uncorrelated with participant characteristics and particular types of environments.

A less technical, but equally important, gain from this approach to social action programs is the understanding on the part of administrators, decision-makers, and legislators that if we are to learn anything from experience it is necessary to hold the design of the program (that is the designed project differentials in treatment variables) constant for a long enough period of time to allow for the "settling down" of the program and the collection and analysis of the data. *A commitment to hold to design for a long enough period so that we could learn from experience is a central element in the experimental approach to social action.*

The idea that social action programs should be experimental is simple, but we cannot be sanguine about the speed with which the full implications of this simple idea will be accepted by decision-makers and the public as a whole. The view that programs can be large-scale *action* programs and still be designed as intentional experiments has not been easy to get across, even to those trained in experimental methods in the social sciences, with its tradition of small-scale research.

The emphasis on *ex post* evaluation is evidence of the fact that at some level legislators understand that social action programs are "testing" concepts. But it will require more explicit acceptance of the idea that some aspects of programs "tested" in action will fail before the full advantages of the intentionally experimental approach can be realized. It takes restraint to mount a program with a built-in experimental design and wait for it to mature before deciding on a single program concept, but we emphasize that restraint does not mean small-scale or limited action.

It is not unfair, we think, to characterize the approach to social action programs that has been taken in the past as one of serial experimentation through program failure. A program is built around a single concept, eventually it is realized that it does not work, so the program is scrapped (or allowed to fade away) and a new program and concept is tried. Certainly serial experimentation through failure is the hard way to learn. An intentionally experimental approach would allow us to learn faster by trying alternative concepts *simultaneously* and would make it more likely that we could determine not only *that* a particular concept failed, but also *why* it failed.

THE ACCEPTABILITY OF EVALUATION RESULTS

It does little violence to the facts to state that few decisions about social action programs have been made on the basis of the types of evaluations we have been discussing thus far in this paper. A major reason for this, we feel, is an inadequate taste for rigor (or an overweening penchant for visceral judgments) by administrators and legislators and excessive taste for the purely scientific standards by academics. It often seems that the scholars conspire with the legislators to beat down any attempt to bring to bear more orderly evidence about the effectiveness of alternative programs. It is not at all difficult to find experts who will testify that virtually any evaluation study is not adequately "scientific" to provide a sound basis for making program decisions. There is a reasonable and appropriate fear on the part of academics that sophisticated techniques of analysis will be used as deceptive wrapping around an essentially political kernal to mislead administrators or the public. This fear, however, often leads to the setting of standards of "proof" which cannot, at present, given the state of the art of social sciences, or perhaps never, given the inherent nature of social action programs, be satisfied. The result generally is that the evaluation is discredited, the information it provides ignored, and the decision-maker and legislator can resume the exercise of their visceral talents.

A first step toward creating a more favorable atmosphere for evaluation studies is to recognize that they will not be final arbiters of the worth of a program. A positive but more modest role for evaluation research was recently stated by Kenneth Arrow in a discussion of the relative virtues of the traditional processes of public decision-making (characterized as an adversary process) and the recently developed procedure of the Programming, Planning, Budgeting

System (characterized as a rationalistic or "synoptic process").[20] Arrow advocated an approach in between forensics and synoptics.[21] He illustrated his argument by making an analogy with the court system, suggesting that what was happening through the introduction of the more rationalistic processes was the creation of a body of "rules of evidence." The use of systematic evaluation (along with the other elements of the PPBS) represents an attempt to raise the standards of what is admissible as evidence in a decision process that is inherently likely to remain adversary in nature. Higher standards of evaluation will lessen the role of "hearsay" testimony in the decision process, but they are not meant to provide a hard and fast decision rule in and of themselves. The public decision-making process is still a long way from the point at which the evidence from a hard evaluation is the primary or even the significant factor in the totality of factors which determine major decisions about programs. Therefore, the fear of many academics that poorly understood evaluations will exercise an inordinate influence on public decisions is, to say the least, extremely premature. But if standards for the acceptance of evaluation results are viewed in terms of the "rules of evidence" analogy, we can begin to move toward the judicious mix of rigor and pragmatism that is so badly needed in evaluation analysis.

The predominant view of the role of "serious," independent evaluations [22] (particularly in the eyes of harried administrators), seems to be that of a trial (to continue the analogy) aimed at finding a program guilty of failure. In a sense this paranoid view of evaluation is correct. The statistical procedures used usually start with a null hypothesis of "no effect," and the burden of the analysis is to provide evidence that is sufficiently strong to overturn the null hypothesis. As we have pointed out, however, problems of data, organization, and methods conspire to make clear-cut positive findings in evaluations difficult to demonstrate.

The atmosphere for evaluations would be much healthier if the underlying stance were shifted from this old world juridical rule. Let the program be assumed innocent of failure until proven guilty through clear-cut negative findings. In more precise terms, we sould try to avoid commiting what are called in statistical theory Type II errors. Thus, an evaluation that does not permit rejection of the null hypothesis (of a zero effect of the program), at customary levels of statistical significance, may be consistent with a finding that a very large

---

[20] For a more complete discussion of this terminology, see H. Rowen, "Recent Developments in the Measurement of Public Outputs," to be published in a Universities-National Bureau of Economic Research Conference volume, *The Economics of Public Output.*

[21] Remarks by Kenneth Arrow during the NBER conference cited in the previous footnote.

[22] We mean here to exclude the quick and casual sort of evaluations, mainly "in-house" evaluations, that more often than not are meant to provide a gloss of technical justification for a program.

positive effect may be just as likely as a zero or negative effect.[23] "Rules of evidence" which emphasize the avoidance of Type II errors are equivalent to an attitude which we have characterized as "innocent until proven guilty." (We must frankly admit that, like court rules of evidence, this basic stance may provide incentives to the program administrators to provide data which are sufficient only for arriving at a "no conclusion" evaluative outcome.)

As a final conciliatory comment; when we talk about evaluation studies leading to verdicts of "success" or "failure," it should be recognized that we are greatly simplifying and abbreviating the typical results. Most social action programs are so complex in the variety of inputs and the multiplicity of objectives, that simple over-all judgments are not likely to lead to quick decisions to dump programs. In combination with more detailed studies, the purpose of the evidence provided by the analysts will instead usually be to suggest modifications in the program—to shift the composition of inputs, perhaps to reemphasize some objectives and deemphasize others—and to suggest marginal additions or subtractions in the total scale of the program. It is worth emphasizing these modest objectives because the trust and cooperation of program administrators are indispensable to an evaluation of the program.

[23] Harold Watts has stressed this point in conversations with the authors. See G. G. Cain and H. W. Watts, The controversy about the Coleman Report: Comment, *Journal of Human Resources* **3** (Summer), 389-392 (1968): also H. W. Watts and D. L. Horner, *The Educational Benefits of Head Start: A Quantitative Analysis,* Discuss. Pap. Ser. Institute for Research on Poverty, University of Wisconsin, Madison, 19DD.

III

EVALUATIVE RESEARCH: PRACTICE

8

EVALUATION IN PRACTICE:

Compensatory Education*

Edward L. McDill, Mary S. McDill,
and J. Timothy Sprehe

INTRODUCTION

The civil rights movement of the late 1950's and early 1960's succeeded in asserting that minority groups within the United States had the right to equal educational opportunity. The movement could not, however, guarantee that minority group members would be able to take full advantage of these asserted rights, for a large proportion of American minorities was encumbered with educational deficits which precluded their successful performance in the classroom and in the occupational world beyond. Realization of this condition gave birth to a massive effort to rectify the educational inadequacies. Large-scale

*Some of the material in this document was first presented in a paper at the American Academy of Arts and Sciences Conference on Evaluation of Social Action Programs, May 2-3, 1969, under a grant from the Ford Foundation. That paper was modified and expanded into *Strategies for Success in Compensatory Education: An Appraisal of Evaluation Research,* 1969, published by The Johns Hopkins Press, Baltimore, Maryland. The authors are indebted to The Johns Hopkins Press for permission to reprint in this paper portions of the material presented in that volume. The first author's contributions to this paper were facilitated by support from the Center for the Social Organization of Schools, The Johns Hopkins University, and NSF Grant GS-29873.

programs were mounted for affording preschool instruction to inner-city blacks; special efforts were directed at lowering the dropout rate among Puerto Rican teenagers, at providing better teachers for American Indians or vocational training for residents of Appalachia, and at helping other minority groups in a host of ways.

Essentially, compensatory education has been a movement aimed at compensating for deficiencies in the learning experiences of minority group members. The movement has been strongly sociopolitical, but it has also had its scientific base. The belief that IQ was almost totally a function of genetic factors had been challenged, at least implicitly, in the early 1960's in the writings of J. McV. Hunt (1961) and Bloom (1964), among others. Significantly, the most recent chapter in the nature-nurture debate, the work of Arthur Jensen (1969), was occasioned by controversy surrounding the success or failure of compensatory education programs. Thus the social concern for education of disadvantaged Americans has been paralleled by intellectual ferment in educational psychology and other academic disciplines. The parallelism is not accidental; as White (1970) has pointed out, the social action in compensatory education has been dictated "not by grass roots demands but by the social diagnostician" (p. 164), the professional reformer who operates out of an academic environment and who manifested during the 1960's a growing desire to take an active hand in remaking American education.

Compensatory education has indeed been a massive, nationwide effort, mounted with both staggering suddenness and monumental resources. From virtually no national effort in 1960, compensatory education zoomed to unusual levels of funding. To take three of the best-known national programs, Head Start had a budget of $330 million in fiscal year (FY) 1969 and was reaching over 650,000 students; expenditures under Title I of the Elementary and Secondary Education Act (ESEA) of 1966 totaled $1.123 billion in FY 1969, and Upward Bound was $31 million for the same period.

Despite the enormous investment in compensatory education, there are still few indicators which show unequivocally whether the investment has been fruitful or has been in vain. Evaluation research in the areas has not by and large yielded clear-cut results. This condition is an anomaly, for almost all programs in compensatory education contain—often by law—provision for evaluation of their impact. Agencies responsible for carrying out the programs have attempted to obtain scientific evidence to determine whether or not they have effected the desired changes.

These voluminous evaluation studies are the "data" to which we have directed our attention. They cover small projects involving only fifteen preschool students and vast federal programs reaching hundreds of cities and millions of students with budgets in the billions. As might be expected, the quality of the research is, at the very least, uneven, ranging from carefully conceived experimental designs to solicited testimonials.

Using this large body of evaluation research, we have addressed ourselves in this paper to the following important tasks concerning compensatory educational programs: (1) The kinds of programs resulting from local and national efforts—descriptions of programs under both types of conditions; (2) a detailed examination of the evaluations of four national programs representing a maturational gamut from preschool to college; (3) the controversies among social scientists about the interpretation of the evidence from these studies; and (4) implications for future efforts, both in the design and implementation of programs and in the evaluation of them.

DESCRIPTIONS AND ANALYSES OF PROGRAMS

There have been two types of responses to the need for compensatory education for disadvantaged groups: local and national programs. In this section, most of our attention is given to the global programs although a brief summary of the smaller scale, localized efforts is included.

Local Programs

In an earlier publication (McDill *et al.*, 1969), we gave a brief profile of the rationale, design, and outcome of eleven local programs.[1] These were not intended to be representative of total efforts in this realm. They were rather selected in order to illustrate the diversity of the programs in compensatory education. These programs vary immensely as indicated by the summary of characteristics presented below:

Size

The size of target population for local compensatory education programs has varied from over 60,000 students per year in the Higher Horizons project in New York City to less than 25 students in a program which was conducted by Bereiter and Engelmann at the University of Illinois.

---

[1] These programs are Banneker, St. Louis, Missouri; Higher Horizons, New York City; More Effective Schools, New York City; Early Training Project, Peabody College, Nashville, Tennessee; Bereiter-Engelmann, Academic Preschool Program, Champaign, Illinois; Institute for Developmental Studies, New York City; Perry Pre-School Project, Ypsilanti, Michigan; Computer Assisted Instruction, Stanford University; Diagnostically Based Curriculum for Preschool Deprived Children, Bloomington, Indiana; Homework Helpers, New York City; Small Group Basic Education Program, Albion, Pennsylvania.

Cost Per Pupil

Where information is available, it appears that costs range from a lower boundary of zero—that is, nothing above usual school expenses—as in the Banneker project in St. Louis, to annual, per-pupil expenditures of nearly $1500 in the Perry Preschool Project.

Intensity of Treatment

Some programs seem to be disseminated throughout an entire school system, so pervasively in fact that in one instance investigators found that New York teachers in the program were not even aware there *was* a program in operation! In others, groups of children are singled out and bombarded with cognitive materials in drill-like precision.

Types of Treatment

In some programs there is total immersion of the student. Elsewhere, the program is designed to give only ancillary, out-of-class assistance to the pupil. In the Homework Helpers Project, for instance, teenagers participated in out-of-school tutoring of elementary students.

Length of Exposure

Six weeks in the summer has been the extent of some programs while others have continued over 3 or 4 years.

Parental Involvement

In the Early Training Project at Peabody College, parental involvement was quite extensive; weekly visits by staff members extended the program's influence into the home. In other programs, there is no evidence of any parental contact.

National Programs

The principal response to the need for compensatory education has come from federal agencies with comprehensive multipurpose objectives that were created as a part of the war on poverty legislation during the Johnson Administration. These agencies do not implement action programs to achieve their goals; they are primarily funding and administrative units whose most important function is policy determination and who use external agencies in implementing these goals.

We will present descriptive information concerning three compensatory programs encompassing the preschool, elementary, and secondary range of special education: Head Start, Title I, and Upward Bound. A fourth new program, funded from both public and private sources, will also be discussed.

This is Sesame Street, the educational television program which has won such wide acclaim in the past 2 years.

Upward Bound

Upward Bound began under the auspices of the Office of Economic Opportunity (OEO) and in 1969 was transferred to the Division of Student Special Services of the U.S. Office of Education (USOE). It started on a nationwide basis after an experimental summer program showed that provision of a precollege experience for selected disadvantaged students had some promise of success. In its first year of full-scale operation, which began in June of 1966, 218 educational institutions were involved. Upward Bound projects were established in most of the 50 states. There were approximately 20,000 secondary school students enrolled in the initial program; by 1971, the number of participating institutions had grown to nearly 300, with over 24,000 pupils enrolled.

Colleges and universities or secondary schools with residential facilities run Upward Bound projects through cooperative arrangements with high school and community action programs. The program is designed to identify as potential college students those high school students who would be overlooked by routine school procedures. The recruitment guidelines set forth by the federal government emphasize the use of diverse sources of recommendations, including former Upward Bound students, neighborhood groups, and clergy. It also specifies that the students must come from families whose annual incomes are below the poverty line.

The program usually recruits students during their sophomore and junior years of high school. Once recruited, they remain in the program through the summer following their senior year of high school. It has as its objectives supplying sustained support and encouragement to the participants, motivating them to seek higher education, and helping them maintain college aspirations. It attempts to generate the necessary motivation and, where needed, to develop the basic skills necessary for the successful pursuit of a college education. There has been some effort to involve parents of the enrollees in Upward Bound through adult education programs, discussion groups, and advisory conferences.

The "treatment" usually takes the form of intensive summer and after-school contact in tutorial programs and enrichment activities and meetings with both secondary school and college faculty members. One of the goals is to establish a relationship between the enrollee and one specific college campus, both with respect to its personnel and facilities. The program has as an integral part of its design "sponsoring" colleges, and almost all of the enrollees spend some time, usually during the summer, in residence on the campus of a sponsoring institution.

The routine through which this acquaintance with a college takes place is fairly well established. However, the process through which high school students are to be motivated and their areas of difficulty identified and alleviated are primarily under the jurisdiction of the local program administration. This autonomy is intended to allow flexibility in meeting the particular needs of individual populations. Few restrictions are placed on a sponsoring institution's curriculum and program design, and thus each project serves its population in a unique way. Although the program does not provide support for students once they enter college, the Upward Bound staff is expected to help them gain admission to a postsecondary institution and to assist them in finding appropriate financial support.[2]

During FY 1971, the cost of the program to the federal government was approximately $28.5 million. The national average was somewhat less than $1200 per student per year of participation in 1971. Budget cuts in recent years have affected the per-pupil expenditures; for example, in 1969, the program was reaching 1200 fewer students at the somewhat higher cost of $1331 per pupil.[3]

Of the limited number of studies of Upward Bound available, most do not present evaluation data; that is, much of the information is in the form of rhetoric. One simple criterion in the success of the program is the proportion of its participants who enroll in college. The latest figures, though only approximate, indicate that, out of some 64,000 pupils involved in the program over the 5-year period, 1965-1969, 73.4% were verified as having been graduated from high school. Of these (approximately 47,000), 76.4% indicated that they planned post-secondary education of some type. USOE has verified that 66.5% of those who participated in the years 1966-1969 actually did enroll in 2- or 4-year colleges.[4] Other estimates show that slightly more than 50% of those entering remained in college, which is approximately the national retention rate (Shea, 1967; Froomkin, 1968; Gardenhire, 1968; Kornegay, 1968a). This does not, of course, indicate anything about the quality of the institutions in which Upward Bound students enroll or the conditions under which they are retained. For example, one study has shown that most Upward Bound students go to predominantly black southern institutions (Kornegay, 1968b), although this trend seems to have been reduced, if not reversed, in the last several years (Greenleigh

[2]American College Testing Program (Saunders and Jones, 1968) conducted a comprehensive study of financial needs of Upward Bound students and concluded that a linkage of the program with necessary student aid funding was essential to survival of Upward Bound. This study was brought to our attention by Greenleigh Associates (1970).

[3]Data for 1971 were supplied by USOE. The source of the 1969 data is *An Evaluation of Upward Bound: Findings and Conclusions* (U.S. Office of Economic Opportunity, n.d.).

[4]An additional 5.1% indicated their intention to attend vocational or technical schools, institutions which USOE did not include in its verification study. Also, 0.3% were in a 5-year high school or preparatory school program and 5.7% of those who had planned to attend postsecondary institutions were not verified. The source of this information is a personal communication from a staff member, Upward Bound Branch, Division of Student Special Services, USOE.

Associates, 1970, p. 106). It is also possible that students going to other types of institutions have received special concessions. Some would argue, however, that the important point is simply getting the disadvantaged student a college degree which will help lift him, and his family after him, out of the "culture of poverty" (Greenleigh Associates, 1970, p. 70).

Attempts have been made to measure changes in perceptions and attitudes at some date after a participant enters a program. The D. E. Hunt and Hardt (1966-1968) series of three studies focuses on attitudinal, perceptual, and achievement charges of high school students during enrollment in the Upward Bound program. Attitudinal measures purporting to predict success in college with some accuracy showed small but statistically significant changes in Upward Bound students in comparison with a control group. Their high school grade point averages, however, did not change. In a more recent publication, D. E. Hunt and Hardt (1969) report more detailed analyses on a small subsample of the high school students enrolled in Upward Bound for whom they had longitudinal data on attitudes and motivation at six points in time and grade-point averages at four points in time over a period of 21 months. The primary objective of the study was to compare the differential effects of the Upward Bound experience on blacks and whites in educational attitudes, academic motivation, and academic performance. Although the students came from a national representative sample of 21 Upward Bound centers, they cannot be considered to be representative of all Upward Bound students (1) because only black and white students were included and (2) because of attrition of subjects over the study period. Two less-than-adequate types of control groups were used in the analysis. Significant positive differences between Upward Bound and non-Upward Bound students were found for both races on self-esteem and internal control. However, such differences were not discovered for academic performance. In fact, the GPA's of both the black Upward Bound students and their controls significantly decreased[5] while those of white Upward Bound students and their counterparts increased, though not significantly.

Greenleigh Associates performed for OEO a history and synthesis of data on Upward Bound for the years 1965-1969 (Greenleigh Associates, 1970). They present first a highly illuminating history of Upward Bound, a significant case study of the bureaucratic turmoils and triumphs affecting one federal antipoverty program. One finds, for example, that OEO sponsored very little intensive

---

[5] Posner (1968, p. 25) notes that in several Upward Bound projects intensive summer work designed to raise academic performance has been followed by a decrease in the participants' grade point averages during the following regular school year. He offers as one explanation for this anomalous finding the suggestion that perhaps teachers "punish" students whose academic interest has been stimulated to the point where they no longer are able to tolerate a rather stultifying classroom situation. Another explanation is that Upward Bound students are more likely to change into more academically demanding high school programs, such as a college preparatory curriculum.

research concerning Upward Bound. This condition, according to Greenleigh Associates (1970, p. 63),

> ... does not result from any fear that its research would reveal basic weaknesses and inadequacies in the program that would jeopardize its continuation. It would appear, rather, that the lack of research was due to policy decisions of both national directors and their staffs who, given the funding limitations for Upward Bound, felt strongly that program considerations needed every appropriated dollar.

This contingency is one we have seen before in other forms; for example, program administrators have refused the use of control groups so that every child could have benefit of the program treatment. In Greenleigh Associates' own survey, program directors strongly recommended more research (pp. 128-129).

As for findings, Greenleigh Associates affirm that Upward Bound was indeed recruiting from its target population the academically underachieving and economically disadvantaged youth in this country. Program participation operated as a considerable restraint to dropping out of high school. One study showed that 5% of Upward Bound students contrasted with 35% for the total low-income population dropped out of high school. Even so, retention of students in the Upward Bound program was a major problem.

The Greenleigh Associates' study, as well as one performed by Research Management Corporation (Cohen and Yonkers, 1969), utilized older siblings as a control group. If older siblings are properly selected, the authors argue, one has "... a group whose members, paired with Upward Bound students, would be of the same sex and race, would have been reared in the same families and in the same community environment, would perhaps have on the average the same intelligence, and would have, in most cases, attended the same schools. For a real-life situation, it is hard to conceive of a better control group" (Greenleigh Associates, 1970, pp. 170-171).[6] Using this procedure, investigators found that Upward Bound students have significantly higher retantion rates (D. E. Hunt and Hardt, 1966-1968). When there is failure to complete college, the principal cause seems to be academic failure, although financial need is sometimes an important factor. Upward Bound seems quite successful in getting students to remain in high school and to enroll in college; yet it appears to have far less impact on developing the basic academic skills necessary to attain the college degree.

Greenleigh Associates used their data primarily to carry out a cost-benefit analysis of Upward Bound. Benefits and costs were viewed both from the standpoint of the individual and of the government. Regarding the individual, they conclude: "... for all groups at all discount rates, regardless of one's assumptions about the percentage of income differentials caused by education,

---

[6] Greenleigh Associates also discuss the biases to which this procedure is prone (1970, pp. 173-174).

the Upward Bound program is beneficial for the individual. In all cases the present value of benefits received is at least twice the present value of costs to the individual" (p. 196). The government would find the program only marginally successful, however, when considering Upward Bound by itself. The authors argue that the government should view costs and benefits in relation to alternative programs, and when thus viewed, they suggest Upward Bound would come out well (p. 217).

Title I

Title I of the ESEA, launched in 1965 under the administrative cognizance of USOE, has as its ultimate goal the overcoming of educational deprivation associated with poverty and race. Since these objectives were specified in the broadest of terms, the determination of more specific goals was left to state departments of education and local school districts.

Most governmental poverty programs have earmarked federal funds to be used in an area of recognized need but have left the determination of the means and goals to be pursued almost entirely to those at the local level. Thus the individual programs "purchased" with these monies and the rationales behind them are diffuse, a point which must always be kept in mind when a national program is evaluated. This is especially true of Title I because it provides bloc grants to school districts for a variety of purposes. Nevertheless, there is a need to determine the benefit to individuals under the presently structured Title I program.

The dimensions of Title I can be described by some of the following specifications. During 1968-1969, there were almost 12 million elementary school children enrolled in schools receiving Title I support. These schools are situated in every state in the United States. Although not each of these children was in a Title I program, and was never intended to be, there has been some indication that children without critical needs were also enrollees in the program. Title I schools are located in rural, urban, and suburban areas, although about half the pupils in the program were in schools in rural areas. About 70% of the pupils in these schools were white, 23% were Negro, and 7% comprised ethnic minorities, such as American Indians, Spanish Americans, and Orientals.

These latter percentages do not represent the breakdown of the participants in the program; there was a much more equal percentage from each of these groups who were enrollees in Title I programs. The national allocation of Title I funds was $156.90 per program participant in 1968-1969, but this varied from $142 to $257 per pupil.[7]

During FY 1970 the appropriation was $1.339 billion, and to give some idea of the numbers of pupils involved, in the preschool group alone there were

[7] The statistical information in this paragraph was taken from Glass (1970).

about 7,271,000 children in the program. In the following fiscal year there was an increase in funds to $1.478 billion, with the number of preschoolers affected increasing to 7,746,000.[8]

Title I has as its target populations students at the pre-school, elementary, and secondary levels, including dropouts. However, it has thus far concentrated on the early elementary years. At the preschool level it has made possible the development of special curricula focusing on cognitive skills—especially reading, arithmetic, and language. Its other efforts include an extended school day or year to help counteract the typical "cumulative deficits" accruing over the conventional 9-month school year. Funds are used for classroom aides, often parents of disadvantaged children, whose responsibilities range from child-tending to clerical and tutorial work with individual students. Funds are also used for recruiting and training teachers whose specialty is teaching socially disadvantaged children. In terms of dollar investments and number of students participating, Title I is the largest compensatory education program in existence.

There has been some research conducted at both local and national levels on Title I since its beginning in 1965. Some of this earlier work has been summarized in *Strategies for Success in Compensatory Education* (McDill *et al.* 1969), and may be reviewed there. In general, the studies have been plagued by a great many difficulties which have made their value questionable in determining the efficacy of Title I.

The latest national level evaluation of the effectiveness of Title I is Glass's (1970)[9], and the following is based on his analysis of data from a field survey conducted by the Bureau of Elementary and Secondary Education, USOE. There are two national objectives, one of which is to provide the same educational *opportunity* for all children. The other concerns reducing the deficiencies in educational *attainment* which are associated with social class membership. The first concerns an equal provision of resources so that there is at least equal and perhaps even greater availability and accessibility to those for whom the

[8] Personal communication with Title I official, USOE.

[9] The methodology of this study is too complex to present here in detail. In brief, the sampling design developed by the National Center for Educational Statistics of USOE was multistage, beginning with school districts as the primary sampling units and students within school classes as the smallest units. The populations to which the data were generalized consisted of Title I participating school districts with enrollments of at least 300 (and the elementary schools, teachers, and pupils in grades 1-6 with an enrollment of 15+ students per grade) which participated in the Title I program during the 1968-1969 school year. The sample consisted of 2900 principals and 22,000 teachers who reported on 104,000 pupils in 438 school districts receiving Title I aid. Data were obtained from questionnaires administered to teachers, principals, and district superintendents. As Glass notes, the most important weakness of the research design is that there were no data obtained from comparative schools (those not participating in Title I). "In absence of such experimental control, the results of any *ex post facto* analysis of program impact must remain tentative and open to question" (1970, p. 225).

usual types and quantities of resources have proven unsuccessful. External "resources" (skilled teachers, classroom materials) either directly or indirectly are essential in eliciting the desired response from the target population.

Thus the first objective is fairly easy to achieve—given a national commitment to do so—and its successful attainment can more or less be shown by documenting that those for whom the resources were intended—in this case the educationally and economically deprived—have been the actual recipients of program resources.

The second objective is, of course, a much more difficult goal by its very nature, for even though external resources are provided, there is still the question of the effectiveness that can be attributed to them. In the final analysis, no matter how well-intentioned educational activities are, they can only be turned into individual gains if there is the availability of needed resources, the proper utilization of them, and the appropriate response by the target population. This latter national objective of the successful eradication of educational deficits is proving to be a very difficult one to document.

Most of the analysis in the Glass study centers around the question of whether participants in the Title I program were those for whom the program was intended (first national objective).

In this study, there was a specification of program activities for which Title I funds were spent in three areas of critical needs. The first concerned the need for life-support services, entailing such activities as the provision of food, clothing, medical or dental services. A second kind of concentration of effort went toward meeting needs for personal and social development. Regular school attendance, good relationship with peers, attentiveness in class, positive concepts of self, and higher educational aspirations are the kinds of objectives pursued in this area. The third kind of program activities was in recognition of the need to develop basic skills of reading, mathematics, and language. Not all schools, of course, expended efforts in each of these areas and hence can be held accountable only in those areas in which activities were implemented.

The Glass study attempted to measure needs in each of these three areas and relate them to program participation in order to ascertain the degree of participation by students having needs (an evaluation of the first national objective). An evaluation of the second national objective entails the determination of the effectiveness of participation—that is, the outcome of the program efforts.

In an attempt to objectively specify "need," several measures were used, such as ethnicity, previous failure to attain the expected grade-level reading score, teacher assessment of family income (economic deprivation), and teacher designation of child as a dropout before completion of high school (educational deprivation).

Program outcomes were measures such as reading scores, teacher judgment of "change" in pupils, and teacher assessment of the value of compensatory education programs.

According to Glass, an indication of need was not a strong determinant of participation in either health or cultural enrichment programs since rate of participation seemed to be about the same for those without critical needs as for those with such needs.

When compared with whites, blacks were more likely to be in districts spending more money per pupil. This might be seen as an indication of funds channeled to those schools having pupils with more needs, for Glass, as well as other researchers, indicates that blacks are more likely to have educational needs when scores on achievement tests or economic status are used as an assessment of these needs.

His evidence indicates that some students in Title I schools whose needs indicated less than critical levels were participants in the programs. For example, in about 20% of those schools that reported reading scores there was a larger percentage of students enrolled in academic programs than the percentage of students who scored one or more years below their grade level in reading. One might argue that this represented a diversion of funds intended for students with needs and thereby decreased the resources available to the target population. However, this is difficult to support without having such fundamental information as whether a program could as easily accommodate 15 as 10 pupils, for instance, or if these additional pupils were even necessary to the functioning of the program. The question though of whether target pupils were being replaced by less needy students is not addressed in the Glass study.

Turning now to the question of the effects of program participation, there seemed to be some gains over nonparticipants in personal and social growth when measured by teacher assessment. These are, of course, areas in which both need and outcome are presently more difficult to assess than needs and outcomes concerning basic academic skills.

The primary criteria used for determining academic gains were scores on standardized reading tests. As Glass states, information concerning scores on such tests has an important place in defining a pupil's educational deficits in academic areas and in the future assessment of his improvement. When teachers indicated the areas they thought were needed by Title I students, they chose reading, language, and mathematics in that order with a greater frequency rather than food, health, cultural enrichment, psychological testing, or special education programs. Specifically, the greatest perceived need by the teacher was for compensatory reading programs.

Did resources go to meet these needs? Glass reports that for the two preceding years more Title I money was spent for reading programs than in any other single academic area. So priority seems to have been given to supporting reading programs. As far as participation, the percentages of the whites and of the Orientals in the academic programs were smaller than the percentage of blacks. That is, there was a higher participation among those ethnic groups with the greatest need. Further, there was assignment of the more extensively trained teachers to classes with higher concentrations of pupils on welfare. Additionally, evidence indicates that about 9% of the participants compared with slightly less than 6% of nonparticipants received individualized reading instruction. This evidence suggests that reading programs were provided for those who needed them.

When teachers were asked their judgments about the detection of either "some or large changes" in pupils, in their views more (that is, 50% vs. 44%) participating than nonparticipating pupils had improved in reading performance. However, this difference on the basis of teacher judgment did not hold true for gains in mathematics.

Level of reading is, of course, one of the skills which it is thought possible to objectively measure by means of standardized tests. The lack of systematic attainment of these objective measures is one of the most disappointing features of this study. "Of the 104,080 pupil records obtained in the 1969 survey, only 7½% contained achievement test scores analyzable for reading gain-score analyses" (p. 248). With the realization that there are obvious weaknesses in the data, the analysis does not give any indication that reading programs are effective. In a further analysis, to see if there are particular types of students (using fourteen personal characteristics) who benefit from the program, the conclusion is again negative about effectiveness. "No conclusions are warranted by the data beyond those that pupils in Title I appear to be reading below grade level at a higher rate than pupils generally and that their reading deficit may be increasing over the course of the school year" (pp. 165-166).

With this type of data, one would hardly be justified in feeling that the conclusions from this analysis were very firm. The author himself makes only the most cautious of statements about the study's conclusions.

When teachers were asked, 90% of them gave unqualified or qualified support of the general worth of compensatory programs for the academically disadvantaged, but, as Glass has indicated, his and other studies have failed to document this worth. We will later discuss the explanations being given for why there has been such a failure. (See the section on Controversy Concerning Evaluation Results.)

This evaluation by Glass is subject to all the shortcomings of the most well-planned research in the area of compensatory education for children. In addition, though, his study has even more limiting factors attached to it which are serious enough to bring the value of the study into question. There is not even one objectively obtained measure of outcome, for instance, which has been obtained in a manner which would leave one with the usual amount of confidence to be attached to some of the more important parts of the analysis.

Head Start

Head Start was defined as an intervention program for disadvantaged preschool children to prepare them to cope successfully with later school life and to prevent developmental deficits which would hamper their success. In order to achieve this objective, the program adopted a multifaceted mission, involving efforts to improve intellectual and academic performance and physical health, and to provide social services and psychological services as well as to involve parents in the program itself (McDavid *et al.,* n.d.).

Head Start was initiated as an 8-week program in the summer of 1965, under the administrative authority of OEO, with an enrollment of approximately 560,000 children. At the end of the summer the program was expanded to include full-year services. In 1969 the program had expanded to an enrollment of 450,000 in summer centers and 214,000 in the full-year program.

In FY 1970 roughly half the summer centers were converted into full-year operations. Enrollments were then approximately 263,000 full-year students and 209,000 summer enrollees. The number of students in each of the two types of programs has remained constant since. Head Start had a total operating budget of approximately $360 million for FY 1971 and an estimated allocation of $376.8 million for FY 1972. Since the inception of the program, some $2.5 million to $3.0 million have been allocated annually for evaluation purposes.[10]

The program is conducted in local centers, totaling more than 13,000 in 1967. The emphasis appears to have varied considerably both in terms of organization and services provided, thus rendering systematic evaluation a difficult task. However, OEO maintained its own research and evaluation unit from the inception of the program and made attempts, subject to restrictions imposed by financial and personnel limitations, to appraise the work of the multitude of local centers with different objectives and to generate ideas for innovation in the program. The same appears to hold true for OCD which has inherited some of the research and evaluation studies undertaken while Head Start was located in OEO (and which are still in progress) while launching its own evaluation efforts of the program.

The volume of available evaluation studies completed, those in progress, and those planned far exceeds that of either Upward Bound or Title I program.[11]

[10] The information in this paragraph was supplied to us by personal communication with officials of the Office of Child Development (OCD), DHEW, which was established by the Nixon Administration in 1969 to administer the Head Start program and coordinate a number of other federal programs for preschool children.

[11] In an earlier publication (McDill *et al.,* 1969, pp. 16-18), we summarized the number of completed and ongoing studies arranged according to subject matter (e.g.,

There are at least two reasons for this. First, a more innovative approach has been taken because it has represented a national effort to extend formal or systematic education "downward," providing preschool education where none existed for the vast majority of disadvantaged children. It was also innovative in that heretofore there had been little interest in training the preschool child to acquire cognitive or school skills. Of course, this was partly because of the middle-class orientation toward socioemotional development which dominated preschool institutions. Second, national interest and enthusiasm were expressed for Head Start right from the beginning, with attendant expectations beyond the capabilities of any program and certainly beyond those of any newly created effort.

The national assessment of Head Start which is both the most comprehensive and systematic to date is *The Impact of Head Start* (Cicirelli *et al.* 1969). This evaluation was conducted by the Westinghouse Learning Corporation and Ohio University under contract with the Office of Evaluation of OEO between June 1968 and June 1969. The primary question to which the evaluation was addressed was as follows: To what extent has the Head Start program at the national level had an impact on the affective and cognitive development of children which persisted into the elementary school? The authors of the report and the social scientists in the Office of Research Plans, Programs, and Evaluation (RPP&E) of OEO were acutely aware of the methodological limitations of the study and its restricted focus on affective and cognitive criteria, as they indicate both in the original report and in a number of publications subsequent to the report. Nevertheless, as White (1970, pp. 169-170 and 177) has noted, OEO officials made the justifiable decision that a comprehensive national evaluation needed to be conducted quickly since the program had been in operation as a national effort for 3 years, at an annual cost of more than 300 million dollars, with knowledge of its effectiveness based only on either short-term studies or a limited number of local, long-range studies. Such a decision by OEO made it necessary to sacrifice the advantages of a longitudinal study (employing, for example, an experimental design) and also to forego an assessment of the program's effect on other objectives, such as health and nutritional services to children and social services to the child and to his family.

The Westinghouse study produced immediate and sometimes emotional criticism among social scientists, congressmen, federal executives, and journalists. Subsequent to this initial flurry of visceral reactions, there have been some more reasoned, critical evaluations of the study published. This study, like the

---

curriculum, motivation, and cognitive performance) which had been prepared by the Evaluation and Research Unit of Head Start. In addition, we reviewed the summaries of 66 studies of Head Start activities for the years 1965-1967—relying primarily on *Head Start Childhood Research Information Bulletin* (1969) prepared by the Eric Center of the National Laboratory on Early Childhood Education—in an attempt to assess the effects of the program on cognitive growth.

Equality of Educational Opportunity survey (Coleman *et al.*, 1966) and the Jensen report (1969), has evoked a degree of interest and controversy among educators, social scientists, politicians, and the lay public much greater than other educational research of the last decade. For this reason, it is important to review in some detail the design and findings of the study and its criticisms and then attempt to assess the validity of both.

The sample consisted of 1980 first, second, and third-grade students who had attended Head Start centers and a matched sample of nonparticipating children from the same "target areas"[12] as a comparison group. These subjects were selected from a random sample of 104 centers out of the total of almost 13,000 in existence in 1966-1967. Seventy-five of the centers had only summer programs, and the remaining 29 were full-year facilities. This proportion of summer and full-year centers corresponded very closely to the 70/30 proportion in the universe of existing centers (White, 1970, p. 171). From each of the local centers an attempt was made to select eight Head Start participants at each of the three grade levels and an equal number of control children who had not attended Head Start but were residents of the target area at the time the center was instituted. The two groups of subjects were matched on the important variates of age, sex, race/ethnicity, and kindergarten attendance. No attempt was made to match the two groups on socioeconomic background. Instead, a covariance technique was employed in the analysis to adjust SES differences.

A battery of mental aptitude, scholastic achievement, and attitudinal tests was administered to both groups of students. In addition, interview data were obtained from the students, their parents, and officials of Head Start centers. Finally, the students' elementary teachers completed rating forms on such student characteristics as desire for achievement and motivation for learning and the social and intellectual climates of the schools.

Two different approaches were utilized in analyzing the data. The first, and primary, was covariance analysis using both Head Start centers and students as units of analysis. The second approach involved the use of a nonparametric technique, the rationale for which we will discuss below. In addition to the Westinghouse report, several other publications[13] have summarized its important findings on both cognitive and affective tests, based on separate analyses of summer and full-year programs and for each grade. Therefore, suffice it to state here that for the national sample only one statistically significant difference was found favoring Head Start students when thirty comparisons were made by grade and summer *vs.* full-year programs on the following six different mental tests: the Illinois Test of Psycholinguistic Abilities (ITPA), the Metropolitan

---

[12] The target area was a defined geographical area which had a Head Start center and an elementary school which served children from the given residential area.

[13] See, for example, McDill *et al.* (1969); Williams and Evans (1969); Smith and Bissell (1970); and Cicirelli *et al.* (1970).

Reading Tests, Stanford Achievement Tests, Children's Self-Concept Index, Children's Attitudinal Range Indicator (a measure of attitudes toward peers, parents, and society), and Classroom Behavior Inventory (a measure of desire for achievement in school).[14]

Limited analyses were also conducted on subgroups of centers—broad geographical region, size of community, and ethnic/racial composition of centers. There was some evidence to suggest that predominantly black centers, centers located in the southeastern region of the United States, and those located in central cities tended to be more effective than other types of centers.

Given these results, we believe the following conclusion from the Westinghouse study accurately summarizes the impact of the Head Start experience on two different categories of criteria:

> In sum, Head Start children cannot be said to be appreciably different from their peers in the elementary grades who did not attend Head Start in most aspects of cognitive and affective development measured in this study, with the exception of the slight, but nonetheless significant, superiority of full-year Head Start children on certain measures of cognitive development (Cicirelli et al., 1969, p. 8).

As noted above, the Westinghouse study has been subjected to several types of criticisms both shortly after the report was issued (by both scientists and nonscientists) and more recently by behavioral scientists and educationists poring over the results more systematically (and in certain instances engaging in further analyses of the data). On some points, the "instant" criticisms and the delayed, more systematic critical evaluations of the report overlap. In other cases, the more recent criticisms raise new and more fundamental issues about the study. It should be stressed that nearly all of these criticisms have been answered by the authors of the study, by social scientists in the Office of RPP&E of OEO who established the criteria for the evaluation,[15] and in one instance by an academician who served as a consultant for the study (White, 1970).

One of the most frequent criticisms is that the study is too narrow in scope, due to its central concern with cognitive and affective criteria. The Secretary of HEW at the time the report was released is reported to have immediately lodged this charge against the study (New York Times, 1969b, p. 22).

---

[14]This conclusion is based on comparisons of total scores on the tests, not scores on subtests. For a highly intelligible summary of the principal data from the survey, see Cicirelli et al. (1970, Table 4, pp. 122-123).

[15]In an earlier publication (McDill et al., 1969, pp. 23-27), we offered rebuttals to some of the criticisms at the time—responses which are strikingly similar to those of OEO social scientists who had established the guidelines for the evaluation. (See, for example, Williams and Evans 1969, pp. 126-128.) In this section we present again our views, modified and/or expanded, in light of new evidence and opinions of the "proponents" and "opponents" of the study.

Granted that the study did not attempt to assess the impact of Head Start on the child's physical health, nutrition, social services, family stability or larger community—each of which is an important objective of the program—the researchers were completely justified, in our view, in restricting focus to two types of psychological variables. Time and funds allotted made it impossible to assess effects on variables relating to each of the program's objectives. Or, as Williams and Evans (1969, p. 126) note, ". . . One of the reasons for the failure of so many evaluations is that they have aspired to do too much."[16] More importantly, almost everyone positively valuing social action programs agrees that cognitive and affective outcomes are among the cardinal objectives in such programs. Certainly this was agreed upon by the original OEO planning committee for Head Start, a body composed of scientists and academicians who were charged with the task of establishing its objectives and guidelines.

A second early criticism leveled at the study by journalists is that the measures of the criterion variables (especially those tapping affective characteristics of students) are of "dubious validity" (*New Republic*, 1969). The adequacy of the affective tests has also been questioned by respected scientists, including both consultants to the study (Madow, 1969; White, 1970, p. 73) and researchers reanalyzing the Westinghouse data (Smith and Bissell, 1970, p. 53). Earlier (McDill *et al.*, 1969, pp. 11-12) we lamented the lack of adequate measures of cognitive development of young children, and we will broach this topic again in a broader context later in this paper. However, here we feel that it is only proper to assess the reliability and validity of these criterion measures taking into account the handicaps under which Westinghouse researchers were working. They were aware of this problem, and in fact found it necessary to devise their own instruments for measuring affective criteria because existing measures of such variables for preschool children had, at best, limited utility. Furthermore, although the Westinghouse researchers and OEO officials (Williams and Evans, 1969, p. 127) admitted the affective measures were generally of unknown predictive utility, their coefficients of reliability are above the minimum levels of acceptability generally recognized by measurement experts.[17] This information, combined with the fact that the instruments have "face validity,"

---

[16] Stanley (1970, p. 651) shares this view with respect to design and implementation of Head Start: "For example, if Project Head Start had been concerned with determining, say, what is necessary to produce good readers in families where typically the children do not learn to read well, rather than seeing how much good of various sorts (medical, dental, emotional, cognitive, etc.) can be done in a fixed period of time with a prespecified amount of money per child, the project would probably have proceeded quite differently and might have been "much more effective."

[17] Cicirelli *et al.* (1970, pp. 115-116) cite reliability coefficients providing evidence to support our position here. Furthermore, they note that the measure of children's self-concept is based partly on a measure widely used in previous research and having "acknowledged validity."

indicates they are far more scientifically valid than subjective impressions and testimonials often proffered by evaluation researchers or designers of compensatory programs who simply assert that their treatments have had positive impact on the child's self-esteem, attitudes toward school, and academic motivation. Finally, and most important, White (1970, p. 174) makes a cogent observation about the affective instrumentation: "While the attitudes of the child were approached with instruments which were, in my opinion, not proven, it must be understood that in this context of evaluation the value of those attitudes should have been registered in the school achievement measures."

With respect to the cognitive tests, the Westinghouse researchers employed those which have been in use for several years, have been normed on national samples of students, and have been employed extensively in numerous researches where the subject population was students in the same age range as those in Head Start. Furthermore, these tests have shown an overall high level of reliability and predictive validity.[18]

Without question, the aspect of the study which has generated the most important criticisms (Smith and Bissell, 1970; Campbell and Erlebacher, 1970a, b) and responses from the authors and OEO officials (Cicirelli *et al.*, 1970; Cicirelli, 1970; Evans and Schiller, 1970) is the *ex post facto* design, a methodology which the authors were forced to employ because of the short time available for conducting the study, but nevertheless a research design which has inherent weaknesses. Smith and Bissell (1970, pp. 54, 74, and 103) list the *ex post facto* design as one of the two fundamental weaknesses of the study because the authors were unable to obtain treatment and comparison groups which were highly similar on variables relevant to the success of the Head Start experience. The authors were aware of the shortcomings of the *ex post facto* design, and they attempted to match the subjects on a number of important variables, supplemented by a covariance random replications model (Cicirelli *et al.*, 1969, pp. 90-102) to adjust for difference in the socioeconomic background of the students since the parents of the comparison children were higher on educational level, occupation, and income per capita. As we noted above, a second statistical procedure was employed, a nonparametric procedure involving the grouping of subjects within a Head Start center according to three different

---

[18] Smith and Bissell (1970, pp. 79-80) agree that the Metropolitan Readiness Test has high reliability and excellent predictive validity. However, they question the ITPA on the grounds that its validity and reliability for use with disadvantaged children are questionable. A more general criticism of measures of criterion vàriables for all preschool compensatory education programs has been levelled by Zimiles (1970). His indictment has to do with a lack of knowledge base concerning the cognitive growth of young children which fosters an emphasis on "outcome" evaluation rather than "processual" evaluation; i.e., assessment of the cognitive processes and related personality variables which mediate and support the child's intellectual functioning at any given point in time. We will address ourselves to Zimiles' thesis below in the section on evaluation results.

measures of the socioeconomic level of the parents and then calculating a weighted score difference between the treatment and comparison groups (using centers as units of analysis) on the different measures of cognitive and affective performance (Cicirelli *et al.*, 1969, pp. 173-182). This nonparametric technique was introduced as a supplementary test of the hypotheses because it required less stringent assumptions about the data than did covariance analysis. These two different analytical approaches yielded basically the same overall negative findings regarding Head Start experience.

Campbell and Erlebacher (1970a, b) have delivered the most elaborate and sophisticated criticism of *ex post facto* studies, using the Head Start evaluation as a substantive example to demonstrate their weaknesses. Their argument (1970a) is that in the Head Start evaluation [as is "often" (p. 185) true in evaluation studies of compensatory education programs] the nonparticipants (i.e., "controls") were superior to or more able than the participants, making the Head Start experience look less effective (i.e., underestimating the "true" effects) than it really was or even producing spurious negative effects. That is, the matching procedure and subsequent covariance analysis utilized did not successfully adjust the original differences in favor of the nonparticipants on the criterion variables,[19] with the experimental and control groups each regressing toward their respective population means on the dependent variable, producing misleading results. The direction and amount of bias in outcomes for any *ex post facto* study depends upon several conditions such as the difference in the means of "experimental" and "control" groups on a covariate (e.g., socioeconomic background).[20] They demonstrate that matching cannot remove all the artifacts in any empirical study. Furthermore, they point out that analysis of covariance likewise underadjusts the original differences between the two groups unless the data meet a stringent set of assumptions—assumptions not fulfilled in the Westinghouse evaluation according to Campbell and Erlebacher.

The Westinghouse evaluators (Cicirelli, 1970) and OEO officials (Evans and Schiller, 1970) grant the validity of these arguments in the abstract and also concede that the comparison group in the study was superior to the Head Start participants in terms of ability and socioeconomic background. However, they strongly dispute Campbell and Erlebacher's conclusion (1970a, p. 203) that "It is tragic that the social experiment most cited by presidents, most influential in governmental decision making, should have contained such a misleading bias." Cicirelli (1970, p. 213) points out that because the differences in the two groups on socioeconomic background were *small*, one would expect the differences in

---

[19] Madow (1969, p. 250) makes the point that the statistical techniques employed *may* not have successfully adjusted the two groups, perhaps obscuring the effects of Head Start.

[20] We are indebted to James Fennessey of The Johns Hopkins University for aid in clarifying our thinking on regression artifacts in *ex post facto* designs.

performance attributable to the regression artifact also to be small. Similarly, Evans and Schiller (1970, p. 216) contend that the regression artifact was not of sufficient magnitude to materially affect the substantive conclusions of the study.

Campbell and Erlebacher (1970b, p. 221) respond that the degree of bias in the results in favor of the control group cannot be ascertained, primarily because the characteristics of the populations from which the nonparticipants were selected were unknown prior to the matching.

In their discussion of regression artifacts, Campbell and Erlebacher (1970a, p. 195) cite our earlier publication (McDill et al., 1969, pp. 38-42), in which we described evaluations of eleven local programs we listed above, as support for the position that in compensatory education the more rigorously designed studies tend to show the most favorable treatment effects, with the contrary being true in most fields (e.g., pharmacology). Specifically, they note that each of the five local programs we discussed in which true experimentation was used yielded significant cognitive gains for the treatment group, while only one of the five using a quasiexperimental design produced positive results. They offer as one "plausible" explanation for this disparity the speculation that in the nonexperimental studies, the control groups, selected in a nonrandom manner, were superior to the treatment groups. As much as we are in favor of rigorous experimental evaluations of all social action programs where feasible, we submit that an equally plausible explanation for these differences is that the successful programs were more rigorous and sophisticated in terms of conception, design, and implementation of the programs themselves.[21] (See, for example, Hawkridge et al., 1968b, p. 18). Perhaps the *most* plausible explanation is that the successful compensatory programs are the ones which also happen to be most carefully designed and executed *and* happen to have scientifically rigorous evaluations built in as part of the programs themselves. Our interpretation of the evidence available in the literature on compensatory education leads us to this conclusion.

Regardless, Campbell and Erlebacher's substantive stance (1970a, p. 185) that in quasiexperimental or *ex post facto* evaluations of compensatory education the "control" group often is more capable is problematical. In fact, based on the evidence we have examined, especially Head Start evaluations (both local and national), we are of the opinion that the obverse is more likely to be true. If we are correct, then it suggests that the *ex post facto* design of the Westinghouse study did not seriously bias the outcome against the Head Start participants and hence result in "tragically misleading analyses" which Campbell and Erlebacher lament. Rather, conclusions about the effectiveness of Head Start should be based not solely on evidence from this one study but should embrace evidence

---

[21] A classic example of a program adhering to scientific criteria in design, implementation, and evaluation is the Early Training Project, Peabody College, Nashville, Tennessee.

from other studies.[22] As we noted above, in our own search for evidence relating to the cognitive impact of Head Start, we uncovered 66 studies. Only 31 of these used cognitive variables as criteria, and of these only 17 used control groups in a before-after design, with random assignment of subjects being the rare exception. Our conclusion was that only 11 of the 31 studies showed statistically significant effects in favor of Head Start participants.

Schiller and Evans (1968) conducted an independent review of 30 Head Start evaluations completed under contract with the Office of Evaluation and Research of Head Start between 1965-1968. Several of the studies they reviewed focusing on cognitive outcomes were covered in our review, and none of the studies they reviewed involved a true experimental design. On the basis of their review, they reached a conclusion similar to that of the Westinghouse study: "At any rate all we can say with confidence from the studies carried out to date is that most of the ones utilizing follow-up measures and control groups find the Head Start and comparable non-Head Start children performing the same by the end of the first year of school . . ." (p. 8). White (1970, p. 169) reaches basically the same conclusion in his review of evaluation studies conducted prior to the Westinghouse assessment.

Although our review and that of Schiller and Evans do not offer definitive evidence to refute Campbell and Erlebacher's argument that *ex post facto* studies typically involve selection of control groups superior to the treatment groups, these separate assessments of a host of recent evaluation studies suggest that Campbell and Erlebacher's claim is questionable. In fact OEO reported in its national evaluation of Head Start for 1965-1967 that volunteer families of Head Start children were more verbally skilled, better educated, and more likely to be intact than economically comparable non-Head Start families (McDavid *et al.* n.d., p. 4). The evidence seems to be comparable for participants in various other educational reforms. For example, studies show that in school desegregation efforts in the South after the 1954 Supreme Court decision, the black students "selected" or "recruited" were superior academically and came from less disadvantaged homes than those remaining in segregated schools.[23] The same selection process holds true for other educational innovations such as team teaching, PSSC physics, and TV teaching.[24] To conclude this argument we cite a

[22] In sum, we would find it truly remarkable if these independent conclusions were based on evaluations which systematically obtained control groups superior to the Head Start control groups. Campbell and Erlebacher (1970, p. 202) seem to recognize this point: "Selecting a control from a generally less able population would make it [Head Start] look good. There are so many combinations of conditions that would produce this bias that we may be sure it has occurred in many studies." The question we pose is how these two biases, one in favor of Head Start participants and the other in favor of non-Head Start children, could produce such similar findings?

[23] For evidence to support this position, see Katz (1964).

[24] We are indebted to Julian Stanley for bringing these examples to our attention.

statement by Miller *et al.* (1970, p. 39) about selection of participants for social ameliorative programs in general: "Efforts to improve the condition of the poor, when effective, generally result in improving the conditions of those at the top of the bottom, leaving the bottommost untouched."

Thus, we grant the technical accuracy of Campbell and Erlebacher's point about the possible biasing effects in the Westinghouse evaluation attributable to the *ex post facto* design, but like the Westinghouse researchers and OEO evaluators, we are of the opinion that they overestimate the actual importance of the regression artifact for that particular study. We are of this opinion because, as we stated earlier, the Westinghouse study produced findings about Head Start which are highly consistent with the weight of evidence from other studies.

Moreover, the diffuse "total effort" approach[25] (Smith and Bissell, 1970, p. 58) subscribed to by a majority of directors of Head Start centers as late as the summer of 1966 contrasts sharply with the highly structured, carefully planned effort (with a primary emphasis on teaching cognitive skills) which appears to distinguish successful preschool programs from the unsuccessful (Hawkridge *et al.*, 1968b, p. 18; Bereiter, 1971, p. 6). In other words, it is quite probable that many of the Head Start participants in the Westinghouse sample were the recipients of a preschool experience characteristic of the middle-class nursery school, and this type of program has failed to produce substantial and persistent cognitive gains in disadvantaged children. Thus, we agree with White (1970, p. 163) that in general the substantive conclusions of the study were sound.

Another criticism which was leveled shortly after the study appeared (*New York Times*, 1969a, p. 11E), and more recently in greater depth (Smith and Bissell, 1970, pp. 54 and 103), is that by focusing on an overall evaluation of the program, the evaluators failed to consider likely variations in quality of local programs which could be of use to planners of future compensatory efforts. This is a criticism of considerable merit, and as we noted earlier (McDill *et al.*, 1969) involves a research question which needs to be answered as quickly as possible.[26] However, the mission of the Westinghouse evaluation was to answer the more fundamental question of the effects of the program at the national level—a

[25] Boyd (1966, p. 38, cited in Smith and Bissell, 1970, p. 58) reported that most directors "reveal a preference for a supportive, unstructured socialization program, rather than a structured informational program."

[26] However, if Bereiter (1971) is correct, it might have been impossible to conduct such an investigation. He reports (pp. 13-14) the following private communication from an official of OEO: ". . . Efforts to study the effects of natural variations amond Head Start programs have had little success because there simply was not enough variation to work with."

summative assessment (White, 1970, pp. 169 and 178)[27] which federal policy makers require to make decisions about future funding levels and/or reorganization of programs.

In their detailed reanalysis of cognitive measures from the Westinghouse survey, Smith and Bissell focus on local and programmatic variations in effectiveness of Head Start centers, and they conclude that the program was more effective than the Westinghouse researchers stated. Specifically, they take the position that the Head Start experience is of clear "educational importance" (p. 101) for full-year Head Start centers and for urban black centers. In a reply to this reanalysis and criticism of the Westinghouse conclusions, Cicirelli *et al.* (1970) take strong issue with Smith and Bissell's conclusions. The disagreement between the two groups regarding the differential effectiveness of varying types of Head Start centers seems to be one of degree, not kind. Their controversy is too lengthy and complex to treat systematically here. However, after carefully reading both documents, we are convinced that Smith and Bissell's reanalysis provides no startling revelations about differential effects. In fact as Cicirelli *et al.* note (1970, p. 124), the types of differences among programs which Smith and Bissell isolate are for the most part the ones noted in the original study; namely, full-year centers are statistically more effective in producing cognitive gains which are detectable in the first three grades of elementary school, and black centers located in central cities appear to have more impact on cognitive criteria than other facilities. Their disagreement about the magnitude of cognitive effects for the above types of centers reduces to a matter of professional opinion about how large differences in scores must be in order to be labeled as educationally significant. However, given the selective nature of Smith and Bissell's reanalysis, we think the following conclusion by Cicirelli *et al.* (1970, p. 124) is not inappropriate: "But it is hard for us to understand how Smith and Bissell can claim their reanalysis has produced any real changes in the Westinghouse findings or how they can regard the difference of a few points on one cognitive measure (out of the three that were studied), in the one small sub-group (out of a national sample), as evidence that the Head Start program has produced significant results."

There are several other criticisms, of varying degrees of validity, directed at the Westinghouse study, which space limitations preclude our even mentioning here.[28] However, there is one which is too important to ignore entirely, namely,

---

[27] As White notes, early in 1968 OEO established an evaluation policy of its programmatic efforts and decided to pursue the following three types of evaluations: *summative* (assessing the impacts of programs at the global level); *formative* (focusing on local efforts to isolate effective strategies which could be used to improve national efforts); and *monitoring* (periodic "custodial" assessments of local programs to determine that minimum federal guidelines were being followed).

[28] We discussed a number of these briefly in an earlier publication (McDill *et al.*, 1969, pp. 22, 23, and 26). A longer list and response to each are presented in Williams and Evans (1969).

that concerning the adequacy of the sample, both in terms of number of centers selected and representativeness of the universe of centers. Both consultants to the study who defended it overall (White, 1970) and those who questioned its overall validity (Madow, 1969) criticized the quality of the sample. In addition, Smith and Bissell deliver the most detailed criticism of the sample. Both Madow and Smith and Bissell criticize the sample for being purely random and not stratified on crucial variables such as full-year *vs.* summer facilities, racial and ethnic composition, geographical region, and size of city. Such a sample, they argue, would have permitted an analysis of the relative effectiveness of various types of centers. Cicirelli *et al.* (1970, pp. 107-108) provide two types of defenses to this criticism. First, they point out that data on the characteristics of the approximately 13,000 centers were not available to permit the selection of a more rigorous stratified sample. Second, they respond that this is not a valid criticism of the sample because the objective of the evaluation was to assess the impact of Head Start at the national level, not to analyze the differential effectiveness of centers. Both groups of critics take the researchers to task because there was a substantial attrition in centers originally selected, leading, they believe, to serious biases in the sample. Specifically, 225 centers had to be chosen in order to obtain the target sample of 104. Cicirelli *et al.* admit that some bias was introduced into the sample because of this attrition (attributable to circumstances beyond the control of the researchers, not to lack of technical skill on their part). However, they point out that of thirty-two characteristics and goals on which the participating and nonparticipating centers[29] were compared, they differed statistically on only five of the attributes. Furthermore, a comparison of the sample centers with a larger sample of centers selected by the Bureau of the Census showed no large differences on characteristics, such as sex ratio of pupils, father's education, and racial/ethnic distribution of pupils.

Finally, both Madow and Smith and Bissell criticize the study for the small number of centers (especially full-year facilities) which they contend require very large differences on the criterion variables to produce statistically significant results, even though the differences could be educationally significant. Evans (1969, p. 255) acknowledges that, in retrospect, the researchers were erroneous in selecting such a small number of full-year centers and if the study were conducted again such facilities would be overselected to permit more systematic analysis of them. However, he argues that the basic findings of the research would not be altered by a larger sample because a "power of the test" was conducted, indicating that with the N and variance of the existing sample the statistical tests employed were capable of detecting differences between the Head Start and comparison groups "below the level of what would be practically meaningful" (p. 255).

---

[29] It should be acknowledged that these comparisons were made on the basis of a questionnaire sent to the 121 nonparticipating centers, with a response rate of only 45%.

In short, Cicirelli *et al.* (1970) and Evans (1969) agree with our earlier conclusion (McDill *et al.*, 1969, pp. 26-27) that although the sample had weaknesses, it was sufficiently adequate to provide valid generalizations for the substantive problems to which the evaluation was addressed.

After assessing the critical evaluations of the Westinghouse study which have appeared since we earlier reviewed the study (McDill *et al.*, 1969), we find no reason to alter our position that it is the most rigorous national assessment of the program which has been conducted, and its conclusions are valid.

Furthermore, the fears of the Westinghouse critics—both those expressed shortly after the report was issued (e.g., *New York Times*, 1969a) or the more recent ones appearing in academic publications (e.g., Madow, 1969, p. 246) that the report would be used by federal officials to eliminate or cut back the program—have proved unfounded. The funding level of Head Start in FY 1968, the year prior to the evaluation was approximately $323 million; in FY 1970, the year the Westinghouse study was conducted it was $326 million; in FY 1971, it is $360 million; and the estimate for FY 1972 is $376.8 million!

One lesson which Head Start ought clearly to bring home is that large-scale federal programs, once initiated, are not easily dismantled. When the national educational and poverty lobbies mobilize for a program which captures the public's imagination and commitment to the extent that Head Start has, it is not abolished or even easily curtailed, even if it does not produce the instant success its adherents had been of sufficient naiveté to hope for. Consequently, for the future, the experience of Head Start would argue for the importance of boldly experimental, yet rigorously evaluated, pilot programs *prior* to initiation of a nationwide effort which often acquires a functional autonomy once launched.

Sesame Street

November 10, 1969, signalled the beginning of a major, new, nonclassroom experiment in compensatory education. On that date the television program Sesame Street began its first 26-week experimental season. Supported by grants totaling $8 million from a variety of public and private sources,[30] Sesame Street is aimed at teaching 3-5-year-old children eight major skills: body parts, letters, forms, numbers, relational terms, sorting skills, classification skills, and problem-solving.

Sesame Street's success in terms of public popularity has made it, and the various characters who appear in the series, household words. To the television

---

[30] Initial support was principally from (1) National Center for Educational Research and Development, (2) National Institute of Child Health and Human Development, both in the U.S. DHEW, (3) U.S. Office of Economic Opportunity, (4) National Foundation on the Arts and Humanities, (5) Carnegie Corporation, (6) Ford Foundation, (7) John and Mary Markle Foundation, and (8) Corporation for Public Broadcasting. The list of donor organizations has since become much longer and includes several large corporations.

world it has demonstrated that educational TV can be commercially successful. In some cases, Sesame Street has outdrawn competing commercial programs in popularity (Culhane, 1970). During the 1970-1971 season, the program was reaching more than six million preschool children over 250 stations. In 1970, Sesame Street won the George Foster Peabody Award for meritorious service to broadcasting.

The Children's Television Workshop (CTW), producers of Sesame Street, began with the ideal of maximizing both audience appeal and quality of instruction without stinting either (Samuels, 1970). The question of audience appeal is best measured by finding out how large an audience is tuning in to the program. A variety of audience surveys have been carried out, ranging from studies commissioned by CTW and conducted by professional pollsters to college class projects. For example, Daniel Yankelovich, Inc. conducted three CTW-sponsored surveys in Bedford-Stuyvesant, East Harlem, and Washington, D.C. in April, 1970. Local black interviewers talked to 97 qualified respondents. Respondents qualified if they had children 2 to 5 years in the house 5 days a week and at least one working television set. The results for Bedford-Stuyvesant indicated that 60% of the children were regular viewers; in East Harlem, 77% watched the program, the vast majority watching it three or more times a week. In Washington, D.C., where the program is shown only on UHF, only 63% of respondents watched the UHF channel and penetration of Sesame Street was 32%. A separate study in Chicago black ghettos indicated that 88% of those interviewed watched the program, and 50% were daily viewers (Samuels, 1970). The reliability of measuring "tuning-in" by respondents' self-reporting is certainly open to question. These high percentages may be overestimates, reflecting some respondent desire to associate oneself with something favorably publicized.

Audience surveys have experienced difficulties in obtaining definitive answers concerning the size of Sesame Street's audience due to factors such as the show's being aired only on UHF, the hours at which the program was aired (10:00 a.m. and 4:00 p.m. being considered ideal by CTW), and whether the viewer can see the program only via cable or only on educational TV. Still, audience response to Sesame Street has clearly been beyond the expectations of the CTW staff. Of the target population of 12 million preschool viewers, estimates for 1971 indicated that the program was being watched on a fairly regular basis by more than 6 million, and some placed the figure as high as 8 million (*Newsweek*, 1971), although reliability of these estimates is not known.

In its continuing efforts to reach Sesame Street's target population, CTW has begun a "utilization" campaign which attempts to mobilize grass roots resources for bringing Sesame Street to every 3-5-year-old in the country. A network of coordinators has been set up in the largest U.S. metropolitan areas. "This team, aided by thousands of volunteers, builds the viewing audience with projects ranging from 'flyer' squads who distribute literature about the show on street corners, in supermarkets and other places where mothers of young children might be reached, to organizing viewing centers in inner-city neighborhoods and enlisting the aid of civic-minded persons and institutions to give of their time and to donate goods such as TV sets" (*Children's Television Workshop*, n.d., p. 14). In addition, a program of "Sesame Mothers" has been begun in California for training mothers in organizing viewing groups and conducting follow-up lessons. The *Sesame Street Magazine* has been given free to inner-city families during the program's second season.

From the outset, CTW avowedly directed attention to the educational impact of Sesame Street. Educational Testing Service (ETS) conducted a before-after evaluative study of the impact of Sesame Street during its first year of programming. ETS studied 943 children (modal age of 4 years) from Boston, Durham, N.C., Philadelphia, Phoenix, and a rural area in northeastern California. The sample contained disproportionate numbers of disadvantaged children (particularly blacks), more boys than girls, and small numbers of advantaged suburban and disadvantaged Spanish-speaking children. The sample was divided into quartiles according to frequency of viewing, although popularity of the program was such that there were few children who had never seen the program.

Children were tested with 203 questions in eight different areas on which the program focuses. These areas range from simple tasks such as naming parts of the human body to higher-order cognitive skills such as classifying and sorting by several criteria (e.g., classification by form and function). The major conclusions of the study were as follows:

1. Children who watched the most, learned the most; amount of viewing time was the most important variable.

2. Skills to which the program devoted most time were the skills best learned.[31]

3. Children watching at home without adult supervision learned as much as—in some cases, more than—children watching in school under teacher supervision.

4. The above findings held true across age, sex, geographical location, SES, whether watched at home or at school, and mental age (IQ).

5. Three-year-olds gained most in learning, relatively more than 5-year-olds.

6. The scores of disadvantaged children who watched a great deal surpassed those of middle-class children who watched only a little.

7. It appears, though only tentatively, that the program may be particularly effective for teaching English-language skills to children whose first lan-

---

[31] This finding is consistent with one of Bereiter's conclusions (1971) regarding the effectiveness of highly structured preschool programs which we present below. That is, outcome of the program is tied closely to its content.

guage is not English and who neither test nor perform well in conventional American classroom settings. The tentativeness of this finding is dictated by the small number of Spanish-speaking children in the sample.

To isolate the effects of amount of viewing time, ETS conducted a special "Age Cohorts" study, using two disadvantaged groups of children none of whom attended nursery school:

> Group 1 was 53 to 58 months of age at the time of pretesting. Group 2 was 53 to 58 months of age at the time of posttesting. In addition to being of the same chronological age at the point of comparison, they were of comparable mental age and they lived in the same communities. There were, in short, no observable differences between the two groups in important matters of previous attainments, IQ, and home background. There were more than 100 disadvantaged children, who were not attending school, in each group (Ball and Bogatz, 1970, p. 8).

Group 1 (N=114) was tested prior to the airing of any Sesame Street shows, so that there was no chance the program could have contaminated their scores. When compared with posttest scores of Group 1, Group 2 children in the two highest quartiles of amount-of-viewing scored some 40 points higher than the comparable children in Group 1 who had never watched the show, indicating that when maturational effects, IQ, previous attainments, and home backgrounds were held constant, the frequent viewers made very large gains. Stated differently, with important confounding variables statistically controlled, this analysis reveals that increase in test scores was a monotonic function of amount of viewing time.[32]

Compared with findings from evaluation research on other compensatory education programs, Sesame Street appears encouraging. Findings to date are consistently positive and relate directly to amount of viewing time. In addition, the test results suggest that transfer of learning is an outcome of the program. In attempting to account for Sesame Street's apparent success, one turns most immediately to the method of preparation of program segments. The program staff, buttressed by eminent educational consultants, adopted and maintained an openly experimental approach to their materials. The staff took the viewpoint that their target group was a difficult audience to reach, one which was highly

---

[32] Parenthetically, the results of this ingenious analysis provide an answer to Campbell and Erlebacher's anticipated weakness (1970a, p. 203) in evaluations of Sesame Street:

> If we look to the probable biases in quasi-experimental evaluations of the 'Sesame Street' preschooler's educational television program, they will no doubt be in this direction. In any given neighborhood, it will be the more competent homes that know of the program's existence and make certain that their children get to see it.

True, the children who were the most frequent viewers of the program had higher pretest and posttest scores and showed the largest gains from pretest to posttest. However, the results of this "Age Cohorts" study show that despite the initial superiority of these children, amount of viewing made a statistically and educationally significant contribution to the intellectual development of these disadvantaged children.

selective in viewing and which had a very short span of attention. They therefore felt that conventional assumptions concerning TV programming for children could not be expected to hold true, and they must find out from the children themselves whether or not the materials were interesting and educational. As Edward Palmer, Sesame Street's director of research and evaluation, explains:

> In one of a number of research methods, we visit a day care center in New York City and show a piece of material to preschoolers, often to one child at a time. We run the piece on a television set tied to a portable video-tape play-back unit and then place a 'distractor'—a television-size rear screen projector which shows a different slide every eight seconds—nearby. We then measure the proportion of each eight-second interval when a child is watching our television presentation as opposed to looking at anything else, including the distractor. The data, accumulated on graphs, is carefully analyzed in company with the program's producers to determine why attention rose or fell during the test pieces (Palmer, 1969, p. 3).

Using these techniques, the researchers found, for example, that "young children are unlikely to remain interested for long if an adult talks full-face to them," or that "talk not directed specifically to the children's level almost instantly causes attention to begin wandering" (Palmer, 1969, p. 4). This experimental approach, utilized in virtually every element of Sesame Street programming, must be considered a key factor in the program's apparent success.

Recently, Sesame Street has come in for criticism from various quarters (Holt, 1971; *Newsweek*, 1971). However, CTW appears to be an organization which is constructively open-minded to its critics. For example, it is reported that CTW has invited John Holt, "noted education critic" (*Newsweek*, 1971, p. 52), to become a consultant[33] to the program after he recently published an article in *The Atlantic* (Holt, 1971) attacking the program. He contends the program is similar to conventional schools which mold students into passive recipients of knowledge, instead of providing them with opportunities to be active participants in the learning process.

Given its initial apparent success, Sesame Street is likely to receive much more attention from evaluation researchers. Future evaluations would benefit from refining the principal explanatory variable utilized in the ETS study, "amount of viewing time." The adequacy of the operational definition of the variable could be questioned since there is no knowledge of factors such as circumstantial distractions which might affect quality of viewing. In addition, although amount of viewing time is a composite measure in the ETS study, it is still subject to the limitations or weaknesses of parents' reporting on their behavior and that of their children given the fact that some of the components of the measure are based on this type of information. Nevertheless, the ETS results lead to the tentative conclusion that Sesame Street is one of the more efficacious compensatory education programs.

[33] Private communication with staff member of USOE.

CONTROVERSY CONCERNING EVALUATION RESULTS

It seems there are persons with a variety of interests, each with his own reasons for wanting to achieve a successful compensatory education program. Child development theorists and educational specialists provided interpretations of the types of programs that needed to be initiated. Administrators made commitments in undertaking the implementation of programs, as did each individual teacher and aide whose efforts in the program were essential to its realization. Perhaps the largest commitment to successful compensatory education programs came from persons who realized the limited horizons of substantial numbers of minority groups.

There were only a few who thought in the early 1960's that a mounted attack on existing educational problems would bring anything but their resolution.[34] However, equally as few today can say that the success of compensatory education has been documented. There is hardly room for objecting to this statement on the basis of the widespread evidence that is available. The explanation of this state of affairs though has brought forth controversial and diametrically opposite opinions as to why evidence of success is lacking. Briefly, these controversies surround (1) the technological aspects of evaluation and (2) the theoretical aspects of program content.

As Manning (1969) has indicated, one of the functions of educational tests has been that of assessment of educational programs such that there could be a systematic basis for comparisons of the outcomes. However, there are those who argue that we are not yet capable of adequately evaluating program effects. Their position is that there is a lack of appropriate measuring devices or a lack of appropriate statistical techniques which are presently available that yield reliable and valid results—or that the limitations of often-used methods have yet to be fully appreciated and taken into consideration by evaluators.

Suchman (1969) reminds us that any evaluation implies "measurement" in some form; it is an inherent and inescapable component. Even the most subjective evaluations have embedded in them a judgment—regardless of how poorly articulated—of the merits or lack thereof that the program has when compared with an alternative program or no program at all. Both intensive and extensive research efforts have been devoted to the measurement of cognitive variables. This has been especially true of the measurement of intelligence.

However, as Jensen (1970, p. 54) notes, critics, since the early years following the development of the Binet test, have voiced concern that the available tests are inadequate measures of intellectual capacity. The controversy, the same today as then, centers on whether these tests, or any existing test of

[34] The *New York Times* (1969a) article reports that a number of researchers had persisted from the beginning in warning that these programs were not likely to bring instant success.

cognitive functioning, actually measure "real" and meaningful differences—cognitive differences—in individuals or are the observed differences meaningless and only a reflection of biases in the tests—test score differences.

This problem is further complicated if the measures are for lower social classes or ethnic minorities. Wilkerson (1970, p. 32) states that the social experiences of minority group children may be different enough that it would be inappropriate to use the same measuring devices and apply the same norms to an assessment of their performance as would be applied to the white, middle-class majority.

Of course, this controversy has been raised anew in evaluations of compensatory education programs. Earlier we discussed some of the criticisms of the quality of the measures used in the Westinghouse evaluation of Head Start. In summarizing the criticisms as they apply to Head Start evaluation, Williams and Evans (1969) state:

> The test instruments used in this study, and indeed all existing instruments for measuring cognitive and affective states of children, are primitive. They were not developed for disadvantaged populations, and they are probably so gross and insensitive that they are unable to pick up many of the real and important changes that Head Start has produced in children (p. 127).

Historically, there has not been the urgency that has been recently felt in attempting to measure important factors in preschool development, and if there is a need for more adequate measures of cognitive development, the need for such measures in the affective domain of development is many times greater. Heretofore, much of the research concerned with affective factors has been a result of academic curiosity. There has not been the powerful stimulus of acquiring knowledge in this domain in order to have a basis for modification of the usual outcome. The reader might be reminded that the impetus for the development of intelligence tests stemmed from a pragmatic need for a measure of intelligence—to detect children who were likely not to succeed in school. One of the spin-offs of interest in evaluation of compensatory education programs might be development of reliable and valid affective measures. We previously indicated the need for a self-concept quotient, for example, which would be comparable to the intelligence quotient (McDill et al., p. 12).

This lack of adequate affective tests has given rise to the valid argument that preoccupation with cognitive measures has resulted in a limited focus. Because it is a criticism which can at this time only be acknowledged by evaluators, and never refuted, it may have in fact been used by more critics than are truly concerned about the value which such measures would add to evaluation of compensatory programs. It is difficult at this point to determine the sincerity of the critics who contend that the real program effects have taken place in a change of attitudes, motivation, self-esteem, or peer group relationships and that these are the real and important changes, if only they could be rigorously measured. To be sure, there is merit in their stance, but until the much-needed data instruments are developed, we would only agree with them that important factors have not been measured, but whether these are the *most important* ones is certainly debatable.

Another aspect of the "technological" controversy concerns the design of the evaluation and what techniques are appropriate to give adequate assessment. The explanation given for a lack of significant differences in evaluation is that there has been an unwarranted application of statistical techniques which has masked real program effects. This controversy has recently generated a number of articles concerning the Westinghouse evaluation of Head Start which were covered in detail on pages 155-166. The crux of the controversy is that when true experimental designs with random allocation to control and treatment groups are not used, attempts to equate important factors (ability or social class, for instance) of the two groups either by matching on these factors or by statistical control (such as covariance), are totally inadequate and do not give a valid assessment of program effects (Campbell and Erlebacher, 1970a, b). This position concerns the necessity of adherence to appropriate evaluation designs and analysis and remains silent about whether appropriate content design has been used.

A second explanation of why compensatory education programs have failed has to do with program content. Some argue that the wrong objectives are being pursued, that is, the program content needs modification; others argue that the program needs to be extended in time—that it is too condensed and should be extended to different age levels.

One such explanation of intervention programs having failed because of the programs' having a wrong approach—that is, the program content needed modification—is presented by Baratz and Baratz (1970). According to them, intervention programs have been designed by "social pathologists" who have consistently taken the viewpoint that the attitudes and behavior of the target population are deficient rather than just different. To them programs have been developed to overcome deficits which do not exist; what is needed are programs designed to capitalize on these differences. "Then and only then can programs be created that utilize the child's differences as a means of furthering his acculturation to the mainstream while maintaining his individual identity and cultural heritage" (p. 47). While most of their disagreement with the more well-known childhood intervention programs appears to be purely semantic in nature, the importance of their argument lies in the authors' call for a different kind of program before success can be achieved.

J. McV. Hunt (1969b) calls for continued program modification of content on the basis of research. While he acknowledges that structured programs aimed at cognitive development do have some success, "Yet, we still have a long way to go before we shall have learned what an appropriate curriculum from birth to five might be" (p. 149). This idea is further elaborated in *The Challenge of Incompetence and Poverty* (J. McV. Hunt, 1969a) where he repeatedly states that compensatory education programs have been developed without having had the benefit of a firm theoretical foundation. Action has been called for before sufficient research was accomplished. Thus what is needed is continuing research on the basis of which intervention programs could be tailored which would be capable of accomplishing the goals set out for them.

Jensen (1969) presents the lack of success of compensatory education as a consequence of differences in patterns of learning. His position is that compensatory programs must take these into consideration insofar as content of program is concerned and instead of a lockstep method and uniform curricular content, there should be diversity in educational programs, such that success can be achieved via a number of educational routes.

Zimiles (1970) stands somewhat between the two camps of controversy on evaluation methods and program content. His main objection is to the present approach to evaluating progress because to him the focus is currently on only a very narrow band of cognitive functioning, such as stored information and ability to follow simple instructions. His thesis is that programs should concentrate on, and thus effectiveness should be judged by, measures of the more important functions of "process," such as development of initiative or of perseverance, which are examples of the personality characteristics crucial to developing a valid theory of intellectual growth necessary to remedy the academic and affective deficits of disadvantaged children. To do this, according to him, requires a much different approach to assessment. His contention is that this kind of evaluation would require observation under a variety of conditions and times. Although expressing the need for process evaluation, he does admit the lack of a knowledge base which hampers giving straightforward and usable alternative suggestions for program content. In other words, what he seems to be calling for is both a concentration in the programs on different cognitive functions as well as the needed measures for evaluating them.

CONCLUSIONS

Strategies for Success in Compensatory Education

The evidence regarding the effectiveness of compensatory education is ambiguous. In both previous and current work in this area, we, like Posner (1968, p. ii) and Hawkridge *et al.* (1968a)[35] have discovered few projects which demonstrated persistent and consistent results. However, it is debatable whether

[35] Hawkridge and his associates (1968a, Part 1, p. 11) conducted a literature and mail search of over a thousand compensatory education programs and discovered only approximately a hundred which met the following criteria: (a) the program report was completed in

this ambiguity is a consequence of the inadequacy of the programs or of the evaluations, for little of the evidence has been obtained from tightly conceived research designs and adequate samples, testing, and data interpretation.

Despite the paucity of documentation regarding the success of compensatory education programs, there are strategies which should be carefully considered. An extensive comparison of "successful" and "unsuccessful" programs has been conducted by Hawkridge *et al.* (1968b), and another less ambitious, yet highly informative study was made by Posner (1968).[36] In neither study do the authors claim that their samples are representative of all successful or unsuccessful compensatory education programs. However, it is our conviction that of the studies comparing several compensatory programs, these two are among the most important to date.[37]

The following is a synthesis of the recommendations made in these two studies:

a. Meticulous planning and lucidly stated program objectives.
b. Very low student-faculty ratio—individualization of instruction.
c. Instructional activities and materials that are closely tied to program objectives.
d. High intensity of treatment.
e. Rigorous training of teachers in the methods and content of the program.

The recommendations emanating from these two studies are quite congruent and are generally consistent with the observations and suggestions of a variety of persons concerned with compensatory education; for example, journalists (Pines, 1967), experts in human learning (Jensen, 1969), and academicians who developed some of the more widely acclaimed compensatory programs (Bereiter, 1967). We add our agreement to the others about these recommendations.

Perhaps the best approach to a discussion of these recommendations is to summarize a program which we strongly feel is an outstanding example of a

---

1963 or later; (b) the program was directed toward disadvantaged children at the preschool, elementary, or secondary level; (c) the enrollees gained in cognitive achievement, with the primary focus upon reading or language arts, mathematics, or IQ; and (d) the program showed evidence of research design good enough to justify some degree of confidence in the findings.

[36] Fifteen successful compensatory programs were investigated in an attempt to identify the features that made for success. Three criteria were used in selecting the programs: (a) the quality of the research design and evidence of objective results persisting over time, as defined by experienced observers of compensatory education efforts; (b) objectives differing from those of other programs selected; and (c) accessibility of programs for site visits.

[37] More detailed information on these two studies is presented in McDill *et al.* (1969, pp. 56-58).

successful compensatory education venture.[38] This is the Bereiter-Engelmann Academic Preschool Program, originating at the Institute for Research on Exceptional Children, University of Illinois. Although Bereiter is no longer at Illinois, the program has been continued, in modified form, by Engelmann and others (Bereiter, 1971; Engelmann, 1970). Bereiter has also modified and expanded his earlier approach, now known as the Conceptual Skills Program (Crittenden, 1970), at the Ontario Institute for Studies in Education. Our presentation here is restricted to the original Bereiter-Engelmann program because it is the one for which the most detailed information on characteristics and outcomes is available.

The program was launched in 1964 and had as its objectives the teaching of language, reading, and arithmetic skills to preschool children of low socioeconomic background, most of whom were blacks. More precisely, the goal of the endeavor ". . . was to achieve changes of such magnitude that there could be little doubt (statistically or otherwise) that the changes were a function of instruction" (Engelmann, 1970, p. 343). The students received equal amounts of instruction in each of the three subject areas based on task analysis and programming of tasks (Bereiter and Engelmann, 1966; Rusk, 1969). Stated differently, the designers developed specific learning objectives and instructional methods to achieve these goals. These methods involved the specification of well-defined concepts and operations for each curriculum, with strong emphasis on constructions and intensive, repetitive drills in predetermined sequences. Thus, for example, the language curriculum was based on the premise that the rules of language require understanding and generalizing analogies and was, therefore, focused on dramatizing analogies. Children attended classes for 2 hours daily, 5 days a week for the entire year, supplemented with a limited number of field trips. In classes the students were continuously and explicitly informed of what they were to learn, what the criteria of learning were, and the utility of the curriculum to the larger social world. This information was communicated through examples and careful control of teachers' responses. The students were taught in small groups (homogeneous in ability) using a highly structured curriculum emphasizing cognitive growth, not socioemotional development.[39] Both positive and negative sanctions were employed, with the empha-

[38] A second successfully conducted program which has been continuously monitored and evaluated in a search for a practical solution to the problems of educating the disadvantaged is The Early Training Project at Peabody College (Klaus and Gray, 1968; and annual reports from the project at George Peabody College for Teachers, Nashville, Tennessee). We briefly described the objectives, methods, and outcomes of this program in an earlier publication (McDill *et al.*, 1969, pp. 61-65). Space limitations preclude our presenting updated evidence on both programs. We chose the Bereiter-Engelmann program for presentation here because it appears to have been tested in more locales and compared with other types of preschool programs more frequently than the Peabody program.

[39] Bereiter (1971, p. 6) himself, states the following in discussing the controversy about preschool education focusing on the unstructured nursery approach *vs.* the more

sis on positive reinforcement using material rewards until the children were able to react directly to praise by teachers (Engelmann, 1970). Teachers were carefully selected and intensively trained in the methods, rationale, and philosophy of the program. In addition, parental involvement was an important component of the program. Meetings with parents were held in the course of the academic year to explain the program and to encourage them to accept this preschool activity as a serious academic enterprise, not a "baby-tending" service (Bereiter and Engelmann, 1966, p. 73).

Bereiter and Engelmann and others who have used this approach have consistently obtained measurable, positive results which have been presented in a number of publications. Rusk (1969) summarizes the results on three different cohorts of preschool students at the University of Illinois which showed significant positive gains over an academic year. The first group maintained its original gains during a kindergarten year,[40] and the second cohort improved upon its first year gains. Engelmann (1970) presents more detailed data on this second cohort of students. A group of 12 disadvantaged students was taught 2 years (preschool and then kindergarten). The control group consisted of 28 disadvantaged students who were placed in a traditional preschool curriculum. The assignment of subjects to the two groups was random, resulting in their being comparable on IQ and race-sex composition. The mean IQ for the experimental group increased from 95 to 121 during the 2 years, while the control group increased their IQ's only five points to a mean of 99.6. Furthermore, the standardized achievement scores of the experimental group at the end of the second year of treatment (i.e., after kindergarten) were well above national averages in reading, arithmetic, and spelling—2.6, 2.5, and 1.6 respectively.[41] The 1-year gains for the third-year cohort in IQ, reading, arithmetic, and spelling are roughly comparable to those for the second cohort.[42]

These second and third cohorts were also included as part of a larger study conducted by Karnes (1968) in Champaign-Urbana, Illinois (cited in Rusk, 1969) involving five different approaches to preschool training. Karnes concluded that the two highly structured programs, Bereiter-Engelmann's and hers, were more effective in enhancing and maintaining cognitive functioning than the other three.

Rusk's own research adds further support for the Bereiter-Engelmann "pressure cooker" (Pines, 1967) approach. The purpose of his study was to

---

structured method: ". . . I think there would be little disagreement that the Bereiter-Engelmann program stands as the most extreme and clear-cut version of a 'highly structured, detailed method of instruction.' "

[40] No control groups were used for this first cohort.

[41] The control group was not administered these three tests because they were not taught these skills in kindergarten.

[42] At the time Rusk (1969) published his summary, data were not available on the second-year performance of this third cohort, that is, the end of their kindergarten year.

determine whether in a 6-week summer curriculum, using the Bereiter-Engelmann method, Head Start children would make significant gains over students in a control group (i.e., random assignment to treatments) exposed to a traditional, unstructured approach. The pretest-posttest measures of concept acquisition for the two groups supported the conclusion that children in the academically oriented curriculum made statistically significant cognitive gains over children in the program "emphasizing social objectives and the broadening of experience with the world" (Rusk, 1969, p. 3). One of the most important aspects of Rusk's research is that these differences between the two groups were achieved in the short span of a summer. The differences were attributed primarily to the differences in the teacher-training programs.

In a recent informative paper, drawing conclusions from the evidence to date on the effectiveness of the original Bereiter-Engelmann approach, Bereiter (1971) lists five studies[43] in different localities which compared it with other types of preschool efforts (both structured and unstructured) and with no treatments. These studies employed heterogeneous samples of disadvantaged subjects and diverse criterion measures. Some of the programs with which it was compared are among the more prominent intensive efforts developed during the last decade which have shown success and which we referred to earlier in this paper (e.g., Peabody Early Training Project and Perry Preschool Project). With only one partial exception, each of the studies employed random assignment of students to the treatment and control groups.

Bereiter draws several important generalizations from a synthesis of results from these five studies. First, the Bereiter-Engelmann program has significantly more effect on IQ and achievement than the unstructured child-centered approach, "but not necessarily more impact than other programs with a strong instructional emphasis" (p. 6). He does not take the position that the various structured programs are identical in their accomplishments. To the contrary, he takes the reassuring and plausible position that the differences in outcome are a function of differences in content of instruction. Thus, his program, which places heavy emphasis on verbal reasoning and problem-solving, appears to result in larger IQ gains than the other structured programs which show larger, immediate effects on such criteria as reading readiness (Karnes) and Peabody Picture Vocabulary (Peabody Early Training Project).

Second, the various structured programs are superior to the cultural enrichment programs in transferring skills to later school learning, but again no one of these structured efforts stands out as a better predictor of later school success than the others.

Third, the traditional approach appears to be characterized by a much lower frequency of teaching acts of any kind than any of the structured

---

[43] One of the five was the Karnes study (1968) discussed above.

programs. Thus, he describes the traditional approach as one that is more "custodial" and less educational—not one which represents a different approach to teaching but one which involves a lower order of pedagogical effort.[44]

From this brief description and presentation of results of various evaluations of the Bereiter-Engelmann program, it seems evident that it contains the essential features which characterize successful programs according to Hawkridge and associates and Posner. However, one might detect what is an apparent exception involving Posner's recommendation that compensatory education funds should not be concentrated on any one age group: Bereiter and Engelmann have been classified as belonging to the "cognitive" school whose members purportedly adhere to the position that disadvantaged children deprived of early sensory stimulation are unlikely to fulfill their inherent academic potential. To this assumed disagreement there are two meaningful responses. First, it may be answered that the high school students in some of the successful programs described by Posner may not have been disadvantaged to the extent of those in different samples utilizing the Bereiter-Engelmann or other stuctured, preschool approaches. There is some evidence to suggest this is true. Take for example, the Homework Helper's program in New York City which both Hawkridge and Posner label as successful. In this program, "disadvantaged" high school students who comprised the treatment group were used as tutors for elementary and junior high students. The experimental group achieved significantly higher gains on standardized reading achievement tests than the controls, presumably as consequences of being trained and supervised by master teachers and of being provided economic incentives. It is noteworthy that the average reading level of both the experimental and treatment groups was approximately at the tenth grade.

Second, even though Bereiter is often labeled as a member of the "cognitive" school, he certainly does not adhere to the position that there is rigorous scientific evidence that early sensory deprivation places the child at such a disadvantage that later educational experiences in the elementary years (or even beyond) cannot remediate his deficiencies: "But if it is true that an effective kindergarten program can overcome differences in preschool experience, then it may also be true that an effective first-grade program can overcome differences in kindergarten experience, and so on up to some unknown point where the weight of past experience tips the scales" (Bereiter, 1971, p. 19). One cannot afford to reject promising programs out of hand just because they are not focused on an early maturational level. We would merely buttress Bereiter's position by stressing that at this time compensatory education and its evaluation are an art, not a science.

---

[44] We would add parenthetically that it is small wonder that Head Start evaluations have shown the program to have produced such limited success given its "traditional," "child-centered," or "cultural-enrichment" emphasis.

Given the fact that today the design and implementation of compensatory education programs are not precise, systematic efforts must be made to strengthen their knowledge base. One of the crucial elements in obtaining such knowledge is rigorous evaluation of program effectiveness which can be used to modify programs so as to achieve their objectives. This is the final point of this paper to which we now direct our attention.

Strategies for Evaluation

It seems likely that funds will continue to be provided for compensatory education, as well as for other programs directed at the disadvantaged. The notion that innovation in education is self-justifying is becoming accepted in the United States (Posner, 1968, p. 30), and the various poverty programs spawned in the last 10 years or so have become an integral part of federal, state, and local governmental agencies. To eliminate them might not be politically feasible; they have gained a foothold in the bureaucracies (Moynihan, 1969, pp. 156-157). Our future efforts should be aimed not at determining whether an entire program, such as Head Start, should be abolished because overall it is unsuccessful, for such programs are most likely here to stay. Rather, we should attempt to answer the question of which of the alternative methods appears most successful: For example, are year-round Head Start programs more effective than those lasting only for the summer?[45]

In compensatory education we are still at the stage of trying to identify the problems and their causes. Simultaneously, we are in the embarrassing position of applying solutions and cures to those still unknown problems. Social pressures dictate that we be open to the possibility of finding a workable solution before we understand the mechanisms by which the solution works.

Given both the current ambiguity in the area of special education and the urgency of social forces seeking remedies, we feel that considerable flexibility is required in program approaches. Our advocacy is incompatible with strictly scientific evaluation. We are aware of the incompatibility. Even more, we are stating our approval of it.

The dilemma which we wish to tolerate is that of maximizing program flexibility and at the same time maximizing our knowledge of which is effecting change through evaluation procedures. Where evaluation research shows what will work and will not work, its recommendations should be utilized in program design. Where research shows little or nothing concerning the variables to be manipulated, evaluation research will learn from innovative programs that appear to have worked, in order to pass on this knowledge to other program areas.

---

[45] Evidence from the Westinghouse study (Cicirelli et al., 1969) indicates that full-year Head Start programs are superior to summer programs. It recommends that summer programs be converted into full-year or extended year programs.

We would suggest, then, that a number of programs continue to be locally based and funded and staffed with project directors who might be long on ideas and experience but short on methods for justifying the ideas. It has to be recognized, of course, that such relatively independent projects, established to promote creative venturing, constitute a high-risk activity. The risk lies in the fact that the yield from such programs is apt to be quite low, that funds may appear to be wasted. But that yield is also more apt to be one of finding a workable solution without being distracted by details accompanying the minute specifications of the causes of program success. The rationale for these high-risk programs is that they are more likely to shortcut the time-consuming academic approach—including the built-in evaluation—and arrive at a solution which can then be subjected to questions as to why it works.

Taking into consideration the dilemma which we chose to tolerate, namely, that of wanting both sophisticated, carefully evaluated projects on which to base decisions concerning existence and adjustments of individual projects, and at the same time encouraging high-risk projects which maximize individual directors' innovative abilities, we suggested that the variable with which we are dealing is program specificity. The following continuum is a reasonable reflection of the way in which we have conceptualized the situation.

That is, programs which are not highly structured present difficulties for evaluation research, but they also present the opportunity for maximum innovation. At the other end, highly specific programs yield a great deal of evaluative information, but their structure precludes the flexibility necessary for innovation.

In consideration of the dilemma discussed above, we would like to encourage three lines of action. First, as part of fund allocation and jurisdiction, a group of programs should be sponsored in which the method of evaluation is specified by an evaluation committee. This would give the evaluation committee a group of controlled programs from which they could maximize the yield of data of the type best suited to answer specific substantive questions while minimizing the interference of methodological weaknesses in the interpretation of the results. Such a pool of control programs would be small and the programs themselves viewed as part of the evaluation process. Perhaps the number of control programs would never be large enough to satisfy researchers' demands for untangling the multitude of substantive questions involved, but even a limited attempt would be a step in the right direction and scientific parsimony might result from administrative parsimony.

Second, a small number of programs should be funded at the other end of the program specificity continuum, programs which would be purely speculative and knowingly of high risk. The "high risk" refers to the low probability in program effectiveness payoff. However, the programs could proceed without excessive and slow evaluation. That is, given the social urgency of compensatory education, we think it in the public interest to find solutions quickly, and this means funding, on a small scale, novel, untried programs which do not have to come under immediate evaluational appraisal—giving the innovator a chance to observe his idea in action and to adjust the program on the basis of these "subjective" data before evaluators emerge onto the scene with a more rigorous evaluation plan.

This leaves the large majority of programs in the third area, a compromise area, where any evaluation has to be adjusted to fit in with the ongoing program procedures.

Of course, there are social scientists concerned with the methodology of evaluation who would disagree with this last point, for it implies the use of evaluative methods such as cross-sectional field surveys,[46] ex post facto designs, and some types of longitudinal designs involving the use of statistical techniques for which the data fail to meet strictly the assumptions of the tests. Our reaction to such a position is succinctly stated by Cicirelli et al. (1970, p. 125):

> To rule out ex post facto studies, for example, is to virtually guarantee that the use of social science research for policy decision-making will be even less than it is now. In the real world of government social action programs, decisions are going to be made either in the presence or absence of information. If the social scientist hopes to increase at all the rationality of these decisions he will often have to depart from ideal evaluation requirements. Only rarely if ever, for example, will it be possible in the evaluation of ongoing social action programs to arrange for the random assignment of subjects to experimental and control groups; and time pressures will often make it necessary to forego longitudinal measurements. Of course, such compromises involve risks and the greater the compromises the more likely it is that results will be in error.

Certainly, the overall objective is the moving of programs from the left hand of the continuum toward the right hand side, where we can clearly specify the program and the conditions under which it will be successful.

The foregoing is predicated on the belief that a variety of approaches to compensatory education be planned and tested. It appears to us that no other

---

[46] For useful suggestions about utilizing the field survey for an effective evaluation tool, see Light and Smith (1970).

strategy can hope to extricate compensatory education from the confusion in which it now struggles. At present, compensatory education programs are genuinely burdened with proving their own *raison d'être.*

REFERENCES

Ball, S., and Bogatz, G.A. (1970). *A Summary of the Major Findings in "The First Year of Sesame Street: An Evaluation."* Educational Testing Service, Princeton, New Jersey.

Baratz, S.S., and Baratz, J.C. (1970). Early childhood intervention: The social science base of institutional racism. *Harvard Educational Review* **40**; 29-50.

Bereiter, C. (1967). Instructional planning in early compensatory education. *Phi Delta Kappan* **48**; 355-59.

Bereiter, C. (1971). *An Academic Preschool for Disadvantaged Children: Conclusions from Evaluation Studies.* Paper presented at the Hyman Blumberg Memorial Symposium on Research in Early Childhood Education, Johns Hopkins University, Baltimore, Maryland.

Bereiter, C., and Engelmann, S. (1966). *Teaching Disadvantaged Children in the Preschool.* Prentice-Hall, Englewood Cliffs, New Jersey.

Bloom, B.S. (1964). *Stability and Change in Human Characteristics.* Wiley, New York.

Boyd, J. (1966). *Project Head Start, Summer 1966: Facilities-Resources of Head Start Centers.* Educational Testing Service, Princeton, New Jersey.

Campbell, D.T., and Erlebacher, A. (1970a). How regression artifacts in quasi-experimental evaluations can mistakenly make compensatory education look harmful. In *Disadvantaged Child*, (J. Hellmuth, ed.), Vol. 3. Brunner/Mazel, New York.

Campbell, D.T., and Erlebacher, A. (1970b). Reply to the replies. In *Disadvantaged Child* (J. Hellmuth, ed.), Vol. 3. Brunner/Mazel, New York.

Children's Television Workshop. (n.d.). Brochure printed by CTW, New York.

Cicirelli, V.G. (1970). The relevance of the regression artifact problem to the Westinghouse-Ohio evaluation of head start: Reply to Campbell and Erlebacher. In *Disadvantaged Child* (J. Hellmuth, ed.), Vol. 3. Brunner/Mazel, New York.

Cicirelli, V.G. et al. (1969). *The Impact of Head Start. An Evaluation of the Effects of Head Start on Children's Cognitive and Affective Development*, Vol. 1. Report to the U.S. Office of Economic Opportunity by Westinghouse Learning Corporation and Ohio University.

Cicirelli, V. G. et al. (1970). The impact of head start: A reply to the report analysis. *Harvard Educational Review* **40**; 105-29.

Cohen, B.R., and Yonkers, A.H. (1969). *Evaluation of the War on Poverty, Education Programs.* Research Management Corporation.

Coleman, J.S., et al. (1966). *Equality of Educational Opportunity.* US Govt. Printing Office, Washington, D.C.

Crittenden, B.S. (1970). A critique of the Bereiter-Engelmann preschool program. *School Review* **78**; 145-67.

Culhane, J. (1970). Report card on Sesame Street. *New York Times Magazine* May 24.

Engelmann, S. (1970). The effectiveness of direct instruction on IQ performance and achievement in reading and arithmetic. In *Disadvantaged Child* (J. Hellmuth, ed.), Vol. 3. Brunner/Mazel, New York.

Evans, J.W. (1969). Head Start: Comment on the criticisms. In *Britannica Review of American Education.*

Evans, J.W., and Schiller, J. (1970). How preoccupation with possible regression artifacts can lead to a faulty strategy for the evaluation of social action programs: A reply to Campbell and Erlebacher. In *Disadvantaged Child* (J. Hellmuth, ed.), Vol. 3. Brunner/Mazel, New York.

Froomkin, J. (1968). *Students and Buildings*, Rep. OE-50054. U.S. Office of Education.

Gardenhire, J.F. (1968). *Study of College Retention of 1965 & 1966 UPWARD BOUND Bridge Students.* Report to the U.S. Office of Economic Opportunity by Educational Associates, Inc., Washington, D.C.

Glass, G.V. (1970). *Data Analysis of the 1968-69 Survey of Compensatory Education (Title I),* Final Report on Grant No. OEG 8-8-961860 4003-(058). U.S. Office of Education, Washington, D.C.

Greenleigh Associates. (1970). *Upward Bound 1965-69: A History and Synthesis of Data on the Program in the Office of Economic Opportunity.* Report to the U.S. Office of Economic Opportunity, Washington, D.C.

Hawkridge, D.G.; Chalupsky, A.B.; and Roberts, A.O.H. (1968a). *A Study of Selected Exemplary Programs for the Education of Disadvantaged Children.* Final Report on Project No. 089013. U.S. Office of Education, Washington D.C.

Hawkridge, D.G., Tallmadge, G.K., and Larsen, J.K. (1968b). *Foundations for Success in Educating Disadvantaged Children*, Final Report on Project No. 107143. U.S. Office of Education, Washington, D.C.

Headstart Childhood Research Information Bulletin. (1969). Vol. 1. National Laboratory on Early Childhood Education, ERIC Center, Washington, D.C.

Holt, J. (May 1971). Big bird meet Dick and Jane. *Atlantic,* pp. 72-78.

Hunt, D.E., and Hardt, R.H. (1966-1968). *Characterization of UPWARD BOUND Summer 1966; Characterization of UPWARD BOUND Academic Year 1967; Characterization of UPWARD BOUND 1967-1968.* Syracuse University Youth Development Center, Syracuse, New York.

Hunt, D.E., and Hardt, R.H. (1969). The effect of upward bound programs on the attitudes, motivation, and academic achievement of Negro students. *Journal of Social Issues* **25**; 117-29.

Hunt, J. McV. (1961). *Intelligence and Experience.* Ronald Press, New York.

Hunt, J. McV. (1969a). *The Challenge of Incompetence and Poverty.* University of Illinois Press, Urbana.

Hunt, J. McV. (1969b). Has compensatory education failed? In *Environment, Heredity, and Intelligence.* Compiled from the *Harvard Educational Review,* Reprint Ser. No. 2.

Jensen, A.R. (1970). Another look at culture-fair testing. In *Disadvantaged Child* (J. Hellmuth, ed.), Vol. 3. Brunner/Mazel, New York.

Jensen, A.R. (1969). How much can we boost IQ and scholastic achievement? *Harvard Educational Review* **39**; 1-123.

Karnes, M.B. (1968). *A Research Program to Determine the Effects of Various Preschool Intervention Programs on the Development of Disadvantaged Children and the Strategic Age for Such Intervention.* Paper presented at A.E.R.A. meeting, Chicago, Illinois.

Katz, I. (1964). Review of evidence relating to effects of desegregation on the intellectual performance of Negroes. *American Psychologist* **19**, 381-99.

Klaus, R.A., and Gray, S.W. (1968). The early training project for disadvantaged children: A report after five years. *Monographs of the Society for Research in Child Development* **33**, No. 4.

Kornegay, F.A. (1968a). College enrollment of former upward bound students: A profile and summary. *Idea Exchange* **3**, No. 11, 24-26.

Kornegay, F.A. (1968b). *Sample Study of 1967 Bridge Students into Spring Semester 1968.* Report to the U.S. Office of Economic Opportunity by Educational Associates, Inc., Washington, D.C.

Light, R.J., and Smith, P.V. (1970). Choosing a future: Strategies for designing and evaluating new programs. *Harvard Educational Review* **40**, 1-28.

McDavid, J.W., *et al.* (n.d.). *Project Headstart Evaluation and Research Summary, 1965-1967.* U.S. Office of Economic Opportunity, Project Headstart, Division of Research and Evaluation, Washington, D.C.

McDill, E.L., McDill, M.S., and Sprehe, J.T. (1969). *Strategies for Success in Compensatory Education.* Johns Hopkins Press, Baltimore, Maryland.

Madow, W.G. (1969). Head start: Methodological critique. In *Britannica Review of American Education.*

Manning, W.H. (1969). The functions and uses of educational measurement. *Proceedings of the 1969 Invitational Conference on Testing Problems: Toward a Theory of Achievement Measurement.* Princeton, N.J.: Educational testing service.

Miller, S.M., *et al.* (1970). Creaming the poor. *Transaction* **7**, 38-45.

Moynihan, D.P. (1969). *Maximum Feasible Misunderstanding.* Free Press, Glencoe, Illinois.

New Republic. (1969). How head a head start? April 26, pp. 8-9.

Newsweek. (1971). 'Sesame' under attack. May 24, p. 52.

New York Times. (1969a). Dispute over value of head start. April 20, p. 11E.

New York Times. (1969b). Finch criticizes head start study. April 25, p. 22.

Palmer, E. (Aug.-Sept. 1969). Can television really teach? Reprint from *American Education,* pp. 1-5.

Pines, M. (1967). *Revolution in Learning: The Years from Birth to Six.* Harper, New York.

Posner, J. (1968). *Evaluation of "Successful" Projects in Compensatory Education,* Occas. Pap. No. 8. U.S. Office of Education, Office of Planning and Evaluation, Washington, D.C.

Rusk, B.A. (1969). *An Evaluation of a Six-Week Headstart Program Using an Academically Oriented Curriculum: Canton, 1967.* Paper presented at A.E.R.A. meeting, Los Angeles, California.

Samuels, B. (1970). *The First Year of Sesame Street: A Summary of Audience Surveys,* Vol. IV, Final Report on Grant No. OEG-0-8-080475-3743(007). U.S. Office of Education, Washington, D.C.

Saunders, H.R., and Jones, S.S. (1968). *A Study of Financial Need of Upward Bound Students: The 1968-1969 Bridge Class.* American College Testing Program.

Schiller, J., and Evans, J. (1968). *Where We Stand in the Evaluation of Head Start* (Mimeo). Office of Research, Plans, Programs, and Evaluation, U.S. Office of Economic Opportunity, Washington, D.C.

Shea, P. (1967). *Upward Bound Early Progress, Problems and Promise in Educational Escape from Poverty.* Report to the U.S. Office of Economic Opportunity.

Smith, M.S., and Bissell, J.S. (1970). Report analysis: The impact of head start. *Harvard Educational Review* **40**, 51-104.

Stanley, J.C. (1970). Review of E.L. McDill *et al.* (1969). *American Educational Research Journal* **7**, 649-51.

Suchman, E.A. (1969). Evaluating educational programs. *Urban Review* **3**, 15-17.

U.S. Office of Economic Opportunity. (n.d.) *An Evaluation of Upward Bound: Findings and Conclusions.* Office of Economic Opportunity, Washington, D.C.

White, S. (1970). The national impact study of head start. In *Disadvantaged Child* Vol. 3 (J. Hellmuth, ed), Vol. 3. Brunner/Mazel, New York.

Wilkerson, D.A. (1970). Compensatory education: Defining the issues. In *Disadvantaged Child* (J. Hellmuth, ed.), Vol. 3. Brunner/Mazel, New York.

Williams, W., and Evans, J.W. (1969). The politics of evaluation: The case of head start. *Annals of the American Academy of Political and Social Sciences* **385**, 118-32.

Zimiles, H. (1970). Has evaluation failed compensatory education? In *Disadvantaged Child* (J. Hellmuth, ed.), Vol. 3. Brunner/Mazel, New York.

9

EVALUATING FEDERAL MANPOWER

PROGRAMS: Notes and Observations*

Thomas K. Glennan, Jr.

INTRODUCTION

Five years have passed since the signing of the Economic Opportunity Act and an explicit declaration of a War on Poverty. Even more time has elapsed since the first specific social action programs were undertaken in an effort to help the poor or ameliorate the adverse consequences of the workings of our economic and social system. Much is known about the inputs to these programs. We know how much has been spent. We have a fairly good idea of how many people have participated in these programs and the characteristics of these people. We know remarkably little about the effects of these programs. Indeed, in many instances, we do not know or cannot agree about the dimensions by which to measure these effects.

The experience of the present and past social action programs should be the best source of information to guide our future programs. Programs that are "working" should be sustained or expanded. Programs that are "not working"

*First printed as RAND Corp. memorandum, RM-5743-OEO, Santa Monica, California, 1969. The research reported herein was performed under contract with the Office of Economic Opportunity, Executive Office of the President, Washington, D.C., 20506. The opinions expressed herein are those of the author and should not be construed as representing the opinions or policy of any agency of the United States Government.

should either be curtailed or restructured. Within a program, the most effective features should be emphasized and the least effective discarded or modified. The most effective projects should be expanded, the least effective cut back or reoriented. The performance of new programs, suggested by research or demonstration activities, should be compared with that of existing programs.[1]

In fact, few systematic efforts to extract information from existing programs and demonstration activities have been made. Those that have been made have generally had severe conceptual and methodological shortcomings. As a result, the decisions about program design and relative funding of these programs have usually been based upon hunches, anecdotal evidence, and political bargaining. Perhaps this is the best that could have been expected. Certainly a well-defined and reliable scheme for extracting timely information on program effects did not and does not exist. Evaluation of social action programs is an art, and a not very well developed one at that.

It is interesting and useful to speculate on the reasons for the failure to pursue evaluation efforts more vigorously in the earlier days of the War on Poverty. Clearly, the initial efforts of OEO were, and had to be focused on, initiating a number of large and ill-defined programs. It was a time for innovators, activists, and operators—not evaluators—and rightly so. In the first few years the programs were changing rapidly as the operators gained greater intuitive understanding of the possibilities and limitations of the program designs. Had evaluations been undertaken, they would have been largely irrelevant by the time they were completed.

From the beginning, OEO had an Office of Research, Plans, Programs and Evaluation (RPP/E) which had an ill-defined mandate to evaluate programs. In its initial years, the evaluation function of the Office of RPP/E was lodged in the Programming Division. In large part, the evaluations that were performed were carried out by the programs themselves although on occasions the Office of RPP/E took a strong lead in initiating particular studies. The Office did place considerable emphasis on developing information systems, anticipating that after a few years, when program operations had settled down, these systems would provide information that would support studies of program impact. In retrospect, this may have been a mistake. The information systems, developed without much guidance from "specialists" in evaluation, have failed to provide adequate and reliable information for studying the effectiveness of the programs.

Since most of the evaluation work was carried out by the programs themselves, it was natural that the evaluators focused on gathering information

---

[1] The term program in this paper is used to designate a collection of local projects that are developed and managed according to a set of guidelines mandated by the federal government. The Job Corps or the Neighborhood Youth Corps are examples of manpower programs.

that would support program improvements. They sought out projects that seemed to be functioning smoothly, were using innovative techniques, or were experiencing great difficulty. The insights gained, usually in quite informal ways, were used to guide program operators in making changes in guidelines, in seeking new local sponsors or in justifying the program to Congress and the public. With one or two exceptions, the analysts did not question the existence of any given program or whether the objectives of their program could be better achieved by other existing or potential programs. If they had, it is unlikely that the program operators would have chosen to continue supporting such analytical efforts.

This is not intended as a criticism. It is unrealistic and probably undesirable to ask a program organization to question its own existence. It is even more unrealistic to ask it to do so in its initial years. But it is not unrealistic to ask that someone in the government attempt to determine the relative effectiveness of the multitudes of federal programs and make decisions on which ones to enlarge or cut back or to specify where totally new approaches are needed. Some individuals within the Office of RPP/E felt that this function in OEO should be strengthened and that RPP/E had the mandate to do so.

In the fall of 1966, a number of evaluations of program effectiveness were initiated by RPP/E. In the course of attempts to carry out these analyses, it became clear that the kind of information required to support decisions about which programs should be continued and expanded and which should be cut back or changed was not being generated. The next summer, a separate division of RPP/E was set up and, after several months, procedures dividing evaluation responsibilities between RPP/E and the programs themselves were developed. The OEO Instruction setting out these procedures suggested that there were three kinds of evaluations:

> Evaluations are categorized into three major types. The *first* is the overall assessment of program impact and effectiveness where the emphasis is on determining the extent to which programs are successful in achieving basic objectives. The *second* is the evaluation of the relative effectiveness of different program strategies and variables where the emphasis is on determining which of the alternative techniques for carrying out a program are most productive. The *third* is the evaluation of individual projects where the emphasis is on assessing managerial and operational efficiency.[2]

The project monitoring or "Type III" evaluation obviously should be the responsibility of the program manager. This function provides him with information needed to enable him to carry out his day-to-day management tasks. "Type II" evaluations are intended to support improvements in overall program effectiveness by identifying superior project designs, curricula, or types of project personnel. This information can be used to modify program guidelines or to suggest better procedures to project directors. Because information needed to

---

[2] OEO Instruction Number 72-8, March 6, 1968.

structure such evaluations should be available at the program level and because the resulting information will be used by program managers, responsibility for Type II evaluations should also rest with the program manager.

Responsibility for overall impact or "Type I" evaluations is assigned to RPP/E. Type I evaluations are intended to help determine the relative impact or effectiveness of national programs as a (partial) basis of allocating resources to programs. A minimum of 1% of program funds is to be set aside for evaluation, with one-sixth of 1% being used by RPP/E for Type I evaluation. Although RPP/E has not yet completed a sufficient number of evaluations to support a final judgment, it appears that the establishment of the evaluation division represents an important step toward a more systematic examination of program experiences as a basis for program planning.

But the organizational history just discussed should not be cited as the sole explanation for the failure to mount more systematic evaluation efforts. The fact is that evaluation in practice falls far short of the ideal. It is easy to say that an agency should determine the impact of its programs. It is extraordinarily difficult to do so. Surely a part of the reason that more systematic impact evaluations have not been mounted is the lack of confidence that they can be mounted. The quantification of program outcomes and the measurement of these outcomes pose significant conceptual and practical problems. Members of poverty populations are increasingly hard to survey.[3] The impact of many of the programs is expected to be felt only over a period of years.

This chapter deals with evaluation and its potential use in the planning process. In particular, the focus is on the use of evaluation in manpower programs. Conceptually, this is one of the easiest areas of the War on Poverty in which to do evaluation. The purpose of manpower programs is to help people obtain better jobs, or maybe just any job. The increase in a man's or a woman's income as a result of participating in a program would seem a pretty good (even if incomplete) measure of the program outcome. Moreover, there is a sizable literature in economics dealing with the value of training and education that provides the theoretical underpinnings for studies to determine the benefits and costs of training. Despite these favorable factors, none of the overall impact evaluations that have been done to date should serve as a basis for planning future program activities. The few overall impact evaluations that have been completed are characterized by the use of very poor data and inconsistent analytical assumptions. This chapter will suggest ways in which evaluations can be made more relevant and useful. In the next section a benefit-cost framework for evaluation is developed. Following this, several methodological problems

---

[3] In large part, this is the result of the intensive surveying that has already occurred in ghetto areas. Growing militancy among blacks has also increased the resistance to being interviewed.

associated with and limiting the quality of program evaluations are examined. Program evaluation efforts are related to the planning process, placing particular emphasis on whether straightforward impact (Type I) evaluations can constitute a useful input to this process. Conclusions and suggestions for potential program evaluators are contained in the final section.

This chapter treats the role of program evaluation in planning. Its tone will often seem to imply that program funding levels and program designs should be based solely upon evaluation data. This clearly is not and cannot be the case. Planning decisions are the result of a complex bargaining process. The outcome of such a bargaining process will reflect many factors, only one of which is information concerning past program performance. This is as it should be. Even the most sophisticated evaluations provide but crude guides to action. As will be seen, they consider only a part of the program outcomes. They must usually utilize less than adequate data. They ignore many of the factors that must go into decisions on program funding levels and designs. Thus, program evaluations must be viewed as only one of a number of inputs to the planning process.

But two points need to be made. It is my judgment that program evaluations can be improved and, if improved, should play a larger role in the planning process. Second, the process of carrying out evaluation projects is likely to have a useful effect upon program planners. It can force a more careful examination of program objectives, as well as provide clues about how to improve program operations.

BENEFIT-COST EVALUATION OF MANPOWER PROGRAMS

In this section, a number of issues concerning the measurement and interpretation of benefits and costs are considered. For the moment, it is assumed that the major purpose for carrying out benefit-cost evaluations is to support the allocation of resources among a group of national manpower programs. A subsidiary purpose may be the justification of requests for additional funds to be utilized by manpower programs. Evaluations carried out for this purpose fit into the category earlier referred to as Type I evaluations.

If all programs have exactly the same objectives, it is fairly simple, conceptually, to specify the questions that evaluations should answer. Suppose, for example, that the sole objective of all manpower programs is to increase the national output. If this is the case, the evaluations should determine which program is providing the greatest increase in national output per dollar spent.

To accomplish this, the economist utilizes a form of analysis called benefit-cost analysis which attempts to support judgments concerning the economic efficiency of a program. The effects of the program must be translated into increments in national or collective output. This increment in output is then compared with the costs. The program producing the greatest increment of output per dollar is the most efficient in the sense that the increase in national output per dollar of input is greater than that of all other programs. Presumably, if resources are shifted from other programs to this program, total output will be increased.

Most program evaluations have attempted to obtain a measure of total program benefits or perhaps an average benefit per trainee. These evaluations have not focused on the problem of predicting the effects of an increase or decrease in program funding. Only under rather exceptional circumstances could measures of total or average benefits and costs be used to predict the effects of expanding or contracting a program.

The relevant benefit-cost ratios are those associated with marginal increments (or decrements) in the funding of these alternatives. Consider two programs, Program X and Program Y. Suppose a tentative decision has been made to add $50 million to these two programs and the problem is to choose whether to add it to X or to Y. The problem is not to determine whether the current benefit-cost ratio is higher for one or the other program but to estimate the benefit associated with adding resources to one or the other program. The problem is illustrated in Fig. 1 where the relation between benefits and costs for a program is portrayed. Suppose the program is currently operating at a level represented by cost C and benefits B. The average benefit-cost ratio is given by

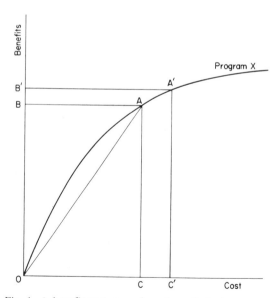

Fig. 1. A benefit-cost curve for a hypothetical program.

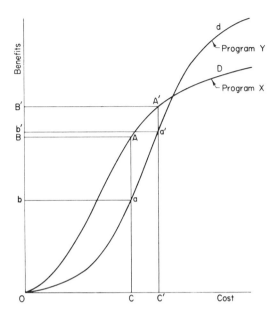

Fig. 2. Benefit-cost curves for two programs.

the slope of the line segment OA or $\frac{OB}{OC}$. If the decision is whether or not to add resources equal to CC′, the relevant (marginal) benefit-cost ratio is that represented by the slope of AA′ which is equal to $\frac{BB'}{CC'}$. The use of the average benefit-cost ratio could be quite misleading. This is illustrated in Fig. 2 in which two programs are compared. At current funding levels (C for both programs), Program X, represented by line OAA′D, has a higher average benefit-cost ratio than the program represented by Oaa′d. That is, $\frac{OB}{OC}$ is greater than $\frac{Ob}{OC}$. However, if the same increment of resources (CC′) is added to both programs, the incremental or marginal benefit-cost ratio is greater for Y than for program X. We see that $\frac{bb'}{CC'}$ is greater than $\frac{BB'}{CC'}$; thus, the increment of resources should be allocated to program Y.[4]

There are a number of reasons for expecting marginal benefit-cost ratios to differ from average benefit-cost ratios. For example, as a youth program is enlarged it may reach deeper into the ranks of the disadvantaged. Such youths may require more services in order to achieve a given increment in income, or putting it another way, they may derive less benefit for a given quantity of services.

[4] The optimal allocation of resources occurs when the marginal benefits associated with a small increase in expenditures are the same for all programs. In the example shown in Fig. 2, the allocations shown are not optimal. In general, we have insufficient information to describe these curves accurately.

If a program requires administrative and professional personnel who are in scarce supply, increases in program activity levels should be associated with either the hiring of lower quality personnel or the necessity of paying more for equivalent quality personnel. If the added personnel are of lower quality, the benefits to program enrollees associated with specific number of hours of professional services should decrease.

To my knowledge, no explicit attempts to estimate marginal benefit-cost ratios have been made for social action programs. However, the possibility that there will be decreasing marginal returns to additional investments in a program is frequently recognized. One reason for the steady movement toward on-the-job training programs rather than institutional training programs is the recognition that there is a shortage of high quality vocational teachers available in the nation's public school programs, whereas industry potentially has many skilled workers capable of teaching the necessary skills in their plants.

A crude analysis, closer to the type considered in this chapter has been carried out by the Job Corps. Experience has shown that any increase in Job Corps enrollment would be likely to consist largely of 16-year-olds. It appears to be difficult or impossible to attract increased numbers of older youths. The Job Corps appears to be less successful in dealing with 16-year-olds than with older youth. They stay a shorter time. Because there are a large number of initial costs (for health services, clothing and testing, and so forth) the cost per month of Job Corps experience for a 16-year-old youth is higher than for other age groups. Since expected benefits are thought to increase with the length of the Job Corps experience, the benefits accruing to 16-year-olds are expected to be less. Hence, the marginal benefit-cost ratio for an increase in Job Corps activities should be lower than its average benefit-cost ratio.

This example suggests that attempts to measure the costs and benefits for different segments of the client population may have a significant payoff for policy planning activities. Such data would support not only decisions concerning gross resource allocation among programs, but also decisions on program guidelines and target populations. If information on costs and benefits associated with providing services to different segments of the population were available, guidance could be provided which, if followed, would increase the benefits associated with the program, while holding costs constant. In terms of Figs. 1 and 2, this would be equivalent to shifting the benefit versus cost curves upward. Such evaluations would combine the functions of Type I impact evaluations and Type II evaluations aimed at program improvement. This combined evaluation might be called a Type I-plus evaluation and will be discussed in the section on the relationship of program evaluation to the planning process.

Distribution of Costs and Benefits
Among Economic and Social Classes

Statements about the economic efficiency of a social program do not take into account who pays for the program and who receives its benefits.[5] Clearly, in the poverty program the issue of who receives benefits is a crucial one. The introduction of these issues complicates benefit-cost analysis because of the necessity of weighing gains and losses of one group (the poor) against the gains and losses of another group (the non-poor).

When programs have objectives that go beyond simply maximizing the return on public investments irrespective of who receives the benefits, a simple benefit-cost ratio is an insufficient indicator of program outcome. Several alternative approaches to this problem have been suggested. Perhaps the most frequently advanced idea is the use of a system of weights reflecting the relative value society places on increases in the well-being of specific groups in society. For example, a given increase in income to very poor families might be considered more significant or valuable than a similar increase in income to a "barely" poor family. An increase in the income of the barely poor is in turn more valuable than a similar increase in income of the nonpoor. Or increases in the income of Negroes may be valued more highly by society than increases in the income of whites. If such a set of weights could be specified, a new figure of merit for the program's impact could be formed that consisted of the weighted sum of the benefits to differing segments of society. A similar weighted sum of the costs would also be needed.

It is difficult to conceive of a feasible way to arrive at an explicit set of weights. Clearly, however, a set of weights is implicit in the actions of Congress and various executive departments.[6] Because of the difficulty in arriving at a set of weights, the best the evaluator can do may be to simply portray the costs and benefits of a program for different subgroups in society. Thus, for example, analysis of poverty program outcomes might consider two groups, the poor and the nonpoor (roughly speaking, these latter are the taxpayers). The benefits to the poor would include increased earnings resulting from program participation plus other increases in income from sources such as welfare or training allowances. Costs to the poor would include earnings foregone while in training plus out-of-pocket expenses for transportation or baby-sitting services.

---

[5] In many respects, my comments on treatment of distributional objectives parallels that of Rothenberg. See Rothenberg (1967), particularly Chapter II.

[6] For a discussion of the need to integrate distributional effects and efficiency in assessing the cost and benefits of a program, see Weisbrod (1968).

For the taxpayers the primary benefit of the program is probably the satisfaction that is derived from seeing the welfare of the poor improved. The value of this satisfaction is hard to determine. However, there are also tangible benefits. The increased earnings of the poor may be accompanied by a decrease in welfare payments, by decreases in crime against the taxpayer or more generally, decreases in the cost of social services from levels that would have existed in the absence of the program. The cost to the taxpayer is the cost of the program including training allowances (if any), net of decreases in other payments such as welfare that result from the existence of the program.

When the outcomes of programs are portrayed in terms of their consequences for various segments of society, many of the questions concerning the treatment of elements of costs and benefits are simplified. Transfer payments such as welfare payments, for example, are usually not considered either a cost or a benefit in benefit-cost analyses because such a transfer simply represents a shift of consumption from one group to another. No consumption is foregone by society as a whole. However, it is clear that such transfers have significant consequences for different groups in society and form an important effect of most social action programs.

Although a tabulation of costs and benefits to various segments of society is important, it is clear that the policymaker is likely to want a figure of merit for the program that summarizes its performance. This desire is part of the reason for the popularity of the benefit-cost ratio. The construction of such a figure of merit should depend upon the objectives of the program. For manpower programs targeted on poverty populations, the following formulation might be used. Basically the objective of the program is the increase in the economic welfare of the target population. The costs are the foregone consumption of the rest of society. With such a formulation the benefits are:

1. The increased earnings (net of taxes) of the target population resulting from participation in the program
2. plus the net increase in transfer payments to the target population during participation in the program
3. less decreases in transfer payments to the target population because of higher earnings subsequent to program participation
4. less losses of earnings from work that would have been performed if enrollee had not been in program
5. less losses of earnings of poor individuals displaced by trainees.

The sum of these changes is simply the stream of increments (or decrements) or real income both during and after the program which are attributable to the program.

The costs should include:

1. The direct costs of the program including subsistence payments
2. less any decreases in other transfer payments occasioned by the existence of the program
3. plus losses of income of the nonpoor if they are displaced by the program enrollees
4. plus any decreases in income to the nonpoor that occur because trainees are temporarily withdrawn from the work force
5. less long-term decreases in transfer payments because of the higher earnings of target population resulting from program
6. less net external benefits which accrue to the nonpoor and are not reflected in earnings of target population
7. less the increases in taxes paid by the target population on earnings increments resulting from the program.

Numerous assumptions must be made in order to obtain estimates of many of the cost components. This is particularly true for items 3, 4, 6, and 7. For example, increased taxes paid by program participants have value to the nonpoor only if they result in lower taxes for the nonpoor or the support of other government programs that benefit the nonpoor. Calculation of such quantities depends upon assumptions concerning level of economic activity, the reaction of the government to increases (or potential increases) in tax revenues, and the disruption of the benefits of government programs among the poor and nonpoor.

Costs and benefits occur over a considerable period of time. In order to compare costs with benefits, both streams are discounted back to the present time using some value of discount rate. The proper value of discount rate to use has been the subject of considerable debate, a debate I do not choose to enter.[7] It is worth noting, however, that the relative ranking of programs will not be affected by the choice of a discount rate unless the temporal patterns of costs and benefits differ between the programs. The absolute ratio of benefits to costs will be significantly affected by the choice of discount rates.

Because of the many assumptions that must be made, the probability that an evaluation by one investigator will be comparable to that of another is not high. Comparison of two programs using figures generated by two different analysts is usually unwise. Two practical suggestions to improve this situation can be advanced. First, whenever practical, programs having similar or over-

---

[7] The choice of a proper rate of discount is extensively discussed in Hearings Before a Subcommittee on Economy in Government of the Joint Economic Committee (1968).

lapping objectives should be simultaneously evaluated·using identical assumptions (and if possible identical data collection efforts). Second, efforts should be made to develop an agreed-upon set of conventions for the evaluation of social action programs similar in concept to those contained in the "Green Book" for water resource projects.

Nonmonetary Benefits

The discussion has proceeded as if all program benefits could be reflected in monetary terms. This is clearly not the case. There are benefits to the poor that are not measurable in dollar terms. Improvements in self-image, improved access to public services because of better knowledge, less alienation from the world of work or from other segments of society, better health or improved reading and computational skill are but a few of the nonmonetary benefits that are thought to accrue to participants in various manpower programs. To some extent some of these may be positively associated with income increases. Hence, comparison of programs in terms of their impact on increasing incomes will implicitly consider these factors. There is no simple way to include those factors that are more directly associated with program experience in the calculation of benefits.

If two programs have the same monetary benefits relative to costs, it might be possible to choose between them on the basis of the probable relative impact on other nonmonetary benefits. For situations where the benefit-cost ratios differ, the judgment is much more difficult. Consider, for example, a comparison of the Job Corps and the Neighborhood Youth Corps (NYC). Suppose the youths from both programs gain the same benefits in terms of increased income. The youths from Job Corps receive extensive medical and dental care, considerable counseling, remedial education and some vocational skills, all in a residential environment. The youths in NYC, on the other hand, receive only work experience with generally limited amounts of remedial education and counseling. The Job Corps costs about four times as much per trainee as the NYC. Hence, with the assumption of equal monetary benefits, the benefit-cost ratio of Job Corps would be one quarter of NYC's. How much of this difference can be attributed to the failure to adequately account for the improved individual welfare associated with good health or reading capability? This is a matter of judgment that is now made, in the case of manpower programs, by an ill-defined set of decision-makers in OEO, the Department of Labor, the Budget Bureau, the White House, and Congress.

This problem must be carefully separated from the one in which these nonmonetary program outcomes are thought to lead to subsequent increases in income. The benefits described in the previous paragraph are what the economist calls "consumption" benefits to program participants leading to improvements in his current well-being. However, many of these benefits, such as health status, reading skills, or degree of alienation from various groups in society may be related to long-term work experience. Improvements along these lines may improve the capacity of the individual to find and keep a job, but this improvement may not be clearly discernible in the proximate work experience of the individual. In this case if the Job Corps provides the individual with capabilities that become useful only after some work experience or when the youth is older, then comparing the monetary benefits of the two programs only on the basis of proximate work experience is inappropriate. Unfortunately, there is little basis for determining the impact of many factors, such as health, upon the lifetime earnings of an individual. The analyst has to retreat to the rather unsatisfying activity of specifying the size of the improvement in employment or wage rates that would be required to equate the benefit-cost ratios so that the policymaker can more easily make a judgment about the probability that such a future difference can be expected to occur.

Conclusions

This section has touched on a few conceptual problems associated with benefit-cost analysis. A glance at any group of evaluations of manpower programs will be sufficient to indicate the great variety of ways analysts have approached the problems noted here. This variability has rendered the studies incomparable and to some extent has discredited benefit-cost analysis.[8] Steps should be taken to reduce this variability, perhaps by establishing conventions under which benefit-cost or cost effectiveness studies of human resource programs would be conducted.

THE MEASUREMENT OF BENEFITS AND COSTS

In the previous section elements of a conceptual framework were established for comparing the costs and benefits of undertaking a manpower program. It was implicitly assumed that data on both the costs and benefits were available and that the major task of the evaluator was specifying what data to aggregate to obtain meaningful measures of costs and benefits.

Although it is true that many evaluations utilize questionable assumptions in calculating costs or benefits, the major difficulties seem to lie in empirically estimating these figures. Data produced routinely as a by-product of program operations suffer from two major flaws. They tend to be unreliable. Data for

---

[8] For example, three evaluations of the Job Corps using essentially the same data yielded estimates of benefit-cost ratios ranging from 0.3 to 5.0. See Regelson. (1969).

many projects are missing or contain numerous errors. More serious is the fact that few projects follow enrollees after the training period and hence are in a position to report earnings or employment histories.[9] Hence, the fundamental data required to assess benefits of a training program, the earnings of the trainee, must be obtained by other means. In most cases, the other means is some form of survey.

In general, the increase in national output is measured by the increase in income of the trainee. The use of this measure can be justified by the assumption that wages are equal to the marginal product of the worker. Two further assumptions are required. First, wages should represent total compensation. If extensive fringe benefits are also "paid," the use of only wages understates the program benefits. Second, it must be assumed that the enhanced employment and income status of the trainee has not been at the expense of someone else—that there is no displacement of workers by the trainees. This is a hard assumption to validate, for displacement is difficult or impossible to measure. Displacement should be less during periods of high employment (labor shortages) than during periods of economic slack.[10]

If the objective of the program being evaluated is to enhance the economic welfare of a target population, increases in income experienced by the trainee as a result of his training must be measured. However, the change in income is made up of many more factors than simply changes in employment rate and wages. Changes in welfare payments, unemployment compensation, and other forms of transfer payments that result from program participation must be measured. Taxes must be netted out. Decreases in economic welfare of other members of the target population who are displaced by the trainee should be accounted for if such displacement takes place.

Measurement of all these effects poses significant problems. How much of the change in the wage income of a trainee should properly be attributed to his training? In many instances, individuals can expect normal increases in their income. During periods of increasing economic activity, labor markets tighten and unemployment rates decrease; wages frequently rise. In such circumstances, the income of most of the work force may be expected to increase. Young workers just entering the labor force typically experience considerable unemployment and only low wages, partly as a result of laws that prohibit them from taking certain jobs. More important, perhaps, is the fact that a youth is trying out jobs in search for work that appeals to him, a process that often leads to

---

[9] The reporting system for the Manpower Development and Training Act includes data on work histories of enrollees subsequent to enrollment. These data are supposed to be collected by the Employment Service but the return rates are quite low.

[10] The displacement effect has an analog on the cost side. Opportunity costs to society due to the withdrawal of labor from the work force depend upon the employment level. In

unemployment. As he ages, his wages and employment increase. If a training program has a large number of youths, much of the observed increase of income of the trainees can be attributed to this maturation process.

The ideal measure of the increase in trainee income is a comparison of his actual income subsequent to training with what his income would have been without training—clearly an impossible comparison. In the absence of this measure, the best substitute is the work experience and earnings of a control group of individuals who are similar to the trainees in all respects except for the receipt of training. The most satisfactory control group is that formed when potential trainees are randomly assigned to either training or the control group. Such assignments are generally held to be socially unacceptable and I know of no case where such a procedure has been used to construct a control group for a large social action program evaluation.

Many other types of controls have been tried—none of which is very satisfactory. These include:

1. The program enrollees themselves (before and after comparisons).
2. Groups of individuals who signed up but failed to enter the program.
3. Groups of individuals who stayed in the program only a short time.
4. Groups of individuals having similar backgrounds who for one reason or another did not sign up for training.

The first type of control, the experiences of the enrollees prior to enrollment, has already been discussed. It has very limited credibility at times when labor market conditions change rapidly or in the evaluation of programs serving a large number of youths. The second, third, and fourth types of groups have grave problems of their own; the most pervasive and yet unanalyzable problem is the so-called self-selection problem. Because the trainee group chose to enter the program and the control group chose not to, the two groups may differ in systematic yet unmeasurable ways. In general, the dimensions of these unmeasurable differences are considered to be attitude and motivation.

RAND's experience in examining a comprehensive youth program illustrates this problem (Holliday, 1967). A retrospective survey of program enrollees was made. Short-term enrollees, those staying less than a week, were used as a control group. Their average stay was less than 2 days. By various criteria, those in the control group did better than the longer term enrollees. In seeking an explanation for this, the analysts reached the tentative conclusion that the "controls" were typically more motivated than the long-term program participants. They left the program quickly because they felt they could do better

---

conditions of high unemployment, opportunity costs should be much less than the earnings that would have been received by the trainee if he had not been working, since other labor stands ready to fill the demand the trainee does not meet.

elsewhere—in this case, by seeking a job by themselves. Indeed, there was some suggestion that the program facilitated this by providing placement counseling.

In contemplating this finding, however, we decided that had the result turned out otherwise, we would have had little confidence in the result. There appears to be an equally plausible set of arguments that would hold that short-term stayers or no-shows (the second and third types of control groups listed on the previous page) are less motivated and able. Perhaps the distribution of motivation and attitude for this group is really bimodel. It includes both the least and most motivated individuals in the population served by the program. One or the other type may predominate in any particular case.

Of the four types of control groups listed, the most satisfactory appears to be the last, a group of individuals who have similar work histories but have never come in contact with the program being evaluated. The choice of such a group has been accomplished in several ways. The Somers study in West Virginia utilized a random sampling of individuals in the files of the employment service (Somers, 1968). Earl D. Main used a control group of friends, neighbors, or relatives of the trainee whose names were obtained from the trainee. Page and Gooding used persons who filed regular claims for unemployment compensation who reportedly had similar demographic characteristics (Hardin, 1969).

Although the last type of control seems most satisfactory, it is by no means obvious that it eliminates the self-selection bias. For this reason, lingering and reasonable doubts about the validity of the estimates of program effects will remain.

Longitudinal versus Retrospective Studies

Further steps can be taken to satisfy doubts about the adequacy of a control group if the study is longitudinal and the control group is actually chosen *before* the trainees whose experiences are to be examined enter the program. Such a prospective and longitudinal study of a major manpower program has not to my knowledge been made, although OEO is now in the process of implementing one.

All of the studies reviewed in the course of preparing this chapter were retrospective and most obtained their data at only one point in time. The major limitation of a retrospective nonlongitudinal sample is the inability to measure attitudes at different points in time. As a consequence, a control group can be compared with an enrollee group only on objective factors such as age, race, sex, or work experience. Questions about current attitudes or expectations are difficult to phrase and interpret but there is even less reason to place credence in such questions when they refer to a much earlier point in time. Thus, in none of the benefit-cost studies examined were attitudinal questions used to control for differences between a control group and the enrollee group.

In a prospective and longitudinal study, of course, attempts can be made to ascertain the attitudes and expectations of the two groups and differences in these dimensions can conceivably be controlled in comparing the work experiences of the two groups. Such control, however, is hampered by the absence of any well-developed and accepted theory concerning the relationship of attitudes and expectations to job search and retention behavior.[11]

Longitudinal studies can have other advantages of course. If repeated interviews are made, they may result in more reliable estimates of the sample's work experience because the respondent is not asked to recall information over long periods of time. Program experiences can be monitored in greater detail than that provided by program records. But such studies have disadvantages also. Most important perhaps is their expense. They take place over a longer period of time which means the evaluation staff has to be kept intact for a longer period. Longitudinal studies are susceptible to sample degradation as members of the original sample are lost because of moves, death, or simply because they cannot be found. This may result either in small ultimate sample sizes or a larger initial sample.[12] Since a prospective, longitudinal evaluation of a large social action program has yet to take place, the importance of both the potential benefits and problems cannot be realistically assessed.

One frequently voiced complaint about prospective and longitudinal studies is that they require longer to complete, increasing the probability that the evaluated programs will have changed; the chance that the evaluation will be irrelevant is higher than would be the case in a retrospective study. This complaint must be examined carefully. If a program is to be evaluated on the basis of the experiences of individuals entering in or terminating from a program during a specified period of time, either type of study will provide data at approximately the same time. But, the decision to undertake the longitudinal study must be made much earlier—sometime prior to when the enrollees whose experiences are to be examined enter the program.

Up to now, evaluation has been a fairly *ad hoc* activity. Once it was decided that an evaluation was to take place, there were substantial pressures to obtain information as soon as possible. If, however, evaluation becomes more routine, longitudinal study designs become more feasible with a continuing succession of such efforts in being at any given time. With such a commitment, longitudinal studies could provide data to decision-makers at least as quickly as retrospective studies.

[11] Preliminary example of such a study is contained in two publications by Underhill (1967, 1968).

[12] Such loss also results in biases because the lost group may be different from those that are found. But these biases are also present in retrospective surveys with low response rates. At least in the longitudinal survey, earlier data can be used to compare the characteristics of the group that is lost with those that are found.

Clearly the desirability of instituting such a continuing program depends upon a variety of factors. Since such studies have not been carried out, we have little evidence on these factors. What is the cost per subject in the sample? Does the probable increase in confidence in the validity of control group/trainee comparisons seem worth the increase in cost? What is the probability that a major program reorganization will render the evaluation results irrelevant? The current OEO evaluation of manpower programs should clarify many of these questions.[13]

The Projection of Benefits

Whether or not a study is retrospective or prospective and longitudinal, it will examine work experiences only during a short period of time, perhaps 6 months to a year. It is generally felt that benefits are likely to accrue over a period of years and hence some techniques must be applied to project the proximate work experience into the future. The number of ways in which benefits have been projected is approximately equal to the number of studies that have been carried out. The assumptions concerning the projections are usually dependent upon the data available. For example, Cain in his study of the Job Corps has inadequate data on employment rates so he assumes a constant and equal employment rate for both control and enrollee groups. Differences in income are due entirely to wage rate differentials. On the other hand, Borus and Somers have observations on income and project the observed differences. Borus chooses to project these for 10 years and assume no benefits accure to trainees if they leave jobs for which they were trained. Cain and Stromsdorfer project the earnings over a lifetime, correcting for mortality and assuming a decreasing differential between the controls and trainees. This decreasing differential was used because longitudinal data in the West Virginia studies suggested that the differentials faded (see Cain, 1967; Borus, 1964G; Cain and Stromsdorfer, 1964).

Clearly, the method of projecting benefits will be important in determining the absolute value of the benefit-cost ratio. But, if the same methods are used to project proximate earnings for each of several programs, the choice of method will not affect the relative levels of the ratios of proximate benefits to costs. Thus, if the evaluation is being undertaken to examine the relative effectiveness of several programs in achieving an objective, there appears to be little to be gained in projecting the observed income differentials over a lifetime *unless* there is solid evidence that income differentials will behave differently through time for the different programs.

---

[13]OEO is currently carrying out a longitudinal evaluation of five manpower programs. Program enrollees in ten cities will be interviewed several times during a period of 18-20

As soon as the need to aggregate program outcomes into a unique and undimensional measure is relaxed, it is possible to compare programs against a variety of criteria. For example, programs could be compared on the basis of their contributions to lowering unemployment or increasing wage rates or perhaps changing rates of family desertion. Typically, such analyses are called cost-effectiveness analyses and are appropriate when comparing alternative means for achieving the same ends.

The Examination of Alternative Designs

There are relatively few national manpower programs. Moreover, these have been established with only vague hypotheses concerning the combinations of services that are likely to be successful. It is tempting therefore to structure an evaluation in such a way as to provide insight on alternative designs. Suppose the projects examined differ in the mix of services provided or the type of personnel utilized. Would it be useful to view these projects as a form of natural experiment that could be used to cast light on superior project demands and hence suggest changes that should be made in program guidelines?

Two major problems limit the value of the natural experiment. The first problem has to do with multiple causality. In RAND's examination of a comprehensive youth program there was some indication that successful labor market performance was inversely related to length of stay in the program. There are a number of plausible explanations for such a phenomenon. Perhaps the most reasonable is that youths with more severe problems tend to stay in the program longer and also to have worse labor market performance after they leave the program. Ascribing all of the poor labor market performances to the length of stay rather than to some unmeasured personal characteristics of the enrollee results in the conclusion that the program may be detrimental.

The same may be true for attempts to relate the success of a project to the mix of services it provides. To the extent that the mix of services reflects the peculiar and unique (but unmeasured) needs of the enrollees of the project, attempts to relate success of the project to the mix of services will be frustrated. It will be impossible to separate the impact of the service mix of the project on the labor market performance from the impact of the quality of the enrollees.

Multiple causality frequently plagues the social sciences. Basically, this problem arises because of the lack of a theory of human behavior that relates measurable psychological variables to various forms of human performance. In the absence of such theory, it will be impossible to separate the effects of the multiple causes in natural experiments. This has led to suggestions that more

---

months. The evaluators also hope to examine the impact of local labor market characteristics on program outcomes.

formal experiments be carried out (Cain and Hollister, 1969). In such experiments a more systematic attempt would be made to vary project inputs independently of the enrollee characteristics and so lessen the problems of multiple causality.[14]

The use of experimental projects as a means of systematic program development is likely to be more common in the future. Certainly OEO's experience with rapidly initiating large national programs on the basis of "theory" rather than proven experience would not support the contention that this approach to program development should be continued. Yet the value of experimental projects or social experiments as a means of program development and as a source of planning information remains to be demonstrated. Such experimentation will be expensive and may not lead to replicable designs. It will take considerable periods of time and require an uncommon cooperation between project operators and evaluators. While the use of social experiments for program development and planning remains an exciting possibility, it should not be viewed as a panacea for the planner seeking to improve program design.

Summary

These comments on problems associated with carrying out meaningful program evaluations are intended to convey the impression that evaluators still have a long way to go before they can routinely produce evaluations that are unassailable and reproducible. In the near future, evaluation will remain an art. New efforts should be viewed in part as attempts to improve methodology.[15]

How then, in light of these potential and actual shortcomings of actual evaluations, should an agency proceed to utilize such evaluations in its planning efforts? This problem will be considered in the next section.

THE RELATIONSHIP OF PROGRAM EVALUATION TO THE PLANNING PROCESS

The previous section considered the conceptual underpinnings of program evaluation, particularly as they apply to manpower programs. In general, the discussion assumed that the evaluator was simply trying to compare the benefits with the costs of the program. This perspective characterizes what OEO calls Type I or impact evaluations.

---

[14] The major current example of such an experiment is Project Follow Through which is seeking to try out a substantial variety of programatic approaches to helping disadvantaged youngsters succeed in the early years in school.

[15] Federal agencies that want to improve evaluation efforts would do well to promote continuity and quality of the staffs that carry out these efforts. In informal observations of the staffs carrying out evaluation, one gets some sense that each new evaluation effort starts out fresh with unfortunately little input from previous evaluations.

If a pure Type I evaluation of a single program is undertaken, it will provide a figure of merit, a benefit-cost ratio for the program. What role can this piece of information play in the planning process? By itself, this ratio can do very little. If it is unsatisfactory, that is, if the benefits are low relative to the costs, it may result in initiating a search for better ways to achieve the program's objectives. But such a ratio provides no clue about how to find a better program.

If several programs exist and have the same (or at least overlapping) objectives, simultaneous Type I evaluations may provide information on the relative effectiveness of the two programs. If due attention is placed on distinguishing average from marginal costs and benefits, a planner would recommend a shift of resources away from the program with a low marginal benefit-cost ratio toward the program with a high ratio. As noted in the last section, however, obtaining information on marginal as opposed to average benefits and costs may require posing questions about the effectiveness of components of a program with different parts of the target population. This type of question requires what OEO calls a Type II evaluation.

The planner obviously has a much greater menu of alternatives than just increasing or decreasing the funding levels of existing programs. He can:

1. Add new programs and/or delete old programs,
2. Change the management of existing programs,
3. Change the design of existing programs, including the mix of services and/or the target population,
4. Change the mix of local projects within the national program, as well as
5. Reallocate resouces among the programs.

In the context of the analytic structure presented in the last section, Type I evaluations can provide guidance only for decisions relating to reallocation among the programs. In many instances, however, decisions falling within the first four categories may be more appropriate. Such decisions require richer information than that provided by a "pure" Type I evaluation.

In light of the shortcomings of Type I evaluations for real world decision-making, is it worthwhile carrying them out? Does it really make sense to do studies that examine only the impact of a total program, not the impact of the program on subgroups of the target population or variations in impact as a function of variations in project design? The experiences of the Office of Research, Plans, Programs and Evaluation (RPP/E) with its initial major program evaluation is instructive in this regard, and suggest both the bureaucratic and methodological difficulties associated with program evaluation.

An evaluation conducted by the Westinghouse Learning Corporation and Ohio University sought to examine the national impact of Project Head Start, the major OEO-sponsored program dealing with preschool education. Project Head Start itself has a substantial research and evaluation activity and several large national evaluations were conducted in the early years of the program. These evaluations had, in the eyes of RPP/E, a number of shortcomings, many of which were beyond the control of the evaluators or Head Start itself. They did suggest that children experience gains in cognitive and affective behavior during their exposure to the Head Start program, but they indicated that these gains might not be sustained once the Head Start youngsters entered public school. There has been a good deal of debate on this "fade-out" or "catch-up" phenomena. Advocates of Head Start argued that what was occurring was that other children in the schools were catching up with the Head Start children and, consequently, that the program was having a useful effect. Critics or skeptics suggested that these gains were fading out, either because the program did not have sufficient impact or lasting effect or because the nation's public school systems were so unresponsive to the needs of disadvantaged youngsters that they could not capitalize upon gains the youngsters had made during Head Start.

One question that RPP/E wanted to answer was whether the total program had a positive effect. It is clear that in any program such as Head Start there are local projects that are very successful in preparing preschool youngsters to function more effectively in the school environment. There are also poorly run projects which provide almost nothing for the youngsters. Head Start sprang into existence in a great hurry, enrolling some 250,000 youngsters within a period of a few months in the summer of 1965. Any program that is inaugurated and expanded at such a rapid rate is bound to lack the kind of careful planning that might lead to relative homogeneity of the outcomes of the numerous projects. This, combined with the lack of proven theories concerning learning by preschool youngsters, gave rise to a reasonable doubt about the overall impact of Head Start.

In light of these possibilities and because the national Head Start program was not carrying out a national evolution, RPP/E decided to inaugurate a nationwide impact evaluation. The study was intended to provide indications of the performance of a national probability sample of youngsters who had participated in Head Start over a period of 3 years. The desire for fairly rapid results led the evaluators to choose an *ex-post* design. About one hundred projects were chosen randomly and students who had entered local public schools after some Head Start exposure were studied. The evaluation team attempted to find a group of comparable children to use as a control group who had not been in Head Start and who were currently in the same classrooms. In order to obtain reasonable national coverage with economically feasible sample size, eight students at each grade level (first, second, and third grades) from each project were examined, together with a comparable group of control students. Not all projects had existed for the entire 3 years so the sample size of third graders is smaller than that of the second graders, which in turn is somewhat smaller than that of the first graders. The number of students examined for each of these individual projects is too small to allow one to reliably characterize the effects of an individual project and this was not intended to be the objective of the evaluation. Instead, the project results were aggregated to give a total national estimate of impact. While a determination of national impact was the major focus, subsidiary analyses examined differences between the program impact by regions of the country, by racial groups, and by whether the youngster was in the summer or the full-year program.

This study represented a classical retrospective "impact-only" design. It provided an estimate of the impact of Head Start along a large number of dimensions of cognitive and affective development. The impact of the program was determined by comparing the scores of the children who had had Head Start experiences with the scores of a control group selected from the same school system who had been eligible for Head Start but who had not been enrolled. The control group was matched to the experimental group on sex, racial or ethnic group, and whether or not kindergarden was attended. It was impossible to match the control group with the experimental group on socioeconomic status because such data were not available at the time of sampling. However, extensive interviews were conducted with parents of both groups which, among other things, provided the socioeconomic data required to match these groups. Co-variance analysis was used to effect this match.

During the planning stage for this evaluation study, the Head Start organization argued that the study should not be carried out. They felt the design focused on too narrow a set of objectives, utilized instruments that could not properly assess the psychological and educational development of young children and, because it was *ex post,* ran a significant risk of utilizing an imperfectly chosen control group. They felt adverse findings of dubious scientific worth were likely and that such findings would have unfortunate impacts upon the development of the program because of their effect on the morale of national and local Head Start organizations and on public support for the program.

The RPP/E response made several points. First, whatever the multiplicity of program objectives established by Head Start itself, the prime objective of the program is to help improve the functioning of the disadvantaged youngster in the school. The important functions are cognitive and affective (or attiudinal) development. Second, they admitted the possible shortcomings of the *expost* design but felt that an adequate control could be constructed or if not, that this fact would be detectable. Finally, they argued that OEO had the responsibility to make some judgments concerning Head Start's effectiveness and that the then current Head Start research program was not producing any data on the program's effectiveness.

It is important to note that the statements on both sides are potentially valid. They are also to some extent self-serving. A politically popular program such as Head Start which has reason to suspect an evaluation will turn out negatively is unlikely to want to be evaluated. An organization such as RPP/E that aspires to provide rational advice concerning the allocation of resources among programs based upon "hard" data will want an overall program evaluation done. Since the programming organization can only affect major resource allocations it cares little about time-consuming data collection and analysis efforts that seek to answer more complex questions than simply "is the program working?" On the other hand, the program managers will be concerned with all the nuances of program design and, if evaluation must be carried out, will seek a richness of information that will support decisions on program design. A well-publicized national evaluation that is negative may well have adverse consequences on the morale of program personnel and hence it is reasonable for program managers who feel they are still developing and improving the program to resist such an evaluation. But despite this possibility, a failure to assess the validity of claims of effectiveness breeds complacency and leads to the development of an entrenched bureaucracy committed to the status quo.

Head Start was developing a major longitudinal study which, in the minds of the program administrators, overcame most of the problems of a quick retrospective design; they proposed that their study constitute the evaluation. This study involved only three or four sites and required 5-7 years to complete. RPP/E felt that such a study, while potentially useful for program development, was neither timely nor sufficiently representative of the national impact to constitute an evaluation of the program.

The RPP/E study results were indeed unfavorable to Head Start. There was little indication that Head Start youngsters did any better than non-Head Start youngsters. Predictably, the study was attacked by advocates of Head Start on methodological grounds. Early versions of the study reached President Nixon's advisors and appear to have been instrumental in shaping the rhetoric of his pronouncements on the program. It is still too early to assess whether the evaluation will have a useful impact in forcing changes in the program design. It is clear, however, *that the study provides little guidance on what changes should be made.* A study that could provide such guidance would require a substantially more elaborate design, a larger sample size (hence more expense), and a longer execution period. No study that purports to be a national impact evaluation that will also provide clues to what program changes should be made has yet been mounted—perhaps it cannot be.[16]

Conceptually and tactically, a simple impact evaluation is the easiest to carry out. The question posed in such an evaluation is simple: Does the program, as represented by a national probability sample, have a discernible impact along

---

[16] The study did indicate that the summer Head Start program appeared to have less impact than the year-round program, suggesting that reallocation of funds from summer to year-round projects would lead to improved outcomes.

some specified dimensions, or does it not? Although there will be debate on dimensions, the sample design is relatively straightforward and the analysis is not terribly difficult. If, however, one wants to pose additional questions to be answered by the evaluative activities, the design becomes more complex. If it is desired to determine what kinds of treatments are effective, what types of teachers are effective, or what kinds of institutional environment seem most productive in achieving the project ends, one must not only describe these factors and determine which ones the child has been exposed to, but one must also design a sample that is of sufficient size and structure to allow meaningful statistical generalizations to be drawn. If as is generally the case in large social action programs, there is an absence of well-developed and concrete hypotheses about these factors, the design of the sample and of the survey instruments must proceed with a great deal of uncertainty. No doubt the sample sizes will be larger and consequently, the costs of evaluation wil be substantially greater. These are not the only problems, of course. The length of time required to prepare for data collection and subsequently to analyze the data collected, will be greater. The problems of effecting a bargaining agreement between the evaluator and the program to be evaluated will take longer because more agreements will have to be reached. Simplicity of design is lost and the possibilities of disagreement and argument over the design are substantially increased. Finally, the interpretation of the data is far more difficult and complex. Indeed, it is likely that there will be something in the data for everyone; for every conclusion one draws about the effects of the program, someone else can draw a different conclusion. It is hard to refute the Head Start evaluation's conclusion that no perceptible and consistent gains have been experienced by Head Start children in a national probability sample. But if that same study had been able to say that children of a certain background or sponsors of a certian type had been effective, surely the emphasis placed on the evaluation by proponents of the program would have been substantially different and might have obscured the overall pessimistic conclusion.

The qualities of impact-only evaluations designed solely to determine whether or not a program is having effects along relevant outcome dimensions can be summarized as follows:

Impact-only evaluations are relatively easy to mount and interpret because only a single hypotheses is being investigated.

This simplicity translates into an ability to mount such an evaluation relatively quickly and to carry out the analyses associated with it relatively quickly.

Impact-only evaluations are politically dangerous because of their go/no-go quality. There is little capacity in the design to point out directions in which the program should be changed in order to improve its effectiveness, if indeed it proves ineffective. By the same token, it is the hardest type of evaluation for program managers to shrug off because of the straightforwardness of its conclusions.

The impact-plus evaluation contrasts with the impact-only evaluation in the following ways:

It examines a wider range of questions (in particular, what is working for whom) and consequently, it requires a longer setup time.

The additional hypotheses to be tested mean that larger sample sizes are required, and with some survey designs these studies may require reductions in the number of sites examined and a reduction in the representativeness of the total sample examined.

Results are more equivocal and subject to many differing interpretations and hence are likely to be more politically acceptable but possibly less effective in producing change.

The choice between the two types of designs, or more properly along the continuum between the two types of designs, will depend upon the particular case. As a general rule, it would appear that the more complex impact-plus evaluation is appropriate to the early years of a program when adaptation is taking place. Later, the impact-only evaluation may be more appropriate, particularly when the evaluation is intended to support the allocation of resources among programs having similar objectives.

Program versus Project Evaluation

The point of view explicitly taken in this chapter is that of a senior planner in a federal agency who seeks to allocate resources among a number of programs. This is the usual view of evaluators at the federal level. Bateman (1968) has commented on this:

The development of PPB [Planning, Programming and Budgeting Systems] has, in most instances, been characterized by an almost exclusive concern with efforts to more optimally allocate resources among programs. Very little attention has been given to the problems of program management; that is, the organization of resources within a program to achieve the greatest effect. This is not unexpected in a department like Health, Education, and Welfare where the bulk of Federal financial resources are channeled through State and local administrative hierarchies, a circumstance which precludes extensive involvement in the day-to-day management and direction of program operations. In a sense, PPB has followed a natural course in emphasizing, through the legislative and budget process, the resource allocation issues among programs since it is precisely in those areas that able people have had the greatest power to produce identifiable change.

In the National Manpower training effort, on the other hand, the need for rigorous project evaluation may soon become quite acute, while at the same time the value of program evaluations is reduced. The reason for this is the Department of Labor's attempt to decentralize the operations of the manpower program and to emphasize comprehensive local manpower programs. It will be important to seek methods of carrying out the evaluation of local projects.

It is beyond the scope of this chapter to treat this problem in any detail. However, several important points can be made. The comparison of the effectiveness of a number of projects requires far more data then an examination of overall program effectiveness. Not only must each project be examined, but the records of a sufficient number of enrollees to characterize the local program's effectiveness must be collected. This puts a very great premium on finding an inexpensive means of following up on enrollees—clearly interviews at 10 to 50 dollars apiece are much too expensive. At least two alternatives are available. One is the time-honored practive of using placement rates or other proximate criteria as the measure of program effects. This appears to be the measure used in the system Bateman has described. The problems with using such project-reported measures are well known. If a project knows that the placement rate is being used in judging its performance, it will tend to find ways to inflate this figure.[17] The more nearly the criterion approximates the true program objectives, the better it will be. The true objective of a manpower program is not high reported placement rates or even truly high placement rate; rather, its goal is continuing high employment rates or earnings for its trainees. Observations on employment or earnings clearly are superior to observations on reported placements.

One method of obtaining such information on a routine and continuing basis is to tap either the Social Security Administration or Internal Revenue Service files. These files have wide (though not total) coverage, are relatively inexpensive to search, and could provide a basis for a useful project evaluation system. Both the Department of Labor and OEO are investigating the use of such data.

Even after such data have been obtained, important conceptual problems remain. Local labor market conditions, patterns of discrimination, or geographic structure will materially affect project outcome. Very little work has been done on local labor market phenomena and even less work has been done on these phenomena as they apply to the types of populations served by manpower training programs.[18] In the near future, therefore, it is likely to be impossible to separate the impact of project design and execution from the impact of labor

[17] RAND's experience in using placement data as a means of tracking individuals did not provide great confidence in the validity of these statistics. In one case, as many as 50% of the individuals reported as placed had never been at the firm. In many instances, individuals left after only a day or two of work.

[18] RAND is currently undertaking a group of studies of the impact of local labor market phenomena on the poverty population.

market conditions in any very satisfactory way. The data and analytic problems make it unlikely that objective cost-effectiveness or benefit-cost evaluations can play a large role in guiding local project funding in the near future.

CONCLUSIONS AND RECOMMENDATIONS

On the basis of the foregoing analysis, this section seeks to advance a few words of advice to would-be evaluators. It seems far too early in the history of social action program evaluation to view these conclusions as more than sugges-tions for next steps to be taken, so perhaps the most important recommendation is that evaluations undertaken in the near future should be viewed as vehicles for the development of evaluation methodology as well as providing information on program outcomes.

It is important to reemphasize that my perspective is that of the planner who seeks information to guide his decisions. For the most part, my model of the planners' world is one where he has a group of program alternatives among which he can allocate resources. The role of evaluation, then, is to guide the resource allocation. But, as has been noted, this is too narrow a concept. If a program is not doing well, the solution may be to change its management or to improve certain types of services or to change its target population or even to redefine the objectives of the program. Indeed, as the Department of Labor moves toward increasingly comprehensive designs, such as the Concentrated Employment Program, there will be no obvious alternative programs in which to invest and the only decision alternatives are changed program designs.

In my judgment, planners and evaluators should informally conduct a "contingency" analysis before they start an evaluation. Such an analysis would pose questions about decisions to be made if one or another result is obtained. If such an analysis is carried out, I suspect one would seldom find an evaluation designed *solely* to estimate the overall impact of a program. If the evaluation shows a negligible impact, the consequences are simply too harsh for a govern-ment agency to take and the results will be suppressed if possible. A far more realistic approach is to propose a set of hypotheses that have implications for program planning. For example, it could be hypothesized that a program works better with youths than adults, males rather than females, or in loose labor rather than tight labor markets. Answers to such questions provide guidance to the planner and, even if the overall program impact appears small, the planner is in the position to indicate how its impact can be improved.

An alternative approach is to sample program experiences in such a manner that exemplary projects can be identified. These exemplary projects then provide some information on the *potential* program effects as well as guidance on changes that can and should be made in the less effective projects. At present, this choice must be made on a subjective basis because little hard data are available on project outcomes.

There are no doubt other ways in which to structure program evaluations. I am convinced, however, that if the evaluator and the planner were to sit down and ask what will happen if the results show one thing as opposed to another, the quality of evaluation would improve, its relevance would increase, and its results would be more likely to be used.

Objectives

The objectives against which the programs are to be evaluated have generally been inadequately specified. Much of the confusion over what is a cost and what is a benefit results, in part, from the lack of explicit statements concerning the program objectives. I have argued that two types of objectives dominate manpower programs. One is the increase of the national product through increases of the productivity of the labor force. The other is a distributional objective, to improve the welfare of one segment of society by increasing its labor market productivity. Legislative or administrative intent may suggest that secondary benefits be considered.

There is no reason why a program should be evaluated against only one objective. Indeed, there frequently is a mandate in the legislation supporting manpower programs to consider several objectives. As a consequence, specifications for evaluation efforts should include explicit statements of program objectives and, if possible, criteria by which to measure the degree to which the programs achieve those objectives. There is no need to insist that all program effects be combined into a single measure of program impact. The world is a complex and messy place. Within reason, evaluations should reflect this complexity.

Marginal versus Average Effects

In principle, it is important to consider marginal rather than average effects. In practice, this is generally infeasible. Program evaluations deal with what exists (or more properly what existed at the time of the evaluation) rather than what might exist if the program were expanded or contracted. In putting evaluation results to use, however, marginal effects can often be taken into account. If increases or decreases in program enrollment will be limited to particular demographic subgroups, data on the average program effect on that subgroup are likely to be a better estimate of marginal effects than the average outcome for the program as a whole. Again, contingency analysis on the part of the planner and the evaluator should lead to better evaluation designs which, in turn, should improve the usefulness of the evaluation for making estimates of marginal impacts.

The Need for a Set of Conventions

The results of the studies examined during the research for this paper are not comparable. In part, this noncomparability results from differences in the data available to each analyst. More important, however, each analyst uses his own set of assumptions concerning such phenomena as displacement effects, opportunity costs, social rates of discount, and transfer payments. Clarification of program objectives should help resolve part of the problem, but there is still a great deal of scope for arbitrary judgment. Consequently, a set of conventions for carrying out benefit-cost or cost-effectiveness evaluations or manpower training programs should be developed and published.

Data Systems

Little evidence has been found during this study to suggest that data systems currently used by manpower programs will ultimately develop information that will support program or project evaluation. The data produced are unreliable and do not provide any useful output measures. As a consequence, in the short run, data produced by these systems should not play a large role in the planning for evaluations. Evaluations should rely upon sample surveys. The results obtained will be less subject to unknown biases.

In the long run, however, data systems should be designed with evaluation needs as well as the needs of local projects in mind. Much of the lack of reliability of information systems at the local level appears to come because these systems are of little or no use in program operations. Much of the data that must be fed into these systems are of little current use to project managers—in part because they are not retrievable and are often out of date.

Several steps should be taken to improve the data systems. Their design should be explicitly tailored to the needs of local projects. If they fulfill a need, they will probably be used and the data will be more reliable. They should in all probability be automated. One of the factors that will facilitate their use is timeliness, which may most easily be obtained through modern data processing techniques. It may well be that the government should consider setting up regional computer centers that will support these systems. It seems likely that once such local systems are in being, they can be routinely tapped to provide the national reporting desired.

These developments still will not solve the problem of following up on the individual trainee. For this purpose, it appears that tapping into one of the national reporting systems such as those of the Social Security Administration or the Internal Revenue Service may well be the best approach.

Longitudinal Studies

For several reasons, longitudinal studies have significant advantages for the evaluation of any social action program. When performed on an *ad hoc* basis, they have two significant disadvantages. They take a long time to perform and they are expensive. If the information systems suggested above were developed and if evaluation was routinized, the disadvantages of longitudinal studies could be substantially reduced. The data could be timely and the costs significantly lessened. Such a set of changes will not come about without positive action. Whether the benefits of such design are great enough to warrant such action is not clear. These benefits are, after all, emphasized particularly by deficiencies of the more commonly used retrospective designs. Whether longitudinal designs in practice will turn out to realize their theoretical advantages remains to be demonstrated. For this reason, the current OEO effort to evaluate several manpower programs using a longitudinal design should be carefully monitored.

Systematic Experimentation

For reasons that are quite similar to those militating for longitudinal studies, systematic experimentation with varying program designs has great appeal. Again, it is an appeal that grows largely out of the shortcomings of current efforts to learn from what I have called natural experiments. Certainly evaluations of current programs, even when the programs appear to have benefits exceeding their costs, leave many questions unanswered. Is there a less expensive design that will do much the same thing, for example?

Somers (1968, p. 15) in an introduction to a collection of studies that show consistently favorable outcomes for MDTA projects, states:

> These benefits of retraining programs are impressive. Their worth would seem to be well established. But there are still some nagging questions. One unanswered question is whether on-the-job training would provide even better benefit-cost ratios and whether methods can be found for encouraging on-the-job training of the disadvantaged. Another is whether non-training job development and human resource programs might do as well for the disadvantaged unemployed, without the higher costs of vocational training courses.

Questions such as these suggest the need to systematically establish a set of demonstration programs that examine program design alternatives that are not currently a part of our national programs. Such projects would not be the same as the current demonstration projects. These tend to be established as a result of a proposal from an individual or organization. There tend to be many idiosyncratic factors associated with the operation of the projects. Moreover, they are generally poorly evaluated. A program of systematic experimentation would seek to establish projects having a range of characteristics. There should be some replication of project designs to reduce the impact of particular personalities or localities.

Again, there is a current activity that deserves monitoring as a guide to the benefits of such an effort. The OEO-funded, and HEW-run, Follow Through program is attempting to simultaneously examine a variety of project designs utilizing, in part, a common evaluation design to assess the outcome.

A Final Note

It is clear that evaluations of program outcome at the national level have not been of sufficient quality to justify their use as a major input in planning a national manpower program. This is, as I have argued, only partly due to the very large methodological problems facing the evaluator. More important as an explanation are two organizational factors: (1) Most programs and most agencies are reluctant to be evaluated; (2) if they must be evaluated, they will seek to find evaluation designs that have the greatest probability of supporting the status quo.

But the evaluators themselves are also at fault. Too little effort has been placed on relating evaluation to the planning process. Too little concern has been given to identifying the decisions that evaluative efforts should be designed to clarify. Too often the evaluator has either chosen to or by default had to define his own evaluation objectives with little continuing interaction with the programs or agency. Too often the evaluation results in a final report whose summary and conclusion are read but whose data are left largely unanalyzed.

Solutions to these two problems (the reluctance to be evaluated and the irrelevance of the evaluations) push in opposite directions. The first argues for separating the evaluation function more sharply from the operating programs because otherwise the program managers will tend to render them useless. The second argues for bringing them closer in order to make the information generated by the evaluation more relevant and useful.

This is a quandry that requires close attention by senior agency administrators. There is no simple solution.

REFERENCES

Bateman, W. (1968). 'New techniques of federal program management.' In *Federal Programs for the Development of Human Resources.* Vol. I. A compendium of papers submitted to the Subcommittee on Economic Progress of the Joint Economic Committee, Congress of the United States, Washington, D.C.

Borus, M. E. (1964a). *The Economic Effectiveness of Retraining the Unemployed, A Study of the Benefits and Costs of Retraining the Unemployed Based on the Experience of Workers in Conneticut.* Unpublished dissertation, submitted to Yale University Graduate School, New Haven, Connecticut.

Borus, M. E. (1964b). 'A benefit/cost analysis of the economic effectiveness of retraining the unemployed.' in *Yale Economic Essays* 4.

Borus, M. E. (1968). 'Time trends and the benefits from retraining in Connecticut.' *The Development and Use of Manpower*. Proceedings of the 20th annual winter meetings of the Industrial Relations Research Association, Wisconsin.

Cain, G. G. (1967). *Benefit/Cost Estimates for Job Corps*. Department of Economics and the Institute for Research on Poverty, University of Wisconsin, Madison.

Cain, G. G., and Hollister, R. G. (1969). Evaluating Manpower Programs for the Disadvantaged. A paper presented at the North American Conference on Cost-Benefit Analysis of Manpower Policies, University of Wisconsin, Madison.

Cain, G. G., and Stromsdorfer, W. (1964). An economic evaluation of government retraining programs in West Virginia. In *Retraining the Unemployed*, (G. G. Somers, ed.), University of Wisconsin Press, Madison.

Center for the Study of Unemployed Youth (1968). *A Study of the Meaning and Effects of the Neighgorhood Youth Corps on Negro Youths Who are Seeking Employment*. Graduate School of Social Work, New York University.

Committee on Administration of Training Programs (1968). *Report of the Committee on Administration of Training Programs*. Submitted to the Secretary of Health, Education and Welfare, Washington, D.C.

Dorfman, R. (1965). *Measuring Benefits of Government Investments*. Brookings Institute, Washington, D.C.

Dunlap and Associates, Inc. (1967). *Survey of Terminees from Out-of-School Neighborhood Youth Corps Projects*. Final Report prepared for Department of Labor, Bureau of Work Programs, Washington, D.C.

Hanson, W. L., Weisbrod, B., and Scanlon, W. J. (1968). *Determinants of Earnings: Does Schooling Really Count?*, Economics of Human Resources, Working Paper 5A. Department of Economics, University of Wisconsin, Madison.

Hardin, E. (1969). *Benefit-Cost Analysis of Occupational Training Programs: A Comparison of Recent Studies*. A paper presented at the North American Conference on Cost-Benefit Analysis of Manpower Policies, University of Wisconsin, Madison.

Harris, L. *et al.* (1967a). A study of August 1966 terminations from the Job Corps, Conducted for the Job Corps.

Harris, L. *et al.* (1967b). A study of the status of August 1966 Job Corps terminees—12 months after termination (revision).

Harris, L., *et al.* (1967c). A study of job corps no-shows: Accepted applicants who did not go to a training center.

Hearings Before a Subcommittee on Economy in Government of the Joint Economic Committee. (1968). *Economic Analysis of Public Investment Decisions: Interest Rate Policy and Discounting Analysis,* 90th Congress, 2nd Session, Washington, D.C.

Holliday, L. P. (1967). *Appraising Selected Manpower Training Programs in the Los Angeles Area,* RM-5746-OEO, pp. 8-9. The Rand Corp., Santa Monica, California.

McKean, R. N. (1958). *Efficiency in Government Through Systems Analysis*. Wiley, New York. (1967).

Mangum, G. L. (1967). *Contributions and Costs of Manpower Development and Training,* Policy Papers in Human Resources and Industrial Relations, No. 5. National Manpower Policy Task Force, Washington, D.C.

Planning Research Corporation. (1967). *Cost/Effectiveness Analysis of On-the-Job and Institutional Training Courses*. Prepared for the U. S. Department of Labor.

Regelson, L. (1969). *Applications of Cost-Benefit Analysis to Federal Manpower Program*. Paper presented to Operations Research Society of America, Denver.

Ribich, T. I. (1968). *Education and Poverty*. Brookings Institution, Washington, D.C.

Rothenberg, J. (1967). *Economic Evaluation of Urban Renewal*. Brookings Institution, Washington, D.C.

Somers, G. G., and Stromsdorfer, E. (1964). *A Benefit Cost Analysis of Manpower Retraining.* Proceedings of the Industrial Relations Research Association.

Somers, G. G. ed. (1968). *Retraining the Unemployed.* University of Wisconsin Press, Madison.

Suchman, E. A., (1967). *Evaluative Research.* Russell Sage Foundation, New York.

Underhill, R. (1967). *Youth in Poor Neighborhoods.* National Opinion Research Center, Chicago, Illinois.

Underhill, R. (1968). *Methods in the Evaluation of Programs for Poor Youth.* National Opinion Research Center, Chicago, Illinois.

Walther, R. H. (1968). *A Study of the Effectiveness of Selected Out-of-School Neighborhood Youth Corps Programs: Methodological Considerations in Evaluative Research Involving Disadvantaged Populations* (Draft) Social Science Research Group, George Washington University, Washington, D.C. (Mimeo).

Walther, R. H. and Magnusson, M. L. (1967). *A Study of the Effectiveness of Selected Out-of-School Neighborhood Youth Corps Programs: Retrospective Studies of the Effectiveness of Out-of-School Neighborhood Youth Corps Programs in Four Urban Sites.* Social Research Group, George Washington University, Washington, D.C.

Weisbrod, B. A. (1968). Income redistribution effects and benefit cost analysis. In *Problems in Public Expenditure Analysis* (B. Chase, Jr., ed.), Brookings Institution, Washington, D.C.

10

ISSUES IN INCOME
MAINTENANCE EXPERIMENTATION

David N. Kershaw

This paper discusses some of the major "operational" (as opposed to methodological or conceptual) problems encountered in implementing the New Jersey Negative Income Tax Experiment. The focus is upon the set of problems involved in implementing a major social experiment in the field—those issues to be faced after the complex questions of the basic conceptual and methodological design are resolved sufficiently to begin field experimentation. In the New Jersey experiment the design and methodological issues were extremely complex, but they were similar in kind—if not in degree—to those treated in the past by experienced researchers. The operational issues however, often were completely new—how families were going to be selected, how they were to be paid, how local communities would react, how families which were not selected would behave, how we could communicate with sample families in such a way that they would learn to administer the system themselves, how we would verify incomes without real sanctions, what relationship would/should we have with various government agencies.

It has become increasingly clear during the course of the New Jersey experiment that a substantial interconnection exists between the operational and the methodological aspects of the experiment. Not only do various practical problems such as community reaction, difficulty in locating certain kinds of respondents, and cost constrain the implementation of some conceptual notions, but the various possible resolutions of operational questions often become conceptual issues themselves as the experiment progresses. Particularly in the case of administrative costs and techniques, regarded as a relatively unimportant side issue at the outset, operating aspects of the experiment were converted into important questions for experimental investigation. We have redefined a large number of our operating procedures in order to gain insights applicable both to future experiments and to a national income maintenance system.

Despite this overlap between operational and methodological issues, I have tried to restrict my comments principally to operational problems. The first section of this paper provides a brief description of the Negative Income Tax and some of the major methodological issues underlying the design of the New Jersey experiment. The remainder considers a variety of problems that had to be treated in getting the experiment into the field. The paper is a case study of one attempt to do large-scale social experimentation in a complex urban setting. But it goes beyond case specifics in the sense that many of the problems encountered will be faced again—certainly in other income maintenance projects and probably in other experiments that must be conducted in neighborhoods composed of poor ethnic or racial minorities.

THE NEGATIVE INCOME TAX AND THE NEW JERSEY EXPERIMENT

The negative income tax concept is one of a number of guaranteed income proposals which have been seriously advanced in the past 5 or 10 years to replace the current patchwork of welfare programs. Its virtues include simplicity of administration (it is a self-administered program which makes use of forms similar to those used by the Internal Revenue Service), equity (it is paid to all whose incomes fall below a prescribed level), dignity (there are no indiscriminate investigations or compulsory "services" provided), and the creation of conditions conducive to individual initiative (the negative tax grant is not taken away from a recipient dollar for dollar as his earned income increases). The way the negative income tax scheme works is quite simple. An individual or family whose earned income is zero is granted a standard amount of money (the "guarantee"). No matter what the family does with the money, where it lives, or who administers the program, the family income will never fall below the guaranteed amount. If the family earns additional income of its own, the initial guaranteed amount is reduced at some established rate (the "rate of reduction"). As the family continues to increase its earnings, the guaranteed amount continues to be reduced until the family reaches a point at which the guarantee has been completely used up (the "breakeven point"). Beyond this point, the family receives no more supplementary funds unless and until its income falls below the breakeven point again, in which case the supplement would be paid according to the same formula.

There have been a number of negative income tax "plans" advanced, but all are essentially like the one described above. Differences stem from varying the rate of reduction, making the rate of reduction nonlinear, changing the guarantee, introducing a "disregard" on some proportion of initial earnings, paying different amounts to different families depending on the composition of the family, and so forth. Nevertheless, all combine the concepts of an income guarantee, a rate of reduction, and a breakeven point.

The negative income tax idea is very appealing conceptually, whether one's major interest is in seeing a guaranteed income introduced or whether one is frustrated at the mushrooming welfare bureaucracy. However, a substantial number of serious issues have been raised which need at least partial answers before vast amounts of resources are committed to a new system based on the negative tax concept.

The primary issues are work incentive and cost, the latter clearly a function of the former. If *all* families below the breakeven income level are eligible, the system will include many families with a partially or fully employed earner. By what amount will this earner's work effort be reduced in response to the receipt of supplementary income? Once this group of "working poor" are included in a national income maintenance program, this question of work incentive becomes a key one. Because there are so many families having incomes between, say $4000 and $8000, a slight reduction in their work effort could have a devastating impact on the cost of a national program.

When early discussion of the negative tax idea took place at OEO in 1965, officials felt that they could predict costs for the traditional public assistance recipients under a negative income tax scheme: the aged, disabled, the very young, and the families headed by a woman with small children could exercise few labor market choices which would influence the cost of a national program. The male-headed families with an earner, however, raised substantially more serious questions: To what extent does a work-leisure trade-off operate at these income levels? Does the tax applied to a supplement have the same impact as one applied to earnings? Will a 70% tax on the supplement produce a different reaction than a 50% rate? Will secondary earners leave the labor force when offered partial reimbursement through a supplement?

The New Jersey experiment was conceived in order to answer questions like those posed above. Primarily, it was designed to address the questions of work response and attitudes toward work, although the experiment deals also with related issues such as consumption and savings behavior, mobility, family stability, use of government services, social integration, and so forth.

In order to measure these and other variables, MATHEMATICA, a Princeton, New Jersey, research firm and the Institute for Research on Poverty at the University of Wisconsin jointly designed the New Jersey experiment. For the experiment, 1359 low-income, male-headed families in five metropolitan areas—Trenton, Paterson, Passaic and Jersey City, New Jersey and Scranton, Pennsylvania—were selected and randomly assigned to one of eight different negative tax plans (defined by some combinations of four guarantee levels and three tax rates) or to a control group. The sample families are interviewed once every 3 months throughout the 3-year experiment. Each family in the experimental (as distinct from the control) group which files an income report correctly receives a check in the mail every 2 weeks. The check is computed using the family's plan and its income for the appropriate period. Experimental families who file correctly continue to receive payments even if they move to distant parts of the country (and some have), and all families continue to be interviewed if they move elsewhere in the country. Those families which break up continue to receive payments separately as new filing units.

In order to administer the experiment, MATHEMATICA staffed an office in Princeton to direct the field activities and a small office in each of the five cities. Each year the experiment administers 5000, 350-question interviews, writes over $800,000 in checks to experimental families, processes 10,000 family Income Report Forms and adds over 30 million words of data to the computer records.

As the discussion which follows shows, the size and complexity of the New Jersey experiment has enabled us to address a broad range of operational issues, important by-products of the original methodological and conceptual aspects of the experiment.

MAJOR OPERATIONAL ISSUES[1]

The Local Political Context

Urban experimentation carries with it the most difficult operating problem of all: the work must be done in a city.[2] By its nature, an income maintenance experiment in an urban area is first exposed to the community at its most

---

[1] *Editors' note*: This section was taken from a longer draft by Kershaw that in part was meant to serve as a guide for other researchers engaging in income maintenance experimentation. Kershaw, who is the chief of field operations for the experiment, is often recounting how he and others faced up to a great variety of problems and how he thinks they should be faced again, given his first-hand experience. In preparing this paper, Kershaw has eliminated much of the detail found in the earlier draft but has retained the earlier style *(at our urging)*. This means that the paper at times reads like a "how-to-do-it" or "how-we-did-it" manual. It is the detail (the many little things that must be done) that in sum dramatically brings home the complexity of a major field experiment in a way that a general theoretical discussion cannot.

[2] The experiment faced some very difficult hurdles in several of the New Jersey cities. In particular, the larger the city, the more difficult were the political problems with the community. In Scranton, which approaches a rural location in some respects, few such community problems were encountered.

sensitive experimental stage: while the families are being selected. The potential for bias or fraud or both at this stage is great and care must be taken to ensure that the integrity of the sample is maintained. Several operating rules were developed in New Jersey to get us past this crucial point.

First, decisions had to be made regarding whom we should inform before the selection process began. It is of great advantage here if the sites selected for the experiment are not known outside of the research staff and if, additionally, there are some alternative sites. The experimenters are in a far stronger position if they have some options which they can exercise during the initial experimental phases. There are two kinds of contacts which are important at this stage: those people who can help the experiment get underway and those people who can do it harm if they so choose. In the first category are individuals with either technical expertise and knowledge of the city (planning departments, Model Cities, local universities) or an official role in the community (the mayor and the chief of police). These people should be told that there is some thought regarding conducting an experiment in the city and that an investigation is currently underway to determine whether the city is a suitable site. The general outlines of the experiment can be spelled out, particularly with respect to an estimate of how much money would be coming into the community if it is selected. It does not seem to be necessary to be very specific about eligibility criteria and it is usually a good idea to refrain from doing so. If supplied with a few general descriptions of the experiment and a personal visit, these officials are usually cooperative.[3]

The more difficult liaison problem is with "community leaders." These can be loosely defined as unofficial representatives of various segments of the community, where community means community of dwellings, views, ethnic backgrounds, or incomes. Locating some of these people is easy; ensuring that everyone who should be contacted has been contacted is more difficult. The approach should be similar to that with the officials of the community: a general description of the experiment (omitting any detailed discussion of eligibility criteria) and what it can do for the community on a short term basis (community people will be hired to interview and to supervise, and community people will be the recipients of the income transfers) and a long term basis (we're going to help get rid of the current welfare system which we all agree is terrible).

The important thing about informing these leaders is to reinforce their leadership positions in the community. Most of them neither understand nor care about the experiment itself. What they do care about is being neglected by any organization that is working in their territory. Serious trouble may arise if

---

[3]The chief of police needs to be informed because most cities require either a special permit for large-scale interviewing or a letter of introduction from the police carried by each interviewer. To avoid interviewer arrests (some of which are inevitable in any case), close cooperation with the police is a necessity.

several people who have been interviewed approach one of these leaders to ask him what is going on and he does not know. Two things may happen, both of which we have experienced in New Jersey. First, he may instruct as many people as he can not to submit to the interview. (In Passaic, N.J., virtually an entire public housing project refused to cooperate until we discovered who the leader was and spoke with him.) Second, he may decide that the operation represents a threat to his position and attempt to take more drastic action. (In Paterson, members of several community groups infiltrated the interviewing staff with a view toward destroying the organization; in the end they realized that the experimenters had no designs on community control and, more importantly, that the interviewer salaries were supporting a number of their members.)

The process of identifying contacts should continue through the initial selection process. It was our experience that very general pamphlets stressing the help being given to the community and the long-range goal of income maintenance worked very well and that most individuals who were originally either very interested or suspicious of the operation lost interest. Getting as many local people as possible to lose interest in the operation should be a primary goal.

Later, during the sample enrollment phase, these same contacts can be used to legitimize the experiment for the recipients. When enrolling families initially our interviewers carried the names of three of four such persons who should be known and respected by the selected families. If a family was suspicious or hesitant, they were urged to telephone or write one of these people for assurance.

As the experiment continues, the unofficial contacts should be kept informed of its progress; some of them may also be called upon to provide inside information about the city, to help families cash their checks or to locate lost families.

A major complication in the urban political context is the existence of violently competing power centers. It is not enough, for example, to locate a Puerto Rican leader and consider the "Puerto Rican community" fully informed. It is often the case that intense rivalries exist within the community (as we discovered in Trenton and Paterson), and between the community leaders and their previous peers who are now in local government positions (as we discovered in Passaic). The important lesson here is that while the organization operating the experiment should attempt to contact various groups and individuals within the local area, it should also be extremely careful not to be identified with any one of them.

Organizational Considerations

Important to the determination of organization structure are three issues: (1) what type of organization should operate the experiment in the field; (2) what type should be responsible for the research, analysis, and overall supervision of the experiment; and (3) what relationships should exist between the operating, research, funding, and other organizations involved. I have not arrived at any clear answers to the whole question of the organization most suitable to operate an income maintenance experiment, but I do have a few observations which may be helpful.

With respect to the relationship between the organizations and the various levels of government, it now seems clear that unless the number of actors is kept to a minimum, substantial, and perhaps insurmountable, operational problems will arise. Experimentation with income maintenance is exceedingly complex and delicate: dealing with a panel study of relatively long duration, making variable payments to families in the sample, operating in a volatile political environment, and making constant adjustments in the experimental parameters as a result of things that are learned in the experiment or outside occurrences, means that the entire organization must be extremely flexible. Decisions must be made quickly and scientifically and new policies implemented rapidly. In view of this I feel that, insofar as possible, income maintenance experiments should be funded from one level of government directly to an operating agency or organization which has full power to make decisions and act on them.

A second important consideration is that the organization operating the experiment should have virtually no connection with any local agency or organization at the experimental site. On numerous occasions in New Jersey, the fact that the experiment was funded by OEO in *Washington* (as distinct from the local Community Action Agency, for example) got us out of very difficult situations. There is tremendous pressure by many local groups to help select the sample. First, this is the way things are done in most cities: those in power give out the jobs and decide on how the pie is to be divided. If any local agency is responsible in the least for the experiment, it will be impossible to draw distinctions in the public's mind between sample selection and other (nonrandom) selections made routinely by the city government, and the experiment itself will become a political plum. Second, it is important to establish at the outset that this is a *scientific* undertaking, not only to allay possible charges of rigging the selection process, but to deal with families who were not selected, to reassure local officials that the experiment is not a political threat (again, because anybody giving out money is automatically regarded as having good political leverage), and, as we will discuss later, to provide the firmest possible grounds for keeping the press and general public away from the families. The fact that it is an experiment run by scientists has the additional advantage of diminishing ideological opposition to it among those in the area who might make it difficult to operate. ("We are certainly not committed to the idea of a guaranteed income, but we think it is important to find out about it once and for all," etc.) It was extremely helpful to us in New Jersey in this regard to use the names of the Institute for *Research* on Poverty at Wisconsin, and *Research* and Plans Division of OEO.

The third important consideration is the organization which actually deals with the families and the local community. The staff in such an organization should have two main qualities: they should be academically oriented to the extent that they understand the purpose of experimentation and are constantly attuned to analyzing, researching, and discovering, as opposed to merely operating; second, they should be oriented toward the attitudes, views, and activities of the community, both because they must operate a program in that environment and because research is more effective if the researcher understands the experimental environment. The major difficulty here is that these two sets of qualities are rarely found in the same person. A community person who is excellent at dealing with the sorts of problems which arise in an urban area may never really grasp the nuances of experimentation. Over the course of the last year we have tried a number of different techniques, including operating a field office with strictly community people who receive light supervision from the central (research) office, operating with strictly research people, and a combination of these. Our feeling now is the organization should continue to hire locally, although this can be a function of how important this factor is considered by each local community. (In our experience, for example, it appears very important in Paterson while it is of no importance in Scranton.) Along with local staff members, a field coordinator should be used: a person who is primarily research-oriented but understands the problems of the local community. This person can provide continuous research direction to the field staff, bring his own research capabilities to bear in the local area, and maintain a standard set of practices by the field staff. A very delicate balance must be maintained between an office which is in and of the local community, and a scientific experiment which maintains some distance from involvement in local community problems and entanglements.

To sum up, a limited number of agencies or organizations should be involved, distant from any local relationships, research oriented but with the clear capability of operating with the blessing of the local community.

Enrollment Techniques

The enrollment period is the time the families have their first contact with the experimental agency as opposed to the interviewing organization. Experience in New Jersey indicates that misunderstandings, misconceptions, and attitudes created during enrollment are exceedingly difficult to change as the experiment progresses.

The enrollment process for participants should include the following:

1. A general introduction to the experiment—Who sponsors it, why, how long it will last?

2. A statement concerning the general benefits to recipients and under what circumstances they will continue to be members of the experiment (they

may move, the family may split up, they may spend the money in any way they choose, etc).

3. A discussion of the obligations of recipients, including accurate reporting, change of address information, etc.

4. Instruction in making out the first Income Report Form to begin the process of filing.

5. General encouragement to take advantage of the local office for assistance with filing or any other problems related to the experiment.

6. A careful explanation of the recipient's rights, including a brief explanation of the rules and information regarding rights of appeal in cases of disagreement with a policy of the experimental agency.

The most general lessons learned in New Jersey about the enrollment process relate to the kind of personnel who do the best job and the nature of the training to be provided to them. The first approach in New Jersey was that enrollers had to have a thorough theoretical background which would enable them to explain the Negative Income Tax concept in detail to recipients. Accordingly, graduate students in the social sciences were used extensively for enrollment in Trenton, and largely in Paterson and Passaic. As in interviewing, however, it became clear that contact with the families should be made by staff members who understand the concept well enough, but who in addition thoroughly understand the attitudes and problems of recipients. Hiring was therefore changed from college students to local community people.

The training procedures also evolved over the course of the experiment until they included the following stages:[4]

1. Introduction to the concept of income maintenance—most enrollers have been interviewers and are very interested in the part they are playing in a larger national effort. It is important, therefore, to discuss in some detail the notion of income maintenance, what it is supposed to do and not do, who supports it, how it works, etc.

2. Review of enrollment procedures—a thorough review of techniques, policies, and approaches for enrollment, including a detailed discussion of each of the items in the enrollment packet. In New Jersey these include: a brochure explaining the basic aims of the experiment, Rules of Operation in brief for the families, a Basic Payments Table for the family's plan, an enrollment agreement for the husband and wife to sign, a calendar for the next 6 months with filing

---

[4] Tangible evidence of improvements in both personnel and technique can be demonstrated from the fact that the refusal rate in Trenton (early training with graduate students) was 10%, in Paterson and Passaic (some community personnel with slightly refined training) was 8%, in Jersey City (all community people with new training scheme) was just under 2% and in Scranton (community people with final training technique) there was one refusal out of an enrollment of 165 families.

dates noted on it, an explanation of the method for filling out an income report form, an identification card for the family to enable them to cash their checks more easily, their first income report form which is filled out by them and given to the enroller to take back to the office, an information sheet on the family for reference by the enroller, a list of local contacts who would be known to the family that the family can call if there is doubt as to the legitimacy of the program, an enroller observation form on which any questions or problems or observations are noted by the enroller for inclusion in the family's file, and the family's first check.

3. A demonstration of enrollment by members of the staff—a brief run-through showing the approach method and a few typical problems is enacted by members of the staff for the benefit of enrollers.

4. A dry run by enrollers—before sending enrollers into the field, a detailed set of practice sessions is administered to enrollers. The best procedure we found included an assembly line arrangement in which enrollers begin by introducing themselves and explaining the program to a member of the staff who made the face-to-face situation appropriately difficult. Enrollers then proceed to another staff member highly experienced with the use of the income report to tell them how to fill out the report (again, typical problems are posed to the enrollers). Finally, they have a session with other staff members who ask questions which are most likely to be asked during actual enrollment. Each enroller is then given a list of questions which have been asked most often in the various New Jersey cities. The enroller studies the questions and asks about any of them which he finds puzzling. This activity takes each enroller about 1 hour.

5. A final pep talk—to avoid overwhelming the enrollers with the amount of information, a brief session is held either with a group or individually to assure enrollers that the process is very easy, that difficult problems arise only rarely, and that they are well prepared. This helps them to relax.

6. Retraining—after the first few enrollments have taken place, it is advisable to get together with the enrollers again and discuss any unusual problems. At this point, the enrollers will want to do most of the talking. This session serves to review any difficulties as well as to build enthusiasm for the enrollment process in general.

Counterattrition Methods

Income maintenance experiments combine the attrition problems normally associated with panel studies with added problems resulting from the fact that different families are receiving different payments, expectations may not be met, and various economic circumstances change during the course of the experiment. There are three distinct attrition stages: (1) refusals at the initial (screening or preenrollment) interviews; (2) refusals to be interviewed or dropouts during the experiment; and (3) changes in address without word to the agency. The first of these require preventive action, the latter two remedial.

Initial refusals create bias problems for any study and are particularly troublesome at the beginning of a panel study of long duration. There are a number of steps which can be taken to minimize the refusal rate. The most effective is to use interviewers who can relate easily to respondents, since a relatively large number of refusals occur after a few minutes in a respondent's home. Assuming that interviewers are well trained and sensitive to respondent attitudes, it may still be necessary to "race-match" in some areas. Care should be taken during initial interviewing efforts to determine whether there is any evidence that refusals are a function of racial differences between respondent and interviewer. A further technique is to pay respondents for the time they take to answer questions. We discovered that five dollars for each hour of respondent time got good results: five dollars was enough above the average hourly wage rate of respondents to seem attractive, but not so much higher that it made respondents suspicious.

Another way of fostering respondent receptivity is to leave a write-up about the program at the doors of respondents who refuse to speak at all, who are not home, or who do not want to answer the questions. A few days later another interviewer can return and try again. This technique was very successful in Jersey City where a large initial refusal rate created some fears of substantial bias.

At the community level the interviewing organization should be careful to make the proper contacts to ensure that various community leaders know about the study and can respond positively if asked about it by potential respondents.

Finally, a well-written and thoroughly tested interview instrument ensures that refusals are kept down by eliminating confusing, sensitive, or otherwise unsatisfactory questions.

Having taken whatever steps are necessary to minimize bias, it is still vital to determine what kinds of bias refusals are presenting. In order to do this in New Jersey, a sample of Jersey City respondents is being studied, including some who refused to be interviewed at the initial contact, to determine the extent to which refusals are a function of income level, home ownership, race, age, ethnic group, or other characteristics.

Following sample selection, counterattrition measures should be immediately instituted to minimize attrition during the panel study. A few lessons have been learned in New Jersey, although a great deal of work remains to be done on counterattrition methods in panel studies.

The most important step is to develop an interest in participating or a sense of responsibility to the study without undue involvement which would tend to create a "Hawthorne effect." The best way of accomplishing this is to maintain brief, regular, remunerative contact with sample families, refrain from bothering them with long, taxing, sensitive interviews as much as possible, and make special provisions for notification of change of address. It is, of course, just as important for sample members to remember to notify the agency of address changes as it is for them to continue to open their doors when interviewers arrive. The New Jersey study makes a regular monthly payment to control group families in exchange for a postcard giving their current address. Another payment is given in return for the quarterly interview. It is too early to determine the effectiveness of this method. However, a yearly bonus system, increasing for each year of participation, was found to be unsatisfactory, primarily because remuneration was deferred. Deferring a payment of $50.00 for a year makes it virtually useless as a counterattrition procedure. Other techniques that were considered include: (1) a lottery for the sample families where a few members become eligible for a very large payment (e.g., a car or house)—rejected because of some legal difficulties and the problem of injecting a "gimicky" quality into the study; (2) much larger interview payments—rejected because of the doubtfulness of responses elicited with a payment so large that sample members get suspicious or uneasy; and (3) a regular communication or "newsletter" to maintain interest—rejected because it was nonremunerative and might create "Hawthorne" type bias. By far the most successful techniques have been small, regular payments in cash and an attempt to keep the interviews brief.

After taking whatever steps are possible to elicit cooperation from the families in maintaining contact, the most difficult counterattrition problem still remains: locating those families who move and do not inform the agency. A number of successful techniques have been developed in the New Jersey study. Some examples are:

1. Inquire of neighbor's children—get the names of the children from the interviews and ask other children where their friends have gone (this eliminates the suspicion problem among the adults, and has been our single most successful technique).

2. Talk to others of the same name—many moves are within the same area and several families have been located by calling all of the names in the phone book corresponding to the lost family's name (relatives are often located in this way and are willing to give the new address of the family).

3. Checking at the post office—change of address forms are available at the post office or through the use of a postcard requesting change of address information on an individual.

4. Dial the same phone number—numbers are often left unchanged.

5. Inquiries of a variety of institutional and individual services—these might include stores and bars in the neighborhood (this has proved to be very effective); the public housing authority; the Department of Public Assistance or other assistance agencies in the community; the police; the Division of

Employment Security; the local churches; state agencies for migrant workers; employers; and landlords.

6. Use of a savvy community contact—there are a number of individuals in every city who know virtually everything that is going on, and we have had great success in locating families, both those who have moved within the city and those who have moved farther, through such people.

Field office personnel should be extremely careful to use these techniques with sensitivity. They should be aware that families do not want some people to know where they are, and staff members should never discuss the experiment with any of the people with whom they are inquiring.

Confidentiality

The problem of maintaining the integrity of the sample population by protecting it from outside influences is central to social experimentation. Aside from the problem of families telling one another that they are recipients (which does not seem to create serious difficulties for the experiment outside of some Hawthorne effect considerations), the sample is threatened primarily from the mass media and from existing governmental agencies whose aims may conflict with those of the experiment.

The major problem with the media is the assessment many of its representatives make about their audience: they are uninterested in why there is an experiment, what it is designed to find out, what a guaranteed income is and what it means for the problems of poverty. The orientation is toward "human interest" and, in many cases, toward public reinforcement of widely held (negative) stereotypes. In this regard, a newsman would usually prefer to interview a family himself rather than talk about the experiment with someone who understands what it is designed to do. Indeed, a great many newsmen have decided not to do a story at all after being refused access to families. Barring a personal interview in which he can use the name of the family (very important for human interest), a newsman would like the following, in decreasing order of preference: an interview using no name, a telephone call to a family, a talk with someone on the staff who has just seen a family, a set of quotes from families, a set of family profiles, a description of the experiment. As one gets to the bottom of this list, the accuracy of the story increases, since the newsman discusses the experiment with people who view it with some perspective. Given the built-in conflict between accuracy and human interest, it is not surprising that there have been few accurate and comprehensive articles or news programs about the experiment.

The real problem, however, is not the lack of accuracy, which we seem to have been able to absorb, but the critical difficulty in keeping representatives of the press, radio, and television away from the families. As we began the experiment, we held rather vague fears regarding the impact of the media on families made available for interviews. Our primary concern centered around the fact that they might no longer react in the same way to the receipt of our payments and would therefore cease to provide valid experimental observations. Our experience to date is too limited to speak definitively about such reactions, although we have increasing reason to believe that our original assumptions about it were correct.

The New Jersey experiment's experiences with newsmen makes clear that it is essential to be publically firm about interviews with families from the beginning. We had a long series of arguments regarding whether we should make a limited number of families available to the media for interviews (with their permission, of course). Most of us felt that since this was an important national experiment using public funds, and since we wanted to educate the public about the concept of income maintenance, it would be wise to provide some means for satisfying requests by the media ("satisfying" being defined as access to families). We therefore identified a few "typical" families and cooperated with one of the television networks in producing an interview. As some of us had feared, this indicated to all other newsmen that the only way to do a story is to talk to families. The others are not satisfied without talking to families and would, of course, like to speak with individuals who have not as yet been interviewed so that their responses will be "spontaneous."

Our current policy has been that no access is given to any families. The names of families already interviewed, while they are technically "in the public domain," are not given out either. *But it is very difficult for us to hold this line after initially having given way.* Future experimenters should decide on a policy in the beginning and follow it. We feel strongly that an income maintenance experiment is delicate and should be insulated as much as possible.

In addition, the extent of the responsibility to the families selected cannot be overemphasized. Too often we have a tendency to consider them "lucky winners," forgetting both the contribution they make as individuals to the experiment and the extent to which the experiment has an impact on their lives. The money from the experiment is not "extra" payment for having been selected to participate in an interesting undertaking; for many it represents a substantial percentage of their incomes. Under these circumstances tampering from the outside can have, from their point of view, an impact of major proportions. The experimenters have an ethical, as well as legal, obligation to tread very carefully with the rights of privacy of the families in the sample.

A second major area where confidentiality is important is in the relationship of the experiment to existing public agencies, in our case with welfare and public housing. We made some assumptions in New Jersey which appear to have been relatively serious mistakes.

First, we based some of our policies on the assumption that families would react in economically rational ways to the interaction of our payments with those of other agencies. The best example is the public housing case. Since we impute rent to families with subsidized housing, their payments increase when public housing raises their rents (although not by as much as their rents). Accordingly, we obtained a waiver from the various public housing authorities regarding the *eligibility* of our families for the 3-year experimental period (i.e., they would be able to remain in the project despite an increase in income), but agreed with public housing that there was no reason for the rents to remain at the same level. We explained this to the families. It now appears, however, that many families exhibit a basic fear of investigation by any government agency for any reason. Despite the fact that the family is much better off with a higher rent and our payments, the decision on the part of public housing to raise the rent constitutes a perceived threat of broader proportions. Similarly, the possibility of a welfare investigation represents a threat large enough for some families that they would prefer not to receive our payments at all. Several of our families have dropped out (and lost benefits) over the public housing and welfare problems; in addition, some families refused to enroll initially for the same reason. The best approach to this problem now appears to us to be a more rigid and formal agreement with public housing people either not to raise the rents at all or, if that is not feasible, to have the experimental agency make up the difference in rent without involving the family. The relationship between public housing and a national income maintenance system will, of course, be carefully worked out. Our experience has implications for further experimentation, however, since an experiment represents an additional, unofficial, and sometimes puzzling outside agency. The idea of our coming in for a 3-year period and inducing agencies of government to begin investigation is troubling to the families.

A second problem stemmed from the erroneous assumption which we made in New Jersey that various welfare agencies would be well-intentioned, cooperative and attuned to the national importance of our efforts. Although we have developed a workable relationship with a number of agencies throughout the state, the possibility that a family may not report accurately and thereby have fraud charges brought against it and the experimental agency remains a very serious problem. Experimenters do not want to be in the position of continually forcing the families to report. (Indeed, one legitimate experimental area is the accuracy of self-reporting.) In addition, it now appears that some families may not report payments accurately to the requisite agency at some point in the experiment, usually due to oversight, but sometimes intentionally. If the welfare agencies appreciated the problems of experimentation and had an interest in scientific inquiry, these situations could be worked out jointly. In many agencies, investigation is a goal in itself, however, and zealous caseworkers and investigators are a continuing threat to the experiment. The result may be the creation of legal difficulties for some of the families on the basis of their participation in the experiment. To avoid this, some formal arrangement of a legal nature should be reached at a high level, temporarily waiving the rights of the local agencies to investigate families who are participating. The agreement should not be intended to exonerate in advance illegal behavior, but to give the experimental agency operating latitude.[5]

Finally, very serious problems can arise in cases where the substance of the experiment suddenly becomes highly relevant in the political arena. In New Jersey, the introduction of the Nixon Family Assistance Plan in August of 1969 posed a critical set of challenges to maintaining the integrity of the sample and the "purity" of the experimental environment. A preliminary report released through OEO in February of 1970 set off a chain of events, including a major investigation by the General Accounting Office, renewed press interest, a Congressional Hearing before both the House Ways and Means Committee and the Senate Finance Committee, and a set of insistent requests for data on individual families by one senator. While the coincidence of the experiment and major legislation on the topic inevitably thrust the experiment once more into the spotlight, such coincidences can be expected to occur with increasing frequency in the future as social science experimentation becomes a more common and legitimate tool of policymaking. Some balance, still being sought in New Jersey, must be found between allowing the experiment to progress uninterrupted and unprotested and sharing evidence, however preliminary and fragmentary, with policymakers when they most need it.

A particularly troublesome aspect of the events following the February OEO Report was the lack of legal protection afforded to the confidentiality of family records. Despite provisions of confidentiality in MATHEMATICA's and the University of Wisconsin's contracts with OEO, and in MATHEMATICA's agreements with the families themselves, it is not clear whether or not those records (and the families) could be successfully subpoenaed by either Congress

---

[5] Editors' note: Long after this paper was completed and at the time we were getting the volume ready to send to the publisher, Dave Kershaw sent this note:

At the moment, I am preparing to appear before the Mercer County Grand Jury for allegedly conspiring with experimental families to misreport our payments to welfare. I have enclosed a statement which I intend to make to the Grand Jury, which expands some parts of the original paper. I have absolutely no time to incorporate this into the paper but if you would like to do so and send me a draft, I would be perfectly happy to read it.

We have included part of Kershaw's statement (the excluded part duplicates the present paper) as an addendum. In his next note (who would have imagined that an experimental project would contain elements amenable to conversion into a continuing soap opera), Kershaw indicated that his 4-hour testimony before the Grand Jury seems to have dispelled the conspiracy charges but that harrassment from local law enforcement officials continues to threaten experimental operations.

or the GAO. The lack of legal precedent for protection (indeed precedent would seem to indicate they *may* be subpoenaed) makes relevant social science research with human subjects highly sensitive, if not risky.

It may be that legislation of the kind which now protects individual Census files needs to be passed before other large-scale efforts like the New Jersey experiment can be undertaken with assurances of privacy to participants. Members of the New Jersey staff have discussed guidelines and regulations with the Office of Statistical Standards of the Office of Management and Budget in order to try to develop safeguards for future experimentation.

The Effect of the Experiment Itself on Responses

One of the most common criticisms of the New Jersey experiment is that it will not last long enough to allow families to react to the receipt of the transfers in a "natural way," that is, in the same way they would were the payments part of a permanent national income maintenance program. Within the larger area of uncertainty surrounding an experiment of relatively short duration are a number of related, specific criticisms: (1) the families will feel like guinea pigs and will react simply because they are part of an experiment ("Hawthorne effect"); (2) they will react to the aims of the experiment and use the money in atypical ways ("funny money"); (3) they will develop a conditioned pattern of responses to the quarterly interviews during the experiment and thus their answers will be a function of the fact that they have been interviewed previously; and (4) the relatively short duration of the experiment will make responses unnatural and atypical (they will be either getting used to it or looking toward the termination date).

At this early stage we cannot say a great deal that is definitive about any of these criticisms. With regard to the first point, we have developed an interview which will determine the participants' awareness to being part of an experiment, how they feel about it, how it affects their behavior, and so forth. In the absence of tabulated results from this interview we have examined evidence collected from the contacts of our field office staff with the families. Our current impression from this source is that the families view us essentially as another agency; indeed, many of them are financially dependent upon the regular receipt of the biweekly checks. The efforts we have made to separate the interviews (Urban Opinion Surveys) from the payments (Council for Grants to Families) appear to have been largely successful; the families themselves seldom confuse the two (i.e., ask an interviewer a question about their payments) and appear to be largely oblivious to our regular scrutiny of their activities. While none of these impressions is systematic enough to depend on, we do not think we are facing serious difficulties. In addition, we are attempting to develop other means for measuring the extent of the Hawthorne effect.

Second, we had been very wary that families would use our payments to do special things (i.e., socially valued activities like clothes for the children, home furnishings, saving) because of its source and because of the nature of the experiment.[6] However, it now appears that this is not going to be a problem. For families close to the poverty level, the luxury of regarding any payment as "funny money" simply does not exist. From a large number of office staff contacts with families, it is reasonably clear that our payments are added to any others the family receives and are used for things the family typically buys. From these preliminary indications, our payments do not appear to be segregated from other income, although the interview currently being administered is designed to obtain more systematic information on this point.

The nature of the responses on the quarterly interviews is a little more disturbing. As several members of the research staff had feared, we are beginning to see some of the problems often encountered in a relatively lengthy panel study. In an early pretest of the in-depth interview currently being administered in Trenton, one of the respondents indicated that he had never really thought about some of the things covered in the questionnaires and was now reading the newspaper and watching television more so that he would be better prepared for the questions. This is obviously a serious problem and must be countered in any panel study. The standard answer is to use two control groups, one interviewed as often as the experimental group and the other rarely, perhaps only at the beginning and the end of the study.

The final specific criticism that these families have a longer time horizon than 3 years and therefore none of their responses are particularly meaningful, is much more difficult to deal with. My current view is that the time horizon of families in the experiment is short enough to yield meaningful and "natural" responses similar to those which would be encountered in a national program. Suspicions, uneasiness, and other reactions tend to vanish after the first few months of the experiment.

Nevertheless, the question of whether responses are valid in a 3-year experiment and, if so, when are they most so, continues to worry us. The special interview which I discussed above addresses the issue of time horizon, although it is not clear whether one can deal with that sort of question in an interview. We may decide that depth interviews with a relatively small group of families is the answer, or that we need to administer a special battery of psychological tests to determine whether or not we can depend on the responses.

The rather indecisive point of this section is that there appears to be some cause for concern on Hawthorne effect grounds. Nor are we sure that we will be

---

[6] Some families agreed to enroll after being told that their participation was important; they had been selected to participate in the first try at a national income maintenance program. Under those circumstances, some families may have felt an obligation to spend the money in certain ways to support the overall goal.

able to develop suitable techniques for testing the extent of bias imposed by the experiment itself.[7] In any case, future experiments should investigate such techniques with care.

Conclusion

Experimentation now appears to be a useful and powerful analytical tool for policymakers. Getting its start with income maintenance experiments, it is a technique which is clearly applicable to a wide range of policy issues.

As with most things, we must be concerned about the creation of "fads." Experimentation is by no means the only way to collect data and it is easy to disregard some of the most important limitations of experimentations: it is costly, time-consuming, politically sensitive, difficult to control, and difficult to replicate with ongoing national programs. However, if we use experimentation as a "last resort"—when other analytical techniques have been exhausted—we can provide an increasingly better set of data to policymakers which will enable them to avoid serious errors in the early years of major new programs.

In view of both the usefulness and the risks of experimentation, it seems to me important for those of us involved in experiments to pay a great deal of attention to developing better ways of *doing* them, so that our mistakes (and, occasionally, our insights) can be translated into more effective techniques for others in the future.

ADDENDUM: EXPERIMENTATION WITHIN THE WELFARE CONTEXT

The Trenton (New Jersey) Experience[8]

This paper reviews our administrative relationship and problems with the Mercer County Welfare Board since the beginning of the Trenton pilot phase of the experiment in August of 1968. In addition, there is a brief discussion of the potential impact of various reporting (or misreporting) options on the families and the implication of some of these for the analysis.

BACKGROUND

The New Jersey Experiment was designed to deal with an exclusively nonwelfare population, the "working-poor." By restricting eligible households to

---

[7] A particularly troublesome point is the fact that these techniques may themselves result in Hawthorne-like effects. The administration of a special interview may have a great deal more impact on the respondents than the quarterly interviews. We are therefore proceeding with our new questionnaire with great care, using only a small subsample of the experimental group.

[8] Statement by D. N. Kershaw, March 24, 1971.

those containing nonaged, employable males, we sought both to collect data on a previously ignored subset of the poor and to avoid the potential difficulties of direct conflict with the existing welfare system.[9] We realized, of course, that some experimental families would, during the course of the 3-year study, become eligible for AFDC by virtue of changes in family composition resulting from death, desertion, divorce, separation, and so forth. Consequently, detailed rules were developed to handle the few expected cases of joint eligibility— providing that experimental families were required to report all welfare income to us, but that our payments would not be reduced as a result of such income. This avoided placing experimental families in any "squeeze" created by a simultaneous reduction in a family's payment on the part of both welfare and the experiment.

The experiment also attempted to develop a working relationship with the three relevant welfare agencies for the Trenton sample (City of Trenton, Mercer County, State of New Jersey), through a series of early meetings.

In January of 1969, the State of New Jersey introduced a new public assistance program, Aid to Families with Dependent Children—Unemployed Parent (AFDC-UP). This new program not only expanded public assistance eligibility to families with an *un*employed male present in the household, but also to families with an *under*-employed male, where under-employed was defined simply on the basis of insufficient earnings. Whereas the Department of Health, Education and Welfare had matching provisions which required AFDC-UP recipients to work less than 35 hours per week to qualify, the more liberal New Jersey regulations had no such restrictions. This meant, of course, that all families previously selected for the experiment would now be theoretically eligible for the more generous AFDC-UP program (AFDC provided a legislated maximum grant of approximately $4160 per year for a family of four, as compared to annual guarantee levels in the experiment of $3686, $2764, and $1843).

The overlapping eligibility problem was complicated, however, by several things. In the first place, families simply below their AFDC-UP breakeven points were not automatically eligible for AFDC-UP payments. In order to qualify, a family had to start (or drop) below the *guarantee level* and demonstrate that such a drop was not engineered in order to get on the rolls. It was therefore unclear how many of our working poor families would actually be affected by the new law. Second, New Jersey was in financial trouble. Without any broad-based tax until a 3% sales tax was levied in 1968, it was unlikely that the State

---

[9] In 1968 when the field work began on the experiment, there was no AFDC-UP segment in New Jersey so that overlap appeared minimal. Accordingly, the early brochures and procedures tended to neglect the problem of overlap with welfare payments.

Comparison of Annual Benefits under New Jersey AFDC and under
Alternative Experimental Plans for Different Earned
Income Levels[a]

Level of earned income	0	2000	3000	4000
AFDC (average benefit)[1]	3000	1310	640	30
AFDC (maximum benefit)[2]	4160	2470	1800	1130
Experimental plans[3]				
$G = .5P; r = .3$(A)	1843	1243	943*	643*
$G = .5P; r = .5$(B)	1843	843	343	0
$G = .75P; r = .3$(C)	2765	2165*	1865**	1565**
$G = .75P; r = .5$(D)	2765	1765*	1265**	765*
$G = .75P; r = .7$(E)	2765	1365*	665*	0
$G = P; r = .5$(F)	3686*[4]	2686**	2186**	1686**
$G = P; r = .7$(G)	3686*	2286*	1586**	886*
$G = 1.25P; r = .5$(H)	4606**[5]	3606**	3108**	2608**

[a]Notes:

1. Source: National Center for Social Statistics, U.S. Department of Health, Education and Welfare, Report D-2, July, 1970.
2. National Center for Social Statistics, Report A-2, June, 1970.
3. Each plan is defined by a guarantee level *(G)*, which is a fraction of the poverty line (at the time the experiment began in 1967) and a tax rate *(r)*, which determines the rate at which the guarantee is reduced by earnings.
4. * Indicates that the plan dominates (that is, offers more money than) the average AFDC payment at that income level.
5. ** Indicates that the plan dominates both the average and the maximum AFDC payment at that income level.

could support for long such an expensive welfare program, part of which was not federally matched. Our estimate was that the rolls would be severely restricted either by a repeal of the liberal segment of the UP law (which I may note, is now occurring), or by restricting eligibility at the county level.

Third, the difference in the tax rates of the experiment and AFDC was an important factor. As the Table shows, while the maximum AFDC payment exceeds all experimental plans at zero income (except the "H" Plan, added later) it is exceeded by the experimental plans over some part of the income range for 43% of the families. And the average AFDC payment is exceeded by our treatments for almost 90% of the families. Moreover, the dominance of the experiment occurs where it is most important, among the working poor with some income. If families were allowed to change back and forth with few or no restrictions, then the introduction of AFDC-UP would mean that families in or dropping into the lower income range would be supported by welfare and could be simply analyzed as one more treatment.

Finally, it was not clear that the caseload would expand rapidly enough to provide real competition for the experiment. In order to measure this as well as we could we asked Joseph Heffernan, Professor of Social Work at the University of Wisconsin and an expert on the AFDC-UP program, to come to New Jersey and speak to welfare officials and caseworkers. Heffernan reported:

> Certainly there is a possibility that New Jersey will move in 1969-70 or 70-71 to provide substantial relief (through the welfare mechanism) to unemployed, under-employed, and low wage earners. It is, however, most unlikely that New Jersey will move fast enough to threaten the experimental design—unless the entire nation picks up enough speed to threaten it. . . . Despite the broad language of the statute, there appears little likelihood that New Jersey will have a significant AFDC-UP program in the coming year.[10]

Taken altogether, then, the introduction of AFDC-UP appeared to pose a set of problems, but not a threat to the operation of the experiment.

Nevertheless, two major precautionary measures were taken. First, an eighth treatment was introduced in all cities but Trenton, with a guarantee level of 4606 dollars and a tax rate of 50 percent—this dominated welfare payments at all income levels. Twenty-two percent of the experimental families enrolled in the next cities were assigned to this treatment. Second, a new set of rules was developed for the other cities, providing that no family could receive payments from the experiment and from welfare at the same time, although a family was permitted to change back and forth as often as desired. Interviews would continue to be conducted with welfare recipients in the experiment and the filing fee would be sent whenever income reports were filed.

We estimated that these changes, in any case, would restrict the welfare population within the experiment to from 15 to 20 percent of the sample and permit us to carry on the analysis as planned. In statistical terms, the percentage remains well within tolerance levels.[11]

Cross-Checking Income with the Local Public Assistance Agencies

Families enrolled in Paterson, Passaic, Jersey City, and Scranton were told that they could not receive experimental payments at the same time that they received cash benefits from a public assistance agency and that both welfare and the experiment should be kept faithfully informed of the family's status. The rules for the Trenton families were not changed, since we were reluctant to institute such a change for families in the middle of the experiment. However, they were advised that they were required to report payments from the experiment to the welfare agency and to report their welfare payments to us.

[10] J. Heffernan, Memorandum of September 26, 1968, "Best Guesses from New Jersey."
[11] It has risen from approximately 12 percent in the beginning to 23 percent currently.

We recognized at once that the single most important ingredient for success in this new system was a frank and cooperative relationship with the public assistance agencies involved and a careful scrutiny of the reporting habits of our own families. Neither of these appeared excessively difficult, since families seemed to be reporting public assistance and other transfers faithfully and the welfare agencies seemed receptive to our overtures for cooperation. Because of our strict confidentiality agreements with the Office of Economic Opportunity, the University of Wisconsin and the families themselves, we did not give lists of names of experimental families to the welfare agencies. Instead, we asked that the agencies request information about a specific family or families and we pledged to respond.

In all of this, we made two major assumptions: (1) that spelling out the rules to the experimental families at the beginning of the experiment and then reminding them every 6 months or so would be sufficient to ensure that all would report correctly to us and to welfare; (2) that welfare officials would be sufficiently interested in the experiment and in the concept of welfare reform to cooperate with us, iron out initial operating difficulties, and develop a procedure for mutually beneficial coexistence. As the situation in Mercer County (Trenton sample) shows, we were at least partially in error with respect to both assumptions. The following review of the events which occurs is instructive, and provides interesting insights both into how the current system operates and how a "new" system is likely to fare.

Trenton

Our first indication that there were problems came in November 1969 when we learned that the Mercer County prosecutor's office was investigating an alleged case of overlapping welfare and experimental payments. We attempted to convince both the prosecutor's office and the welfare officials that the existence of two similar transfer programs was confusing to the families, and that in the interest of experimentation on an important public issue we should try to settle the problem without prosecuting. Our main concern in Trenton was our fear that a public investigation of a family would cause other families to drop out of the experiment. Since the Trenton sample was small (87 families), and was a pilot for the rest of the experiment and could not be replaced without setting back the whole timetable severely, we were very sensitive about anything which would cause attrition.

The prosecutor subpoenaed the records of the family in question. We complied by providing information on payments made to the family by the experiment, and he decided to take the case to the Grand Jury. The Mercer County Welfare Board then requested from us the names of other families on our experiment who were also on welfare. We cooperated by supplying them with a list of 13 additional families reporting welfare income; and we indicated a willingness to meet with them and check on each of these families for overlap. The prosecutor's response was to issue 13 more subpoenas, one for each new family record.

In view of the small size of the Trenton sample and our fears about attrition, we felt it would endanger the experiment seriously to release the records of these families and thus frighten them out of the program. Moreover, our contract with OEO had tight confidentiality clauses in it and we felt bound not to release information without a court order. Accordingly, I sought legal advice and my counsel moved to quash the subpoenas. The Prosecutor's office countered with a court order to show cause why I should not be held in contempt of court.

Our motion to quash the subpoenas claimed: (1) that the information sought was confidential; (2) that the experiment was in the national interest (its contribution to planning for the President's Family Assistance Plan); (3) that Trenton was the key city (longest duration); (4) that losing families in Trenton would damage our whole experiment by destroying our pilot site (we would lose those families prosecuted for sure and probably others); and (5) that the action would be detrimental to the whole experiment. Prior to an actual hearing on these matters, we explained the entire background to the prosecutor and sought an amicable settlement without the damaging effect of publicity.

After several weeks of negotiating with the prosecutor's office, it was agreed that the best solution would be for the families with an overlap to repay the amount of the overlap to the welfare department. As it turned out, all of the families in question had had some overlap during the 18-month period since the beginning of the experiment (amounting to approximately $20,000 in payments the welfare department need not have paid had the families reported correctly). In order to provide as little disruption to the experiment as possible, it was decided that the Council for Grants to Families would make the repayment to the welfare department on behalf of the families. This was considered a legitimate charge to the experiment by OEO. We therefore filed a Stipulation with the Court, with the approval of the Court, which provided in part:

Based upon the affidavits filed in the above two motions and other available information, it appears that there may be a reasonable doubt as to whether any or all of the 14 families affected by the subpoenas were culpable or were honestly confused by a change in the statutory eligibility for (AFDC), which took effect January 1, 1969, or by incomplete casework by the county social workers, or by inadequate administrative controls as a result of the very experimental nature of the Graduated Work Incentive Experiment.

The Council for Grants to Families will re-examine and tighten all of its administrative procedures and will suggest complementary action by the County Welfare Board so as to assure as fully as possible the elimination of duplicate payments by the experimental program and the county welfare agency.

In addition to making repayment on behalf of the families, we decided to change the Rules of Operation with respect to welfare in Trenton. Our Trenton families could no longer receive experimental and welfare payments simultaneously, and a system of quarterly checks was proposed to the County Welfare Department and instituted with the approval of the Department.

ACKNOWLEDGMENT

The author wishes to thank Heather Ross, Arnold Shore, Jerilyn Fair, and Gwendolyn Cavanaugh. In particular, special thanks are due to Cheri Marshall, Director of Interview Development for Urban Opinion Surveys, who made many helpful editorial and substantive changes in the paper.

THE POLITICS OF EVALUATION:

The Case of Head Start*

Walter Williams and John W. Evans

ABSTRACT: In his Economic Opportunity Message to the Congress on February 19, 1969, President Nixon mentioned briefly that the preliminary results of a Westinghouse Learning Corporation–Ohio University evaluation indicated that "the long-term effect of Head Start appears to be extremely weak." This terse announcement triggered a major public controversy that ranged over the Congress, the executive branch, and the educational research community. Much of the debate focused on the esoteric techniques of modern statistical analysis, but the issues were far larger than the particular study. In conflict were two basic premises—one concerned with how to start programs and the other concerned with how to analyze them—that emerged independently in the mid-1960's. For the notion underlying much of the war on poverty—that effective programs could be developed quickly and launched full-scale (and Head Start was a prime case)—was being called into question by the type of evaluative analysis that lay at the base of the Planning, Programming, Budgeting System

* Reprinted from *The Annals of the American Academy of Political and Social Science,* **385** (September, 1969), pp. 118-132. Robert A. Levine, The Urban Institute, and Tom Glennan, The RAND Corporation, have provided helpful comments on earlier drafts of this paper. The views expressed are those of the authors, and not necessarily those of the organizations with which they are affiliated.

initiated in late 1965. The outcome of the clash will have profound implications for governmental procedures for developing new large-scale programs and measuring their results. This paper traces both the events that led up to the controversy and the controversy itself in order to look at the implications for future policy.

Walter Williams, is currently the Scholar-in-Residence, National Manpower Policy Task Force, and on leave from the Office of Economic Opportunity, where he is the Chief of the Research and Plans Division, Office of Research, Plans, Programs, and Evaluation. He previously taught at Indiana University and the University of Kentucky.

John W. Evans, is the Chief of the Evaluation Division, Office of Research, Plans, Programs, and Evaluation. He was previously with the U.S. Information Agency and Ohio State University.

A far-reaching controversy has flared over a recent Westinghouse Learning Corporation–Ohio University evaluation study showing that Head Start children now in the first, second, and third grades differed little, on a series of academic achievement and attitudinal measures, from comparable children who did not attend Head Start.

In the heat of the public controversy, there have been some old-fashioned political innuendos based on vile motives, but, in the main, the principal weapons in the battle have been the esoteric paraphernalia of modern statistical analysis. This is appropriate; the methodological validity of the Head Start study is a critical part of the debate. However, the real battle is not over the methodological purity of this particular study, but, rather, involves fundamental issues of how the federal government will develop large-scale programs and evaluate their results.

At this deeper level of the debate, what we are seeing is a head-on collision between two sets of ideas developed in the mid-1960's. On the one hand, there was the implicit premise of the early years of the War on Poverty that effective programs could be launched *full-scale,* and could yield significant improvements in the lives of the poor. Head Start was the archetype of this hope. Born in late 1964, the program was serving over a half-million children by the end of the following summer. On the other hand, the federal government, during roughly the same period, implemented the Planning, Programming, Budgeting System (PPBS), founded on the premise that rigorous analysis could produce a flow of information that would greatly improve the basis for decision-making. And the notion of evaluating both ongoing programs and new program ideas was fundamental to this type of thinking.

To see the dimensions and ramifications of this clash, it is necessary to return to those halcyon days in which the basic ideas of the War on Poverty and PPBS were formulated. Only then can we explore the present Head Start controversy to see what we may learn from it for the future.

THE EARLY DAYS OF THE WAR ON POVERTY

On June 4, 1965, President Johnson said in his Howard University Address, entitled "To Fulfill These Rights":

> To move beyond opportunity to achievement . . . I pledge you tonight this will be a chief goal of my administration, and of my program next year, and in years to come. And I hope, and I pray, and I believe, it will be a part of the program of all America. . . . It is the glorious opportunity of this generation to end the one huge wrong of the American Nation and, in so doing, to find America for ourselves, with the same immense thrill of discovery, which gripped those who first began to realize that here, at last, was a home for freedom.

The speech rang with hope—a call for basic changes that seemed well within our grasp. Viewed from the present, the address marked a distinct watershed. It was the crest of our domestic tranquility, based on the strong belief that black and white could work together in harmony as a nation. The speech also marked the high point of our faith in our ability to bring about significant change. Despite some of the rhetoric of the time to the effect that change would not be easy, it is fair to say that the faith was there that giant steps could be taken quickly. On that June day, there was the strong belief that the concentrated effort of the war on poverty, launched less than a year before, could bind the nation together.

This faith had two dimensions—first, that there could be a redistribution of funds and power toward the disadvantaged and, second, that, with such a redistribution, new programs could bring substantial improvement in the lot of the disadvantaged. The first was both more clearly perceived and more glamorous. To wrest power and money from the entrenched forces was heady stuff. Less clearly perceived was that redistribution was a necessary, but not a sufficient, condition of progress. New programs had to be devised, not just in broad brush strokes, but in the nitty-gritty detail of techniques and organization. Taking young black men from the ghettos to the wilderness of an isolated Job Corps Center was not a solution in itself. One had to worry about such mundane things as curriculum and the morale of these young men in a Spartan, female-absent environment. This atmosphere of confidence and enthusiasm led us to push aside the fact that we had neither the benefit of experience in such programs nor much realization of the difficulties involved in developing effective techniques.

Standing in 1969 on the battle-scarred ground of the War on Poverty, it is easy to see the naïveté and innocence of that time—scarely half a decade ago. Events were to crash upon us quickly. Vietnam was to end any hope for large funds. Riots, militancy, and the rise of separatism made the earlier ideas of harmony seem quaint. Those with established power did not yield easily either to moral suasion or to more forceful means. Real power is still a well-guarded commodity.

Most important for this discussion, we have found, over a wide range of social-action programs, both how unyielding the causes of poverty are and how little we really know about workable techniques for helping the disadvantaged. The point is not that we are unable to derive "reasonable" programs from bits and pieces of information and hard thinking. We *can*, we *have*. But our experience seems to point up, over and over again, the almost insurmountable difficulty of bridging the gap between brilliantly conceived programs and those which work in the field. Great pressures exist for new "solutions" to social problems to be rushed into national implementation as soon as they are conceived. But the attempts to go directly from sound ideas to full-scale programs seem so often to end in frustration and disappointment.

THE ORIGINS OF ANALYSIS WITHIN THE GOVERNMENT

In the early 1960's, Secretary Robert McNamara relied on a conceptual framework, formulated at the RAND Corporation, to make analysis a critical factor in the decision-making process of the Department of Defense. In October 1965, drawing on this experience, the Bureau of the Budget issued Bulletin No. 66-3, establishing the Planning, Programming, Budgeting System within all federal departments and agencies. The departments and agencies were instructed to "establish an adequate central staff or staffs for analysis, planning, and programming [with] ... the head of the central analytical staff ... directly responsible to the head of the agency or his deputy." These central offices were to be interposed between the head of the agency and the operating programs and were charged with undertaking analysis that would provide a hard quantitative basis on which to make decisions. For social-action agencies, this was a radical change in the way of doing business.

Before PPBS, not much progress had been made in analyzing social-action programs. Although the broad approach developed at the Department of Defense might be used in such analyses, the relevance of particular methodological tools was less clear. For example, there was little actual experience with the kinds of evaluations which seek to measure the effects of a social-action program on its participants or the external world. And a host of formidable problems existed, such as the lack of good operational definitions for key variables, the shortage of adequate test instruments, and the difficulties of developing valid control groups. Thus, the usefulness of evaluative analysis for social-action programs would have to be proved in particular situations.

Beyond this was the political question of bringing analysis into the agency's policy-making process. As analytical studies were quite new to social-action programs, their results—especially those measuring the effectiveness of ongoing programs—were seen as a threat by those with established decision-making positions. Unfavorable evaluation results have a potential either to restrict a program's funds or to force major changes in the direction of the program. One can hardly assume passive acceptance of such an outcome by the managers and operators of programs.

Thus, one can see how the tiny dark cloud of the Head Start controversy formed at this early date. The push toward new operating programs and the emerging PPBS brought about a role conflict between those who ran programs (and believed in them) and those who analyzed these programs (and whose job it was to be skeptical of them). As former Director of the Bureau of the Budget Charles L. Schultze has observed:

> [In the] relationship between the political process and the decision-making process as envisaged by PPB . . . I do not believe that there is an irreconcilable conflict. . . . But they are different kinds of systems representing different ways of arriving at decisions. The two systems are so closely interrelated that PPB and its associated analytic method can be an effective tool for aiding decisions only when its relationships with the political process have been carefully articulated and the appropriate roles of each defined. . . . It may, indeed, be necessary to guard against the naïveté of the system analyst who ignores *political* constraints and believes that efficiency alone produces virtue. But it is equally necessary to guard against the naïveté of the decision maker who ignores *resource* constraints and believes that virtue alone produces efficiency.[1]

Looking in retrospect, at the early PPBS vis-à-vis social-action programs, it may be said that: (1) the absolute power of analysis was oversold and (2) the conflicts in the system between the analytical staff and the operators of the programs was underestimated. Hence, the politics of evaluation—in essence, the clash between methodology, political forces, and bureaucracy—looms much larger than was imagined in those early days. At the same time, knowing more today about how difficult it is to develop and operate effective programs, the need for analysis—the need to assess both our current operations and our new ideas—seems even more pressing in the less troubled days of 1965.[2]

---

[1] Charles L. Schultze, *The Politics and Economics of Public Spending* (Washington, D.C.: Brookings Institution, 1968), pp. 16-17, 76.

[2] PPBS has recently been subjected to a searching appraisal by a number of scholars (including several major practitioners) in the Joint Economic Committee's three-volume study *The Analysis and Evaluation of Public Expenditures: The PPBS System,* (Washington, D.C.: Government Printing Office, 1969). The weight of opinion is that PPBS—the formal system in which analysis is carried out—is having its problems and may well be in political trouble. At the same time, there is general agreement concerning the urgent need for sound analysis. What is at issue, then, is the format for analysis. For example: Should analysis such as that of PPBS be tied to the budget process? But this issue need not be addressed here, for the main concern of the paper is analysis, and not necessarily its particular formal wrapping. Of course, whatever the formal structure, analysis will still have to confront politics and bureaucracy.

BACKGROUND OF THE HEAD START STUDY

With these general considerations as background, we now need to look briefly at the key elements within OEO: the Head Start program; OEO's analytical office, the Office of Research, Plans, Programs, and Evaluation (RPP&E); and the general state of evaluation of the antipoverty programs prior to the Westinghouse study.

Head Start

The concepts underlying Head Start were based on the thinking of some of the best people in the child-development area and on a variety of research findings (probably relatively rich compared to most other new programs) suggesting a real potential for early childhood training, but offering few and often conflicting guidelines as to the detailed types of programs to be developed. In fact, the original concept of Head Start was that it was to be an explicitly experimental program reaching a limited number of children. The idea, however, was too good. It was an ideal symbol for the new war on poverty. It generated immediate national support and produced few political opponents. In this atmosphere, one decision led easily to another, and Head Start was quickly expanded to a $100 million national program serving a half-million children. In the beginning, Head Start consisted mainly of six-to-eight-week summer projects under a variety of sponsors (school systems, churches, and community-action agencies, for example) with a high degree of local autonomy concerning how the project was to be carried out. Later, Head Start funded a significant number of full-year projects with a similar policy of flexibility and local autonomy.

The immense popularity of the early days carried over. Head Start remained OEO's showcase program, supported strongly by the Congress, communities, poor mothers, and a deeply committed band of educators (many with a significant personal involvement in the program).

RPP&E

Analysis came early to OEO because its Office of Research, Plans, Programs, and Evaluation was one of the original independent staff offices reporting directly to the head of the agency. RPP&E predated the *PPBS Bulletin,* but was, in many ways, the epitome of the PPBS analytical staff, in that it was headed by RAND alumni who stressed the power of analysis. RPP&E was both a major developer of analytical data and a key factor in the agency's decision-making process. As one might expect, in this role it had more than once clashed with program-operators.

Evaluation at OEO

Critical to our discussion is the fact that RPP&E did not establish a separate Evaluation Division until the autumn of 1967. Prior to that time, most of the responsibility for evaluation rested with the programs, but RPP&E had had some involvement, particularly in trying to use data developed by the programs to make overall program-assessments.

In the case of Head Start, the program itself had initiated a large number of individual project-evaluations, mainly of the summer program. Across a wide range of these projects it was found that, in general, participants who had been given various cognitive and affective tests at the beginning of the Head Start program showed gains when tested again at the end of the program. However, virtually all the follow-up studies found that any differences which had been observed between the Head Start and control groups immediately after the end of Head Start were largely gone by the end of the first year of school. The meaning of this "catch up" by the control group has been and still is subject to considerable debate, ranging from doubts that the immediate post-program gains were anything more than test-retest artifacts, to assertions that the superior Head Start children raise the performance levels of their non–Head Start classmates.

RPP&E had tried fairly early to develop its own national assessments of Head Start, but found little support for such undertakings withing the program. Two such studies were developed, but the results were marred by technical and analytical problems. At the time of the establishment of the Evaluation Division, therefore, no good evidence existed as to overall Head Start effectiveness–a fact that was beginning to concern the agency, the Bureau of the Budget, and some members of Congress.[3]

As one might guess, the program offices hardly greeted the newly created Evaluation Division with enthusiasm–no one was happy with a staff office looking over his shoulder. In a formal division of labor, three types of evaluation were recognized. RPP&E was given primary responsibility for evaluation of the overall effectiveness of all OEO programs (Type I). The programs retained primary responsibility for both the evaluation of the relative effectiveness of different program strategies and techniques, for example, different curricula in Head Start (Type II) and the on-site monitoring of individual projects (Type III). The basic logic of this division of labor was to ensure that Type I overall evaluations would be carried out, to locate the responsibility for these evaluations at a staff-office level removed from the programs, and, at the same time, to place the Type II and Type III evaluation responsibilities at the program level because of the greater need for detailed program knowledge that these kinds of evaluation require.

This division of labor also matches the type of evaluation with the types of decisions for which different levels within the organization have primary respon-

[3] Later, Head Start made its own attempt at national evaluation through its network of university-based evaluation and research centers. But failure to create control groups and comparable procedures made the results unsatisfactory, and the evaluation component of these centers was discontinued in 1969.

sibility—the overall mixture of programs and resource allocation at the top (Type I), and program design (Type II) and management (Type III) at the program level.

THE WESTINGHOUSE STUDY

Thus, it was out of this total complex of conditions that the Westinghouse evaluation of Head Start originated:

The explosive expansion of Head Start from what was originally conceived as a limited experimental program to a large national program almost overnight.

A developing commitment throughout the government to increasing analysis and assessment of all government programs.

The national popularity of the Head Start program and the widespread equation of this popularity with effectiveness.

Previous evaluations of Head Start that did not provide adequate information on the program's overall impact.

The development of a new staff-level evaluation function at OEO charged with producing timely and policy-relevant evaluations of the overall impact of all OEO programs.

As one in a series of national evaluations of the major OEO programs, the new RPP&E Evaluation Division proposed for the Head Start program an *ex post facto* study design in which former Head Start children, now in the first, second, and third grades of school, were to be tested on a series of cognitive and affective measures, and their scores compared with those of a control group. Because the program was in its third year and there was, as yet, no useful assessment of its overall effects, time was an important consideration in deciding on an *ex post facto* design. Such a design would produce results relatively soon (less than a year), as compared with a methodologically more desirable longitudinal study which would take considerably longer.

Within the agency, Head Start administrators opposed the study on a number of grounds, including the inadequacy of the *ex post facto* design, the weakness of available test instruments, and the failure to include other Head Start goals such as health, nutrition, and community involvement. In sum, Head Start contended that this limited study might yield misleading negative results which could shake the morale of those associated with Head Start and bring unwarranted cutbacks in the program. RPP&E evaluators did not deny the multiplicity of goals, but maintained that cognitive improvement was a primary goal of Head Start and, moreover, was an outcome which reflected, indirectly, the success of certain other activities (for example, better health should facilitate better school performance). Further, the study's proponents in RPP&E recognized the risks outlined by Head Start officials, but argued that the need for evaluative evidence in order to improve the decision-making process makes it necessary to run these risks. After much internal debate, the Director of OEO ordered that the study should be done, and a contract was made in June 1968 with the Westinghouse Learning Corporation and Ohio University.

The study proceeded in relative quiet, but as it neared completion, hints came out of its negative findings. Because President Nixon was preparing to make a major address on the poverty program, including a discussion of Head Start, the White House inquired about the study and was alerted to the preliminary negative results. In his Economic Opportunity Message to the Congress on February 19, 1969, President Nixon alluded to the study and noted that "the long-term effect of Head Start appears to be extremely weak."

This teaser caused a flood of requests for a full disclosure of the study's findings. In the Congress, where hearings were being held on OEO legislation, strong claims were made that OEO was holding back the results to protect Head Start. This was not the case, but the demands did present a real dilemma for the agency—particularly RPP&E. For the results at that time were quite preliminary, and Westinghouse was in the process of performing further analysis and verification of the data. Hence, RPP&E, which, in general, was anxious for evaluative analysis to have an impact at the highest levels of government, did not want to suffer the embarrassment of a national debate over tentative results that might change materially in the later analysis. However, after much pressure, an early, incomplete version of the study was released. In June, the final report was published, and it confirmed the preliminary findings.

These background facts are important in order to understand why the controversy rose to such a crescendo, as it ranged over the executive branch and the Congress, with wide coverage in the press. The Westinghouse study is, perhaps unfortunately, an instructive example of public reaction to evaluations of social-action programs. As we turn now to a brief description of the study, its findings, and a discussion of its methodological and conceptual base, this milieu must be kept in mind.

The study and its major conclusions are summarized succinctly in the following statement by the contractor:

The basic question posed by the study was:

To what extent are the children now in the first, second, and third grades who attended Head Start programs different in their intellectual and social-personal development from comparable children who did not attend?

To answer this question, a sample of one hundred and four Head Start centers across the country was chosen. A sample of children from these centers who had gone on to the first, second, and third grades in local area schools and a matched sample of control children from the same grades and schools who had not attended Head Start were administered a series of tests covering various aspects of cognitive and affective development [The Metropolitan Readiness Test, the Illinois Test of Psycholinguistic Abilities, the Stanford Achievement Test, the Children's Self-Concept Index, and the like]. The parents of both the former Head Start enrollees and the control children were interviewed and a broad range of attitudinal, social, and economic data was collected. Directors or other officials of all the centers were interviewed and information was collected on various characteristics of the current local Head Start programs. The primary grade teachers rated both groups of children on achievement motivation and supplied a description of the intellectual and emotional environment of their elementary schools.

Viewed in broad perspective, the major conclusions of the study are:

1. Summer programs appear to be ineffective in producing any gains in cognitive and affective development that persist into the early elementary grades.

2. Full-year programs appear to be ineffective as measured by the tests of affective development used in the study, but are marginally effective in producing gains in cognitive development that could be detected in grades one, two, and three. Programs appeared to be of greated effectiveness for certain subgroups of centers, notably in mainly Negro centers, in scattered programs in the central cities, and in Southeastern centers.

3. Head Start children, whether from summer or from full-year programs, still appear to be considerably below national norms for the standardized tests of language development and scholastic achievement, while performance on school readiness at grade one approaches the national norm.

4. Parents of Head Start enrollees voiced strong approval of the program and its influence on their children. They reported substantial participation in the activities of the centers.

In sum, the Head Start children cannot be said to be *appreciably* different from their peers in the elementary grades who did not attend Head Start in most aspects of cognitive and affective development measured in this study, with the exception of the slight, but nonetheless significant, superiority of full-year Head Start children on certain measures of cognitive development.[4]

METHODOLOGICAL ISSUES

We now turn to the methodological and conceptual validity of the study—the *explicit* focal point of the controversy—and this presents difficult problems of exposition. First, both of us are protagonists on one side of the controversy, with Evans being one of the major participants in the debate. Second, a presentation of the methodological questions in sufficient detail to allow the reader to form his own opinions would require an extensive discussion. The final Westinghouse report comprises several hundred pages, with a significant portion

[4] *The Impact of Head Start: An Evaluation of the Effects of Head Start on Children's Cognitive and Affective Development,* Westinghouse Learning Corporation–Ohio University, July 12, 1969, pp. 2, 7-8.

of it directed specifically to methodological issues. Under these circumstances, we will summarize the major criticisms that have been made of the study and comment on them briefly in this section. Then, in the next major section, we will set out *our* judgment as to the overall technical adequacy of the report and its usefulness for decision-making.

Criticisms of the Study

1. The study is too narrow. It focuses only on cognitive and affective outcomes. Head Start is a much broader program which includes health, nutrition, and community objectives, and any proper evaluation must evaluate it on all these objectives.

Our experience has been that one of the reasons for the failure of so many evaluations is that they have aspired to do too much. We did not think that it was possible to cover all of the Head Start objectives in the same study; therefore, we purposely limited the study's focus to those which we considered most important. Despite its many other objectives, in the final analysis Head Start should be evaluated mainly on the basis of the extent to which it has affected the life-chances of the children involved. In order to achieve such effects, cognitive and motivational changes seem essential.

2. The study fails to give adequate attention to variations among the Head Start programs. It lumps the programs together into an overall average and does not explore what variation there may be in effectiveness as a function of differing program styles and characteristics. The study, therefore, fails to give any guidance concerning what detailed changes (for example, types of curricula) should be made in the program.

This is essentially correct. As discussed earlier, the purpose of the evaluation was to measure the overall effectiveness of the Head Start program in a reasonably short period of time. This in no way denies the need for a study to get at the question of variation among the programs. The fact is that both overall and detailed information are frequently needed, but the latter generally takes much longer to develop.

3. The sample of full-year centers in the study is too small to provide confidence in the study's findings. Because of such a small sample, the lack of statistically significant differences between the Head Start and control groups is to be expected, and gives a misleading indication that the programs had no effect. With such a small sample, it would take quite large differences to reach a satisfactory level of statistical significance.

The 104 Head Start centers, selected at random, were chosen in order to provide an adequate *total* sample. This was then broken down into an approximate 70-30 division in order to approximate the actual distribution of summer and full-year programs. If we were doing the study over, we would select a larger number of full-year centers. The main advantage, however, would be to allow more analysis of subgroups within the full-year sample. It is very unlikely that the study's principal conclusions about the overall effectiveness of the program would be altered by a larger sample. A detailed "power of the test" analysis showed that with the present sample size and variance, the statistical tests are capable of detecting differences between the experimental and control groups below the level of what would be practically meaningful. Forgetting the statistical complexities for a minute, the simple fact is that the differences between Head Start and control-group scores were quite small. Even in the cases in which differences were statistically significant, they were so small as to have little practical importance.

4. The sample is not representative. Many of the original randomly chosen centers had to be eliminated.

The study suffered a loss of some of the centers specified in the original sample because (1) some small rural areas had all their eligible children in the Head Start program (and hence no controls could be found) and (2) some communities prohibited the testing of children in the school system. Centers were substituted randomly, and a comparison of the final chosen sample with the total universe of Head Start centers showed the two to be very similar on a large number of factors (for example, rural-urban location, racial composition, and the like).

5. The test instruments used in this study, and indeed all existing instruments for measuring cognitive and affective states in children, are primitive. They were not developed for disadvantaged populations, and they are probably so gross and insensitive that they are unable to pick up many of the real and important changes that Head Start has produced in children.

It is entirely possible that this is true. However, most of the cognitive measures are the same ones being used by other child-development and Head Start researchers doing work on disadvantaged children. In those cases (relatively few) where previous studies have shown positive changes on these very same measures, they have seldom been questioned or disregarded because of the inadequacy of the instruments. In the affective area, Westinghouse found no appropriate test instruments and had to devise its own. Hence, the results should be viewed as suggestive, but no more. The Westinghouse study used the best instruments available, and with these instruments, few appreciable differences are found between children who had been part of a Head Start program and those who had not.

6. The study is based on an *ex post facto* design which is inherently faulty because it attempts to generate a control group by matching former Head Start children with other non-Head Start children. A vast number of factors, either alone or acting together, could produce a superior non-Head Start group which would obscure the effect of the program.

It is always possible in any *ex post facto* study that failure to achieve adequate matching on all relevant variables (particularly self-selectivity factors) can occur. *Ex post facto* studies, however, are a respected and widely used scientific procedure, although one which does not provide the greater certainty which results from the classic before-after experimental design carried out in controlled laboratory conditions.

In the Westinghouse study, the two groups were matched on age, sex, race, and kindergarten attendance. Any residual differences in socioeconomic status were equated by two different statistical procedures: a random-replication-covariance analysis and a nonparametric matching procedure. Both statistical techniques, which equated the two groups on parent's occupation, education, and per capita income, yielded the same basic results on the cognitive and affective comparisons between Head Start and control-group children.

7. The study tested the children in the first, second, and third grades of elementary school—after they had left Head Start. Its findings merely demonstrate that Head Start achievements do not persist after the children return to poverty homes and ghetto schools. Rather than demonstrating that Head Start does not have appreciable effects, the study merely shows that there effects tend to fade out when the Head Start children return to a poverty environment.

It is possible that poor teachers, impoverished environment, and other similar factors, eliminated a significant cognitive advantage gained by Head Start children during the Head Start period. But even if this is true, we must have real doubts about the current course of the program. Unless Head Start *alone* can be improved so as to have positive effects which do not disappear, or unless Follow Through or some other program can be developed to provide subsequent reinforcement that solidifies the gains of Head Start children, the *present* worth of the gains seem negligible. Whatever the cause, the fact that the learning gains are transitory is a most compelling fact for determining future policy.

8. The study's comparison of Head Start with non-Head Start children in the same classrooms fails to take into account secondary or spillover effects from the Head Start children. The children who have had Head Start are likely to infect their non-Head Start peers with their own greater motivation and interest in learning. Their presence in the classroom is also likely to cause the elementary school teacher to upgrade her entire level of teaching or to give more attention to, and therefore produce greater gains in, the less advanced non-Head Start group. Thus, the study minimizes Head Start's effect by comparing the Head Start children with another group of children which has been indirectly improved by the Head Start children themselves.

This is certainly a possibility. However, most of the previous before-after studies of Head Start's cognitive effects have shown, at most, small gains—so small that it is hard to imagine their having such major secondary effect on teachers and peers. Moreover, the first-grade children in the Westinghouse study were tested during the early part of their first-grade year—prior to the time when such secondary influence on teachers or peer children would have had a chance to occur. In results of direct measurements of the children (Metropolitan Readiness Test, Illinois Test of Psycholinguistic Abilities, and the like), there were only marginal differences between the Head Start and control-group children at that time. Also, on the Children's Behavior Inventory, an instrument which obtained teachers' ratings of the children, there were few significant differences between the two groups, indicating that the teachers were not able to perceive any differences between the motivation of the Head Start and non-Head Start children. In the light of these findings, it is hard to see how spillover or secondary effects could have occurred to an extent which contaminated the control group.

AN ASSESSMENT

Our overall assessment of the study is as follows:

1. In terms of its methodological and conceptual base, the study is a *relatively* good one. This in no way denies that many of the criticisms made of the study are valid. However, for the most part, they are the kind of criticisms that can be made of most pieces of social science research conducted outside the laboratory, in a real-world setting, with all of the logistical and measurement problems that such studies entail. And these methodological flaws open the door to the more political issues. Thus, one needs not only to examine the methodological substance of the criticisms which have been made of the study, but also to understand the social concern which lies behind them as well. Head Start has elicited national sympathy and has had the support and involvement of the educational profession. It is understandable that so many should rush to the defense of such a popular and humane program. But how many of the concerns over the size of the sample, control-group equivalency, and the appropriateness of covariance analysis, for example, would have been registered if the study had found positive differences in favor of Head Start?

2. The scope of the study was *limited,* and it therefore failed to provide the answers to many questions which would have been useful in determining what specific changes should be made in the programs.

3. Longitudinal studies, based on larger samples and covering a broader range of objectives, would be better, and should be undertaken. But until they are instituted, this study provides a useful piece of information that we can fit into a pattern of other reasonable evidence to improve our basis for decision-making. Thus, the Westinghouse study extends our knowledge, but does not fly in the face of past evidence. For the summer program, the study of a national sample shows what smaller studies have indicated—no lasting gain for the Head

Start children relative to their peers. This may deflate some myths, but does not affect any hard facts. For the full-year program, the evidence of some limited effect is about as favorable as any we have found to date.

We imagine that this type of positive, but qualified assessment will fit any *relatively* good evaluation for some time to come. For we have never seen a field evaluation of a social-action program that could not be faulted legitimately by good methodologists, and we may never see one. But, if we are willing to accept real-world imperfections, and to use evaluative analysis with prudence, then such analysis can provide a far better basis for decision-making than we have had in the past.

What, then, does the Westinghouse study provide that will help in making decisions? First, the negative findings indicate that the program is failing, on the average, to produce discernible school success for its participants. Put more bluntly, the study shows that along the key cognitive and affective dimension, the program is not working at all well. And from this, one can infer, directly, that we should search hard for, and test, new techniques to make learning gains in the Head Start classroom more permanent and, indirectly, that the years before and after Head Start should also be looked at carefully. Second, the evidence suggests the superiority of the full-year over the summer programs. Most of all, we believe that the value of the study consists in the credible, validating evidence which it provides that the honeymoon of the last few years really ought to be over, and that the hard work of finding effective techniques should start in earnest.

Thus, the study pushes policymakers toward certain decisions, particularly those involving within-program tradeoffs—more experimentation and more full-year projects in place of summer projects. Yet, and this would be true no matter how good the study was, the evidence is not a sufficient condition for major program decisions. The last statement holds even for the within-program choices (tradeoffs, but not overall cutbacks) and takes on greater cogency when one seeks implications for decisions concerning the need for more, or fewer, re-sources. The evaluative evidence must be considered in the light of other pieces of information and various highly important political judgments. For example: How deleterious would a program cutback be for program morale, or for our commitment to increase the outlays going to the disadvantaged for education? Surely, no reasonable person would claim that evaluative evidence alone is sufficient. Rather, such choices ought to be political, in the broad sense of that term, with credible evaluative data—a commodity heretofore in short supply—being considered as one of the inputs in the choice process.[5]

---

[5] It is important to note that Mr. Nixon's speech which first suggested the negative results called, not for a cutback in Head Start, but for continuing commitment to early childhood programs and an extensive effort to find new ways to meet the educational needs of the disadvantaged. For what it is worth, this is also the author's view.

CONCLUSIONS

In this section, we shall first present a number of inferences which, in our opinion, can be drawn concerning the larger issues of this controversy and then touch on the unknowns that still plague us. The former fall into two categories—program operations and evaluation.

Operations

1. We should be far more skeptical than in the past of our technical capability to mount effective large-scale programs, particularly in those areas in which the main program goal is to provide a material, positive change in an individual's capacity to earn or to learn. We should distinguish clearly between such "opportunity" programs and maintenance programs in which the primary goal is to deliver a service that is itself a highly valued commodity, for example, money and food. The technical problems of the latter are relatively simple compared to those of programs which attempt to offer earning or educational opportunities. For example, politics aside, it would not be difficult, *technically,* to mount a large-scale food or income-maintenance program far superior to the ones we have presently. But in programs which specialize in opportunity, we often simply do not know what to do technically in order to reach our goals.

2. For opportunity programs, we need to start, as a highest-priority activity, a systematic, concerted effort to develop new ideas for restructuring ongoing programs or creating new ones, and to test the merits of these ideas, on a small scale, before mounting large-scale national programs. Clearly, political concerns will often override this dictum of testing on a small scale. A government program cannot be managed by the procedures which are effective in a research laboratory. Large-scale programs will often start without a prior tested model. But, at the margin, an effort to test may both produce useful tested models and make us think harder about starting large-scale programs without such testing. It is our belief that a commitment by the government to the systematic search for new ideas is a key point which has great potential for improving opportunity programs. Analysis cannot (and should not) replace politics, but it can, over time, facilitate better political decisions.

Evaluation

We urgently need to evaluate the effectiveness of present programs.

In many areas, we now have methodological tools that will allow us to do evaluations much superior to those done in the past.

These evaluations will have limitations, both in terms of scope and in terms of techniques. However, if used in conjunction with other reasonable evidence, such studies can materially improve our base of decision-making information.

The milieu for meaningful program-evaluation involves an interaction of methodology, bureaucracy, and politics; it will therefore often be the case that attacks which are methodological in form but ideological in concern will be made against evaluations.

Major evaluations of programs should be performed by an office and staff removed from the operating program. Self-evaluation is an almost impossible task for a manager who has strong convictions about the value of his program. A separate office can at least institutionalize a relative degree of objectivity, in that it can be charged specifically, within the agency, with the task of program measurement, not program defense. Some people, however, feel that even this may be illusory inasmuch as the staff office will be serving the agency head, who, after all, is the program's chief manager. One cannot escape the fact that evaluation, with its potential for indicating that a program is not working, is a weapon of the arsenal of analysis which is difficult to handle.

Finally, for those of us who urge more evaluation, it is well to remember that evaluation is only one of many inputs—political, bureaucratic, and the like—in the decision-making process, and does not serve as a substitute for good judgment.

The Remaining Unknowns

We have come down strongly on the side of analysis—measuring ongoing programs and testing new ones. At the same time, we have recognized the technical limitations of evaluation and have warned that they must be used with prudence in the light of these limitations. But is this not a politically naïve warning, and hence really a below-the-belt punch to the argument for expanding social programs? As the *New York Times* reported on April 18, 1969: "A number of social scientists . . . have expressed fears that Congress or the Administration will seize upon the [Westinghouse] report's generally negative conclusions as an excuse to downgrade or discard the Head Start Program." Even when administrators and legislators are pure of heart (but relatively ignorant of the limitations of analytical techniques), will they not overvalue, and hence overreact to, quantitative evaluations because of their aura of scientific accuracy? Will the guideline "test and prove before operating on a large scale" become a façade for disparaging all new ideas and retrenching our commitment to the disadvantaged?

These are profound and difficult problems for which there are no simple solutions. For example, a legitimate question to ask us, on the basis of our stated convictions, is whether we would have opted for a large-scale Head Start program at its inception. Even given today's knowledge, we might have done so, because the redistributive kinds of changes, which we discussed earlier, are a critical need. At the same time, we would not today urge either an increase in the program, as now constituted, or new starts on a large scale in the educational area, withour prior testing.

We recognize the danger that the results of evaluation and systematic testing can be ill used. But what course of action is not dangerous? What "good" approach cannot be turned to evil? Is it not even more hazardous to proceed boldly—as if we know, when we do not? Does it seem wise to launch new large-scale opportunity programs—amid verbal paeans, but with no solid evidence of success—and to continue to believe our earlier words without a thought of investigating the outcome?

As we pose these questions, we trail off into gray areas of nagging doubts, without a burst of penetrating truth. This seems fitting—for to stand unsurely in a morass of conflicting issues simply mirrors the larger reality of today. The confidence of 1965 is literally light years behind us.

IV

ORGANIZING FOR LARGE-SCALE
EVALUATIVE RESEARCH

12

OBSERVATIONS ON THE ORGANIZATION

OF SOCIAL RESEARCH*

Peter H. Rossi

INTRODUCTION

When social scientists think of their intellectual ancestors, they usually conjure up an image of a man alternating between the classroom and his study, with side excursions to the library. Only a few means of production were at his disposal—comfortable Victorian armchairs, pigeonhole desks, scratchy pens and stiff paper, and the reference volumes of his extensive private library. At least, this is the nostalgic image of the nineteenth and early twentieth-century sociologist.

There is some evidence that this myth is somewhat overdrawn. Many of our more prominent ancestors engaged in extensive firsthand data collection: We have only to think of Booth and Le Play to conjure up alternative images of Victorian figures interviewing the poor. However, even those who are known today mainly for their "theoretical" work, also engaged in some data grubbing: Max Weber played an important role in the early social survey movement in Germany and Durkheim and his students played similar roles in France.[1] In this

*From R. O'Toole (Ed.), *The Organization Management and Tactics of Social Research*. Cambridge, Mass.: Schenkman Publishing Company, 1971.

[1] For a fascinating account of the beginnings of empirical social research in Germany centering around the *Verein für Sozial Politik*, in which Max Weber played an important

country, Ward, Ross, Giddings, and their students dabbled, although not as extensively, in generating social data directly from observations "in the field."

Nevertheless, the predominant work styles of our intellectual forebearers were not too far from the mythical image of nostalgic recall; or, at least, they were closer to that image than we are today. The art and practice of social science has changed. We are in a period in which empirical social research is the predominant style of sociology and social psychology. For better or for worse, we are committed to a style of social science which regards the collection and analysis of empirical data very highly. Indeed, we emphasize empirical work so strongly that it often appears that social researchers prefer to collect their *own* data even when suitable equivalent data already exist.

The shift to empirical social research as a style of scientific activity has also meant a change in the organization of scientific activity. While there are still many social scientists who are essentially solo practitioners with perhaps a few students as assistants and junior colleagues, the era of collaborative research has arrived. Teams of researchers formed for *ad hoc* purposes are very common. But even more important has been the growth of relatively permanent research organizations whose existence extends beyond the life of specific research projects and in which there may also be an extensive division of labor.

In addition, the means of production have changed and become more technically sophisticated. The typewriter has replaced the pen; the research institute's building has superseded the scholar's study; and the computer has replaced the tallysheets. The most recent technical advance, the copying machine, has had an impact on the use of written documents. Dissemination of research findings occurs more through the use of private printing means, with journal publication serving more as an archive function than as a means for diffusing new knowledge.

This change in the means of production has occurred so recently that we have not yet had the time to observe its full empirical richness and to speculate on its meaning for our field and the institutions, particularly the university, to which it is closely related. In particular, we know that social research is more complexly organized now than it was even a decade ago, let alone 30 years ago, but the forms that the organization of social research have taken have yet to be cataloged or assessed. It is clear that we have borrowed from the experiences of older disciplines who went empirical earlier, and it is equally clear that we have developed new organizational forms especially adapted to our own needs and technology.

---

role, see Anthony Oberschall, *Empirical Social Research in Germany, 1849-1914* (Basic Books, New York, 1965). A similar account of empirical research in France can be found in the doctoral dissertation of Terry N. Clark, *"Empirical Social Research in France,"* Columbia University, 1966.

The organization of social research is the main concern of this paper. Three central questions will be raised in the pages which follow:

First, what are the forces that foster the organization of research into centers and institutes and for the more informal organization of research into efforts by collaborating teams?

Secondly, what are forms taken by research organizations in the present period and the advantages and disadvantages of each form in relation to the functions for which organizations are apparently devised?

Thirdly, can we make some statements concerning optimal organizational forms for research purposes of different sorts?

GAINS FROM ORGANIZED SOCIAL RESEARCH

Clearly, a large part of human activity is organized in at least the minimal sense of at least two human actors jointly contributing to a shared activity. The forces which sustain organized activity are the gains to participants arising from participation in organizations as against pursuing an activity on their own. That man is a social animal is attested to by the fact that one of the major gains to participants in organized activity comes form the satisfactions arising from interaction *per se*.

These are very general formulations, applying with equal force to the most trivial and to the most critical activities. Furthermore, they do not help to understand in a specific instance either the form of organization that develops nor the degree of organization. In the broadest sense, there are no solitary scholars or researchers; indeed, even the mythical Robinson Crusoe survived on the gains from past organized human activity that he retained in his memory (let alone the help he got from Friday). The solitary sociologist scholar relies on a more organized form of memory residing in the volumes of his library, on the results obtained by censuses, surveys, etc. The critical issue, therefore, is not whether empirical research is organized, but to what extent? Furthermore, what are the benefits (and costs) to be gleaned (or suffered) from entering into relatively enduring forms of interaction with other persons in the pursuit of empirical social research?

Part of the gains from organization stem from ease in dealing with the accomplishment of research tasks. These may be called the "internal" gains from organization. There are also gains in the area of "foreign relations," that is, gains in the ability to deal effectively with exogenous elements in the environment. We will deal first with the internal gains.

Perhaps the most obvious gains from enduring collaboration among social researchers are those which flow from collegiality. To have a set of peers who share the same interests and goals and who therefore provide an engaged audience as well as a source of advice and ideas is a gain of some appreciable magnitude.

Of course, many social scientists are to be found "naturally" within environments which provide them with peers, especially those who are within academic departments of sociology.[2] What is to be gained from organization in this respect that could not be obtained from departmental colleagues? The problem lies in that departmental colleagues are bound together in a set of varied relationships, some of which may inhibit collegiality. The formation of a research organization segregates out those relationships which are bound up with common interests in research and facilitates collegiality by providing a context in which those bonds of interest held in common are stressed and other relationships (which may be competitive or fraught with some conflict) are suppressed. A research organization provides each member with the legitimate right to access to the other members in a role which is task oriented and specific rather than possibly affectively oriented and diffuse. Thus, department members may and often do form a research organization whose main function it is to provide a context wherein the ordinary forms of relating to one another as departmental colleagues are suspended in favor of more task oriented relationships, at the same time reinforcing the solidarity that arises when men share some goal in common.

Another gain to organization lies in the development of equity in the distribution of resources. In some cases, the resources may be access to computational facilities; in other cases, it may be access to students that is the main resource; in still others, actual funds may be at stake.[3] In cases where resources are scarce, a research organization may help to provide at least the appearance of equity by whatever distribution may have to take place.

In some fields the distribution of resources is particularly important. For example, in astronomy, time on a telescope is limited, with more demand for its use than can be accommodated easily. Observatory organization takes on the function of making equitable allocations. In the social science fields, computers, social psychology laboratories, secretarial help, research space, or research assistants are the main types of resources around which organization may grow to ensure adherence to a "proper" division of resources.[4]

---

[2] The importance of the social and intellectual support provided by a group of professional peers can be seen most dramatically in the low attractiveness of work contexts in which the individual is the sole sociologist or social psychologist in the organization. Thus, research positions in medical schools, schools of public health, health and welfare agencies, in small liberal arts colleges, etc., suffer particular disabilities in recruiting social researchers when the organizations are unable to provide an environment which contains a sufficient number of social researchers to at least have the potential to provide a congenial professional peer environment.

[3] The conflicts that may arise over division of resources are among the most important of the centrifugal forces in organized research. Indeed, it is almost always possible to detect when an organized research project is going poorly because this is the point at

Perhaps the greatest gain to participation in organized research arises out of the potential efficiencies of a division of labor. At the simplest level, providing secretarial and clerical help can make the difference between easy progress in research and one which requires many side excursions into nonessential tasks. At a more complex level, a division of labor among an administrative cadre (who keep the books, hire lower level personnel and make sure that there is plenty of coffee), research assistants, technical personnel (e.g., computer programmers, sampling statisticians, machine tenders, etc.) and, as in the case of survey research, maintaining a field staff capable of running sample surveys, can make it possible for a researcher to do research on a much larger scale and with greater efficiency than would be possible were he to attempt research on his own.

In social research, the division of labor arising in connection with the conduct of sample surveys provides the basis for the development of its most complex research organizations. The conduct of sample surveys requires the coordination of various specialized experts plus the deployment and management of a large field staff. Sample surveys are labor intensive and the coordination of the labors involved leads to lines of authority, responsibility, and control which are not to be found ordinarily in connection with social research.

Research also has its "foreign relations" problems. Financing has to be obtained from outside sources. Legitimation as a responsible and competent researcher has to be established. Competition for other uses of scarce resources within a university has to be met. Research organizations help to meet the "foreign relations" needs of researchers by packaging and thereby multiplying the political and professional resources of the individual researchers involved.

The multiplier effect on political power can be seen in the formal research organization's reputedly greater ability to command the attention of university administrations, private foundations, and government agencies. It is supposed to

---

which hostility becomes generated among project members. A project going well has lots of resources (i.e., good data and interesting findings) to go around but one which is going poorly generates intense concern in individual members whether each will have a sufficient "cut" of the research findings to recoup the investments they have made in time and money. In one such project that I know of, project members began to lock up their computer runs to prevent other members of the project from "stealing" their findings!

[4] The practice of "bulk budgeting" can help to create a very strong organization with a high level of participation by members. Thus, there is at least one university which allocates monies to its departments in lump sums to be divided among professional salaries, staff salaries, stationery, etc., by the department itself. The Dean stated to me that this practice tended to result in either strengthening the hand of the department chairman enormously or in producing a very strong democratic organization within departments. The R & D Centers and regional laboratories supported by the Office of Education enjoy (or suffer from) a modified form of bulk budgeting with much the same effects on the position of the director and of staff members.

be easier for a formal research organization to obtain a research grant than an individual researcher, just as it is easier for a research organization successfully to advance a claim for space and research budget with a university administration than it is for an individual faculty member. Whether it is *in fact* easier for formal research organizations to obtain grants than individuals is not clear,[5] although I am quite sure that university administrations pay more attention to research organizations than they do to individual researchers.

Perhaps the truth of the matter is that formal research organizations are more useful to some than to others. Research centers are probably especially helpful to young persons just starting out on their careers for whom the centers can provide the stamps of legitimacy and guarantees of competence which their names may not yet carry.

For senior persons with relatively well-established reputations, affiliation with a center may not provide more leverage with a foundation or government agency than such a person would have on his own. For example, my own university recently established an Urban Affairs Center which will eventually subsume some of my own activities, but these were started without the Center being in existence and would neither be harmed nor helped by being part of the Center. Yet the Center "package" did manage to attract a fairly sizable Ford Foundation grant and some financial support from the local business community, none of which I could have attracted on my own. To the outside world, a formal research organization is more than the sum of its parts, representing something more attractive than an individual could possibly be.

A research organization is also viewed as somehow more responsible than an individual. An individual researcher may leave to take another position, an administrator may defect to teaching, but a research organization will ordinarily carry on their commitments, recruit new personnel, and transfer the tasks involved to new people. Furthermore, a research organization has a responsibility to respond to demands and hence may be more sensitive to the needs and wishes of potential clients and benefactors. This latter point is particularly important when it comes to applied research. For example, a Center for Research on Poverty would find it harder to turn down a prospective research contract on poverty problems than an individual who is doing research in poverty.

In short, a research organization pools and magnifies the political, charismatic, technical, and responsibility potentials of its individual staff members. In

---

[5] Of course, some granting agencies take a very different view, regarding with some suspicion applications that come in from research organizations and giving preference to those submitted by individuals. The Russell Sage Foundation, for example, argues that an individual's grant is easier to evaluate than that of a research organization because in the latter case it is not clear who has drafted the proposal, who is really the principal investigator, and who will actually carry out the research involved.

this sense the position of individual staff members is thereby enhanced vis-a-vis their environments of universities, grant-giving agencies, and potential contracting agencies.

Note that both the internal and the external gains accruing from the organization of research are greater for researchers at the very top and at the bottom of the research reputation hierarchy. A man of considerable reputation, by reconstituting his activities as a research organization, enhances considerably his ability to get work done. The division of labor possible within a center means that it is possible for him to hire junior personnel in a context wherein he can tell them what to do and thereby multiply his own efforts. For the senior man of considerable reputation, a research organization reconstitutes the authority structure of the old-fashioned graduate departments with its senior members directing the work of junior members in a coordinated division of labor.

For the very junior man starting out on his research career, a research organization provides funds, amenities, leverage in the world of benefactors that is not available to him on his own. In return, he has to give up some degree of independence.

In contrast, for the middling man, participation in a research organization is a maximum gain only if the organization has a minimal hierarchical structure. If he participates as a junior in a division of labor he has lost status and it is not clear that he gains that much more in his "foreign relations" with universities and with potential benefactors. For the man in the middle, research organizations with equal status and minimal division of labor are more attractive.

It should be clear from the discussion of the last few paragraphs that there are costs to participation in research organizations, as well as gains. If a social scientist who works by himself does so at a low level of efficiency, he does have greater autonomy than one who works within an organized context. His ability to say "no" or "yes" to demands on his time is greater. He has more control over the amount of access others can have to him: of course, he has less rights of access to others.

There are other potential losses as well. Large-scale research organizations do not fit well within the academic grooves. The tensions that have arisen between research centers and traditional departments have not yet given rise to academic novels, although the intrigue, conflict, and tension is often high enough and complex enough to seem worthy of a C. P. Snow novel. Perhaps it is because the novelists tend to be humanists and the conflicts between research centers and traditional departments have been going on in the physical and social sciences.

Traditionally academic departments regard the large-scale centers as rich imperialists. Such centers, according to this view, compete unfairly for graduate students, swallow up junior faculty members, and engage in questionable research activities, usually of an applied nature. Center directors are seen as powerful men seeking constantly to enlarge their spheres of control with many followers who would swamp the democratic processes of departmental organizations if they were allowed in too close to departments. On the other side, Center personnel see departments as concerned mainly with protecting their status, only dabbling in research rather than being totally dedicated to research activity, and being overly protective of the "orgainzational integrity" of their departments.

Not all research organizations engage in running battles with traditional departments. The minimum complexity organization of the "brown bag" lunch group or the *ad hoc* research project varieties do not engender conflict with departments. It is the large-scale center, with its hierarchical structure, extensive division of labor, and large-scale funding that produces bones for contention.

Of course, research organizations are not exclusively sources of troubles to the academic departments with which they may be affiliated. The training of graduate students in the craft lore of social research and in the technical aspects of research practice is better accomplished in the doing of research than in the classroom. The better schools have attached research institutes because they are committed to the apprenticeship mode of research training and the formal research institute is a suitable means for accomplishing this end.

Furthermore, formal research organizations may enhance the status of a department in the field and within a university. The publications of a research center add to the collective *curriculum vitae* of a department and the publicity given to such centers in the press and in professional publications make some impact on the world.

VARIETIES OF RESEARCH ORGANIZATIONS

The gains and losses accruing to the organization of research reviewed in the last section implies that research organizations can take on a variety of forms depending upon which gains are being maximized and correspondingly which losses are being minimized. Not all that appears on the academic scene, the titles of "center," "institute," or "laboratory" are identical. They vary in size, amount of funding, but even more crucially in structural characteristics.

As we have indicated in the previous section, perhaps the most simple of all research organizations are the solidary, equal status groups, existing in most primitive form as "brown bag" lunch groups and in most extensive form as professional associations. An appropriate name for such informal research groups is the *collegium.*

The most salient structural characteristics of such collegia are that members tend to be of equal status, and engage in few concerted research efforts. The collegium exists mainly to provide a context in which persons interested in the same area of research can meet, exchange ideas, and perhaps cooperate on an *ad hoc* basis in specific research projects. Decision-making rules in such organizations tend to be democratic in character, perhaps with rotating chairman, or in the case of large-scale professional associations, elected officers and legislative bodies, but with little or no power over the activities of members except the power to admit or reject applications for membership. *Collegia* are research organizations which stress collegiality as a gain for their members and may confer some degree of status upon members.[6]

The next level of complexity of research organization, the consortium,[7] is represented by perhaps a majority of the organizations that go under the names of institutes and centers. Consortia are organizations designed primarily to maximize the foreign relations gains from organizing research and have a minimum division of labor. They are essentially collections of faculty members, each pursuing his own research interests, using the center to provide letterheads, secretarial service, and political leverage within the university and with funding agencies. The directors of such centers have little authority over members and the main division of labor within such centers involves the provision of minor clerical and secretarial services to members.

Almost every major university department of sociology has one or more such consortia. At Berkeley there are so many that it looks almost as if each senior member of the faculty has his own. Chicago, too, has its share. Some are co-terminous with the department or departments to which they are attached: the Laboratory of Social Relations at Harvard includes every member of the department, as does the Institute for Social Research at North Carolina.

It is the consortium form that departments have in mind when they indicate that they wish to start a research center. Such centers are mainly regroupings of faculty members under a different name but without fundamentally altering the authority relationships among members. They are attractive regroupings because of the leverage they provide on university administrations for funds and space and on grant-giving agencies for funds. Such organizations

---

[6] An interesting and somewhat pathetic example of how an organization which was formed to maximize collegiality among social scientists and remains mainly to confer status is the Sociological Research Association. The Association was formed in the 1930's by a group of young sociologists mainly to foster the development of empirical social research. For reasons which are obscure to me, it restricted membership to 100 people, a device which made the Association a prestige conferring organization. The Association persists even now when its initial aims have largely been achieved—most sociologists if they do not engage in empirical research are at least in favor of it—and its membership consists largely of aging sociologists who meet once a year to hear usually unexciting papers read by one of its members after the usual hotel banquet dinner. The Sociological Research Association no longer is in the forefront of anything, but persists to administer its *numerus clausus*, conferring status by membership but offering members hardly anything more.

[7] Used with apologies to the interuniversity consortium on political behavior, which on an inter-institutional basis is similar to what is meant here.

present no problems to departmental structures and have potential benefits of the "foreign relations" gains variety.

It should also be evident that there is no particular benefit to research *qua* research from the consortium form. Whether my own research is carried out under the auspices of the Group for Research on Social Policy, as my little research consortium is called, or under no title at all makes little difference to the research. As GROSP, my young graduate student associates and I have a letterhead, some claim on research space, perhaps a greater degree of solidarity, but the division of labor among us remains the same as before we adopted a name. GROSP may not live much longer than the research project to which it provides an umbrella, especially since the graduate students hopefully will get their degrees and move on to other institutions, and, when I engage in my next project, perhaps the name will not be as appropriate as some other.

The next level of complexity is represented by *"Institutes,"* centers which arise around the use and maintenance and distribution of a scarce resource, access to which has to be regulated in the name of equity. Several social psychologists may band together in an institute to regulate the use of interaction rooms and the accompanying electronic equipment. Or, in the days of punched cards, an institute may arise around the use of a computer—sorter or IBM 101. Or, in some cases, the resources involved may be funds: R & D Centers funded by the Office of Education have sometimes taken on the institute form. Or, a grant from Ford may foster the establishment of an Urban Affairs Center in the form of an institute because decisions have to be made on how the funds are to be allocated.

The allocation decisions made by such organizations tend to resemble existing principles of differentiation in the host organization. Thus, the grants given by the Rockefeller Foundation in the 1920's to several universities to foster the development of social research tended to be allocated among the faculty according to their rank and prestige, not necessarily according to need and merit.[8] If anything, such organizations tend therefore to end up strengthening existing arrangements; if they accomplish something above and beyond what individual members could do on their own, it is only because existing arrangements of status and authority coincided with merit and research competence.

The highest level of complexity is shown by "research firms,"[9] those research organizations which have elaborate divisions of labor, hierarchies of

---

[8] Indeed, this is one of the major reasons why some of the private foundations, notably Rockefeller and Carnegie, stopped giving grants to institutions for the institutions to allocate among faculty and moved instead to grants given for specific projects.

[9] I have used this term in the full realization that in the context of academia "firm" has the negative connotations of profit seeking and commercialism. Yet the term seems quite appropriate since their structures so closely resemble the business firms we are more familiar with.

authority and status within their professional cadres, and whose personnel do not coincide with departmental structures. Perhaps the best examples are the Institute for Social Research at the University of Michigan, the National Opinion Research Center at the University of Chicago, and the Bureau of Applied Social Research at Columbia University.

The critical differences between the "research firms" and the centers previously considered in this paper lie in the development of separate professional staffs and a relatively stringent line of authority. The directors of research firms have a great deal more authority, particularly over the professional staff which has no faculty status. The gains of research firms are primarily in the foreign relations area and also those which derive from the more intensive division of labor; hence, it is no accident that the best examples of research firms are those that have arisen around the research activity in the social sciences which requires the most extensive division of labor—the conduct of sample surveys. Properly to conduct a survey one needs to assemble at a minimum the following skills: sampling of human populations, questionnaire construction (an art rather than a science and hence highly dependent for its highest development on extensive practical experience), interviewing, data processing, and data analysis. All of these would be needed to conduct sample surveys of any size, but they become particularly crucial when sample surveys are to be conducted that cover more than a small neighborhood or small community. Specialization becomes absolutely essential when the surveys are to cover a large geographic area, such as a region or the nation as a whole.

It is still possible for the individual researcher or for a small group of researchers plus their acolyte graduate students to conduct sample surveys of institutionalized populations (e.g., the freshman class at Michigan State University) or of odd at-hand types of universes (e.g., Flint, Michigan). Indeed, most of what passes for social research that gets into professional journals is based upon such odd universe research.[10]

It is no longer possible (indeed, if it ever was) for a social scientist to do anything more extensive without setting up at least an *ad hoc* bureaucratic apparatus of considerable size and complexity. The startup costs for a national survey are too great to be absorbed by a single survey alone; hence, only the specialized national survey organizations have the capability of undertaking them. For example, assembling materials and drawing an area probability of the United States would cost somewhere between $50,000 and $75,000. Hiring and

[10] Because the universe samples are not terribly relevant or maximally appropriate ones, most social research leaves much to be desired as far as generalizability is concerned. The limitation of coverage gives rise to bewilderingly contradictory findings, for after all, Flint, Michigan is not the United States nor does the freshman class at Michigan State represent college freshmen in the United States.

training a national staff of interviewers (even if you employed persons who had previous interviewing experience) would cost somewhere around $50,000 additional. No single national survey can sustain those costs and such startup costs have to be spread out over a number of national surveys. Thus, the specialized national survey organization, in the form of research firms, has come into existence.

It is very significant that large-scale survey research did not develop within universities but was grafted onto universities after it had passed through the critical periods of infancy. Thus, the National Opinion Research Center is still a separate corporation which affiliated itself with the University of Chicago after it had become a going concern. Michigan's Survey Research Center was set up initially by a group of researchers who had worked together as a team running a survey research organization within the Department of Agriculture during World War II. Columbia's Bureau of Applied Social Research in its earlier manifestations had been the Office of Radio Research and had shuttled from Princeton to the University of Newark and occupied a very marginal status at Columbia until it was finally fully absorbed by the university in the middle 1950's.

Developing a research firm—a large-scale organization with an extensive division of labor—does not come naturally to a university department. Indeed, the principle of organization of a university department abhors all but the most minimal division of labor. Essentially, an academic department is a collection of scholars whose work is only minimally integrated in a division of labor sense. Professors are required to teach courses, and these courses are supposed to be integrated in some sort of rational way to form a curriculum. But there is very little supervision over what is taught in courses or the way courses are taught, and most curricula remain plans which are implemented only vaguely.[11]

In American universities, departments do not engage in common scholarly enterprises in which a research task may be broken down into component tasks, each member taking a component as his contribution to a common research project.[12] Indeed, when an academician refers to the independence of academic

---

[11] Indeed this is part of the reason why students are demonstrating such dissatisfaction with university teaching today. The division of labor within departments has deteriorated so far under the pressure of a labor market which has made relaxation of teaching duties one of the major means for attracting faculty that students are confronted with lackadaisical teaching in poorly planned courses within anarchic curricula.

[12] In contrast, some European universities have maintained an internal rank system implying a division of labor in which senior men direct the work of junior men. Nor was faculty autonomy always the case in American universities: The design of the Social Science Research Building at the University of Chicago provided for suites of offices in which a senior man (occupying the largest office) would be surrounded by his juniors (in smaller offices) with a common foyer to be shared by secretaries and research assistants. The architect designed the building in the 1920's to facilitate the division of labor that was then current in the social sciences.

life, he refers to the fact that once he has met his teaching obligations (over which he has a great deal of control, the amounts of which have been in a steep secular decline), he is free to pursue his own intellectual interests within the limits set by local production standards and the amount of research funds he is able to obtain from granting agencies. His presence on the campus is not taken for granted outside of teaching duties. At certain seasons of the year, when research review committees of the National Science Foundation and the National Institutes of Health are meeting in Washington D.C., a better set of academics than exists on the staff of any American university can be put together by routing visiting faculty members out of the hotels and motels in the D.C. area.

It is the independence of the academician and his reluctance to engage in an extensive division of labor which has led to the grafting onto university structures of research firms rather than attempting to impose a division of labor on existing departmental structures. Characteristically, research firms have "directors" while departments have "chairmen"[13] expressing in the titles of their chief administrative officers the greater authority of the one as compared with the other. Because of his greater authority the director is much more important to the functioning of a research firm than a chairman is to the functioning of a department, a large factor in the difficulty many departments now experience in finding someone who is willing to take over the chair.[14] A research firm functions best when its director provides both intellectual and administrative leadership, but a department functions best when its chairman knows how to sense departmental consensus, to summarize the consensus in policy, and to guard the independence of individual members from encroachment by either university administration or students.

The radically different organizational principles of the research firm and the academic department lie at the root of the controversies that often characterize the relationships between such centers and the departments to which they are closely related intellectually. On the one hand, the departments regard the centers as potentially imperialist organizations, sopping up scarce resources, providing a haven for second-rate personnel (no first-rate person would submit himself to being part of a division of labor), and generally accruing too much power. On the other hand, the research firm personnel often develop a stance which characterizes the academicians as amateurs and dilettantes in research,

[13] Chief administrative officers of academic departments were not always named "chairmen." Nor were they always elected by their departments for limited terms as is predominantly the case today. The title used frequently a few decades ago was "head" and the office was often held for indefinite terms.

[14] Chairmen have little authority, much responsibility, and gain few "brownie" points for pursuing their tasks well. It is a nice post in which to put someone past his prime who needs a good excuse for not producing as much as he once did.

more concerned over guarding the worth of their status than with pursuing knowledge through research of the highest standards.

There is little doubt that being a professor is more prestigious than being a researcher. Tenure—that mysterious state of grace into which a professor is elected by his colleagues in ceremonies only more guarded in secrecy than the election of popes and from which he can fail only by committing crimes of the most revolting character—has not generally been extended to research firm personnel except at the highest levels. Tenure is the source of the greater institutionalized charisma of the faculty. Researchers have generally been paid more—at least as far as salary is concerned. But professors have sources of income from outside sources. One of my former colleagues used to boast (somewhat vulgarly) that he paid his income tax with his university salary. Thus it is not clear that the researchers employed by research firms have a greater income, although it does seem that their salaries are greater, especially in the early stages of career lines.

The cadre of professionals, technicians, and clerks that make up a research firm constitute an expensive apparatus with a constant if not growing appetite for funds. To keep a national survey center going at a level of activity which is a minimum for the maintenance of survey quality requires an annual budget of close to two million dollars. This level of funding would provide that there is sufficient field work to retain a sampling staff, provide work for interviewers (so that they do not drift into some other part-time activity) and keep the staff occupied. This funding exigency is a source of one of the major problems of a survey center. Large-scale surveys are expensive and there are few sources of funds to which one can turn for support. In effect, unless universities allocate continuing support, survey centers tend to become more and more closely tied to the needs of potential big clients. The big client of this historical period is the federal government and the major source of funding lies in the welfare and education branches. More surveys are being conducted on the problems of the poor than on almost any other topic at the moment.

The price of having a large-scale survey center is the necessity to take on "projects" in order to keep the apparatus functioning at least at minimum levels of efficiency. The intellectual quality of applied research is not necessarily lower than that of "pure" research, but its prestige is lower. Hence the attractiveness of research firm positions to professional social scientists is less than that of academic positions. Were it not for marginal types of professionals—men who do not like to teach, women who are barred from the university because of nepotism rules, individuals who are over-age in grade, etc.—it would be difficult to staff such centers with any but less than first-rate personnel. Indeed, it is often the contention of the departments that institute personnel are in fact less than first-rate and hence ought to be insulated from the department by being kept out of teaching, access to graduate students, etc.[15]

In an earlier article on a related topic,[16] significantly written while I was Director of the National Opinion Research Center, I referred to the practice of "robin-hooding," a term coined to cover the practice of smuggling "pure" research interests into applied research projects, sometimes with the connivance and knowledge of the clients but more often without their knowledge and informed consent. At the time, I was overly impressed by the opportunities "robin-hooding" appeared to present. In retrospect, it seems like a very inefficient way of pursuing a line of research interests, involving making many detours and following a very crooked line toward an objective.

It appears to me to be unlikely that research firms involving extensive divisions of labor will be started at other universities. The existing research firms are being converted to the patterns congenial to traditional university forms, as in the case of the Survey Research Center at Michigan or the Bureau of Applied Social Research at Columbia or gradually being pushed out of the university as in the case of the National Opinion Research Center at Chicago. Both SRC and BASR look more like the minimal division of labor collection of almost equal status individuals than they used to. NORC's historically strong connections with the sociology department are presently very weak and seem unlikely to get stronger.

The future will undoubtedly see sample surveys be undertaken by academic personnel through subcontracting with either commercial or nonprofit institutes connected only very vaguely with universities. The tensions between the groves of academe and the business firm-like structure of the large-scale institute can be solved by decomposing the activities involved in large-scale surveys into those parts which are mainly intellectual in character—survey design and analysis—and those which are mainly administrative in character—sampling and data collection.

Of course, the future may see the development of new research methods which may recapitulate the history of sample surveying. One can imagine, for example, the development of techniques for extending experimental designs into

[15] This problem has been "solved" for some of the applied laboratories in the physical sciences by establishing the laboratories at some physical distance from the campus. The Hopkins Applied Physics Laboratory is 15 miles from the main campus. Lincoln Laboratories at MIT is some 30 miles away, and the Argonne National Laboratory connected with the University of Chicago is also far enough away to make easy moving from laboratory to campus difficult.

[16] "Scholars, Researchers and Policy Makers: The Politics of Large Scale Research," *Daedalus* 93 Fall, 1964.

applications in the field, requiring an extensive division of labor, administrative apparatus, etc. Such a development might foster the establishment of one or two research firms whose problems, in relation to the universities they may be connected with, will resemble those of the survey centers of the recent past.

Lest the impression be left with the reader that these four types of research organizations represent the only ways in which the social research of today is organized, it should be borne in mind that there are many solo researchers who work by themselves or perhaps with one or two research assistants. Indeed, the actual working groups within consortia and even research firms may, on closer inspection, turn out to be such solo or small groups of researchers working on particular projects and drawing upon the resources of the consortium or the research firm just as the solo researcher would draw upon the resources of any other service organization, like the library or the computer center.

There is much to be said for the solo researcher mode of research organization, particularly for those types of research in which an extensive division of labor is neither dictated by the logic of the research activity or the scope of the task involved. Indeed, a good case can be made for the purchase of research services, e.g., interviewing, coding, etc., from either commercial firms or large academic research firms, rather than setting up new research firms in order to meet the needs of particular research projects. The weight of hyperorganization has laid heavily upon research activities. Extensive organization is not a good substitute for intelligence and creativity, and although a whole may be more than the sum of its parts, it is not a great deal more. A social researcher of recognized competence and creativity who engages in research which requires relatively little in the way of a division of labor may lose more than he gains from participation in either a consortium or a research firm.

Although the main concern of this paper is with the social research activities that take place within the academic context or at least on the periphery of the groves of academe, it should be recognized that there are other contexts within which social research is conducted which lie outside the university entirely. Research departments of government and private agencies constitute one such nonacademic mode, as well as the separate research organizations, either profit or nonprofit, represented by organizations like the Educational Testing Service or the Stanford Research Institute. Whether by design, imitation, or accident of history, the forms of organization of such nonacademic research organizations tend to follow those we have discussed above.

Thus, the collegium is represented, for example, by the research committees of health and welfare councils being informal, nonworking meetings of persons interested in sets of common problems. Consortia can be found in the basic research departments of organizations like the Educational Testing Service or may be represented by organizations like the Laboratory for Socio-environmental Studies of N.I.M.H. in which essentially autonomous individuals or small groups work on their own problems supported by the services of the larger organization.

But, the preferred mode of research organization is the research firm, with a director of research, his own staff, and a more or less integrated program of research. The best of research firms in the nonacademic world produce research of considerable importance and stature: The National Merit Scholarship Corporation's research group has a list of research publications which would do honor to any academic department of educational sociology or psychology. Similar statements could be made about the research departments of the National Academy of Science, the National Research Committee which has turned out under Lindsey Harmon such excellent monographs using data from the national roster of scientific personnel. These are examples I have taken primarily from the fields in which I have had some interest. I am sure that other social scientists can find other examples.

The problems of such social research enterprises are considerable. For one thing, although salaries may be higher in such organizations, they have considerable difficulty attracting high-level personnel. Mission-oriented research is not as attractive to autonomy-seeking social scientists as the freedom afforded within academic departments. Hence the nonacademic research organizations, when they work well, tend to be manned by good researchers who happen to be on the margins of academia, women, men with Ph.D.'s from third and fourth rank universities, persons who are wedded for some particular reason to particular local communities, persons who abhor teaching, etc.

A second main problem is how to attain and sustain a critical mass of research personnel. There are few social researchers who are completely solitary workers. At minimum they need research assistants and usually someone with whom to talk about the research and with whom to plan a research endeavor. The single-man research department is more than an anomaly; it is simply unworkable.

A third main problem is how to maintain sufficient control over the setting of research problems, the conduct of research, and the publication and dissemination of research findings. In large part, this is a political problem; research has to compete with other demands on funds. Mission-oriented research can hardly be allowed to raise questions which might find the total enterprise of the sponsoring organization to be fatuous. Hence the best research enterprises tend to be walled off structurally from their parent organizations. Thus the Educational Testing Service's basic research operation is totally divorced organizationally from the operational side of ETS. Or, the Laboratory for Socioenvironmental Studies of N.I.M.H. has little connection with the granting or other operations of the Institute, and is physically located some miles apart from the N.I.M.H. central offices.

The successes of such "captive" social research organizations in this era of short labor supply tend to be fragile and ephemeral. They flourish for a while, and then decline as the men who made them flourish and are enticed away by offers of more money or status, or both. Research budgets are among the first items to be cut back when agency funds are cut. No matter how objective agency administrators appear at the point of hiring researchers, they are still likely to panic when the research begins to cast doubt on the efficacy of the agency's operation.

For these reasons an operating agency is perhaps best advised to contract for research with an existing research firm rather than to start its own research organization. For the same amount of resources, ordinarily, better researchers and perhaps better research could be obtained through control over the conduct of research.

TOWARD A PHILOSOPHY OF
SOCIAL RESEARCH ORGANIZATION

Social research organizations yield both gains and losses to participants. I have tried to indicate what some of the major positive and negative benefit flows are. Obviously the reason we set up research organizations is to obtain potential positive benefits. Similarly, when we dismantle an organization it is because the perceived costs outweigh the benefits, although it does appear that we continue organizations often long past the point when the flow turns from positive to negative.

A research organization, then, is worthwhile when it somehow augments the activities of individuals appreciably beyond what they can do on their own and when the costs of participation are smaller than the benefits. What are the conditions under which such a positive flow can be maintained?

To begin with, let us consider the circumstance under which costs are small. This is the case for the collegium: it uses up time, but hardly any other resources and in turn affects the major part of the individual social scientist's activities very little. It also does not augment the work of individual members by very much. Some may be inspired by discussion with colleagues to do things differently than they would have on their own, and some may enter into collaborative work that might not have occurred under other circumstances. But, by and large, the actual performance of research is untouched by such an organization. Note also that the costs of maintaining such an organization are borne fairly equally by its members, although the benefits may be unequally distributed. It is perhaps for this last reason that senior members of such groups tend to drift away, ostensibly under the pressure of other commitments, and that such groups are most successful when composed of equal age and equal status members.

Consortia of the usual level of complexity, involving primarily machinery for the equitable allocation of resources, e.g., a laboratory or the provision of clerical and administrative services, have a somewhat more durable existence. The benefits are clear, although limited, and the costs are slight. It is useful to be able to hand the administration of research grants over to some competent secretary and the director is not expected to supervise in any intensive way or to "coordinate" research activities. If such a research organization manages to obtain a director without too many ambitions and with a devotion to providing administrative services, benefits will be real although not very large. Problems arise when a director attempts to "direct" or impose too many meetings, or attempts to supervise research which staff members are conducting, or otherwise departs from an essentially supportive role.

The large-scale research firms promise the greatest potentials both for yielding large positive benefits and for imposing great costs on participants and their environments. A large-scale center is at its best with a director of considerable intellectual stature and leadership ability. It is only when such a director is clearly a man of first rank stature that his supervision of research does not raise the hackles of pride on staff members. It is also under such conditions that the foreign relations of the research center, particularly its relations with academic departments, can be handled properly. It is this dependency on charisma which makes a large-scale research center such a vulnerable organization, and so difficult to institutionalize. If one could be sure that a man you appoint as director has charisma, then large-scale research centers would mushroom on every campus. But no one is trained for the role and can only be seen as properly fulfilling the role after he has taken the position itself. By definition charisma is a gift that can only be received by an individual, not earned through work or study.

Large-scale research centers have another disability. They are extremely difficult to dismantle. The commitments to personnel are great. A research center can exist for years on applied research contracts of low intellectual yield. The momentum of a large-scale organization is great and administrators abhor putting an end to anything that has a large gross income. Large-scale research institutes never die: they just wither away intellectually.

The philosophy of research organization toward which this discussion is tending argues for the consortium as a better mode. The research firms are too risky. The collegia yield too low a return. A conservative research organization policy therefore favors the middle ground, with enough organization to make things somewhat easier, but not too much dependency on either the risks deriving from noncharismatic leadership or the weight of a bureaucracy that has to be fed on a month-to-month basis.

In the social research of today the efficiency of the consortium mode is enhanced by the development of organizations like NORC or commercial survey firms who are willing to undertake through subcontracts the very onerous task of gathering data through large-scale surveys. Similar contract services exist with respect to computer soft-and hardware. These contract services make it possible for the solo or the small group of researchers to expand their research capabilities considerably without expanding their immediate research organizations.

THE CAPACITY OF SOCIAL SCIENCE ORGANIZATIONS TO PERFORM LARGE-SCALE EVALUATIVE RESEARCH*

Walter Williams

INTRODUCTION

The principal concern of this paper is with the capacity of social organizations to perform large-scale evaluative research in support of social policy-making. This type of research presents a number of problems for social science organizations. First, the research generally will need to be multidisciplinary in nature, often drawing on both the social and the biological sciences. Second, evaluative studies of major social policies will be complex undertakings requiring a high level of technical, organizational, and administrative skills. Third, the research often will have to conform to a tight time schedule to be useful in policy formulation. Finally, the results, if directly relevant to major policy decisions, may involve the organization in heated political controversy.

Evaluative research includes two types of studies: *outcome evaluations* and *field experiments*. The former are studies intended to measure the effects of an agency's existing projects or programs on their direct participants, other desig-

*First printed as *Public Policy Paper* No. 2, Institute of Governmental Research, University of Washington, Seattle, 1971.

nated groups, and/or specific institutions (e.g., what is the relationship between benefits and costs). Field experiments are designed to assess the merits of *new* policy ideas in terms of *outcomes* in a setting corresponding at least in part to actual field operating conditions.

Few would argue with the normative proposition that a major evaluative effort in the social areas is badly needed, particularly for those programs serving disadvantaged groups.[1] The experience of the 1960's brought serious doubts about the effectiveness of most major social programs and a lessening of confidence in what seemed to be an implicit premise of the early War on Poverty years that programs could be launched full scale without testing and yield significant improvements in the lives of the disadvantaged. Bits and pieces of evidence (some from research), hard thinking, and good will did not necessarily combine to produce programs leading to dramatic breakthroughs in the social areas. Over a wide range of social programs, it has been found how difficult and/or expensive remedies for poverty are, and how little is really known about workable techniques for helping the disadvantaged.

Yet, few sound evaluations and even fewer rigorous small-scale projects have been undertaken by the social agencies serving the disadvantaged. And a corresponding disquiet has set in concerning the existing capacity in the social science research community for large-scale evaluative research in support of social policymaking. In light of the short supply of competent policy-oriented researchers, the inadequacy of methods and concepts for carrying out evaluative research, and the lack of organizational capacity to undertake large-scale evaluative activities, one can ask legitimately whether or not evaluative results used directly in the social policy process may not cause more harm than good. Thus the basic issues of the paper concern:

1. The organizational changes that might be made within the government and the social science community to increase the number of capable policy-oriented researchers, to foster improvements in evaluative concepts and techniques, and to develop more social science organizations capable of carrying out sound, large-scale evaluative investigations and other kinds of research needed for policy formulation.

2. The possible deleterious consequences for society and for social scientists in performing studies directly relevant to social agency policy, and the measures that might be taken to reduce these dangers.

---

[1] The subsequent discussion concerning the methodological capacity to assess project or program outcomes is probably just as pertinent for all social programs as it is for programs aimed at reducing poverty and/or the barriers to equal opportunity. However, my experience is with the latter so that the remarks in the following pages technically refer to social programs and policies for the disadvantaged. For a fuller discussion of my experience, see Williams (1971, pp. xiii-xiv).

A number of factors relevant to the consideration of the two questions set out in the previous paragraph will be discussed. It is important to observe at the outset that we will find far more that is unknown than is known. Certainly no definitive answers will be forthcoming—rather at times the gaps in our knowledge will present barriers even to intelligent discussion. Be that as it may, the questions are too important to ignore. At basic issue is whether or not social science can make a significant contribution to social policymaking while still maintaining its historical role as a relatively independent critic of public policy.

FACTORS RELEVANT TO A CONSIDERATION
OF SOCIAL SCIENCE'S CONTRIBUTION
TO SOCIAL POLICY

The purpose of this section is to discuss in a broad context a number of factors relevant to a consideration of the issue of social science's contribution to social policy. Various factors—many of which would require at a minimum a lengthy paper for a reasonable treatment—are discussed briefly to suggest the nature of the topic. These factors include:

1. *The social policy areas present complexities beyond those that exist elsewhere.*

Rats, pigeons, missiles, genes, and even elementary particles appear to be far easier to understand in a rigorous way than people in complex social situations. At the heart of the matter is the fact that a practical infinity of possible relevant variables exist; all are likely to be related to one another; and it is very difficult to guess on an *a priori* basis which are going to be most pertinent to any given problem. This dilemma must be faced both by researchers in treating intercorrelation and interaction among variables, and by persons responsible for developing programs. For example, consider the area of education for the disadvantaged. First, we do not understand the process of education and the determinants of educational achievement. Second, available evidence indicates that the relevant factors are not limited to those the school itself may be able to control, such as classroom techniques, teachers, school budget, and school organization (and these are complex enough), but include such factors as socioeconomic status, race, community (or neighborhood), and peer group associations. And, of course, policymakers have little or no control over these variables.

The fact that social programs must operate in a complex political and bureaucratic setting complicates matters even more. For example, Title I of the Elementary and Secondary Education Act in deference to the states' prerogatives in the educational field simply made money available for helping the disadvantaged without any very strong stipulations as to how it would be used. The money dribbled into the educational system and mixed with other monies raises real questions about its effective use, and at the same time makes it almost impossible to measure that effectiveness in any kind of rigorous evaluative study. If we add the politics of the Congress, the agencies, and the Executive Office, problems both for the program designer and the researcher almost boggle the mind.

One hardly needs to dwell at length on this complexity in the social program areas as it is a well known phenomenon. Yet it is well to keep in mind that what social science must be organized to do is to address probably the most difficult of all areas of study, that of people interacting with each other in a large, complex society.

2. *Large-scale, multidisciplinary studies will be required to fulfill the data needs of social policymakers; and the need for major outcome evaluations and field experiments that necessitate replication seem certain to usher in an era of "big social science."*

The beginning signs of "big social science"—research requiring relatively large amounts of money and a high level of organizational and administrative skills to operate the project—are already apparent. The OEO/Department of Labor outcome evaluation of five manpower programs has over 10,000 people in the treatment and control groups and is estimated to cost 4½ million dollars; OEO's performance contracting experiment is estimated to cost 6½ million dollars[2]; and the cost of the several negative income tax experiments now in progress will run into the tens of millions of dollars. While it is a central question whether or not social science in either a methodological/conceptual or organizational sense is capable at present of undertaking these large-scale studies, there is little doubt that such studies will ultimately be needed for intelligent social policymaking.

3. *The social sciences have been characterized by a lack of orientation toward and organization for large-scale, multidisciplinary policy research.*

The reward structure of the social sciences in the past militated against policy research in that policy-oriented researchers in the social sciences, except economics (and here the policy orientation has been in traditional areas such as monetary and fiscal policy, not social policy), were viewed as second-class citizens by their disciplinary peers. This point is made strikingly in the recent National Academy of Sciences/Social Science Research Council report (1969, p. 193) on the social and behavioral sciences, which stated:

---

[2] In a performance contract a local school system will enter into an agreement with a private company to provide classroom instruction. Payments to the contractor will be based on measured rates of classroom achievement (e.g., changes in reading levels over a contract year) with bonuses for high overall classroom achievement and penalties for poor performance.

Although there is a close relationship, in principle, between basic research and applied and developmental work, basic research tends to receive more attention from behavioral scientists in universities. Many academic scientists value the prestige that their contributions to basic research and theory give them in the eyes of their peers more than whatever rewards might be obtained from clients who would find their work useful. It is no wonder that university scientists prefer the kind of research that is satisfying in itself (because it is self-initiated and free of restraints) and leads not only to scientific knowledge, but also to respect and status tendered by those whose judgments they value most. It is no wonder, either, that their value systems are passed on to their students. Thus, much of the applied work in disciplinary departments is done by those who for one reason or another do not compete for the highest prizes of their disciplines.[3]

Moreover, there is little tradition in the social sciences of extended multidisciplinary work. Yet social problems in general cut across the established disciplines. For example, an effort to investigate means of increasing the capacity of the public schools to educate minority children may well require research not only by sociologists, psychologists, economists, and linguists, but also biological scientists in areas such as nutrition and brain functioning. Collaboration, however, by members of different social science disciplines—much less joint research with biological scientists—is the rare exception.

Furthermore, the social sciences in general lack organizations with the capacity to perform large-scale field research. Extensive evaluative research requires major organizations with large multidisciplinary staffs. These may in turn need high levels of administrative capability, elaborate divisions of labor and hierarchies of authority and status. Few such organizations exist either in universities or outside of them, and those that do, such as the National Opinion Research Center and the Survey Research Center, have traditionally specialized in sample survey activities. And these organizations certainly do *not* have proven records of high-level evaluative research in the social areas.

This lack of orientation toward and organization for policy studies has produced a severe shortage of policy-oriented researchers; a minimum of graduate preparation aimed at developing competent researchers who view policy as their main area of inquiry; and an inadequate development of concepts (e.g., an explanatory model in the education area), methods, and field procedures for deriving evaluative results.

4. *Present deficiencies in staff size and skills within the government—the Executive Office, the Congress, and the agencies—severely limit the level and quality of evaluative activities in the social program areas.*

Part of the explanation for the dearth of relevant policy research in the social areas derives from the fact that the government has done little to define clearly what types of studies are needed, or to encourage this socially important and methodologically challenging research in the social science community.

---

[3] Currently I suspect that this statement is less true than at publication in 1969. But we simply do not have a systematic study of this question (see point 5, page 4).

Generally, government staffs do not have the technical and administrative capability to determine evaluative needs, design or work with contractors and grantees to design studies, and supervise the ongoing evaluative effort or monitor it in sufficient detail to determine the validity of the results. After studying the status of evaluation in 15 programs in HEW, HUD, OEO, and the Department of Labor, and in the General Accounting Office and the Bureau of the Budget (now Office of Management and Budget), the Urban Institute group under Joseph Wholey observed: "The Social Security Administration's Office of Research and Statistics and the OEO Office of Planning, Research, and Evaluation, each with a substantial in-house evaluation capacity, are notable bright spots in an otherwise bleak staff picture" (Wholey *et al.* 1970).

It would be a distorted picture to stress only weaknesses. In the last few years, the social agencies, the General Accounting Office, and the Executive Office have begun to develop evaluative capability. Such studies as the New Jersey negative income tax experiment, the performance contract experiment developed at OEO, and the OEO/Department of Labor longitudinal evaluation of five manpower programs certainly indicate competence. Furthermore, given the difficulties of assessing social programs and projects, the progress to date may be quite reasonable in terms of developing evaluative capability. Our purpose, however, is not to judge the past but to look toward the future. And in these terms, it would be a most serious mistake not to recognize that the present deficiencies in staff size and skills within the government severely limit the level of evaluative activities in the social program areas.

5. *Little detailed information is available concerning the present capacity of the social sciences to engage in policy-oriented research and teaching.*

While the present deficiencies noted above are quite apparent, it is also true that those concerned with *future* directions in the social sciences must operate with only the most limited information. Now available in published form are broad statements about the lack of social science activity in the policy areas and general descriptions of activities such as the number of Ph.D's graduated each year in the social sciences, but little else. A brief example will illustrate this point.

The 1970 National Register of Scientific and Technical Personnel included in its Specialities List for economists such categories as "Economics of Poverty," "General Welfare Programs," and "Urban Economics and Public Policy." Ten years ago, these categories did not exist, yet what do they imply? The American Economics Association, which administered the questionnaire, asked economists to specify their specialties from a long list that included no more than the name of the category and a number. To paraphrase Humpty Dumpty, "Economics of Poverty means just what I choose it to mean." In short, there is absolutely no qualitative information available, not even a simple description of what research the economist is engaged in, and the lack of information is hardly restricted to economics.

Little effort has been expended to study systematically the social science research community—no one has researched the researchers. In response to perceived pressures to be more relevant, universities have established new schools, new institutes, and new areas of study. Established research organizations and new ones now claim competence in social areas. Yet one can barely find a listing of all of these entities, much less any detailed discussion of their scope of activities and quality. In addition, almost nothing has been written as to whether or not universities are modifying their curricula so as to make their graduates more oriented toward policy questions. There may be some hopeful signs of efforts to study the social science research process, as witnessed by the recent report in *Science* of a study by Karl Deutsch and others (1971) on the conditions that make for research breakthroughs in the social sciences. This type of work, however, is just beginning. And one cannot overemphasize the scant information upon which to develop some notion of the potential supply of policy research for social agencies.

6. *The milieu for scientific activity has changed significantly in recent times. The general attacks of science both for errors of omission and commission, the turmoil in the universities, and the decrease in funds available for research and for university operations seem likely to be important factors, even if we cannot yet predict how they will affect science policy.*

While it is far too early to try to assess the implications of the above changes in terms of their potential effects on policy research, it is not obvious that the effects will necessarily be negative. The looseness of the academic marketplace now may make it much easier to "guide" people toward policy research. As a government staff member in the mid-1960's, I found that in trying to generate policy research one had to beg and make all kinds of concessions to researchers to get them to consider policy issues. Those days may well be gone; the Office of Management and Budget, for example, is now able to push federal granting organizations like the National Science Foundation and the National Institutes of Health much more toward funding "relevant" research. It is not clear that this is necessarily bad in the development of social science as a contributor to social policy.

7. *Particularly at the present low stage of development of evaluative techniques in the social sciences, the use of evaluative studies in social policy-making poses risks both to society and to science.*

The purpose of evaluation itself may be disruptive for program personnel and participants, and bring conflict in an agency between evaluation staffs and operating bureaus. Scientists (avoiding the mystic abstraction "science") can be completely wrong in terms of design of studies or interpretation of results, ignore or not perceive deleterious consequences of their discoveries, or manipulate data and theory in such a way as to support their political beliefs—needless to say, with resultant harm. For example, an outcome evaluation indicating incorrectly that a program is not effective can bring reductions in program funding, unwarranted changes in staff and policies, and a shattering of the morale of staff and participants. Or, the argument that every new operating program ought to be tested and shown to be effective before operating on a large scale can be used as a façade for disparaging all new ideas and retrenching on social commitments. Legislators and administrators relatively ignorant of evaluative techniques may overvalue and hence overreact to quantitative data because of their aura of scientific accuracy.

Conversely, the undertaking of evaluative research may have harmful consequences for individual scientists and the institutions of science. The context in which information is used is very important—the same data cited in a scholarly journal and on the floor of the legislature have different implications. Thus any information including evaluative data which can have a material effect on policy decisions, such as bringing significant cuts in program funding, is best viewed as "political" information. Political sensitivity can bring the researcher into the center of a raging controversy. This is well illustrated by the Westinghouse Learning Corporation evaluation of Head Start in which the debate over the validity of the results was carried on not only in the scholarly journals, but in major newspapers, the Executive office, and the Congress. As I have observed elsewhere (Williams, 1971, p. 123, italics in original):

> [Westinghouse is] a stark illustration of what might be termed the implications of the iron law of absolute evaluation flaws. That is, as a general rule *the absolute methodological and logistical deficiencies in any evaluation make political infighting a near certainty when evaluation results threaten a popular program*. In short, "questionable evaluation practices" can always be attacked on methodological grounds for political and bureaucratic purposes.

Academic independence and objectivity can be threatened by the institutional relationship between the governmental sponsor and the researcher. Sponsors of evaluative studies may attempt to suppress unfavorable findings. They may tell an investigator what to find or to change results, or force the release of preliminary results in support of a particular policy position. Even without overt influence, a close and continuing relationship between an agency and a research organization may either raise doubts concerning the latter's objectivity or blunt its sensitivity to bad policies of the client. Mutual trust and the asking of embarrassing questions that might put basic programs of the agency in jeopardy are difficult to combine over long periods of time.

A COMMON FRAME OF REFERENCE

The above listing of factors—many meriting a long paper which in most cases could be written only in terms of the grossest speculation because of the lack of firm empirical evidence—is so formidable as to make sensible discussion difficult and recommendations concerning how to foster policy-oriented social research hazardous. If one does propose to engage in discussion and to proffer recommendations, what seems to make sense is to first try to establish a common frame of reference. This involves specifying what proves to be a limited number of points about which most of us would agree, and from this common starting point examining my particular experiences, orientation, and biases.

It is pertinent to indicate the reason my biases are stressed in this discussion. I feel very strongly that almost no intelligent discussion has emerged concerning the critical issue of the potential contribution of social science to social policymaking, and that a major barrier to fruitful discussion has been a tendency to work from unstated assumptions concerning matters about which we have little or no solid evidence. Only if our biases and our fears, such as the possible contamination of science by its closeness to policy, are set forth and considered will we ever progress to reasoned debate.

Common Points of Agreement

A strong consensus would emerge in support of the following statements:

1. There are a number of grave social problems for which solutions urgently need to be sought.

2. Results from *soundly* conceived and executed studies that measure the effectiveness of existing programs and assess the merits of new policy ideas on a small scale before new large-scale programs are launched are urgently needed in support of social policymaking.[4]

3. In all likelihood major decisions on social policy will not await research results, nor should decisions be held up for the lack of research evidence.

4. Evaluative evidence *will* be and, even if there were great improvements in its quality, *should* be only one of several kinds of available information in the policy process, with choices ultimately being political in the broad sense of that term.

These statements need only the briefest elaboration. Major decisions about social policy are now being made and are going to be made in the future with only limited empirical evidence. For example, the decision in any budget year to continue programs as they are presently operated is itself a significant decision. Moreover, even major decisions to change programs or introduce new ones will be made without much evidence. In view of the present deficiencies in techniques, personnel, and organizations in social research, it would be ridiculous to suggest that new social programs cannot be started unless there is strong

[4] This is probably the one statement for which there may be disagreement. But I suspect it is more apparent than real in that those who oppose evaluative studies do so more in terms of perceived weaknesses in techniques (*soundly* conceived and executed studies *cannot* now be carried out) than of a rejection in the abstract of the principle of evaluation.

empirical evidence showing their effectiveness. Moreover, great improvements in the development of research information should not make that evidence over-riding. The propositions indicate support for a pluralistic process in which evidence of many types, including political and bureaucratic prerogatives, will be important—often far more important than sound evaluative data. Still, it would be nice to have some of the latter at a time when key social decisions are to be made.

The Author's Experiences and Biases

When I was at the Office of Economic Opportunity, I was on the staff of the Office of Research, Plans, Programs, and Evaluation (RPP&E), the first central analytical office in a social agency. The office was responsible directly to the agency director for overall planning for programs aimed at reducing poverty and the barriers to equal opportunities, and also supported studies by outside researchers. RPP&E was a key office in the policy process in which decisions about social programs involving billions of dollars were made—more often than not without benefit of any hard evidence or with very limited data. Decisions were made with these great gaps in knowledge, not because RPP&E or OEO did not try to find relevant, sound information, but because such information did not exist, and often there was not time (given the regimen of the policy process) to develop the needed data. Yet lack of time was not the only limiting factor; our attempts to develop policy research made clear the difficulties of policy studies both in terms of methodological and conceptual shortcomings and bureaucratic/political barriers.

This experience has made me both tolerant of imperfect, though better than present, information and sensitive to the difficulty and the challenge of social policy research. Let me try to crystallize my perspective by setting out and discussing three propositions that reflect how I approach the problem of developing more policy research:

1. In some substantive areas (e.g., education and manpower) present evaluation methods involving large-scale sample surveys of programs offer a real potential in the near term for increasing materially the useful outcome of information directly pertinent to social policy decisions.

Notwithstanding, there are serious problems in carrying out such work, and the resultant findings will hardly be definitive or substitutes for good judgment. As the author has noted elsewhere (Williams, 1969, p. 457):

> [T]here must be a far greater concern for the requirements of statistical design than has generally been exhibited in the past. These requirements would generally include a well-designed sample, early field interviewing to maximize the retrieval of informa-tion, repeated follow-up to reduce sample attrition, and a reduction in the importance of heroic assumptions in the model. In short, good evaluations are going to need well-qualified evaluators who are funded at "high" levels so that excessive shortcuts

are not required, and who are given realistic planning time to develop a sound evaluation model.

Even under such circumstances, it will be necessary to make arbitrary decisions and to recognize that many crucial questions are beyond our present capabilities. . . .

Further, some caution is needed in interpreting evaluation data which generally will mean fitting the evaluation evidence into a mosaic with other reasonable evidence to "validate" a decision. In general, the present generation of outcome evaluations should be viewed as a piece of evidence, not *the* definitive piece of information that bowls over all other reasonable indications of a different policy decision.

2. While useful evaluations can now be performed with present techniques, they will be time consuming; and in some areas in which concepts and techniques are deficient, only a very long time horizon is realistic.

The time exigencies of program policy needs and the time requirements of sound evaluative studies are certain to be in conflict. Haste is not compatible with the present deficiencies in evaluative methodology and field procedures. Even if one relies essentially on present techniques, it will take significant amounts of effort, time, and money to produce evaluative studies that are significantly better than those of the past.[5] Moreover, the present technology in some areas is sufficiently limited so that study results will not feed directly into the decision process, but will lead in succeeding stages to a decision-making input. Such exploratory activity would be expected over time to increase the capacity to produce significantly better future outcome data. But the payoff in terms of results directly relevant for decision-making may be many years away.

The idea of a long time horizon for some evaluative activities with an initial emphasis on exploratory work not leading directly to inputs into the decision process will be difficult for key officials to accept. Pressures on them to act quickly are tremendous. It would be a sterile exercise to push aside these political considerations. At the same time, if a realistic attitude toward the time required for evaluative research cannot be developed, it is difficult to see how real progress can be made.

3. Evaluative information may be used for policy purposes unless compelling *a priori* reasoning or strong empirical evidence support a claim of potential bias in the results.

To date, there has not been a field evaluation of a social action program that could not be faulted legitimately by good methodologists, and we may

[5] For example, this conservative time estimate would hold for an evaluation using an outside contractor to measure prospectively a manpower training program of 6 months' duration: 2 or 3 months to get bids and award the contract; 2 to 6 months for the contractor to develop the evaluation methodology and sample; 6 months for the manpower training program itself; 6 to 12 months of on-the-job time by participants after the training (depending on acceptance of 6 months or 1-year wage experience); and 2 to 6 months to process the data and prepare a report. This estimate indicates a time range from 1½ to nearly 3 years from the start of an evaluation until results come in. At the minimum, data would be available not for the upcoming fiscal year but for the one after that.

never see one. Only cursory inspection of an evaluative study will generally produce a number of potential biases, e.g., people will refuse to be interviewed, members of the treatment and control groups will disappear, or project directors will not allow random assignments. With some scholarly thought a fantastic number of subtle potential biases can be unearthed. However, policymakers should not reject evaluative results because some bias might possibly exist.

The recent Westinghouse Learning Corporation evaluation of Head Start referred to previously well illustrates this point. In this study, a sample of children who had gone on to the first, second, and third grades after participating in the Head Start program were matched in terms of certain variables, e.g., age, sex, with a "control" (technically, comparison) group of children from the same local area, and both groups were administered a series of tests to ascertain levels of cognitive and affective development. In comparing the test scores of the two groups, covariance techniques were used to adjust for other socioeconomic statue differences.

Surely possible biases in this case may be important. The standard argument in such *ex post facto* investigations is that those who enter the program are more likely to succeed either because they (or in this case, their parents) are more motivated than the controls or because the program personnel "cream" from the applicants, picking the best in order to make the program look good.

In a recent paper, Campbell and Erlebacher (1970) have argued the reverse of this proposition in suggesting that *ex post facto* evaluations in the social areas may be biased *against* the treatment showing a positive effect in that (1) program personnel purposely choose the most needy applicants, and (2) available statistical techniques such as those used in the Westinghouse study do not correct sufficiently for the fact that the treatment group is worse off than the controls. If both parts of the argument hold, an evaluative design requiring significantly higher achievement scores as evidence of Head Start effectiveness would be inappropriate—catching up by the Head Start group might well be an acceptable performance. Given Campbell and Erlebacher's eminence as methodologists, let us simply accept as valid their argument concerning the present inadequacy of techniques to correct biases. However, Campbell and Erlebacher support the first part of the argument only with hypothetical data, not empirical evidence. So, if the alleged bias does not exist, the deficiency of the statistical tools does not matter.

I have my doubts that such biases are important. And these doubts are grounded in observation, if not systematic study. First, the situations in which individuals come to apply for programs are quite "chancy": they may be recruited (at times almost physically dragged in) or get program information almost by pure chance either from a friend or other sources. Second, program assignment procedures, in part, because of the great urgency of getting people into programs within time and fund restrictions, do not leave one with the impression that staff personnel can determine from among a group of individuals with similar objective characteristics (e.g., income, level of education, job experience, etc.) who is more or less likely to succeed in the program. Thus, in *ex post facto* program evaluations with reasonably well-matched treatment and control groups drawn from a large number of projects, I would argue the following: The likelihood is small that the results will be sufficiently biased by the lack of random assignment procedures so as to render them misleading for policy analysis.[6]

In sum, a policymaker faces the inherent dilemma of running risks if he chooses to develop evaluative evidence (e.g., wasting funds on useless studies or, worse, using invalid results) and of incurring other risks if he does *not* undertake evaluative research (continuing ineffective programs or launching new flops). No available information permits a precise and objective weighing of these risks. So we are each reduced to a quite subjective assessment dominated by our own experiences. Mine lead me, on the one hand, toward developing in some program areas evaluations that are expected to be used directly in policymaking. "Fairly good" evaluative results available before decisions must be made will be both a distinct improvement over the past and superior to more rigorous results arriving after the decision. One may well trade quality for speed. For example, in the just-discussed Head Start evaluation, RPP&E chose an *ex post facto* study that would yield evaluation data in a year over a more sophisticated longitudinal design taking at least 3 years. On the other hand, in some areas I would restrict work to developmental studies, and in the longer run would require in all areas quite high standards for policy research. In short, it would be mixed strategy reflecting different needs and different time frames.

WHERE DO WE GO FROM HERE?

The overriding issue in this paper concerns the steps over time that the government (the consumer of policy research) and the social science research community (the main potential supplier) should take to increase materially the

---

[6] This formulation is hardly very elegant and depends heavily upon the matching of treatment-control groups. Some small but consistent differences may exist. There is no rule for saying when the difference is large enough to bias the results for policy. Moreover, in small geographic areas, a program such as Head Start could present problems. To the extent that the poorest people are relatively well known in an area and the program is able to "saturate" that group by getting almost all of the eligible children, the controls may be superior in socioeconomic terms. But, for the great bulk of programs in which the available slots will be far below the need level, saturation seems more unlikely to occur. In general, saturation requires far greater knowledge than present about the population, more sensitive selection techniques, more time available to those who determine participation than generally exists in the real world, and far more money.

development of soundly conceived and executed evaluative studies, and to reduce the dangers attendant upon such development. The following sections will address possible future directions (some of which are clear but most of which are not) and some of the problems they raise. The discussion has three major topics: the federal government's demand function for policy research, the organization of the social sciences for policy research, and the means of minimizing the risks of developing and using evaluative results.

The Federal Government's Demand Function for Policy Research[7]

One thing is most clear—a significant increase in soundly conceived and executed evaluative studies requires that social agencies as the primary developers and users of social program evaluative results within the government establish large, well-trained staffs with sufficient technical and administrative skills to determine evaluative needs, to articulate these needs to outside researchers, to design or work with contractors and grantees to design studies and methodologies, and to supervise the ongoing evaluative effort. The skills and knowledge required for competent evaluation staff members are quite high: substantive knowledge about specialized areas (e.g., education) including the ability to specify evaluative needs; a sound background in designing evaluative studies and using statistical techniques including the ability to translate variables into measurable concepts usable in the field; and beyond these two sets of technical skills, the *administrative* ability to work with program personnel and researchers over time. Despite the fact that such skills in the social program areas are in short supply, the number of people needed for a viable evaluation staff will generally be substantial. For example, Wholey (1970, pp. 82-85) estimates that at least a GS-13 to GS-15 level staff member is required for every two to four (or $500,000 worth of) outside studies, with additional staff needed for special functions such as developing overall evaluative needs.

It cannot be overemphasized that the government policy research staff must be made up of people with sufficient technical training and/or experience to interact with academic social scientists in a peer relationship. While the social scientist may have a national reputation in his discipline (an unlikely status for the government staff person), the latter should be at least a qualified journeyman in his academic specialty. One party may have a comparative advantage in terms of techniques and disciplinary knowledge, and the other in terms of

[7]The concern of this paper is restricted to the government's *technical not* its *political* capability to develop and use evaluative research. So this section will not address such questions as the location and status of the social agency evaluation office; the relationships among the social agencies, the Executive Office, and the Congress concerning evaluative studies; etc. For such a discussion, see Williams (1971).

knowledge about policy and policy needs, *but they must speak the same disciplinary language.*

The Congress and the Executive Office also badly need evaluative data, and at a minimum must have the staff capability to articulate their concerns to the agencies and to be intelligent interpreters and users of evaluative information. Beyond this, both may wish to develop sufficient staff to carry out a limited number of evaluations to keep the agencies honest. The limiting factor— and it may well be an overriding one—is the shortage of competent evaluators. The present situation is analogous to the one existing at the start of the Planning, Programming, Budgeting System in 1965 where a severe shortage of policy analysts thwarted the implementation of a basically sound concept for improving the governmental decision process. Thus, everyone attempting to draw on a limited supply of competent people may result in no staffs of sufficient size and skill to carry on a high level of evaluative activity.

If the federal government is to increase significantly the flow of sound evaluative results in the social areas, it must fund relatively more research directed specifically toward major policy problems and require that the research involve more interaction between government policy research staffs and outside researchers than it has in the past. It is important to stress that the statement does not imply only "applied" work but may also include "basic" research. However, the statement is meant to convey the notion of some structuring of the research both in terms of the areas of concern and of the interaction with government staffs. For example, the adequate education of lower socioeconomic class, minority children is clearly a major social problem that badly needs investigation. In the search for causes of poor education and means of improving it, research might range from studies of the possible relationship between malnutrition and brain damage in a fetus to field experiments testing a new teaching process. Not only may policy-oriented research include "basic" research, it seems likely that in many social areas, major new applications must await the development of new knowledge from fundamental research.

At the same time, policy research should be *structured* at least to the extent that government policy research staffs will specify gaps in knowledge blocking more intelligent policymaking; and that the researcher will be committed to thinking about these needs. This commitment, including interaction with a government policy research staff, is extremely important. The need for interaction rests on the premise that in part the lack of useful social policy research in the past stemmed from ignorance about programs and policies, policy needs, and the form in which research results would prove useful in the policy process. What the government policy research staff should offer relative to the outside scientist is not superior intellect, but superior information about policy needs. This argument holds even for the most fundamental policy studies by social scientists in which the researcher has great freedom to determine the scope, character, and timing of the study; here also the value of the study for policy purposes is likely to be greater when the researcher has an appreciation of policy needs gained through interaction with government staff members.

The above formulation may raise in the mind of the social scientist a specter of government staff members with a new shibboleth, "policy relevance," dictating what scholars need to study and how it should be studied. Such a danger always exists. But if government policy research staffs are upgraded as envisioned, the interaction may for the first time provide researchers with knowledge about policy needs in sufficient detail to permit fruitful policy work.

In this regard, one other point needs to be made. The past has been one of significant interaction between the government and social scientists. But this interaction has been between researchers and government research—not policy research—staffs which themselves were not informed about or oriented toward program and policy concerns. As the author has observed elsewhere (Williams, 1971, pp. 65-6, italics in original):

> The critical point is that the government men of power, themselves, have not been oriented toward policy process needs. That is, the government research bureaucracy, *as isolated from policy as the academic,* frequently shares the academic gestalt of what is proper *(pure exceeds applied)* but in their wisdom define popular pure areas. Thus the long tradition of government funding has supported the academic's distaste for policy-relevant studies while allowing him to believe that he is aware of what social research government does in fact need.

It is critical to recognize, however, given both the weaknesses of government evaluative staffs and the social science community to perform policy studies, that the shift toward policy-directed research should be relatively small and gradual. The great bulk of social research should continue to be guided by the same concerns as in the past, with scientists performing research that in the long run may facilitate policy but which is *not* framed with policy concerns in mind. At the present stage of groping to formulate what research is needed for policy, it would be ridiculous to try to shift a large percentage of research funds toward explicit policy questions. The government simply does *not* have the technical capacity to use vast sums in search of policy relevance. Lots of money can be as destructive as small amounts—agency research managers, just as program operators, must obligate *all* funds before the end of the fiscal year or lose them. The time that might be concentrated on developing a few sound projects with a high potential for producing policy results may instead be widely distributed over many projects of dubious quality and relevance in order to expend all funds.

For this reason, it is not appropriate to try to specify desirable absolute or relative levels of expenditure increases for policy studies or the time path of such increases. What is appropriate is a strong recommendation for a rapid buildup of policy research staffs. *Evidence of staff capability must precede major funding increases.* Also, a firm commitment must be made to more policy-oriented research, particularly evaluative studies, that is "validated" by immediate (but still relatively small) funding increases for policy studies at the expense of other research.

The Organization of the Social Sciences for Policy Research

The types and level of research on social problems now required to facilitate social policymaking strongly indicate the need for more special organizations (e.g., profit and nonprofit research organizations, institutes, academic departments or schools) with explicit missions of large-scale, multidisciplinary research and/or teaching in the social policy areas. Recently the establishment of large-scale social policy organizations has been recommended by a number of groups and individuals, including major committees of the National Science Foundation (1969), the National Academy of Sciences, and the Social Science Research Council (1969). The National Science Foundation, which proposes the creation of "Social Policy Research Institutes" and the combined NAS/SSRC committees which in turn propose new "Graduate Schools of Applied Behavioral Science" develop their recommendations along quite similar lines. But there are differences. The NAS/SSRC proposal suggests that the new organizations be a part of the university and have a regular teaching function. The NSF report leaves the location issue open, neither requiring that the institutes be at universities nor rejecting that location, but stressing a close relationship with government agencies (not a point of emphasis in the other report).

It is the question of location—in or outside of universities and where in the university—that seems to be the most controversial one. There does seem to be a convergence of views on one point about location. Both the NSF and NAS/SSRC reports state explicitly and strongly that the new organizations when on campuses should be financially and administratively *independent* of the established social science departments. And one can certainly make a strong normative argument that disciplinary departments ought not as departments undertake large-scale policy research which may draw researchers from teaching, and present even stronger positive evidence that individual social science departments are not likely to undertake major policy studies, particularly those of a multidisciplinary nature.

It does seem a valid argument that a social policy institute, department, or school should have the same financial and administrative power to choose its professional staff as the disciplinary departments. For example, in its appointments, a social policy institute should not be beholden to a disciplinary department that defines staff acceptability only in terms of theoretical or conceptual elegance validated primarily by publication in a handful of prestige journals. It is also important that social policy organizations not be isolated from the rest of the university, cut off from interaction with disciplinary peers or having lower quality standards for staff. Social policy organizations need not exist in a hostile relationship with the disciplinary departments. An institute in order to have a critical mass for research purposes may hire more people in a special area than a department would to fulfill its teaching functions, and the latter may be happy to make joint appointments (especially if the salary costs are low). A university at the inception or rapid buildup of a social policy organization may want to provide special "quality checks" through a multidisciplinary university committee, and to place a high value on cooperation, with disciplinary departments including joint appointments. What the university should not do, however, is recreate the disciplinary departments (especially ones that consider policy research an inferior good) by giving them a unilateral veto over the hiring of members of their discipline in policy organizations.

Difficulties of performing large-scale policy research in an academic setting and the potential conflict with other university functions have led some to recommend that policy research organizations be separate from the universities. This thesis has been particularly strong in physics where there is a wealth of experience with major applied and basic research centers, some of which have been a regular part of the university, some with peripheral attachments to it, and others with no formal relationships. Alvin Weinberg (1966, p. 176) has observed that "the ecology of the discipline-oriented university encourages the rise of purism and specialization and the denial of scholarship and application in science" and Harvey Brooks (1968, p. 70) has suggested: "Where a more programmed effort is desirable or the social need is so urgent that some technical effort is required, even though no very promising new approaches are evident, it should probably be centered at nonacademic institutions, with academic participation only when interest or ideas appear spontaneously from the academic community." Edward Teller (1966, p. 126) has gone so far as to recommend that even without the collaboration of established universities, applied laboratories should be given the responsibility for the education of applied scientists.

There has been much less discussion of the location of social policy research organizations. However, Peter Rossi (1972) in a provocative paper makes a strong case against locating at universities those types of social research organizations which have elaborate divisions of labor, distinct hierarchies of authority and status, and a professional staff drawn from several academic disciplines. Rossi labels such organizations "research firms," and offers as prime examples the Institute for Social Research at the University of Michigan, the National Opinion Research Center at the University of Chicago (which he directed for several years), and the Bureau of Applied Social Research at Columbia University. He thinks that such organizations do *not* fit well in the university structure.

The basic argument is that having a regular academic appointment is more prestigeful than a nonacademic research status and offers more autonomy than mission-oriented work. Large-scale, social research organizations under these circumstances tend to attract marginal people, some who are very good, but for a number of reasons cannot "qualify" for academic appointments, and more who are second rate. Further, staff members generally have all sorts of status conflict problems on the campus. Rossi suggests that the few successes of large-scale social research organizations based at universities are explained primarily by a charismatic leader whose departure signed their demise. Institutional devices, independent of the strong leader, do not seem to protect the organizations in the hostile environment of the university.

Rossi (1972, p. 275) then proposes that the appropriate research organizations for universities are ones "designed primarily to maximize the foreign relations gains from organizing research . . . [and which] are essentially collections of faculty members, each pursuing his own research interests, and using the center to provide letterheads, secretarial services, and political leverage within the university and with funding agencies." In short, the organization that will function well in the university is one that is unlikely to do large-scale social research and because of its ties to one department is almost certain to be unable to do multidisciplinary work.

That *all* large-scale, multidisciplinary policy research or that the education of "applied" scientists should not be university functions are debatable points even in the physical sciences. In the social sciences with far more limited experience and debate, it would be premature to suggest a divorcing of all large-scale social research and the teaching of policy techniques from the universities.

A distinction, however, can be made as to types of research that may lead to a significant difference in functions between universities and nonuniversity research organizations. For purposes of analysis, research can be distinguished as between studies in which the results are expected to have a *direct* bearing upon major agency policy decisions (e.g., an outcome evaluation of Head Start) and those in which the results are expected to have an impact on decisions only after additional research or testing (e.g., a tightly controlled laboratory experiment in early childhood learning).

As a general rule, "direct decision" and "earlier stage" studies bring a differing set of demands upon the entity conducting the project. First, the former frequently necessitate a massing of staff, including specialists both in substantive areas and administration, a number of whom may work full time or nearly full time on the project in order to meet agency time deadlines. Second, direct decision studies may require methodological short cuts that do not diminish greatly the results in terms of policy relevance but that render the study unfit for a prestige journal, thus lessening its academic worth. Third, direct decision studies have a high potential for bringing the institution conducting the study into a conflict situation within the agency decision-making process, a point well illustrated by the Westinghouse Head Start evaluation. The closer to a key decision, the closer to potential conflict is a good generalization—a controlled laboratory study of learning will no doubt be done in relative quiet compared to an outcome evaluation.

As compared to universities, nonuniversity research organizations such as the RAND Corporation generally seem better able in an institutional sense to perform large-scale research, the results of which are expected to have a direct effect on social agency decisions.[8] At least over the near term, say 5 years, nonuniversity policy research organizations should be more capable of rewarding social policy work both in money and status terms, institutionalizing the "heat" from direct decision studies as a part of doing business, and massing the key substantive area, administrative, and field procedure experts needed to mount a concerned effort. These organizations frequently face the problem of finding top-flight scientists, but here the selective use of members of regular university departments will often supplement the operation.

These nonuniversity organizations seem the likely candidates for expanding the supply of direct decision studies both significantly and relatively quickly. Nor should this comparative advantage rule out more fundamental research since direct decision studies may give the organizations great insight into more basic problems. Further, they may be able to attract competent researchers for any kind of policy studies only if some basic work can be performed.

The universities, however, probably should have the major role in the more fundamental policy-oriented research. Here the articulation of needs and a "good selling job" by the federal government become paramount as many basic social problems fit well in the reward structure of social and behavioral scientists. The key point is that these more basic studies offer the traditional incentives of the past and, as an added attraction, may help overcome national problems to which science itself has oftentimes been a major contributor.

At the same time, the past experience with universities does suggest that funding agencies take a much firmer stance in requiring that university organizations demonstrate policy research commitment and competence. This "suspicion" should, of course, extend to nonuniversity organizations, but historically it has been the universities that have performed most of the social science studies. And funding agencies should be far less willing than in the past to take for granted either university capability or desire to undertake policy research.

---

[8] Institutes located on campuses but having professional staffs whose appointments are not in the established disciplinary departments may be an exception to this statement. In the following general discussion, however, the special and complex issue of such institutes will not be pursued.

One final point needs to be made. The arguments that nonuniversity organizations in the near term may have a comparative advantage in direct decision studies and that funding agencies be less willing to take university capacity for granted should not be expanded to allow the university to "cop out" on social policy research and teaching. *The university presently has a major share of the qualified social science researchers and a virtual monopoly on the education of the social scientist at a critical career stage.* Even if one adopts the thesis advanced in a recent report by the American Academy of Arts and Sciences (1971, pp. 6-7) that research is appropriate at a university only when it facilitates the primary university mission of learning, academics are going to have to get more knowledge than they presently have about policy research in order to train competent social policy researchers. I would rank this training for policy research a highest priority item. It seems to me also that university social scientists ought to engage in the search for means of solving critical social problems; hence social policy research *qua* research is an appropriate university function. But such considerations quickly carry one to a discussion of the university and society—a topic that is difficult to avoid when focusing on the research function but one that is hardly to be treated in a couple of paragraphs at this time. Rather, the basic point is that the arguments of this discussion are not meant to provide—nor, I believe, *do* provide—a basis for letting the university turn away from policy-oriented research and teaching.

Minimizing the Risks of Developing
and Using Evaluative Results

Wide and careful scrutiny of evaluative activities both by various parties at interest (political) and by relatively disinterested researchers (technical) before decisions are made seems the most likely means of minimizing the risks that invalid evaluative results will be used in policy or that sound results will be misused through interpretations of them beyond their legitimate limits. Two comments need to be made concerning this formulation. First, analysis must occur before decisions are made for the obvious reason that after the decision is often too late. What is not obvious is how to get results on the table, given both the real time pressures of fiscal year decision-making and the desires of decision-makers for flexibility. Second, wide discussion and debate will often leave the proper policy choice still debatable. In many ways the situation will resemble a courtroom setting in which each side has experts who score points, with the final verdict resting on contradictory evidence. But better that the validity of the evaluative study design and the interpretation of results be subjected to wide political and technical scrutiny than that it be looked at only in the comparative isolation of an agency or congressional committee.

Agencies supporting research and the researchers themselves are unlikely to want outsiders looking over their shoulders. Steps must be taken to facilitate and institutionalize access to evaluative information at a reasonably early stage. For example, a bill introduced by Senator Abraham Ribicoff would authorize the present General Accounting Office (reconstituted and renamed) to analyze ongoing evaluative studies, going so far as to grant the (undesirable) power to subpoena the records of evaluation contractors, subcontractors, and grantees. Other possible measures might include (1) a legal requirement for public disclosure at the letting of evaluative contracts and grants, not scattered amid a deluge of other announcements, but in a single, readily available source; (2) the requirement that contractors prepare for public distribution interim progress reports, including methodological and procedural discussions, and (3) the establishment of independent bodies (perhaps funded by private foundations or quasipublic entities such as the National Academy of Sciences) to perform thorough methodological critiques. I hold no particular brief for these suggestions. In fact the critical point is that to date little thought has been given to the detailed procedures involved in establishing an institutional structure that will bring evaluative activity under careful scrutiny. At this point the most reasonable proposal is one calling for a search for such institutional means rather than one specifying particular approaches.

Scrutiny is not without its own dangers, as a couple of examples will attest. First, in the New Jersey negative income tax experiment, the news media have made several attempts to interview experiment participants. The threat of "contamination" of the experiment must be apparent, and with a relatively small number of participants, the whole study could be destroyed. Another quite real danger is that almost any type of scrutiny (and consider the even more pervasive power to subpoena) can infringe on the rights of participants. Second, in a search for new alternatives in the education area, OEO has proposed experiments with performance contracting and educational vouchers. The former is now completed, but widespread opposition by the educational community has kept the voucher experiments from starting. It is not necessary to judge the merits of this specific case to see the general dangers deriving from the fact that a concerted effort by an interest group can block an experiment and in so doing effectively block future policy. Yet, it is difficult to see how evaluative evidence itself can be evaluated unless it is made widely available just as other research. And with the potential effect on major decisions, it is imperative that results be subjected to a critique before decisions are made.

There is also an urgent need to investigate institutional means for protecting researchers in policy-oriented studies from government interference that lessens independence and objectivity or unduly restricts the scope of the investigations. In policy studies the federal government should draw on well-regarded (usually academically oriented) researchers, including scholars recognized as outstanding by their disciplinary peers. It should be apparent that with ample funds the government can always get plenty of second-rate research. What is difficult is to bring to policy research top-flight people who in general will and *should* adhere to the academic standards of independence and objectivity.

The above formulation is not meant to suggest a hands-off policy by government staffs. Studies expected to have a direct impact on decisions will often constrain the researcher's effort—and legitimately—in terms of firm time deadlines, the relatively detailed specification of the objectives of the study and methods and procedures to be used, and detailed monitoring of the ongoing work by the agency policy research staff. However, unwarranted restrictions involving attempts to influence the findings, to suppress them, or to force early release of information must be minimized.

Pressures for early release are probably the most likely type of government interference, and have occurred recently in two politically sensitive evaluative studies: the Westinghouse Head Start evaluation and the New Jersey negative income tax experiment. The White House first ordered OEO to send it a copy of the earliest draft of the Westinghouse report and then made these very preliminary findings known in a Presidential message; and second, it forced Westinghouse to make available to the Congress copies of a preliminary report (for a detailed discussion, see Williams, 1971, Chapter 7). In the negative tax experiment, the researchers were asked by the Nixon Administration to analyze preliminary data so results could be provided to the House Ways and Means Committee then considering the Family Assistance Plan. The demand came sufficiently early in the experiment to raise legitimate questions about the wisdom and propriety of the analysis at that time. Further, the request had such severe time constraints that it did not permit a reasonable level of quality control in the analysis (Watts, 1970, pp. 8 and 12). Can anyone doubt that evaluative results are a form of political evidence?

There is little precedent in the social sciences for the problem of releasing preliminary results. The issue is first a methodological rather than a moral question. A researcher may believe for a number of technical reasons that his preliminary findings are not yet amenable to any kind of interpretation. For example, in the Westinghouse evaluation, the contractor, when forced to release a preliminary report, argued that additional statistical analyses were needed before interpretation of the data would be warranted. Individual experts may differ in their appraisal of whether or not it would be premature to release information; and, the question ultimately is judgmental in that a methodological purist might well claim that no preliminary release of results is justified. The issue then is what the researcher should do if he believes that his data should not be released in their present form.

To see the nature of this issue, let us assume that an agency is shown some preliminary findings in the normal course of agency-researcher relationships and sees the potential usefulness in an upcoming political situation. The agency might suggest that the researcher let it have the preliminary results, including various caveats about their use, and that it will take responsibility for the release and interpretation of the information. In such a release the preliminary nature of the results can be played down so as to suggest that the findings strongly support the desired political action.

Should the researcher refuse to provide the preliminary information to the agency? If the agency gives an interpretation that is unwarranted in the view of the researcher, should he warn the public of the questionable interpretation? The situation is quite different from that of a final, readily available evaluative study that presents a sufficiently detailed account of methodology and concepts and enough data for a reader to assess the study's conclusions and draw his own. Under these circumstances the evaluative results are a part of the public domain; the researcher has no general responsibility for unwarranted interpretations of the published results. While it is a debatable point, there even seems to be no strong obligation to correct interpretations by the contracting agency, as long as their validity can be assessed from information in the final report. But with preliminary results, the researcher alone among nongovernment scientists knows the facts. Silence concerning unwarranted interpretations means acceptance. Most certainly, if policy is being made on the basis of the preliminary results, corrections will not suffice in a final report. Yet if the researcher refuses to provide requested data to the agency or warns publically of the agency's interpretation, he may jeopardize both the single project and future funding from a (perhaps, the) major source of his organization's revenue.

Even more difficult to treat than overt pressure may be the subtle threat to research organizations dependent for the bulk of their funding on a single or a small number of government sources. Here the potential influence may be a fear of losing future contracts that leads the research organization to try to "please" the big client. Of course, it is tempting (and not completely unjustified) to observe that those who want chastity should avoid compromising situations. The problem, however, is not simply that of protecting the objectivity of research organizations (and hence letting the imprudent ones suffer the consequences), but of protecting the public against the unwarranted use of evaluative results. When a single evaluative activity can, at the extreme, influence decisions involving billions of dollars and millions of people—to be specific, the New Jersey experiment and the Family Assistance Plan— it is no small problem.[9]

The critical issue is whether or not policy research organizations funded by one or a small number of mission agencies can have extended contact with a funding agency and yet retain objectivity and independence. Enke (1967, pp. 4-5) has argued that in the case of the RAND Corporation and the United States

___

[9] The last few paragraphs draw heavily on Williams (1971, pp. 127-8).

Air Force extended interaction and independence have been blended so as to produce a high level of useful policy work, but that a number of unusual features were required:

> Project RAND's *contract includes several little known peculiarities* that together go far to *explain the extraordinary success of RAND.*

> First, *the terms of reference were and are extremely broad,* initially being "intercontinental warfare other than surface." Within this scope, RAND researchers worked on what they and their supervisors considered important, and not necessarily on what concerned Air Force officers. Many a general in the early days, learning of the existence of an Air Force-supported RAND, visited Santa Monica to announce what research he wanted done only to depart perplexed, having been told politely that RAND was deciding for itself what Air Force problems were important and tractable.

> Second, and a corollary, *RAND decides what completed research to show the USAF.* A Project RAND study does not have to be exposed to the customer until the management considers this desirable. Thus RAND imposes its own deadlines. But more important, it can "bury" those research ideas that lead nowhere. True research includes dead ends. With Project RAND the management does not have to "play it safe" by assigning staff only to prosaic undertakings certain to yield something that can be given the customer.

> Third, again a corollary, *specific projects* within the general terms of reference are *defined by RAND.* Recommendations are less likely to be narrow suboptimizations. Future problems are more likely to be anticipated in time for something to be done: for example, RAND was once criticized for conducting a large project on the defense of North America from air attack, until shortly afterwards when the Soviets detonated their first atomic device.

> Fourth, *Project RAND has had relatively few financial worries.* The initial funding was sufficient for several years. After some difficulties, Project RAND now enjoys something akin to institutional funding as it is given adequate notice of any reduction in level of support. Obviously this is important when recruiting. Also, because RAND does not have to sell research by the project, showing salary charges and rates for each, the management is more able to bid for real talent.

> Fifth, although many of RAND's departments are organized by academic discipline, *the major projects are interdisciplinary* and include members of different departments. Having discipline departments attracts and holds analysts with superior professional qualifications. It takes a mathematician to recruit a mathematician. But more important is the bringing together of economists, mathematicians, and engineers into a single project for 6 to 12 months, having a unique purpose, and forcing them to learn each others' languages and concepts. After initial misunderstandings, the final results are nearly always significant, often surprisingly so. Too many important and unresolved issues seem to remain unattacked in the No Man's Land that lies between established academic disciplines. At a university, it is only the maverick faculty member who strays into strange and suspect areas, and he alone can seldom achieve as much as can an interdisciplinary team.

> Sixth, *RAND's staff* is usually considered by Air Force officers to be *part of the Air Force "family."* This was especially true when Project RAND comprised almost all the activity of The RAND Corporation. Hence RAND staff members had access to sensitive information sometimes of the "skeleton-in-the-closet" variety. This close-yet-independent relationship contributes to productive research. It is another

reason why certain federal agencies each need a "within-the-family" research organization of their own.

Seventh, The *RAND* Corporation (established in 1948), *has always had a Board of Trustees that effectively guided and protected it.* This Board is truly familiar with much research at RAND—listening to three days of briefings twice a year. Even more important, the Board comprises men of such national stature that RAND has been able to preserve its independence through various attempts by the USAF to clip its wings.

The reader may disagree with Enke's claim of RAND's great success, but I suspect that far less controversial is his added argument of RAND's preeminence among the Department of Defense oriented "Think Tanks." None of the others had RAND's autonomy which Enke thinks is explained by the fact that "the USAF has often been more displeased than pleased with what it unexpectedly got for its money for Project RAND. Senior USAF officers have in the past advised their counterparts in the Navy and Army not to make the mistake of creating so independent, influential, and uncontrollable an organization" (Enke, 1967, p. 7).

It will not be easy to create a setting in which researchers can gain significant knowledge about policy problems, have a great deal of autonomy in performing policy research, and be free from undue pressures. This will be especially true for social policy organizations that owe their existence to one or a few mission agencies. The efforts to institutionalize wide public disclosure and scrutiny of evaluative activities may help in establishing such a setting, but clearly the question of the researcher's independence and objectivity requires immediate discussion and debate.

At the same time, I think it is critical that social scientists keep the matter of independence in perspective. Given the dearth of relevant social policy research, it would be wrong to make these potential threats to independence the principal problem. Far more important is the question of getting the social science community moving toward a material contribution to social policy-making.

It has been argued that even the most basic types of policy research will be enhanced if the researcher can gain detailed knowledge of policy problems and concomitant research needs. Such a formulation indicates a major role for the mission agencies in basic policy research even if they are not the funding source; and, under ideal circumstances, the social agencies would be the primary source of basic research funds in their areas of concern. This is true both because of the potential for interaction between agency staff and researcher and because the agencies will be more likely to use research results supported by their own funds.

Funding of basic policy research by the mission agencies is not without its problems. First, the agencies more than organizations such as the National Science Foundation are likely to exert undue influence or put restrictions on research organizations. Second, in times of budget decreases basic research funds in mission agencies are usually cut back significantly. These problems suggest that NSF and the National Institutes of Mental Health (which is part of a mission agency but historically has been considered an independent funding source) support more basic policy research in the social areas. The big problems in making NSF and NIMH major funding sources of basic policy research concern (1) the means of developing greater knowledge about policy problems among potential researchers in light of the fact that these organizations in the past have had only a limited interest in social agency policy needs and (2) the means for getting the research results once they are available considered by the mission agencies in their policy process. These are complex institutional problems for which no ready solutions are apparent.

A shift in funds by NSF and NIMH to basic policy research at the expense of other basic research may have some major "indirect" benefits. The change could increase not only policy information but also fundamental scientific knowledge in the social sciences. Remember, basic policy research differs from other basic research only in requiring that the researcher have an appreciation of policy issues and needs and thinks in terms of the research implications that flow from them. Thus I suspect that the support of basic policy research by NSF and NIMH, if coupled with satisfactory institutional means of imparting policy needs to researchers, will expand the frontiers of knowledge in the social science disciplines more than if only basic, but not policy-oriented, research is funded. This argument derives from my belief that the great social science questions of our times are bound up in the great social issues. Certainly, I cannot prove this thesis, but it is not one that should be rejected out-of-hand.

A Concluding Observation

One final point needs to be made: If there is relatively more funding of policy research, if more interaction occurs between government policy research staffs and researchers, and if more special social policy research organizations are established, it will *not* guarantee a high level of social policy research. To label an organization the Social Policy Research Institute, and to staff it with social scientists from several disciplines ensures neither that the researchers will work together in a multidisciplinary effort nor that they will address relevant social issues more effectively than in the past.

This should come as no surprise. The decision to move toward more policy work must be implemented, and this requires a lot more than a name and a functional statement. However, the move toward more policy-oriented social research seems to be a sound one. Yet the fact remains that success depends on a complex dynamic process involving the government and researchers. Perhaps more than anything else, success depends on social science responding positively to the challenge and making a real commitment to confronting the great social problems of our times.

ACKNOWLEDGMENTS

Several individuals have provided either useful comments on earlier drafts of the paper or discussion on specific points of issue: Brewster Denny, University of Washington; Robert Levine, RAND; Richard Nelson, Yale University; and Peter Rossi, Johns Hopkins University. In addition, I am indebted to the Executive Committee and to Henry David and Stephen Baratz of the Division of Behavioral Sciences, National Academy of Sciences/ National Research Council. During the period I was preparing this paper, I was serving as a consultant on federal evaluation policy for the Executive Committee. The latter activity permitted me to discuss many of the issues in this paper with the Executive Committee and staff of the Division, and contributed to my understanding of them. The views expressed in the paper, however, are those of the author, and not necessarily those of the individuals and institutions mentioned above.

REFERENCES

The Assembly on University Goals and Governance (1971) A First Report. Amer. Acad. Arts Sci. Cambridge, Massachusetts.

Brooks, H. (1968) The future growth of academic research. In *Science Policy and the University* (H. Orlans, ed.). Brookings Institution, Washington, D.C.

Campbell, D. T., and Erlebacher, A. (1970). How regression artifacts in quasi-experimental evaluations can mistakenly make compensatory education look harmful. In *Compensatory Education: A National Debate* (J. Hellmuth, ed.). Brunner/Mazel, New York.

Deutsch, K. W. *et al.* (1971). Conditions favoring major advances in social science. *Science* pp. 450-459.

Enke, S. (1967). *Think Tanks for Better Government*, TEMPO, 67TMP-126. General Electric Company, Santa Barbara, California.

The Behavioral and Social Sciences: Outlooks and Needs (1969). Nat. Acad. Sci., Washington, D.C.

Knowledge into Action: Improving the Nation's Use of the Social Sciences. Nat. Sci. Found. (1969), Washington, D.C.

Rossi, P. H. (1972). Observations on the organization of social research. In *Evaluating Social Programs: Theory, Practice, and Politics* (P. H. Rossi and W. Williams, eds.). Seminar Press, New York.

Teller, E. (1966) Education of the modern inventor. In *Science and the University* (B. R. Keenan, ed.). Columbia Univ. Press, New York.

Watts, H. W. (1970). *Adjusted and Extended Preliminary Results from the Urban Graduated Work Incentive Experiment,* Discuss. Pap. Institute for Research on Poverty, University of Wisconsin, Madison.

Weinberg, A. M. (1966). But is the teacher also a citizen. In *Science and the University* (B. R. Keenan, ed.). Columbia Univ. Press, New York.

Wholey, J. S. *et al.* (1970). *Federal Evaluation Policy.* Urban Institute, Washington, D.C.

Williams, W. (1969). Developing an evaluation strategy for a social action agency. *Journal of Human Resources*, pp. 451-465.

Williams, W. (1971). *Social Policy Research and Analysis: The Experience in the Federal Agencies.* American Elsevier, New York.

AUTHOR INDEX

Numbers in italics refer to the pages on which the complete references are listed.

Wilner, D. M., 54, *65*
Wilson, A., 90, *95*
Wisler, C. E., 104, *107*
Wittich, W. A., 70, *71*

Y

Yonkers, A. H., 148, *183*

Z

Zimiles, H., 159, 174, *185*

SUBJECT INDEX

A

Acceptability of evaluation results, 135-137
Administrative level resistance to experimental designs, 32-33
American Academy of Arts and Sciences, xvii-xviii, 11, 15
American Economics Association, 292
A priori analysis, *see* Policy analysis

B

Behavioral science model, *see* Impact-effectiveness (experimental) model
Behavioral scientists, *see* Social scientists in research organizations and government
Benefit-cost analysis, *see* Outcome evaluations
Bereiter-Engelmann Academic Preschool Program, 176-180
"Bet-coefficients," 88-89, 105
Beta coefficients, 80
Broadly aimed social programs, difficulty of assessing, 33-34
Bureau of Applied Social Research, Columbia, 277-278, 281
Bureau of the Budget
implementing PPBS, 250

C

Carnegie Foundation, 276
Catch-up phenomenon, 208

Central analytical office, 5 *see also* Research, Plans, Programs, and Evaluation (RPP&E), Office of
Child health care programs, 18, 27-28
Children's Television Workshop (CTW), 167-170
Classifications of evaluations, 110-112
see also Types of evaluation
Cognitive measures/development, 164, 171-174
Coleman Report
attitudinal characteristics of students, 89-91
Cain/Watts critique, 73-94
Coleman's defense, 97-106
environmental characteristics, 91-92
Equality of Educational Opportunity survey, 32, 86
interpreting specific variables, 89-94
measuring determinants of achievement, 77-89
need for theoretically justified model relevant to policy, 86-89
objectives of, 75-77
policy issues in general, 73-94
school resources, 93-94
shortcomings, 74-75
teacher quality, 92-93
Community Action Program, 42-44, 114
Community contacts
in experimentation area, 225-233
see also Participants in the New Jersey income tax experiment
Compensatory education evaluations
ambiguity of results, 174-175

319

6
7
8
9
0
F 1
G 2
H 3
I 4
J 5